The Python Wp

Learn to code in Python and kickstart your career in software development or data science

Andrew Bird

Dr Lau Cher Han

Mario Corchero Jiménez

Graham Lee

Corey Wade

The Python Workshop

Authors: Andrew Bird, Dr Lau Cher Han, Mario Corchero Jiménez, Graham Lee, and Corey Wade

Technical Reviewers: Rohan Chikorde, Bert Gollnick, Stephen Klosterman, Tianxiang (Ivan) Liu, Roderick Person, Samik Sen, and Akshay Tharval

Managing Editor: Adrian Cardoza

Acquisitions Editor: Sarah Lawton

Production Editor: Samita Warang

Editorial Board: Shubhopriya Banerjee, Bharat Botle, Ewan Buckingham, Megan Carlisle, Mahesh Dhyani, Manasa Kumar, Alex Mazonowicz, Bridget Neale, Dominic Pereira, Shiny Poojary, Abhishek Rane, Erol Staveley, Ankita Thakur, Nitesh Thakur, and Jonathan Wray

First Published: November 2019

Production Reference: 5220221

ISBN: 978-1-83921-885-9

Published by Packt Publishing Ltd.

Livery Place, 35 Livery Street

Birmingham B3 2PB, UK

Why Learn with a Packt Workshop?

Learn by Doing

Packt Workshops are built around the idea that the best way to learn something new is by getting hands-on experience. We know that learning a language or technology isn't just an academic pursuit. It's a journey towards the effective use of a new tool—whether that's to kickstart your career, automate repetitive tasks, or just build some cool stuff.

That's why Workshops are designed to get you writing code from the very beginning. You'll start fairly small—learning how to implement some basic functionality—but once you've completed that, you'll have the confidence and understanding to move onto something slightly more advanced.

As you work through each chapter, you'll build your understanding in a coherent, logical way, adding new skills to your toolkit and working on increasingly complex and challenging problems.

Context is Key

All new concepts are introduced in the context of realistic use-cases, and then demonstrated practically with guided exercises. At the end of each chapter, you'll find an activity that challenges you to draw together what you've learned and apply your new skills to solve a problem or build something new.

We believe this is the most effective way of building your understanding and confidence. Experiencing real applications of the code will help you get used to the syntax and see how the tools and techniques are applied in real projects.

Build Real-World Understanding

Of course, you do need some theory. But unlike many tutorials, which force you to wade through pages and pages of dry technical explanations and assume too much prior knowledge, Workshops only tell you what you actually need to know to be able to get started making things. Explanations are clear, simple, and to-the-point. So you don't need to worry about how everything works under the hood; you can just get on and use it.

Written by industry professionals, you'll see how concepts are relevant to real-world work, helping to get you beyond "Hello, world!" and build relevant, productive skills. Whether you're studying web development, data science, or a core programming language, you'll start to think like a problem solver and build your understanding and confidence through contextual, targeted practice.

Enjoy the Journey

Learning something new is a journey from where you are now to where you want to be, and this Workshop is just a vehicle to get you there. We hope that you find it to be a productive and enjoyable learning experience.

Packt has a wide range of different Workshops available, covering the following topic areas:

- Programming languages
- Web development
- Data science, machine learning, and artificial intelligence
- Containers

Once you've worked your way through this Workshop, why not continue your journey with another? You can find the full range online at http://packt.live/2MNkuyl.

If you could leave us a review while you're there, that would be great. We value all feedback. It helps us to continually improve and make better books for our readers, and also helps prospective customers make an informed decision about their purchase.

Thank you,
The Packt Workshop Team

Table of Contents

Chapter 2: Python Structures   63

Chapter 6: The Standard Library   229

Chapter 11: Machine Learning 469

Preface

About

This section briefly introduces this course and software requirements in order to complete all of the included activities and exercises.

About the Course

Have you always wanted to learn Python, but never quite known how to start?

More applications than we realize are being developed using Python because it is easy to learn, read, and write. You can now start learning the language quickly and effectively with the help of this interactive tutorial.

The Python Workshop starts by showing you how to correctly apply Python syntax to write simple programs, and how to use appropriate Python structures to store and retrieve data. You'll see how to handle files, deal with errors, and use classes and methods to write concise, reusable, and efficient code.

As you advance, you'll understand how to use the standard library, debug code to troubleshoot problems, and write unit tests to validate application behavior.

You'll gain insights into using the pandas and NumPy libraries for analyzing data, and the graphical libraries of Matplotlib and Seaborn to create impactful data visualizations. By focusing on entry-level data science, you'll build your practical Python skills in a way that mirrors real-world development. Finally, you'll discover the key steps in building and using simple machine learning algorithms.

By the end of this Python book, you'll have the knowledge, skills and confidence to creatively tackle your own ambitious projects with Python.

About the Chapters

Chapter 1, Vital Python: Math, Strings, Conditionals, Loops, explains how to write basic Python programs, and outlines the fundamentals of the Python language.

Chapter 2, Python Structures, covers the essential elements that are used to store and retrieve data in all programming languages.

Chapter 3, Executing Python: Programs, Algorithms, Functions, explains how to write more powerful and concise code through an increased appreciation of well-written algorithms, and an understanding of functions

Chapter 4, Extending Python, Files, Errors, Graphs, covers the basic I/O (input-output) operations for Python and covers using the matplotlib and seaborn libraries to create visualizations.

Chapter 5, Constructing Python: Classes and Methods, introduces one of the most central concepts in object-oriented programming classes, and it will help you write code using classes, which will make your life easier.

Chapter 6, The standard library, covers the importance of the Python standard library. It explains how to navigate in the standard Python libraries and overviews some of the most commonly used modules.

Chapter 7, Becoming Pythonic, covers the Python programming language, with which you will enjoy writing succinct, meaningful code. It also demonstrates some techniques for expressing yourself in ways that are familiar to other Python programmers.

Chapter 8, Software Development, covers how to debug and troubleshoot our applications, how to write tests to validate our code, and the documentation for other developers and users.

Chapter 9, Practical Python: Advanced Topics, explains how to take advantage of parallel programming, how to parse command-line arguments, how to encode and decode Unicode, and how to profile Python to discover and fix performance problems.

Chapter 10, Data Analytics with pandas and NumPy, covers data science, which is the core application of Python. We will be covering NumPy and pandas in this chapter.

Chapter 11, Machine Learning, covers the concept of machine learning and the steps involved in building a machine learning algorithm

Conventions

Code words in text, database table names, folder names, filenames, file extensions, pathnames, dummy URLs, user input, and Twitter handles are shown as follows: "Python provides the `collections.defaultdict` type."

A block of code is set as follows:

```
cubes = [x**3 for x in range(1,6)]
print(cubes)
```

New important words are shown like this: "Typically, standalone **.py** files are either called **scripts** or **modules**".

Words that you see on the screen, for example, in menus or dialog boxes, appear in the text like this: "You can also use Jupyter (`New -> Text File`)."

Long code snippets are truncated and the corresponding names of the code files on GitHub are placed at the top of the truncated code. The permalinks to the entire code are placed below the code snippet. It should look as follows:

Exercise66.ipynb

```
def annotate_heatmap(im, data=None, valfmt="{x:.2f}",
textcolors=["black", "white"],
threshold=None, **textkw):
import matplotlib
if not isinstance(data, (list, np.ndarray)):
```

https://packt.live/2ps1byv

Before You Begin

Each great journey begins with a humble step. Our upcoming adventure in the land of Python is no exception. Before you can begin, you need to be prepared with the most productive environment. In this section, you will see how to do that.

Installing Jupyter on your system

We will be using Python 3.7 (from https://python.org):

To install Jupyter on windows, MacOS and Linux follow these steps:

1. Head to https://www.anaconda.com/distribution/ to install the Anaconda Navigator, which is an interface through which you can access your local Jupyter notebook.

2. Now, based on your Operating system (Windows, macOS or Linux) you need to download the Anaconda Installer.

Have a look at the following figure where we have downloaded the Anaconda files for Windows:

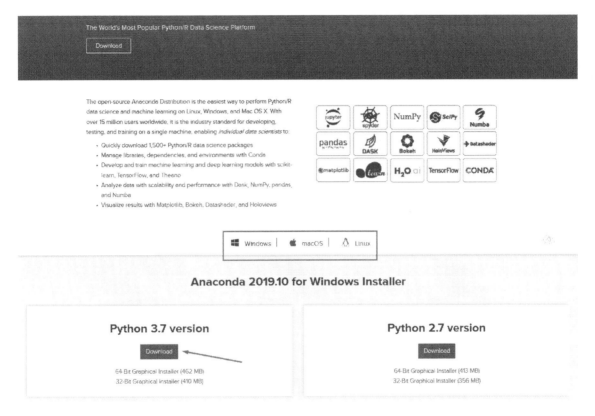

Figure 0.1: The Anaconda homescreen

Launching the Jupyter Notebook

To Launch the Jupyter Notebook frrom the Anaconda Navigator you need to follow the mentioned steps below:

1. Once you install the Anaconda Navigator you will have the following screen at your end as shown in *Figure 0.2*.

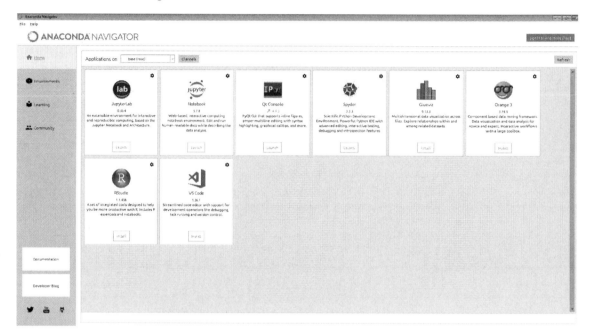

Figure 0.2: Anaconda installation screen

2. Now, click on **Launch** under the Jupyter Notebook option and launch the notebook on your local system:

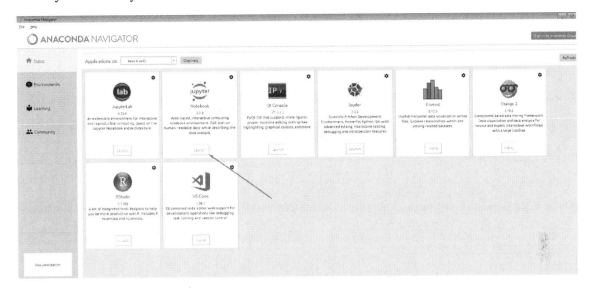

Figure 0.3: Jupyter notebook launch option

Congratulations! You have successfully installed Jupyter Notebook onto your system.

To Install the Python Terminal on your system

To install the Python terminal on your system, follow these steps:

1. Open the following link, which is the Python community website URL: https://www.python.org/downloads/.

2. Select the Operating System (Windows, macOS or Linux) you would be working on as highligthed in the following screenshot:

Figure 0.4: The Python homescreen

3. Once you have downloaded the software, you need to install it.

4. Have a look at the following screenshot in which we have installed the Python terminal on a Windows system. We load it through the Start menu and search for Python and **click** on the software.

   The Python terminal will look like this:

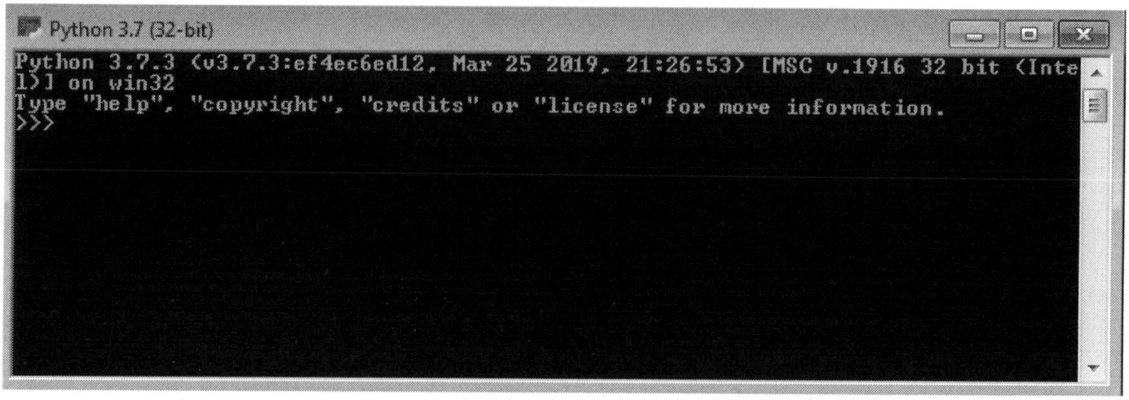

Figure 0.5: Python terminal interface

Congratulations! You have successfully installed the Python terminal onto your system.

A Few Important Packages

Some of the exercises in this chapter require the following packages:

- Matplotlib
- Seaborn
- NumPy

Install them by following this guide. On Windows, open up the command prompt. On macOS or Linux, open up the terminal. Type the following commands:

```
pip install matplotlib seaborn numpy
```

If you prefer to use Anaconda to manage your packages, type in the following:

```
conda install matplotlib seaborn numpy
```

To install Docker

1. Head to https://docs.docker.com/docker-for-windows/install/ to install Docker for Windows.

2. Head to https://docs.docker.com/docker-for-mac/install/ to install Docker for macOS.

3. Head to https://docs.docker.com/v17.12/install/linux/docker-ce/ubuntu/ to install Docker on Linux.

If you have any issues or questions about installation please email us at **workshops@packt.com.**

Installing the Code Bundle

Download the code files from GitHub at https://packt.live/2PfducF and place them in a new folder called **C:\Code** on your local system. Refer to these code files for the complete code bundle.

Vital Python – Math, Strings, Conditionals, and Loops

Overview

By the end of this chapter, you will be able to simplify mathematical expressions with the order of operations using integers and floats; assign variables and change Python types to display and retrieve user information; apply global functions including `len()`, `print()`, and **`input()`**; manipulate strings using indexing, slicing, string concatenation, and string methods; apply Booleans and nested conditionals to solve problems with multiple pathways; utilize 'for loops' and 'while loops' to iterate over strings and repeat mathematical operations and create new programs by combining math, strings, conditionals, and loops.

This chapter covers the fundamentals of the Python language.

Introduction

Welcome to the Python Workshop. This book is for anyone new to the Python programming language. Our objective is to teach you Python so that you can solve real-world problems as a Python developer and data scientist.

This book will combine theory, examples, exercises, questions, and activities for all core concepts; so that you can learn to use Python best practices to solve real-world problems. The exercises and activities have been chosen specifically to help you review the concepts covered and extend your learning. The best way to learn Python is to solve problems on your own.

The material (in this book) is targeted at beginners but will be equally as beneficial to experienced developers who are not yet familiar with Python. We are not teaching computer science per se, but rather Python, the most beautiful and powerful coding language in the world. If you have never studied computer science, you will learn the most important concepts here, and if you have studied computer science, you will discover tools and tricks for Python that you have never seen before.

Python has become the most popular programming language in the world due to its simple syntax, extensive range, and dominance in the field of machine learning. In this book, you will become fluent in Python syntax, and you will take significant steps toward producing Pythonic code. You will gain experience in Python development, data science, and machine learning.

Many introductory Python books provide full introductions to computer science. Learning computer science with Python is an excellent way to start, but it is not the method of this book. Units on software development and data science are rarely covered in such books. They may be touched upon, but here, they represent 40% of our book.

By contrast, many books on software development and data science are not designed for beginners. If they are, the Python fundamentals that they teach are usually summarized in one brief unit. This book devotes considerable space to Python fundamentals and essentials. Beginners are not only welcome; they are guided every step of the way.

In addition to the unique focus on Python fundamentals and essentials, the fact that the content is written by seasoned educators, data scientists, and developers makes this Python book more than just a text or reference.

Python is not the language of tomorrow; Python is the language of today. By learning Python, you will become empowered as a developer, and you will gain a significant edge over the competition. The journey will be fun, compelling, challenging, and ultimately, rewarding.

Vital Python

In this chapter, we present vital Python concepts, the core elements that everyone needs to know before starting to code. You cover a breadth of topics with a focus on math, strings, conditionals, and loops. By the end of this chapter, you will have a strong foundation in Python, and you will be able to write significant Python programs as you continue with the rest of this book.

You will start with a very famous developer example; that is, *Python as a calculator*. In addition to the standard operations of addition, subtraction, multiplication, division, and exponentiation, you will learn integer division and the modulus operator. By using only basic Python, you can outperform most calculators on the market.

Next, you'll learn about **variables**. Python is dynamically typed, meaning that variable types are unknown before the code runs. Python variables do not require special initialization. Our first variables will be **integers**, **floats**, and **strings**. You will identify and convert between types.

Next, in order to work with strings, you will utilize string methods, in addition to **indexing**, **slicing**, and string **concatenation**. You'll also use built-in functions such as `print()` and `input()` to communicate with the user.

Moving ahead, you'll encounter Booleans, `true` or `false` Python types, that precede conditionals, statements with `if` clauses that lead to branching. Booleans and conditionals allow us to write more complex programs by taking a greater number of possibilities into account.

Finally, you close the chapter with loops that allows us to repeat operations. In particular, we apply `while` loops and `for` loops, utilizing `break` and `continue`.

For true beginners, this introductory chapter will get you up to speed with basic programming concepts. If you are new to Python, you will see why the Python language is so clear, powerful, and valuable. By the end of this chapter, you will be comfortable running Python basics on their own, and you will be prepared to tackle more of the advanced concepts ahead.

Let's start coding in Python.

Numbers: Operations, Types, and Variables

In the preface, we installed Anaconda, which comes along with Python 3.7 and the Jupyter Notebook. It's time to open a Jupyter Notebook and begin our Pythonic journey.

To Open a Jupyter Notebook

To begin with this book, you need to make sure that you have a Jupyter Notebook open. Here are the steps.

1. Locate and open your Anaconda Navigator.

2. Search for **Jupyter** Notebook in Anaconda Navigator and click on it.

3. A new window should open in the web browser of your choice.

Figure 1.1: The Jupyter Notebook interface

> **Note**
>
> If you are having trouble, it may mean that your Jupyter Notebook is not set up properly. Go back to the preface or see https://jupyter-notebook.readthedocs.io/en/stable/troubleshooting.html for a troubleshooting guide.

Python as a Calculator

Now that you are all set up, you can begin with the very first interesting topic. Python is an incredibly powerful calculator. By leveraging the `math` library, `numpy`, and `scipy`, Python typically outperforms pre-programmed calculators. In later chapters, you will learn how to use the `numpy` and `scipy` libraries. For now, we'll introduce the calculator tools that most people use daily.

Addition, **subtraction**, **multiplication**, **division**, and **exponentiation** are core operations. In computer science, the `modulus` operator and **integer division** are equally essential as well, so we'll cover them here.

The `modulus` operator is the remainder in mathematical division. **Modular arithmetic** is also called **clock arithmetic**. For instance, in `mod5` which is a modulus of 5, we count 0,1,2,3,4,0,1,2,3,4,0,1... This goes in a circle, like the hands on a clock.

The difference between division and integer division depends on the language. When dividing the integer 9 by the integer 4, some languages return 2; others return 2.25. In your case, Python will return 2.25.

There are many advantages to using Python as your calculator of choice. The first is that you are not limited to using programs that others have written. You can write a program to determine the greatest common divisor or the Euclidean distance between two points.

Other advantages include reliability, precision, and speed. Python generally prints out more decimal places than most calculators, and it always does what you command it to do.

We'll cover a small sample of what Python can calculate. Complex numbers are previewed as a Python type. Great `math` libraries such as **Turtle**, which creates polygons and circles with ease, may be explored in your own time and are mentioned in *Chapter 6, The Standard Library*. The depth of math required for data analysis and machine learning starts with the foundations laid here.

> **Note**
>
> In this book, copy everything that follows >>> in a cell in your Jupyter Notebook; that is, you exclude >>>. To run code, make sure the cell is highlighted, then press *Shift + Enter*. You may also press the **Run** button at the top of the Notebook, but this takes more time. Start thinking like a developer and use keystrokes instead.

Standard Math Operations

You can have a look at the standard math operations and their symbols that we will be using while coding. The following table covers these:

Operation	Symbol
Addition	+
Subtraction	−
Multiplication	*
Division	/
Integer Division	//
Exponentiation	**
Modulo/Remainder	%

Figure 1.2: Standard math operations

Note

The ** symbol is not universally for exponentiation, but it should be. By definition, exponentiation is repeated multiplication. Using the * symbol twice is representative of repeated multiplication. It's terse, fast, and efficient. Other programming languages require functions to exponentiate.

Python provides an optional method from the **math** library, **math.pow()**, but ** is cleaner and easier to use.

Basic Math Operations

We can perform addition on two numbers using the + operator. The following example shows the addition of 5 and 2:

1. Here, we are using the addition operator, + in the code:

```
5 + 2
```

You should get the following output:

```
7
```

We can perform addition on two numbers using the + operator. The following example shows the subtraction of **5** and **2**.

2. Using the subtraction operator in the code, we can perform subtraction on two numbers:

```
5 - 2
```

You should get the following output:

```
3
```

The following example shows the multiplication of 5 by 2.

3. Using the * multiplication operator to multiply the two numbers is done as follows:

```
5 * 2
```

You should get the following output:

```
10
```

4. Now, use the / division operator and observe the output:

```
5 / 2
```

You should get the following output:

```
2.5
```

When dividing two numbers, Python will always return a decimal.

5. Now the same division can be done using the // operator, which is called integer division. Observe the change in the output:

```
5 // 2
```

You should get the following output:

```
2
```

The result of the integer division is the integer before the decimal point.

6. Now, using the ** exponential operator, we can perform exponentiation:

```
5 ** 2
```

You should get the following output:

```
25
```

The next example shows how to use the modulus operator.

7. Finally, use the modulus operator in the code and observe the output:

```
5 % 2
```

You should get the following output:

```
1
```

The modulus operator is performed using the **%** operator, as shown in step 7. It returns the remainder when the first number is divided by the second.

In the aforementioned examples, you have used the different math operators and performed operations with them in a Jupyter Notebook. Next, you move on to the order of operations in Python.

Order of Operations

Parentheses are meaningful in Python. When it comes to computation, Python always computes what is in parentheses first.

The Python language follows the same order of operations as in the math world. You may remember the acronym PEMDAS: parentheses first, exponentiation second, multiplication/division third, and addition/subtraction fourth.

Consider the following expression:**5 + 2 * -3**

The first thing to note is that the negative sign and subtraction sign are the same in Python. Let's have a look at the following example:

1. Python will first multiply **2** and **-3**, and then add **5**:

```
5 + 2 * -3
```

You should get the following output:

```
-1
```

2. If parentheses are placed around the **5** and **2**, we obtain a different result:

```
(5 + 2) * -3
```

You should get the following output:

```
-21
```

If ever in doubt, use parentheses. Parentheses are very helpful for complex expressions, and extra parentheses do not affect code.

In the following exercise, we are going to dive into Python code and work with math operations.

Exercise 1: Getting to Know the Order of Operations

The goal of this exercise is to work with the primary math operations in Python and understand their order of execution. This exercise can be performed on the Python terminal:

1. Subtract **5** to the 3rd power, which is 5^3, from **100** and divide the result by **5**:

```
(100 - 5 ** 3) / 5
```

You should get the following output:

```
-5.0
```

2. Add **6** to the remainder of **15** divided **4**:

```
6 + 15 % 4
```

You should get the following output:

```
9
```

3. Add **2** to the 2nd power, which is 2^2, to the integer division of **24** and **4**:

```
2 ** 2 + 24 // 4
```

You should get the following output:

```
10
```

In this quick exercise, you have used Python to perform basic math using the order of operations. As you can see, Python is an excellent calculator. You will use Python often as a calculator in your career as a developer.

Spacing in Python

You may have wondered about spaces in between numbers and symbols. In Python, spaces after a number or symbol do not carry any meaning. So, **5******3** and **5** ** **3** both result in **125**.

Spaces are meant to enhance readability. Although there is no correct way to space code, spaces are generally encouraged between operands and operators. Thus, **5** ** **3** is preferable.

Trying to follow certain conventions is perfectly acceptable. If you develop good habits early on, it will make the reading and debugging of code easier later.

Number Types: Integers and Floats

Now you will address the difference between an integer and a float. Consider 8 and 8.0. You know that 8 and 8.0 are equivalent mathematically. They both represent the same number, but they are different types. 8 is an integer, and 8.0 is a decimal or float.

An integer in Python is classified as a type of **int**, short for integer. Integers include all positive and negative whole numbers, including 0. Examples of integers include 3, -2, 47, and 10000.

Floats, by contrast, are Python types represented as decimals. All rational numbers expressed as fractions can be represented as floats. Samples of floats include 3.0, -2.0, 47.45, and 200.001.

> **Note**
>
> We are only covering text and numeric types in this chapter. Other types will be discussed in subsequent chapters.

Python types can be obtained explicitly using the **type()** keyword, as you will see in the following exercise.

Exercise 2: Integer and Float Types

The goal of this exercise is to determine types and then change those types in our Python code. This can be performed in the Jupyter Notebook:

1. Begin by explicitly determining the type of **6** using the following code:

```
type(6)
```

   You should get the following output:

```
int
```

2. Now, enter **type(6.0)** in the next cell of your notebook:

```
type(6.0)
```

   You should get the following output:

```
float
```

3. Now, add **5** to **3.14**. Infer the type of their sum:

```
5 + 3.14
```

You should get the following output:

```
8.14
```

It's clear from the output that combining an **int** and a **float** gives us a **float**. This makes sense. If Python returned 8, you would lose information. When possible, Python converts types to preserve information.

You can, however, change types by using the **type** keyword.

4. Now, convert **7.999999999** to an **int**:

```
int(7.999999999)
```

You should get the following output:

```
7
```

5. Convert **6** to a **float**:

```
float(6)
```

You should get the following output:

```
6.0
```

In this exercise, you determined types by using the **type()** keyword, and you changed types between integers and floats. As a developer, you will need to use your knowledge of variable types more often than you might expect. It's not uncommon to be unsure of a type when dealing with hundreds of variables simultaneously, or when editing other people's code.

> **Note**
>
> Type changing will be revisited again in this chapter, referred to as **casting**.

Complex Number Types

Python includes complex numbers as an official type. Complex numbers arise when taking the square roots of negative numbers. There is no real number whose square root is -9, so we say that it equals 3i. Another example of a complex number is 2i + 3. Python uses **j** instead of **i**.

You can take a look at the following code snippet to learn how to work with complex number types.

Divide **2 + 3j** by **1 - 5j**, enclosing both operations within parentheses:

```
(2 + 3j) / (1 - 5j)
```

You should get the following output:

```
-0.5+0.5j
```

For more information on complex numbers, check out https://docs.python.org/3.7/library/cmath.html.

Errors in Python

In programming, errors are not to be feared; errors are to be welcomed. Errors are common not only for beginners but for all developers. You will learn skills to handle errors in *Chapter 4, Extending Python, Files, Errors, and Graphs*. For now, if you get an error, just go back and try again. Python errors in Jupyter Notebooks won't crash your computer or cause any serious problems but they will just stop running the Python code.

Variables

In Python, variables are memory slots that can store elements of any type. The name variable is meant to be suggestive, as the idea behind a variable is that the value can vary throughout a given program.

Variable Assignment

In Python, variables are introduced the same way as in math, by using the equals sign. In most programming languages, however, order matters; that is, x = 3.14 means that the value 3.14 gets assigned to x. However, 3.14 = x will produce an error because it's impossible to assign a variable to a number. In the following exercise, we will implement this concept in code to give you a better understanding of it.

Exercise 3: Assigning Variables

The goal of this exercise is to assign values to variables. Variables can be assigned any value, as you will see in this exercise. This exercise can be performed in the Jupyter Notebook:

1. Set **x** as equal to the number **2**:

```
x = 2
```

In the first step, we assigned the value **2** to the **x** variable.

2. Add **1** to the variable **x**:

```
x + 1
```

You should get the following output:

```
3
```

Once we add **1** to **x**, we get the output of **3**, because the variable has **1** added to it.

3. Change **x** to **3.0** and add **1** to **x**:

```
x = 3.0
x + 1
```

You should get the following output:

```
4.0
```

In this step, we change the value of **x** to **4.0**, and as in the previous 2 steps, we will be adding **1** to the **x** variable.

By the end of this quick exercise, you may have noticed that in programming, you can assign a variable in terms of its previous value. This is a powerful tool, and many developers use it quite often. Furthermore, the type of **x** has changed. **x** started as an **int**, but now x = **3.0** which is a **float**. This is allowed in Python because Python is dynamically typed.

Changing Types

In some languages, it's not possible for a variable to change types. This means that if the **y** variable is an integer, then **y** must always be an integer. Python, however, is dynamically typed, as we saw in *Exercise 3, Assigning Variables* and as illustrated in the following example:

1. **y** starts as an integer:

```
y = 10
```

2. **y** becomes a float:

```
y = y - 10.0
```

3. Check the type of **y**:

```
type(y)
```

You should get the following output:

```
float
```

In the next topic, you will be looking at reassigning variables in terms of themselves.

Reassigning Variables in Terms of Themselves

It's common in programming to add **1** to a variable; for instance, **x = x + 1**. The shorthand for this is to use **+=** as in the following example:

```
x += 1
```

So, if **x** was **6**, **x** is now **7**. The **+=** operator adds the number on the right to the variable and sets the variable equal to the new number.

Activity 1: Assigning Values to Variables

In this activity, you will assign a number to the **x** variable, increment the number, and perform additional operations.

By completing this activity, you will learn how to perform multiple mathematical operations using Python. This activity can be performed in the Jupyter Notebook.

The steps are as follows:

1. First, set **14** to the **x** variable.

2. Now, add **1** to **x**.

3. Finally, divide **x** by **5** and square it.

You should get the following output:

```
9.0
```

> **Note**
>
> The solution for this activity is available on page 516.

Variable Names

To avoid confusion, it's recommended to use variable names that make sense to readers. Instead of using **x**, the variable may be **income** or **age**. Although **x** is shorter, someone else reading the code might not understand what **x** is referring to. Try to use variable names that are indicative of the meaning.

There are some restrictions when naming variables. For instance, variables cannot start with numbers, most special characters, keywords, nor built-in types. Variables also can't contain spaces between letters.

According to Python conventions, it's best to use lowercase letters and to avoid special characters altogether as they will often cause errors.

Python keywords are reserved in the language. They have special meanings. We will go over most of these keywords later.

Running the following two lines always shows a current list of Python keywords:

```
import keyword
print(keyword.kwlist)
```

You should get the following output:

```
['False', 'None', 'True', 'and', 'as', 'assert', 'async', 'await', 'break', 'class', 'continue', 'def', 'del', 'elif', 'els
e', 'except', 'finally', 'for', 'from', 'global', 'if', 'import', 'in', 'is', 'lambda', 'nonlocal', 'not', 'or', 'pass', 'r
aise', 'return', 'try', 'while', 'with', 'yield']
```

Figure 1.3: Output showing the Python keywords

> **Note**
>
> If you use any of the preceding keywords as variable names, Python will throw an error.

Exercise 4: Variable Names

The goal of this exercise is to learn standard ways to name variables by considering good and bad practices. This exercise can be performed in Jupyter:

1. Create a variable called **1st_number** and assign it a value of **1**:

```
1st_number = 1
```

You should get the following output:

```
File "<ipython-input-6-05d80cc97354>", line 1
    1st_number = 1
           ^
SyntaxError: invalid syntax
```

Figure 1.4: Output throwing a syntax error

You'll get the error mentioned in the preceding screenshot because you cannot begin a variable with a number.

2. Now, let's try using letters to begin a variable:

```
first_number = 1
```

3. Now, use special characters in a variable name, as in the following code:

```
my_$ = 1000.00
```

You should get the following output:

```
File "<ipython-input-7-e3c03546ed83>", line 1
    my_$ = 1000.00
         ^
SyntaxError: invalid syntax
```

Figure 1.5: Output throwing a syntax error

You get the error mentioned in Figure 1.4 because you cannot include a variable with a special character.

4. Now, use letters again instead of special characters for the variable name:

```
my_money = 1000.00
```

In this exercise, you have learned to use underscores to separate words when naming variables, and not to start variables' names with numbers nor include any symbols. In Python, you will quickly get used to these conventions.

Multiple Variables

Most programs contain multiple variables. The same rules apply as when working with single variables. You will practice working with multiple variables in the following exercise.

Exercise 5: Multiple Variables in Python

In this exercise, you will perform mathematical operations using more than one variable. This exercise can be performed in the Jupyter Notebook:

1. Assign **5** to **x** and **2** to **y**:

```
x = 5
y = 2
```

2. Add **x** to **x** and subtract **y** to the second power:

```
x + x - y ** 2
```

You should get the following output:

```
6
```

Python has a lot of cool shortcuts, and multiple variable assignment is one of them. Here's the Pythonic way of declaring two variables.

> **Note**
>
> Pythonic is a term used to describe code written in the optimum readable format. This will be covered in *Chapter 7, Becoming Pythonic*.

3. Assign **8** to **x** and **5** to **y** in one line:

```
x, y = 8, 5
```

4. Find the integer division of x and y:

```
x // y
```

You should get the following output:

```
1
```

In this exercise, you practiced working with multiple variables, and you even learned the Pythonic way to assign values to multiple variables in one line. It's rare to only work with one variable in practice.

Comments

Comments are extra blocks of code that do not run. They are meant to clarify code for readers. In Python, any text following the **#** symbol on a single line is a comment. Comments followed by the **#** symbol may be inline or above the text.

> **Note**
>
> Consistent use of comments will make reviewing and debugging code much easier. It's strongly advisable to practice this from here on out.

Exercise 6: Comments in Python

In this exercise, you will learn two different ways to display comments in Python. This exercise can be performed in the Jupyter Notebook:

1. Write a comment that states **This is a comment**:

```
# This is a comment
```

When you execute this cell, nothing should happen.

2. Set the **pi** variable as equal to **3.14**. Add a comment above the line stating what you did:

```
# Set the variable pi equal to 3.14
pi = 3.14
```

Adding the comment clarifies what follows.

3. Now, try setting the **pi** variable as equal to **3.14** again, but add the comment stating what you did on the same line:

```
pi = 3.14  # Set the variable pi equal to 3.14
```

Although it's less common to provide comments on the same line of code, it's acceptable and often appropriate.

You should get the following output from the Jupyter notebook:

```
In [5]:  # This is a comment

In [6]:  # Set the variable pi equal to 3.14
         pi = 3.14

In [7]:  pi = 3.14     # Set the variable pi equal to 3.14
```

Figure 1.6: Output from the Jupyter Notebook using comments

In this exercise, you have learned how to write comments in Python. As a developer, writing comments is essential to make your code legible to others.

Docstrings

Docstrings, short for document strings, state what a given document, such as a program, a function, or a class, actually does. The primary difference in syntax between a docstring and a comment is that docstrings are intended to be written over multiple lines, which can be accomplished with triple quotes """. They also introduce a given document, so they are placed at the top.

Here is an example of a docstring:

```
"""
This document will explore why comments are particularly useful
when writing and reading code.
"""
```

When you execute this cell, nothing really happens. Docstrings, like comments, are designed as information for developers reading and writing code; they have nothing to do with the output of code.

Activity 2: Finding a Solution Using the Pythagorean Theorem in Python

In this activity, you will determine the Pythagorean distance between three points. You will utilize a docstring and comments to clarify the process.

In this activity, you need to assign numbers to the **x**, **y**, and **z** variables, square the variables, and take the square root to obtain the distance, while providing comments along the way and a docstring to introduce the sequence of steps. To complete this activity, you'll utilize multiple variables, comments, and docstrings to determine the Pythagorean distance between three points.

The steps are as follows:

1. Write a docstring that describes what is going to happen.

2. Set x, y, and z as equal to 2, 3, and 4.

3. Determine the Pythagorean distance between x, y, and z.

4. Include comments to clarify each line of code.

    You should get the following output:

```
5.385164807134504
```

> **Note**
>
> The solution for this activity is available on page 516.

So far, in this chapter, you have used Python as a basic calculator, along with the order of operations. You examined the difference between **int** and **float** values and learned how to convert between them. You can implement variable assignment and reassign variables to make programs run more smoothly. You also utilized comments to make code more readable and learned how to identify syntax errors. In addition, you learned a couple of cool Python shortcuts, including assigning multiple variables to one line. As an added bonus, you explored Python's complex number types.

Next, you'll explore Python's other main type, strings.

Strings: Concatenation, Methods, and input()

You have learned how to express numbers, operations, and variables. What about words? In Python, anything that goes between 'single' or "double" quotes is considered a string. Strings are commonly used to express words, but they have many other uses, including displaying information to the user and retrieving information from a user.

Examples include 'hello', "hello", 'HELLoo00', '12345', and 'fun_characters: !@ #$%^&*('.

In this section, you will gain proficiency with strings by examining string methods, string concatenation, and useful built-in functions including **print()** and **len()** with a wide range of examples.

String Syntax

Although strings may use single or double quotes, a given string must be internally consistent. That is, if a string starts with a single quote, it must end with a single quote. The same is true of double quotes.

You can take a look at valid and invalid strings in *Exercise 7, String Error Syntax.*

Exercise 7: String Error Syntax

The goal of this exercise is to learn appropriate string syntax:

1. Open a Jupyter Notebook.

2. Enter a valid string:

```
bookstore = 'City Lights'
```

3. Now enter an invalid string:

```
bookstore = 'City Lights"
```

You should get the following output:

```
File "<ipython-input-2-9c3a3fab8dfa>", line 1
    bookstore = 'City Lights"
                             ^
SyntaxError: EOL while scanning string literal
```

Figure 1.7: Output with invalid string format

If you start with a single quote, you must end with a single quote. Since the string has not been completed, you receive a syntax error.

4. Now you need to enter a valid string format again, as in the following code snippet:

```
bookstore = "Moe's"
```

This is okay. The string starts and ends with double quotes. Anything can be inside the quotation marks, except for more quotation marks.

5. Now add the invalid string again:

```
bookstore = 'Moe's'
```

You should get the following output:

```
File "<ipython-input-4-0ef68cccb92b>", line 1
    bookstore = 'Moe's'
                     ^
SyntaxError: invalid syntax
```

Figure 1.8: Output with the invalid string

This is a problem. You started and ended with single quotes, and then you added an **s** and another single quote.

A couple of questions arise. The first is whether single or double quotes should be used. The answer is that it depends on developer preference. Double quotes are more traditional, and they can be used to avoid potentially problematic situations such as the aforementioned **Moe's** example. Single quotes eliminate the need to press the **Shift** key.

In this exercise, you have learned the correct and incorrect ways of assigning strings to variables, including single and double-quotes.

Python uses the backslash character, \, called an **escape** sequence in strings, to allow for the insertion of any type of quote inside of strings. The character that follows the backslash in an escape sequence may be interpreted as mentioned in Python's official documentation, which follows. Of particular note is **\n**, which is used to create a new line:

Escape Sequence	Meaning
\newline	Ignored
\\	Backslash (\)
\'	Single quote (')
\"	Double quote (")
\a	ASCII Bell (BEL)
\b	ASCII Backspace (BS)
\f	ASCII Formfeed (FF)
\n	ASCII Linefeed (LF)
\r	ASCII Carriage Return (CR)
\t	ASCII Horizontal Tab (TAB)
\v	ASCII Vertical Tab (VT)
\ooo	ASCII character with octal value ooo
\xhh...	ASCII character with hex value hh...

Figure 1.9: Escape sequences and their meaning

Note

For more information on strings, you can refer to https://docs.python.org/2.0/ref/strings.html.

Escape Sequences with Quotes

Here is how an escape sequence works with quotes. The backslash overrides the single quote as an end quote and allows it to be interpreted as a string character:

```
bookstore = 'Moe\'s'
```

Multi-Line Strings

Short strings always display nicely but, what about multi-line strings? It can be cumbersome to define a paragraph variable that includes a string over multiple lines. In some IDEs, the string may run off the screen, and it may be difficult to read. In addition, it might be advantageous to have line breaks at specific points for the user.

> **Note**
>
> Line breaks will not work inside single or double quotes.

When strings need to span multiple lines, Python provides triple quotes, using single or double quotation marks, as a nice option.

Here is an example of triple quotes (''') used to write a multi-line string:

```
vacation_note = '''
During our vacation to San Francisco, we waited in a long line by
Powell St. Station to take the cable car. Tap dancers performed on
wooden boards. By the time our cable car arrived, we started looking
online for a good place to eat. We're heading to North Beach.
'''
```

> **Note**
>
> Multi-line strings take on the same syntax as a docstring. The difference is that a docstring appears at the beginning of a document, and a multi-line string is defined within the program.

The print() Function

The **print()** function is used to display information to the user, or to the developer. It's one of Python's most widely used built-in functions.

Exercise 8: Displaying Strings

In this exercise, you will learn different ways to display strings:

1. Open a new Jupyter Notebook.

2. Define a greeting variable with the value 'Hello'. Display the greeting using the **print()** function:

```
greeting = 'Hello'
print(greeting)
```

You should get the following output:

```
Hello
```

Hello, as shown in the display, does not include single quotes. This is because the **print()** function is generally intended for the user to print the output.

> **Note**
>
> The quotes are for developer syntax, not user syntax.

3. Display the value of **greeting** without using the **print()** function:

```
greeting
```

You should get the following output:

```
'Hello'
```

When we input **greeting** without the **print()** function, we are obtaining the encoded value, hence the quotes.

4. Consider the following sequence of code in a single cell in a Jupyter Notebook:

```
spanish_greeting = 'Hola.'
spanish_greeting
arabic_greeting = 'Ahlan wa sahlan.'
```

When the preceding cell is run, the preceding code does not display **spanish_greeting**. If the code were run on a terminal as three separate lines, it would display **Hola.**, the string assigned to **spanish_greeting**. The same would be true if the preceding sequence of code were run in three separate cells in a Jupyter Notebook. For consistency, it's useful to use **print()** any time information should be displayed.

5. Display the Spanish greeting:

```
spanish_greeting = 'Hola.'
print(spanish_greeting)
```

You should get the following output:

```
Hola.
```

6. Now, display the Arabic greeting message, as mentioned in the following code snippet:

```
arabic_greeting = 'Ahlan wa sahlan.'
print(arabic_greeting)
```

You should get the following output:

```
Ahlan wa sahlan.
```

The compiler runs through each line in order. Every time it arrives at **print()**, it displays information.

In this exercise, you have learned different ways to display strings, including the **print()** function. You will use the **print()** function very frequently as a developer.

String Operations and Concatenation

The multiplication and addition operators work with strings as well. In particular, the + operator combines two strings into one and is referred to as **string concatenation**. The * operator, for multiplication, repeats a string. In the following exercise, you will be looking at string concatenation in our string samples.

Exercise 9: String Concatenation

In this exercise, you will learn how to combine strings using string concatenation:

1. Open a new Jupyter Notebook.

2. Combine the **spanish_greeting** we used in *Exercise 8, Displaying Strings*, with 'Senor.' using the + operator and display the results:

```
spanish_greeting = 'Hola'
print(spanish_greeting + 'Senor.')
```

You should get the following output:

```
HolaSenor.
```

Notice that there are no spaces between **greeting** and name. If we want spaces between strings, we need to explicitly add them.

3. Now, combine **spanish_greeting** with 'Senor.' using the + operator, but this time, include a **space**:

```
spanish_greeting = 'Hola '
print(spanish_greeting + 'Senor.')
```

You should get the following output:

```
Hola Senor.
```

4. Display the greeting 5 times using the * multiplication operator:

```
greeting = 'Hello'
print(greeting * 5)
```

You should get the following output:

```
HelloHelloHelloHelloHello
```

By completing this exercise successfully, you have combined strings using string concatenation using the + and * operators.

String Interpolation

When writing strings, you may want to include variables in the output. String interpolation includes the variable names as placeholders within the string. There are two standard methods for achieving string interpolation: **comma separators** and **format**.

Comma Separators

Variables may be interpolated into strings using commas to separate clauses. It's similar to the + operator, except it adds spacing for you.

You can have a look at an example here, where we add **Ciao** within a **print** statement:

```
italian_greeting = 'Ciao'
print('Should we greet people with', italian_greeting, 'in North Beach?')
```

You should get the following output:

```
Should we greet people with Ciao in North Beach?
```

Format

With **format**, as with commas, Python types, **ints**, **floats**, and so on, are converted into strings upon execution. The **format** is accessed using brackets and dot notation:

```
owner = 'Lawrence Ferlinghetti'
age = 100
print('The founder of City Lights Bookstore, {}, is now {} years old.'.format(owner,
age))
```

You should get the following output:

```
The founder of City Lights Bookstore, Lawrence Ferlinghetti, is now 100 years old.
```

The **format** works as follows: First, define your variables. Next, in the given string, use **{}** in place of each variable. At the end of the string, add a dot (.) followed by the **format** keyword. Then, in parentheses, list each variable in the desired order of appearance. In the next section, you will look at the built-in string functions available to a Python developer.

The len() Function

There are many built-in functions that are particularly useful for strings. One such function is **len()**, which is short for length. The **len()** function determines the number of characters in a given string.

Note that the **len()** function will also count any blank spaces in a given string.

You'll use the **arabic_greeting** variable used in *Exercise 8*, *Displaying Strings*:

```
len(arabic_greeting)
```

You should get the following output:

```
16
```

> **Note**
>
> When entering variables in Jupyter notebooks, you can use **tab completion**. After you type in a letter or two, you can press the *Tab* key. Python then displays all valid continuations that will complete your expression. If done correctly, you should see your variable listed. Then you can highlight the variable and press *Enter*. Using tab completion will limit errors.

String Methods

All Python types, including strings, have their own methods. These methods generally provide shortcuts for implementing useful tasks. Methods in Python, as in many other languages, are accessed via dot notation.

You can use a new variable, **name**, to access a variety of methods. You can see all methods by pressing the *Tab* button after the variable name and a dot.

Exercise 10: String Methods

In this exercise, you will learn how to implement string methods.

1. Set a new variable, called **name**, to any name that you like:

```
name = 'Corey'
```

> **Note**
>
> Access string methods by pressing the **Tab** button after the variable name and dot (.), as demonstrated in the following screenshot:

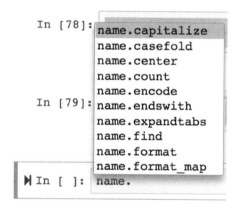

Figure 1.10: Setting a variable name via the dropdown menu

You can scroll down the list to obtain all available string methods.

2. Now, convert the name into lowercase letters using the **lower()** function:

```
name.lower()
```

You should get the following output:

```
'corey'
```

3. Now, capitalize the name using the **capitalize()** function:

```
name.capitalize()
```

You should get the following output:

```
'Corey'
```

4. Convert the name into uppercase letters using **upper()**:

```
name.upper()
```

You should get the following output:

```
'COREY'
```

5. Finally, count the number of **o** instances in the word **'Corey'**:

```
name.count('o')
```

You should get the following output:

```
1
```

In this exercise, you have learned about a variety of string methods, including **lower()**, **capitalize()**, **upper()**, and **count()**.

Methods may only be applied to their representative types. For instance, the **lower()** method only works on strings, not integers or floats. By contrast, built-in functions such as **len()** and **print()** can be applied to a variety of types.

> **Note**
>
> Methods do not change the original variable unless we explicitly reassign the variable. So, the name has not been changed, despite the methods that we have applied.

Casting

It's common for numbers to be expressed as strings when dealing with input and output. Note that **'5'** and **5** are different types. We can easily convert between numbers and strings using the appropriate type keywords. In the following exercise, we are going to be using types and casting to understand the concepts much better.

Exercise 11: Types and Casting

In this exercise, you will learn how types and casting work together:

1. Open a new Jupyter Notebook.

2. Determine the type of **'5'**:

```
type('5')
```

You should get the following output:

```
str
```

3. Now, add '5' and '7':

```
'5' + '7'
```

You should get the following output:

```
'57'
```

The answer is not 12 because, here, **5** and **7** are of type **string**, not of type **int**. Recall that the **+** operator concatenates strings. If we want to add **5** and **7**, we must convert them first.

4. Convert the '5' string to an **int** using the code mentioned in the following code snippet:

```
int('5')
```

You should get the following output:

```
5
```

Now **5** is a number, so it can be combined with other numbers via standard mathematical operations.

5. Add '5' and '7' by converting them to **int** first:

```
int('5') + int('7')
```

You should get the following output:

```
In [4]: int('5') + int('7')

Out[4]: 12
```

Figure 1.11: Output after adding two integers converted from a string

In this exercise, you have learned several ways in which strings work with casting.

The input() Function

The `input()` function is a built-in function that allows user input. It's a little different than what we have seen so far. Let's see how it works in action.

Exercise 12: The input() Function

In this exercise, you will utilize the `input()` function to obtain information from the user:

1. Open a new Jupyter Notebook.

2. Ask a user for their name. Respond with an appropriate greeting:

```
# Choose a question to ask
print('What is your name?')
```

You should get the following output:

```
In [1]:  # Choose a question to ask
         print('What is your name?')

         What is your name?
```

Figure 1.12: The user is prompted to answer a question

3. Now, set a variable that will be equal to the `input()` function, as mentioned in the following code snippet:

```
name = input()
```

You should get the following output:

```
In [*]:  name = input()

         Corey
```

Figure 1.13: The user may type anything into the provided space

4. Finally, select an appropriate output:

```
print('Hello, ' + name + '.')
```

You should get the following output:

```
In [3]: print('Hello, ' + name + '.')

Hello, Corey.
```

Figure 1.14: After pressing Enter, the full sequence is displayed

> **Note**
>
> `input()` can be finicky in Jupyter Notebooks. If an error arises when entering the code, try **restarting** the kernel. Restarting the kernel will erase the current memory and start each cell afresh. This is advisable if the notebook stalls.

In this exercise, you have learned how the `input()` function works.

Activity 3: Using the input() Function to Rate Your Day

In this activity, you need to create an input type where you ask the user to rate their day on a scale of 1 to 10.

Using the `input()` function, you will prompt a user for input and respond with a comment that includes the input. In this activity, you will print a message to the user asking for a number. Then, you will assign the number to a variable and use that variable in a second message that you display to the user.

The steps are as follows:

1. Open a new Jupyter Notebook.

2. Display a question prompting the user to rate their day on a number scale of **1** to **10**.

3. Save the user's input as a variable.

4. Display a statement to the user that includes the number.

> **Note**
>
> The solution for this activity is available on page 517.

String Indexing and Slicing

Indexing and **slicing** are crucial parts of programming. In data analysis, indexing and slicing DataFrames is essential to keep track of rows and columns, something we will practice in *Chapter 10, Data Analytics with pandas and NumPy*. The mechanics behind indexing and slicing dataFrames is the same as indexing and slicing strings, which we will learn in this chapter.

Indexing

The characters of Python strings exist in specific locations; in other words, their order counts. The index is a numerical representation of where each character is located. The first character is at index 0, the second character is at index 1; the third character is at index 2, and so on.

> **Note**
>
> We always start at 0 when indexing.

Consider the following string:

```
destination = 'San Francisco'
```

'S' is in the 0th index, **'a'** is in the 1st index, **'n'** is in the 2nd index, and so on. The characters of each index are accessed using bracket notation as follows:

```
destination[0]
```

You should get the following output:

```
'S'
```

To access the data from the first index, enter the following:

```
destination[1]
```

You should get the following output:

```
'a'
```

To access the data from the second index, enter the following:

```
destination[2]
```

You should get the following output:

```
'n'
```

The character value for **San Francisco** and the corresponding index count is shown in *Figure 1.15*:

Character value	S	a	n
Index Count	0	1	2

Figure 1.15: Diagrammatic representation of the character values and the corresponding positive index values

Now, try adding a -1 as the index value and observe the output:

```
destination[-1]
```

You should get the following output:

```
'o'
```

> **Note**
>
> Negative numbers start at the end of the string. (It makes sense to start with -1 since -0 is the same as 0.)

To access the data from the rear of **San Francisco**, we use the negative sign in this case **-2**:

```
destination[-2]
```

You should get the following output:

```
'c'
```

The following figure 1.16 mentions the characters **sco** from the word **Francisco**, and the corresponding index count:

Character value	s	c	o
Index Count	-3	-2	-1

Figure 1.16: Index value for the negative values for San Francisco

Here is one more example:

```
bridge = 'Golden Gate'
bridge[6]
```

You should get the following output:

```
' '
```

You may be wondering whether you did something wrong because no letter is displayed. On the contrary, it's perfectly fine to have an empty string. In fact, an empty string is one of the most common strings in programming.

Slicing

A **slice** is a subset of a string or other element. A slice could be the whole element or one character, but it's more commonly a group of adjoining characters.

Let's say you want to access the fifth through eleventh letters of a string. So, you start at index 4 and end at index 10, as was explained in the previous *Indexing* section. When slicing, the colon symbol (:) is inserted between indices, like so: [4:10].

There is one caveat. The lower bound of a slice is always included, but the upper bound is not. So, in the preceding example, if you want to include the 10th index, you must use [4:11].

You should now have a look at the following example for slicing.

Retrieve the fifth through eleventh letters of **San Francisco**, which you used in the previous *Indexing* section:

```
destination[4:11]
```

You should get the following output:

```
'Francis'
```

Retrieve the first three letters of **destination**:

```
destination[0:3]
```

You should get the following output:

```
'San'
```

There is a shortcut for getting the first **n** letters of a string. If the first numerical character is omitted, Python will start at the 0th index.

Now, to retrieve the first eight letters of **destination** using the shortcut, use the following code:

```
destination[:8]
```

You should get the following output:

```
'San Fran'
```

Finally, to retrieve the last three letters of **destination**, use this code:

```
destination[-3:]
```

You should get the following output:

```
'sco'
```

The negative sign, -, means that we start at the third-to-last letter, and the colon means that we go to the end.

Strings and Their Methods

You started with string syntax, before moving on to a variety of ways to concatenate strings. You looked at useful built-in functions including **len()** and examined a sample of string methods. Next, you casted numbers as strings and vice versa.

The **input()** function is used to access user input. This really extends what you can do. Responding to user feedback is a core element of programming that you will continue to develop. Finally, you closed with two powerful tools that developers frequently use: indexing and slicing.

There is a great deal more to learn about strings. You will encounter additional problems and methods throughout this book. This introductory chapter is meant to equip you with the basic skills needed to handle strings going forward.

Next, you will learn how to branch programs using conditionals and Booleans.

Booleans and Conditionals

Booleans, named after George Boole, take the values of **True** or **False**. Although the idea behind Booleans is rather simple, they make programming immensely more powerful.

When writing programs, for instance, it's useful to consider multiple cases. If you prompt the user for information, you may want to respond differently depending upon the user's answer.

For instance, if the user gives a rating of 0 or 1, you may give a different response than a rating of 9 or 10. The keyword here is **if**.

Programming based upon multiple cases is referred to as branching. Each branch is represented by a different conditional. Conditionals often start with an 'if' clause, followed by 'else' clauses. The choice of a branch is determined by Booleans, depending on whether the given conditions are **True** or **False**.

Booleans

In Python, a Boolean class object is represented by the **bool** keyword and has a value of **True** or **False**.

> **Note**
>
> Boolean values must be capitalized in Python.

Exercise 13: Boolean Variables

In this short exercise, you will use, assign, and check the type of Boolean variables:

1. Open a new Jupyter Notebook.

2. Now, use a Boolean to classify someone as being over **18** using the following code snippet:

```
over_18 = True
type(over_18)
```

You should get the following output:

```
bool
```

The output is satisfied, and the type is mentioned as a Boolean, that is, **bool**.

3. Use a Boolean to classify someone as not being over **21**:

```
over_21 = False
type(over_21)
```

You should get the following output:

```
bool
```

In this short, quick exercise, you have learned about the **bool** type, one of Python's most important types.

Logical Operators

Booleans may be combined with the **and**, **or**, and **not** logical operators.

For instance, consider the following propositions:

A = True

B = True

Y = False

Z = False

Not simply negates the value, as follows:

not A = False

not Z = True.

And is only true if both propositions are true. Otherwise, it is false:

A and B = True

A and Y = False

Y and Z = False

Or is true if either proposition is true. Otherwise, it is false:

A or B = True

A or Y = True

Y or Z = False

Now let's use them in the following practice example.

Determine whether the following conditions are **True** or **False** given that **over_18 = True** and **over_21 = False**:

- **over_18** and **over_21**
- **over_18** or **over_21**
- not **over_18**
- not **over_21** or (**over_21 or over_18**)

1. You have to put this into code and first assign **True** and **False** to **over_18** and **over_21**:

```
over_18, over_21 = True, False
```

2. Next you can assume the individual is **over_18** and **over_21**:

```
over_18 and over_21
```

You should get the following output:

```
False
```

3. You now assume the individual is **over_18** or **over_21**:

```
over_18 or over_21
```

You should get the following output:

```
True
```

4. You now assume the individual is not **over_18**:

```
not over_18
```

You should get the following output:

```
False
```

5. You assume the individual is not **over_21** or (**over_21 or over_18**):

```
not over_21 or (over_21 or over_18)
```

You should get the following output:

```
True
```

In the next section, we will learn about the comparison operators that go along with Booleans.

Comparison Operators

Python objects may be compared using a variety of symbols that evaluate to Booleans.
Figure 1.17 shows the comparison table with their corresponding operators:

<	less than
<=	less than or equal to
>	greater than
>=	greater than or equal to
==	equivalent to
!=	not equivalent to

Figure 1.17: Comparison table with its corresponding symbols

> **Note**
>
> The = and == symbols are often confused. The = symbol is an assignment symbol. So, **x** = **3** assigns the integer **3** to the **x** variable. The == symbol makes a comparison. Thus **x** == **3** checks to see whether **x** is equivalent to **3**. The result of **x** == **3** will be **True** or **False**.

Exercise 14: Comparison Operators

In this exercise, you will practice using comparison operators. You will start with some basic mathematical examples:

1. Open a new Jupyter Notebook.

2. Now, set **age** as equal to **20** and include a comparison operator to check whether **age** is less than **13**:

```
age = 20
age < 13
```

You should get the following output:

```
False
```

3. Using the following code snippet, you can check whether **age** is greater than or equal to **20** and less than or equal to **21**:

```
age >= 20 and age <= 21
```

You should get the following output:

```
True
```

4. Now check whether **age** is equivalent to **21**:

```
age != 21
```

You should get the following output:

```
True
```

5. Now, check whether **age** is equivalent to **19**:

```
age == 19
```

You should get the following output:

```
False
```

The double equals sign, or the equivalent operator, **==**, is very important in Python. It allows us to determine whether two objects are equal. You can now address the question of whether **6** and **6.0** are the same in Python.

6. Is **6** equivalent to **6.0** in Python? Let's find out:

```
6 == 6.0
```

You should get the following output:

```
True
```

This may come as a bit of a surprise. **6** and **6.0** are different types, but they are equivalent. Why would that be?

Since **6** and **6.0** are equivalent mathematically, it makes sense that they would be equivalent in Python, even though the types are different. Consider whether 6 should be equivalent to 42/7. The mathematical answer is yes. Python often conforms to mathematical truths, even with integer division. You can conclude that it's possible for different types to have equivalent objects.

7. Now find out whether **6** is equivalent to the **'6'** string:

```
6 == '6'
```

You should get the following output:

```
False
```

Here, you emphasize that different types usually do not have equivalent objects. In general, it's a good idea to cast objects as the same type before testing for equivalence.

Next, let's find out whether someone is in their 20's or 30's:

```
(age >= 20 and age < 30) or (age >= 30 and age < 40)
```

You should get the following output:

```
True
```

Parentheses are not necessary when there is only one possible interpretation. When using more than two conditions, parentheses are generally a good idea. Note that parentheses are always permitted. The following is another approach:

```
(20 <= age < 30) or (30 <= age < 40)
```

You should get the following output:

```
True
```

Although the parentheses in the preceding code line are not strictly required, they make the code more readable. A good rule of thumb is to use parentheses for clarity.

By completing this exercise, you have practiced using different comparison operators.

Comparing Strings

Does **'a'** < **'c'** make sense? What about **'New York'** > **'San Francisco'**?

Python uses the convention of alphabetical order to make sense of these comparisons. Think of a dictionary: when comparing two words, the word that comes later in the dictionary is considered greater than the word that comes before.

Exercise 15: Comparing Strings

In this exercise, you will be comparing strings using Python:

1. Open a new Jupyter Notebook.

2. Let's compare single letters:

```
'a' < 'c'
```

You should get the following output:

```
True
```

3. Now, let's compare 'New York' and 'San Francisco':

```
'New York' > 'San Francisco'
```

You should get the following output:

```
False
```

This is **False** because **'New York' < 'San Francisco'**. 'New York' does not come later in the dictionary than 'San Francisco'.

In this exercise, you have learned how to compare strings using comparison operators.

Conditionals

Conditionals are used when we want to express code based upon a set of circumstances or values. Conditionals evaluate Boolean values or Boolean expressions, and they are usually preceded by **'if'**.

Let's say we are writing a voting program, and we want to print something only if the user is under 18.

The if Syntax

```
if age < 18:
    print('You aren\'t old enough to vote.')
```

There are several key components to a condition. Let's break them down.

The first is the **'if'** keyword. Most conditionals start with an **if** clause. Everything between **'if'** and the colon is the condition that we are checking.

The next important piece is the colon :. The colon indicates that the **if** clause has completed. At this point, the compiler decides whether the preceding condition is **True** or **False**.

Syntactically, everything that follows the colon is indented.

Python uses **indentation** instead of brackets. Indentation can be advantageous when dealing with nested conditionals because it avoids cumbersome notation. Python indentation is expected to be **four spaces** and may usually be achieved by pressing **Tab** on your keyboard.

Indented lines will only run if the condition evaluates to **True**. If the condition evaluates to **False**, the indented lines will be skipped over entirely.

Indentation

Indentation is one of Python's singular features. Indentation is used everywhere in Python. Indentation can be liberating. One advantage is the number of keystrokes. It takes one keystroke to tab, and two keystrokes to insert brackets. Another advantage is readability. It's clearer and easier to read code when it all shares the same indentation, meaning the block of code belongs to the same branch.

One potential drawback is that dozens of tabs may draw text offscreen, but this is rare in practice, and can usually be avoided with elegant code. Other concerns, such as indenting or unindenting multiple lines, may be handled via shortcuts. Select all of the text and press **Tab** to indent. Select all of the text and press **Shift + Tab** to unindent.

> **Note**
>
> Indentation is unique to Python. This may result in strong opinions on both sides. In practice, indentation has been shown to be very effective, and developers used to other languages will appreciate its advantages in time.

Exercise 16: Using the if Syntax

In this exercise, you will be using conditionals using the **if** clause:

1. Open a new Jupyter Notebook.

2. Now, run multiple lines of code where you set the **age** variable to **20** and add an **if** clause, as mentioned in the following code snippet:

```
age = 20
if age >= 18 and age < 21:
    print('At least you can vote.')
    print('Poker will have to wait.')
```

You should get the following output:

```
At least you can vote.
Poker will have to wait.
```

There is no limit to the number of indented statements. Each statement will run in order, provided that the preceding condition is **True**.

3. Now, use nested conditionals:

```
if age >= 18:
  print('You can vote.')
  if age >= 21:
    print('You can play poker.')
```

You should get the following output:

```
You can vote.
```

In this case, it's true that **age >= 18**, so the first statement prints **You can vote**. The second condition, age >= **21**, however, is false, so the second statement does not get printed.

In this exercise, you have learned how to use conditionals using the **if** clause. Conditionals will always start with **if**.

if else

if conditionals are commonly joined with **else** clauses. The idea is as follows. Say you want to print something to all users unless the user is under 18. You can address this with an **if-else** conditional. If the user is less than 18, you print one statement. Otherwise, you print another. The otherwise clause is preceded with **else**.

Exercise 17: Using the if-else Syntax

In this exercise, you will learn how to use conditionals that have two options, one following **if**, and one following **else**:

1. Open a new Jupyter Notebook.

2. Introduce a voting program only to users over 18 by using the following code snippet:

```
age = 20
if age < 18:
  print('You aren\'t old enough to vote.')
else:
  print('Welcome to our voting program.')
```

You should get the following output:

```
Welcome to our voting program.
```

> **Note**
>
> Everything after **else** is indented, just like everything after the **if** loop.

3. Now run the following code snippet, which is an alternative to the code mentioned in step 2 of this exercise:

```
if age >= 18:
    print('Welcome to our voting program.')
else:
    print('You aren\'t old enough to vote.')
```

You should get the following output:

```
Welcome to our voting program.
```

In this exercise, you have learned how to use **if-else** in conjunction with loops.

There are many ways to write a program in Python. One is not necessarily better than another. It may be advantageous to write faster programs or more readable programs.

A program is a set of instructions run by a computer to complete a certain task. Programs may be one line of code, or tens of thousands. You will learn important skills and techniques for writing Python programs in various chapters throughout this book.

The elif Statement

elif is short for **else if**. **elif** does not have meaning in isolation. elif appears in between an **if** and **else** clause. An example should make things clearer. Have a look at the following code snippet and copy it into your Jupyter notebook. The explanation for this code is mentioned right after the output:

```
if age <= 10:
    print('Listen, learn, and have fun.')
elif age<= 19:
    print('Go fearlessly forward.')
elif age <= 29:
    print('Seize the day.')
elif age <= 39:
    print('Go for what you want.')
elif age <= 59:
```

```
    print('Stay physically fit and healthy.')
else:
    print('Each day is magical.')
```

You should get the following output:

```
Seize the day.
```

Now, let's break down the code for a better explanation:

1. The first line checks **if** age is less than or equal to **10**. Since this condition is false, the next branch is checked.

2. The next branch is **elif** age <= **19**. This line checks if age is less than or equal to 19. This is also not true, so we move to the next branch.

3. The next branch is **elif** age <= **29**. This is true since **age** = **20**. The indented statement that follows will be printed.

4. Once any branch has been executed, the entire sequence is aborted, none of the subsequent **elif** or else branches are checked.

5. If none of the **if** or **elif** branches were true, the final **else** branch will automatically be executed.

In the next topic, you will be learning about loops.

Loops

"Write the first 100 numbers."

There are several assumptions implicit in this seemingly simple command. The first is that the student knows where to start, namely at number 1. The second assumption is that the student knows where to end, at number 100. And the third is that the student understands that they should count by 1.

In programming, this set of instructions may be executed with a loop.

There are three key components to most loops:

1. The start of the loop

2. The end of the loop

3. The increment between numbers in the loop

Python distinguishes between two fundamental kinds of loops: **while** loops, and **for** loops.

The while Loops

In a **while** loop, a designated segment of code repeats provided that a particular condition is true. When the condition evaluates to false, the **while** loop stops running. The **while** loops print out the first 10 numbers.

You could print the first 10 numbers by implementing the **print** function 10 times, but using a **while** loop is more efficient, and it scales easily. In general, it's not a good idea to copy and paste while coding. If you find yourself copying and pasting, there's probably a more efficient way. Let's have a look at the following example code block:

```
i = 1
while i <= 10:
   print(i)
   i += 1
```

You should get the following output:

```
1
2
3
4
5
6
7
8
9
10
```

You can break down the preceding code block and find out what's happening in concrete steps:

- **Initialize the variable**: Loops need to be initialized with a variable. The variable is going to change throughout the loop. The naming of the variable is up to you. **i** is often chosen because it stands for incrementor. An example is **i = 1**.

- **Set up the while loop**: The **while** loop starts with the **while** keyword. Following **while** is the chosen variable. After the variable comes the condition that must be met for the loop to run. In general, the condition should have some way of being broken. When counting, the condition usually includes an upper limit, but it could also be broken in other ways, such as **i != 10**. This line of code is the most critical piece of the loop. It sets up how many times the loop is expected to run. An example is **while i <= 10:**.

- **Instructions**: The instructions include all indented lines after the colon. Anything could be printed, any function could be called, and any number of lines may be executed. It all depends on the program. As long as the code is syntactically correct, generally speaking, anything goes. This part of the loop is going to run over and over as long as the aforementioned condition is true. An example is `print(i)`.

- **Increment**: The incrementor is a crucial part of this example. Without it, the preceding code will never stop running. It will print 1's endlessly because 1 is always less than 10. Here, you increment by 1, but you could also increment by 2, or any other number. An example is `i += 1`.

Now that you understand the separate pieces, you should look at how it works together:

1. The variable is initialized as **1**. The `while` loop checks the condition. 1 is less than or equal to **10**. 1 is printed. 1 is added to `i`. We increment to `i = 2`.

2. After all indented code after the colon has run, the loop is executed again by returning to the `while` keyword.

3. The `while` loop checks the condition again. **2** is less than or equal to **10**. **2** is printed to the console. **1** is added to `i`. We now increment to `i = 3`.

4. The `while` loop checks the condition again. **3** is less than or equal to **10**. **3** is printed to the console. **1** is added to `i`. We increment to `i = 4`.

5. The while loop continues to increment and print out numbers until reaching the number 10.

6. The `while` loop checks the condition. **10** is less than or equal to **10**. **10** is printed to the console. **1** is added to `i`. Now, increment to `i = 11`.

7. The `while` loop checks the condition. **11** is not less than or equal to **10**. We break out of the loop by moving beyond the indentation.

> **Note**
>
> You will get stuck in infinite loops. It happens to everyone. At some point, you will forget to add the increment, and you will be stuck in an infinite loop. In Jupyter Notebooks, just **restart** the kernel.

An Infinite Loop

Now you should have a look at **infinite** loops. The following code snippet supports this topic:

```
x = 5
while x <= 20:
   print(x)
```

Python often runs very quickly. If something is taking much longer than expected, an infinite loop might be the culprit, as in the aforementioned code snippet. A developer here would be setting all the variables and conditions right to avoid the infinite loop case. An example of a well-written Python code is as follows:

```
x = 5
while x<= 20:
    print(x)
    x += 5
```

break

break is a special keyword in Python that is specifically designed for loops. If placed inside of a loop, commonly in a conditional, **break** will immediately terminate the loop. It doesn't matter what comes before or after the loop. The break is placed on its own line, and it *breaks out of the loop*.

To practice, you should print the first number greater than **100** that is divisible by **17**.

The idea is that you are going to start at 101 and keep counting until you find a number divisible by **17**. Assume you don't know what number to stop at. This is where break comes into play. **break** will terminate the loop. You can set our upper bound at some number that you know you will never reach and break out of the loop when you get there:

```
# Find first number greater than 100 and divisible by 17.
x = 100
while x <= 1000:
   x += 1
   if x % 17 == 0:
     print('', x, 'is the first number greater than 100 that is divisible by 17.')
     break
```

The x += 1 iterator is placed at the beginning of the loop. This allows us to start with 101. The iterator may be placed anywhere in the loop.

Since 101 is not divisible by **17**, the loop repeats, and x = **102**. Since **102** is divisible by **17**, the **print** statement executes and we break out of the loop.

This is the first time you have used **double indentation**. Since the if conditional is inside of a **while** loop, it must be indented as well.

Activity 4: Finding the Least Common Multiple (LCM)

In this activity, you will find the LCM of two divisors. The LCM of two divisors is the first number that both divisors can divide.

For instance, the LCM of 4 and 6 is 12, because 12 is the first number that both 4 and 6 can divide. You will find the LCM of 2 numbers. You will set the variables, then initialize a **while** loop with an iterator and a Boolean that is **True** by default. You will set up a conditional that will break if the iterator divides both numbers. You will increase the iterator and print the results after the loop completes.

In this activity, using the following steps, you need to find the LCM of **24** and **36**.

The steps are as follows:

1. Set a pair of variables as equal to **24** and **36**.

2. Initialize the **while** loop, based on a Boolean that is **True** by default, with an iterator.

3. Set up a conditional to check whether the iterator divides both numbers.

4. Break the while loop when the LCM is found.

5. Increment the iterator at the end of the loop.

6. **Print** the results.

    You should get the following output:

```
The Least Common Multiple of 24 and 36 is 72.
```

> **Note**
>
> The solution for this activity is available on page 518.

Programs

You have been writing programs all through this book. Every chunk of executable code that can be saved and run on demand is a computer program. You have written programs that greeted users, and you just wrote a program to compute the LCM of a given number in *Activity 4, Finding the Least Common Multiple (LCM)*.

Now that you have a lot of tools under our belt, you can combine them to write some pretty interesting programs. You know how to generate input from a user, we know how to convert the input into desired types, and you know how to use conditionals and loops to iterate through cases and print various results depending upon the outcome.

Later in the book, you will get into the details of saving and testing programs. For now, you should work on some interesting examples and exercises. For instance, in the next exercise, you will build a program step by step to identify perfect squares.

Exercise 18: Calculating Perfect Squares

The goal of this exercise is to prompt the user to enter a given number and find out whether it is a perfect square.

The following steps in this exercise will help you with this:

1. Open a new Jupyter Notebook.

2. Prompt the user to enter a number to see if it's a perfect square:

```python
print('Enter a number to see if it\'s a perfect square.')
```

3. Set a variable as equal to **input()**. In this case let's enter 64:

```python
number = input()
```

4. Ensure the user input is a positive integer:

```python
number = abs(int(number))
```

5. Choose an iterator variable:

```python
i = -1
```

6. Initialize a Boolean to check for a perfect square:

```python
square = False
```

7. Initialize a **while** loop from **-1** to the square root of the number:

```
while i <= number**(0.5):
```

8. Increment **i** by **1**:

```
i += 1
```

9. Check the square root of the **number**:

```
if i*i == number:
```

10. Indicate that we have a perfect **square**:

```
square = True
```

11. **break** out of the loop:

```
break
```

12. If the number is **square**, **print** out the result:

```
if square:
    print('The square root of', number, 'is', i, '.')
```

13. If the number is not a square, print out this result:

```
else:
    print('', number, 'is not a perfect square.')
```

You should get the following output:

```
The square root of 64 is 8.
```

In this exercise, you have written a program to check to see whether the user's number is a perfect square.

In the next exercise, you are going to build a similar program that will accept inputs from the user. You need to provide the best possible offer for a real estate and either accept or decline the offer.

Exercise 19: Real Estate Offer

The goal of this exercise is to prompt the user to bid on a house and let them know if and when the bid has been accepted.

The following steps in this exercise will help you with this:

1. Open a new Jupyter Notebook.

2. Begin by stating a market price:

```
print('A one bedroom in the Bay Area is listed at $599,000')
```

3. Prompt the user to make an offer on the house:

```
print('Enter your first offer on the house.')
```

4. Set **offer** as equal to **input()**:

```
offer = abs(int(input()))
```

5. Prompt the user to enter their best offer for the house:

```
print('Enter your best offer on the house.')
```

6. Set **best** as equal to **input()**:

```
best = abs(int(input()))
```

7. Prompt the user to choose increments:

```
print('How much more do you want to offer each time?')
```

8. Set **increment** as equal to **input()**:

```
increment = abs(int(input()))
```

9. Set **offer_accepted** as equal to **False**:

```
offer_accepted = False
```

10. Initialize the **for** loop from **offer** to **best**:

```
while offer <= best:
```

11. If the **offer** is greater than **650000**, they get the house:

```
if offer >= 650000:
    offer_accepted = True
    print('Your offer of', offer, 'has been accepted!')
    break
```

12. If the **offer** does not exceed **650000**, they don't get the house:

```
print('We\'re sorry, you\'re offer of', offer, 'has not been accepted.' )
```

13. Add **increment** to **offer**:

```
offer += increment
```

You should get the following output:

```
A one bedroom in the Bay Area is listed at $599,000
Enter your first offer on the house.
500000
Enter your best offer on the house.
690000
How much more do you want to offer each time?
50000
We're sorry, you're offer of 500000 has not been accepted.
We're sorry, you're offer of 550000 has not been accepted.
We're sorry, you're offer of 600000 has not been accepted.
Your offer of 650000 has been accepted!
```

Figure 1.18: Output showing the conditions mentioned in the code using loops

In this exercise, you have prompted the user to bid for a house and let them know when and if the bid was accepted.

The for Loop

The **for** loops are similar to **while** loops, but they have additional advantages, such as being able to iterate over strings and other objects.

Exercise 20: Using for Loops

In this exercise, you will utilize **for** loops to print the characters in a string in addition to a range of numbers:

1. Open a new Jupyter Notebook.

2. Print out the characters of 'Portland':

```
for i in 'Portland':
    print(i)
```

You should get the following output:

```
P
o
r
t
l
a
n
d
```

The **for** keyword often goes with the in keyword. The **i** variable is generic. The phrase, **for i in**, means that Python is going to check what comes next and look at its individual components. Strings are composed of characters, so Python will do something with each of the individual characters. In this particular case, Python will print out the individual characters, as per the **print(i)** command.

What if we want to do something with a range of numbers? Can **for** loops be used for that? Absolutely. Python provides another keyword, **range**, to access a range of numbers. **range** is often defined by two numbers, the first number, and the last number, and it includes all numbers in between. Interestingly, the output of **range** includes the first number, but not the last number. You will see why in a minute.

3. You use a lower bound of **1** and an upper bound of **10** with range to **print 1-9**:

```
for i in range(1,10):
    print(i)
```

You should get the following output:

```
1
2
3
4
5
6
7
8
9
```

The range does not print the number **10**.

4. Now use **range** with one bound only, the number **10**, to print the first ten numbers:

```
for i in range(10):
    print(i)
```

You should get the following output:

```
0
1
2
3
4
5
6
7
8
9
```

So, **range(10)** will print out the first **10** numbers, starting at **0**, and ending with **9**.

Now let's say that you want to count by increments of **2**. You can add a third bound, a step increment, to count up or down by any number desired.

Use a step increment to count the even numbers through 10:

```
for i in range(1, 11, 2):
    print(i)
```

You should get the following output:

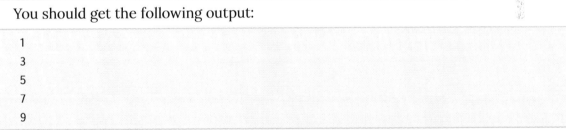

```
1
3
5
7
9
```

Similarly, you can count down using negative numbers, which is shown in the next step.

5. Use a step increment to count down from **3** to **-1**:

```
for i in range(3, 0, -1):
    print(i)
```

You should get the following output:

```
3
2
1
```

And, of course, you can use nested loops, which is shown in the next step.

6. Now, **print** each letter of your **name** three times:

```
name = 'Corey'
for i in range(3):
    for i in name:
        print(i)
```

You should get the following output:

```
C
o
r
e
y
C
o
r
e
y
C
o
r
e
y
```

In this exercise, you have utilized loops to print any given number of integers and characters in a string.

The continue Keyword

continue is another Python keyword designed for loops. When Python reaches the **continue** keyword, it stops the code and goes back to the beginning of the loop. continue is similar to **break** because they both interrupt the loop process, but **break** terminates the loop, **continue** continues the loop from the beginning.

Let's look at an example of **continue** in practice. The following code prints out every two-digit prime number:

```
for num in range(10,100):
  if num % 2 == 0:
    continue
  if num % 3 == 0:
    continue
  if num % 5 == 0:
    continue
  if num % 7 == 0:
    continue
  print(num)
```

You should get the following output:

```
11
13
17
19
23
29
31
37
41
43
47
53
59
61
67
71
73
79
83
89
97
```

Let's go through the beginning of the code. The first number to check is **10**. The first line checks to see if **10** can be divided by **2**. Since **2** does divide **10**, we go inside the conditional and reach the **continue** keyword. Executing **continue** returns to the start of the loop.

The next number that is checked is **11**. Since **2,3,5**, and **7** do not divide **11**, you reach the final line and print the number **11**.

Activity 5: Building Conversational Bots Using Python

You are working as a Python developer and you are building two conversational bots for your clients. You create a list of steps beforehand to help you out, as outlined in the following section. These steps will help you build two bots that take input from the user and produce a coded response.

The aim of this activity is to use **nested** conditionals to build two conversational bots. In this activity, you will build two conversational bots. The first bot will ask the user two questions and include the user's answer in each of its follow-up responses. The second bot will ask a question that requires a numerical answer. Different responses will be given to a different number of scales. The process will be repeated for a second question.

The steps are as follows:

For the first bot, the steps are as follows:

1. Ask the user at least two questions.

2. Respond to each answer. Include the answer in the response.

For the second bot, the steps are as follows:

1. Ask a question that can be answered with a number scale, such as **"On a scale of 1-10…"**.

2. Respond differently depending on the answer given.

3. State a different question following each answer that can be answered with a number scale.

4. Respond differently depending on the answer given.

> **Note**
>
> The second bot should be written with nested conditionals.

Hint - casting may be important.

The expected output for bot 1 is as follows:

```
We're kindred spirits, Corey.Talk later.
```

The expected output for bot 2 is as follows:

```
How intelligent are you? 0 is very dumb. And 10 is a genius
8
Are you human by chance? Wait. Don't answer that.
How human are you? 0 is not at all and 10 is human all the way.
8
I think this courtship is over.
```

Figure 1.19: Expected outcome from one of the possible values entered by the user.

> **Note**
>
> The solution for this activity is available on page 519.

Summary

You have gone over a lot of material in this introductory chapter. You have covered math operations, string concatenation and methods, general Python types, variables, conditionals, and loops. Combining these elements allows us to write programs of real value.

Additionally, we have been learning Python syntax. You now understand some of the most common errors, and you're becoming accustomed to the importance that indentation plays. You're learning how to leverage important keywords such as **range**, **in**, **if**, and **True** and **False**.

Going forward, you now have the key fundamental skills required of all Python programmers. Although there is much to learn, you have a vital foundation in place to build upon the types and techniques discussed here.

Coming up next, you will learn about some of the most important Python types, including lists, dictionaries, tuples, and sets.

2

Python Structures

Overview

By the end of this chapter, you will be able to explain the different types of Python data structures; create lists, dictionaries, and sets and describe the differences between them; create matrices and manipulate both a matrix as a whole and its individual cells; call the `zip()` function to create different Python structures; find what methods are available for lists, dictionaries, and sets; write a program using the most popular methods for lists, dictionaries, and sets and convert between different Python structures.

Introduction

In the previous chapter, you learned the basics of the Python programming language and essential elements such as **string**, **int**, and the use of conditionals and loops that control the flow of a Python program. You should now be familiar with writing programs in Python by utilizing these elements.

In this chapter, you are going to look at how to use data structures to store more complex types of data that help to model the actual data and represent it in the real world.

In programming languages, data structures refer to objects that can hold some data together, which means they are used to store a collection of related data.

For instance, you can use a list to store our to-do items for the day. The following is an example to show you how lists are coded:

```
todo = ["pick up laundry", "buy Groceries", "pay electric bills"]
```

We can also use a dictionary object to store more complex information such as subscribers' details from our mailing list. Here is an example code snippet, but don't worry, we will cover this later in this chapter:

```
User = {
    "first_name": "Jack",
    "last_name":"White",
    "age": 41,
    "email": "jack.white@gmail.com"
}
```

There are four types of data structures in Python: **list**, **tuple**, **dictionary**, and **set**.

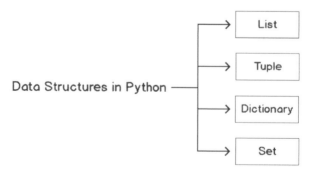

Figure 2.1: The different data structures in Python

These data structures define the relationship between data and the operations that can be performed on data. They are a way of organizing and storing data that can be accessed efficiently under different circumstances.

The Power of Lists

You will now look at the first type of data structure in Python: lists.

A list is a type of container in Python that is used to store multiple data sets at the same time. Python lists are often compared to arrays in other programming languages, but they do a lot more.

Figure 2.2: A Python list with a positive index

A list in Python is written within square brackets, [ ]. Each element in the list has its own distinct **position** and **index**. The elements in a list have a finite sequence. Like other programming languages, the index of the first item of a list is 0, and the second item has an index of 1, and so on. This has to do with how lists are implemented at a lower programming level, so do take note of this when you are writing index-based operations for lists and other iterable objects.

You will now look at the different ways that lists can be useful by completing *Exercise 21, Working with Python Lists*.

Exercise 21: Working with Python Lists

In this exercise, you will learn how to work with a Python list by coding and creating a list and adding items. For example, this could prove useful if, for instance, you have to use a list to store the items that are in a shopping cart:

1. Open a new Jupyter Notebook.

2. Now enter the following code snippet:

```
shopping = ["bread","milk", "eggs"]
print(shopping)
```

You should get the following output:

```
['bread', 'milk', 'eggs']
```

You created a list called **shopping** and added items to your list (**bread**, **milk**, and **eggs**).

Since a list is a type of iterable in Python, you can use a **for** loop to iterate over all of the elements inside a list.

3. Now, enter and execute the code for a **for** loop and observe the output:

```
for item in shopping:
    print(item)
```

You should get the following output:

```
bread
milk
eggs
```

> **Note**
>
> Python lists are different from arrays used in other languages, such as Java and C#. Python actually allows mixed types in a list, that is, **int** and **string**.

4. Now use a **mixed** type of data within the list's content and enter the following code in a new cell:

```
mixed = [365, "days", True]
print(mixed)
```

You should get the following output:

```
[365, 'days', True]
```

But you might be wondering, in that case, shouldn't we be allowed to store a list of lists inside a list? Let's look at that in the next section. This is also known as a **nested list**, which can be used to represent a complex data structure.

In *Exercise 21, Working with Python Lists*, you were introduced to the basics of Python lists.

Later in this chapter, we will dive in deep and learn about the other types of lists that Python provides.

Matrices as Nested Lists

Most of the data we store in the real world is in the form of a tabular data table, that is, **rows** and **columns**, instead of a one-dimensional flat list. Such tables are called **matrices** or **two-dimensional arrays**. Python (and most other programming languages) does not provide a table structure out of the box. Programming languages do not provide table structures as it is not the role of a language to do so. A table structure is simply a way to present data.

What you can do is to present the table structure shown in *Figure* 2.3 using a list of lists; for example, if you want to store the following fruit orders using a list:

Apple	Banana	Orange
5	8	9
7	6	2

Figure 2.3: A representation of lists of lists as a matrix

Mathematically, you can present the information shown in figure 2.3 using a 2 x 3 (2 rows by 3 columns) matrix. This matrix would look like this:

$$\begin{bmatrix} 1 & 2 & 3 \\ 4 & 5 & 6 \end{bmatrix}$$

Figure 2.4: A matrix representation of data

Now you will see how you can store this matrix as a nested list in the following exercise.

Exercise 22: Using a Nested List to Store Data from a Matrix

In this exercise, you will look at working with a nested list, storing values in it, and accessing it using a number of methods:

1. Open a new Jupyter notebook.

2. Enter the following code in a new cell:

```
m = [[1, 2, 3], [4, 5, 6]]
```

We can store the matrix as a series of lists inside a list which is called as a nested list.

3. Now **print** list **m**:

```
print(m[1][1])
```

We can now access the elements using variable **[row][column]** notation.

You should get the following output:

```
5
```

It prints the value of row 2, column 2, which is **5** (remember, we are using a zero-based index offset).

4. Now, access each of the elements in the nested list matrix by retaining their reference index with two variables, **i** and **j**:

```
for i in range(len(m)):
    for j in range(len(m[i])):
        print(m[i][j])
```

The preceding code uses a **for** loop to iterate twice. In the outer loop (**i**), we iterate every single row in matrix **m**, and in the inner loop (**j**), we iterate every column in the row. Finally, we **print** the element in the corresponding position.

You should get the following output:

```
1
2
3
4
5
6
```

5. Use two **for..in** loops to print all the elements within the matrix:

```
for row in m:
    for col in row:
        print(col)
```

The **for** loop in the code used in step 4 iterates both the **row** and **col**. This type of notation does not require us to have prior knowledge of the matrix's dimensions.

You should get the following output:

```
1
2
3
4
5
6
```

At the end of this exercise, you know how a nested list stored as a matrix works. You have also got to know the different ways of accessing values from nested lists. In *Activity 6, Using a Nested List to Store Employee Data*, you will implement the concepts you have learned about lists and nested lists to store employee data.

Activity 6: Using a Nested List to Store Employee Data

You are going to store table data using a nested list. Imagine this: you are currently working in an IT company and are given the following list of employees. You are asked by your manager to use Python to store this data for further company use.

The aim of this activity is to use nested lists to store data and print them as you need them.

The data provided to you by your company is shown in *Figure 2.5*:

Name	Age	Department
John Mckee	38	Sales
Lisa Crawford	29	Marketing
Sujan Patel	33	HR

Figure 2.5: Table consisting of employee data

Follow these steps to complete this activity:

1. Open a new Jupyter Notebook.

2. Create a list and assign it to **employees**.

3. Create three nested lists in **employees** to store the information of each employee, respectively.

4. Print the **employees** variable.

5. Print the details of all employees in a presentable format.

6. Print only the details of **Lisa Crawford**.

By printing the details in a presentable format, you should get the following output:

```
['Lisa Crawford', 29, 'Marketing']
Name: Lisa Crawford
Age: 29
Department: Marketing
--------------------
```

Figure 2.6: Printed details of an employee using lists

Note

The solution for this activity is available on page 524.

In the next topic, you will be discussing a bit more about matrixes and their operations.

Matrix Operations

You will continue to look at how to use nested lists for some basic matrix operations. First, you look at how to add two matrices in Python. Matrix addition requires both matrices to have the same dimensions; the results will also be of the same dimensions.

In *Exercise 23, Implementing Matrix Operations (Addition and Subtraction)*, you will be using the following matrix data, **X** and **Y**, in figures 2.7 and 2.8:

$$X = \begin{bmatrix} 1 & 2 & 3 \\ 4 & 5 & 6 \\ 7 & 8 & 9 \end{bmatrix}$$

Figure 2.7: Matrix data for matrix X

$$Y = \begin{bmatrix} 10 & 11 & 12 \\ 13 & 14 & 15 \\ 16 & 17 & 18 \end{bmatrix}$$

Figure 2.8: Matrix data for matrix Y

Exercise 23: Implementing Matrix Operations (Addition and Subtraction)

In this exercise you will add and subtract the **X** and **Y** matrixes using Python.

The following steps will enable you to complete the exercise:

1. Open a new Jupyter Notebook.

2. Create two nested lists, **X** and **Y**, to store the values:

```
X = [[1,2,3],[4,5,6],[7,8,9]]
Y = [[10,11,12],[13,14,15],[16,17,18]]
```

3. Initialize a 3 x 3 zero matrix called **result** as a placeholder:

```
# Initialize a result placeholder
result = [[0,0,0],
    [0,0,0],
    [0,0,0]]
```

4. Now, implement the algorithm by iterating through the cells and columns of the matrix:

```
# iterate through rows
for i in range(len(X)):
# iterate through columns
   for j in range(len(X[0])):
      result[i][j] = X[i][j] + Y[i][j]


print(result)
```

You'll use the nested list method. As you learned in the previous section, you first iterate the rows in matrix **X**, then iterate the columns. You do not have to iterate matrix **Y** again because both matrixes are of the same dimensions. The result of a particular row (denoted by **i**) and a particular column (denoted by **j**) equals the sum of the respective row and column in matrixes **X** and **Y**.

You should get the following output:

```
[[11, 13, 15], [17, 19, 21], [23, 25, 27]]
```

5. You can also perform subtraction using two matrices using the same algorithm with a different operator. The idea behind this is exactly the same as in *step* 3, except you are doing subtraction. You can implement the following code to try out matrix subtraction:

```
X = [[10,11,12],[13,14,15],[16,17,18]]
Y = [[1,2,3],[4,5,6],[7,8,9]]


# Initialize a result placeholder
result = [[0,0,0],
    [0,0,0],
    [0,0,0]]


# iterate through rows
for i in range(len(X)):
# iterate through columns
   for j in range(len(X[0])):
      result[i][j] = X[i][j] - Y[i][j]


print(result)
```

You should get the following output:

```
[[9, 9, 9], [9, 9, 9], [9, 9, 9]]
```

In this exercise, you were able to perform basic addition and subtraction using two matrices. In the next topic, you will be using multiplication operators for matrixes.

Matrix Multiplication Operations

You can look at how to use nested lists to perform matrix multiplication for the two matrices shown in figures 2.9 and 2.10:

$$X = \begin{bmatrix} 1 & 2 \\ 4 & 5 \\ 7 & 8 \end{bmatrix}$$

Figure 2.9: The data of matrix X

$$Y = \begin{bmatrix} 11 & 12 & 13 & 14 \\ 15 & 16 & 17 & 18 \end{bmatrix}$$

Figure 2.10: The data of matrix Y

For a matrix multiplication operation, the number of columns in the first matrix (X) must be equal the number of rows in the second matrix (Y). The result will have the same number of rows as the first matrix and the same number of columns as the second matrix. In this case, the result matrix will be a 3 x 4 matrix.

Exercise 24: Implementing Matrix Operations (Multiplication)

In this exercise, your end goal will be to multiply two matrixes, **X** and **Y**, and get an output value. The following steps will enable you to complete the exercise:

1. Open a new Jupyter notebook.

2. Create two nested lists, **X** and **Y**, to store the value of matrices **X** and **Y**:

```
X = [[1, 2], [4, 5], [3, 6]]
Y = [[1,2,3,4],[5,6,7,8]]
```

3. Create a zero-matrix placeholder to store the result:

```
result = [[0, 0, 0, 0], [0, 0, 0, 0], [0, 0, 0, 0]]
```

4. Implement the matrix multiplication algorithm to compute the result:

```
# iterating by row of X
for i in range(len(X)):

    # iterating by column by Y
    for j in range(len(Y[0])):

        # iterating by rows of Y
        for k in range(len(Y)):
            result[i][j] += X[i][k] * Y[k][j]
```

You may have noticed that this algorithm is slightly different from the one you used in *Exercise 23, Implementing Matrix Operations (Addition and Subtraction)*, step 3. This is because you need to iterate the rows of the second matrix, **Y**, as the matrixes have different shapes, which is what is mentioned in the preceding code snippet.

5. Now, **print** the final result:

```
for r in result:
    print(r)
```

You should get the following output:

```
[11, 14, 17, 20]
[29, 38, 47, 56]
[33, 42, 51, 60]
```

Figure 2.11: Output of multiplying matrix X and matrix Y

> **Note**
>
> There are packages that data scientists use to perform matrix calculations, such as NumPy. You can find out more at https://docs.scipy.org/doc/numpy/.

List Methods

As discussed before, since a list is a type of sequence, it supports all sequence operations and methods.

Lists are one of the best data structures to use. Python provides a set of list methods that makes it easy for us to store and retrieve values in order to maintain, update, and extract data. These common operations are what Python programmers perform, including **slicing**, **sorting**, **appending**, **searching**, **inserting**, and **removing** data.

The best way to understand this is to see them at work. You will learn about these handy list methods in the following exercises.

Exercise 25: Basic List Operations

In this exercise, you are going to use the basic functions of lists to check the size of a list, combining lists and duplicating lists as well. Follow these steps:

1. Open a new Jupyter notebook.

2. Type the following code

```
shopping = ["bread","milk", "eggs"]
```

3. The length of a list is found using the **len** function.

```
print(len(shopping))
```

> **Note**
>
> The **len()** function returns the number of items in an object. When the object is a string, it returns the number of characters in the string.

You should get the following output:

```
3
```

4. Now concatenate two lists using the **+** operator:

```
list1 = [1,2,3]
list2 = [4,5,6]
final_list = list1 + list2
print(final_list)
```

You should get the following output:

```
[1, 2, 3, 4, 5, 6]
```

As you can see in the output, lists also support many string operations as well, one of which is concatenation, which is joining two or more lists together.

5. Now use the * operator, which can be used for repetition in a list to duplicate elements:

```
list3 = ['oi']
print(list3*3)
```

It will repeat **'oi'** three times, giving us the following output:

```
['oi', 'oi', 'oi']
```

You have now concluded this exercise; the purpose of this exercise was to get you familiar with some common operations that Python programmers use to interact with lists.

Accessing an Item from a List

Just like other programming languages, in Python, you can use the **indexer** method to access elements in a list. You should complete the following exercise by continuing with the previous notebook.

Exercise 26: Accessing an Item from Shopping List Data

In this exercise, you will work with lists and gain an understanding of how you can access items from a list. The following steps will enable you to complete the exercise:

1. Open a new Jupyter Notebook.

2. Enter the following code in a new cell:

```
shopping = ["bread","milk", "eggs"]
print(shopping[1])
```

You should get the following output:

```
milk
```

As you can see, you have printed the value **milk** from the list **shopping** that has the index **1**, as the list begins from **0**.

3. Now, access the **milk** element and replace it with **banana**:

```
shopping[1] = "banana"
print(shopping)
```

You should get the following output:

```
['bread', 'banana', 'eggs']
```

4. Type the following code in a new cell and observe the output:

```
print(shopping[-1])
```

You should get the following output:

```
eggs
```

The output will print **eggs** – the last item.

> **Note**
>
> In Python, a positive index counts forward, and a negative index counts backward. You use a negative index to access an element from the back.

What you have learned so far is more of a traditional way of accessing elements. Python lists also support powerful general indexing, called **slicing**. It uses the : notation in the format of **list[i:j]**, where **i** is the starting element, and **j** is the last element (non-inclusive).

5. Enter the following code to try out a different type of slicing:

```
print(shopping[0:2])
```

This prints the first and second elements, producing the following output:

```
['bread', 'banana']
```

Now, to print from the beginning of the list to the third element

```
print(shopping[:3])
```

You should get the following output:

```
['bread', 'banana', 'eggs']
```

Similarly, to print from the second element of the list until the end

```
print(shopping[1:])
```

You should get the following output:

```
['banana', 'eggs']
```

Having completed this exercise, you are now able to access items from a list in different ways.

Adding an Item to a List

In the previous section and *Exercise 26, Accessing an Item from Shopping List Data*, you learned how to access items from a list. Lists are very powerful and are widely used in many circumstances. However, you often won't know the data your users want to store beforehand, but only after the program is running. Here, you are going to look at various methods for adding items to and inserting items into a list.

Exercise 27: Adding Items to Our Shopping List

The **append** method is the easiest way to add a new element to the end of a list. You will use this method in this exercise to add items to our **shopping** list. The following steps will enable you to complete the exercise:

1. In a new cell, type the following code to add a new element, **apple**, to the end of the list using the **append** method:

```
shopping = ["bread","milk", "eggs"]
shopping.append("apple")
print(shopping)
```

You should get the following output:

```
['bread', 'milk', 'eggs', 'apple']
```

The **append** method is commonly used when you are building a list without knowing what the total number of elements will be. You will start with an empty list and continue to add items to build the list.

2. Now create an empty list, **shopping**, and keep adding items one by one to this empty list:

```
shopping = []
shopping.append('bread')
shopping.append('milk')
shopping.append('eggs')
shopping.append('apple')
print(shopping)
```

You should get the following output:

```
['bread', 'milk', 'eggs', 'apple']
```

This way, you start off by initializing an empty list, and you extend the list dynamically. The end result is exactly the same as the list from the previous code. This is different from some programming languages that require array size to be fixed at the declaration stage.

3. Now use the **insert** method to add elements to the **shopping** list:

```
shopping.insert(2, 'ham')
print(shopping)
```

You should get the following output:

```
['bread', 'milk', 'ham', 'eggs', 'apple']
```

As you coded in step 3, you came across another way to add an element to a list, using the **insert** method. The **insert** method requires a positional index to indicate where the new element should be placed. A positional index is a zero-based number that indicates the position in a list. You can use the following code to insert an item, **ham**, in the third position.

You can see that **ham** is inserted in the third position and shifts every other item one position to the right.

Having concluded this exercise, you are now able to **add** elements to our list, which is shopping. This proves to be very useful when you get data from a customer or client, allowing you to use the methods you have mentioned and add items to your list.

In the next topic, you will work with and learn about dictionary keys and values.

Dictionary Keys and Values

A Python dictionary is an unordered collection. Dictionaries are written with curly brackets, and they have **keys** and **values**.

For instance, have a look at the following example, where you store the details of an employee:

```
employee = {
    'name': "Jack Nelson",
    'age': 32,
    'department': "sales"
}
```

You might have noticed a certain resemblance between Python dictionaries and JSON. Although you can load JSON directly into Python, a Python dictionary is a complete data structure that implements its own algorithms, and JSON is just a pure string written in a similar format..

Python dictionaries are something similar to key-value pairs. They simply map keys to associated values, as shown in *Figure 2.12*:

Key	Value
name	Jack Nelson
age	32
department	sales

Figure 2.12: Mapping keys and values in Python dictionaries

Dictionaries are like lists. They both share the following properties:

- Both can be used to store values.

- Both can be changed in place and can grow and shrink on demand.

- Both can be nested: a dictionary can contain another dictionary, a list can contain another list, and a list can contain a dictionary and vice versa.

The main difference between lists and dictionaries is how elements are accessed. List elements are accessed by their position index, which is [0,1,2...] while dictionary elements are accessed via keys. Therefore, a dictionary is a better choice for representing collections, and mnemonic keys are more suitable when a collection's items are labeled, for instance, a database record such as *Figure 2.13*. The database here is equivalent to a list, and the database list contains a record which can be represented using a dictionary. Within each record, there are fields to store respective values, and a dictionary can be used to store a record with unique keys that are mapped to values:

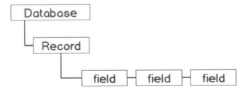

Figure 2.13: A sample database record

There are, however, a few rules that you need to remember with Python dictionaries:

- Keys must be unique – no duplicate keys are allowed.
- Keys must be immutable – they can be a string, a number, or a tuple.

You will work with dictionaries and store a record in *Exercise 28, Using a Dictionary to Store a Movie Record.*

Exercise 28: Using a Dictionary to Store a Movie Record

In this exercise, you will be working with a dictionary to store movie records, and you will also try and access the information in the dictionary using a key. The following steps will enable you to complete the exercise:

1. Open a Jupyter Notebook.

2. Enter the following code in a blank cell:

```
movie = {
    "title": "The Godfather",
    "director": "Francis Ford Coppola",
    "year": 1972,
    "rating": 9.2
}
```

Here, you have created a movie dictionary with a few details, such as **title**, **director**, **year**, and **rating**.

3. Access the information from the dictionary by using a key. For instance, you can use **'year'** to find out when the movie was first released:

```
print(movie['year'])
```

You should get the following output:

```
1972
```

4. Now update a dictionary value:

```
movie['rating'] = (movie['rating'] + 9.3)/2
print(movie['rating'])
```

You should get the following output:

```
9.25
```

As you can see, a dictionary's values can also be updated in place.

5. Construct a `movie` dictionary from scratch and extend it using key-value assignment:

```
movie = {}
movie['title'] = "The Godfather"
movie['director'] = "Francis Ford Coppola"
movie['year'] = 1972
movie['rating'] = 9.2
```

As you may have noticed, similar to a list, a dictionary is flexible in terms of size.

6. You can also store a list inside a dictionary and store a dictionary within that dictionary:

```
movie['actors'] = ['Marlon Brando', 'Al Pacino', 'James Caan']
movie['other_details'] = {
    'runtime': 175,
    'language': 'English'
}
print(movie)
```

You should get the following output:

```
{'title': 'The Godfather', 'director': 'Francis Ford Coppola', 'year': 1972, 'rating': 9.2, 'actors': ['Marlon Brando
', 'Al Pacino', 'James Caan'], 'other_details': {'runtime': 175, 'language': 'English'}}
```

Figure 2.14: Output while storing a dictionary within a dictionary

Up to this point, you have seen how easy it is to implement nesting in both lists and dictionaries. By combining lists and dictionaries creatively, we can store complex real-world information and model structures directly and easily. This is one of the main benefits of scripting languages such as Python.

Activity 7: Storing Company Employee Table Data Using a List and a Dictionary

Remember the employee dataset, which you previously stored using a nested list? Now that you have learned about lists and dictionaries, you will see how you can store and access our data more effectively using these two data types – lists and dictionaries:

Name	Age	Department
John Mckee	38	Sales
Lisa Crawford	29	Marketing
Sujan Patel	33	HR

Figure 2.15: Employee data in a table

Follow these steps to complete this activity:

1. Open a Jupyter notebook (you can create a new one or use an existing one).

2. Create a list named **employees**.

3. Create three dictionary objects inside **employees** to store the information of each **employee**.

4. Print the **employees** variable.

5. Print the details of all employees in a presentable format.

6. Print only the details of **Sujan Patel**.

   You should get the following output:

   ```
   Name: Sujan Patel
   Age: 33
   Department: HR
   --------------------
   ```

Figure 2.16: Output when we only print the employee details of Sujan Patel

> **Note**
>
> The solution for this activity is available on page 526.

Zipping and Unzipping Dictionaries Using zip()

Sometimes, you obtain information from multiple lists. For instance, you might have a list to store the names of products and another list just to store the quantity of those products. What you can do is to aggregate lists using the **zip()** method.

The **zip()** method maps a similar index of multiple containers so that they can be used just as a single object. You will try it out in the following exercise.

Exercise 29: Using the zip() Method to Manipulate Dictionaries

In this exercise, you will be working on the concept of dictionaries, but you will be focusing on manipulating them by combining different types of data structures. You will be using the **zip()** method to manipulate the dictionary with our shopping list. The following steps will help you to understand the **zip()** method:

1. Open up a new Jupyter Notebook.

2. Now create a new cell and type in the following code:

```
items = ['apple', 'orange', 'banana']
quantity = [5,3,2]
```

Here, you have created a list of **items** and a list of **quantity**. Also, you have assigned values to these lists.

3. Now, use the **zip()** function to combine the two lists into a list of tuples:

```
orders = zip(items,quantity)
print(orders)
```

This gives us a **zip()** object with the following output:

```
<zip object at 0x0000000005BF1088>
```

4. Enter the following code to turn that zip object into a **list**:

```
orders = zip(items,quantity)
print(list(orders))
```

You should get the following output:

```
[('apple', 5), ('orange', 3), ('banana', 2)]
```

5. You can also turn a **zip** object into a **tuple**:

```
orders = zip(items,quantity)
print(tuple(orders))
```

You should get the following output:

```
(('apple', 5), ('orange', 3), ('banana', 2))
```

6. You can also turn a **zip()** object into a dictionary:

```
orders = zip(items,quantity)
print(dict(orders))
```

You should get the following output:

```
{'apple': 5, 'orange': 3, 'banana': 2}
```

Did you realize that you have to call **orders = zip(items,quantity)** every time? In this exercise, you will have noticed that a **zip()** object is an iterator and, therefore, once it has been converted to a list, tuple, or dictionary, it is considered a full iteration and it will not be able to generate anymore values.

Dictionary Methods

Now that you have learned about dictionaries and when you should use a dictionary. You will now look at a few other dictionary methods. To start with, you should follow the exercises from here onward to learn how to access the values and other related operations of a dictionary in Python.

Exercise 30: Accessing a Dictionary Using Dictionary Methods

In this exercise, we will learn how to access a dictionary using dictionary methods. The goal of the exercise is to print the order values against the item while accessing the dictionary by using dictionary methods:

1. Open a new Jupyter Notebook.

2. Enter the following code in a new cell:

```
orders = {'apple':5, 'orange':3, 'banana':2}
print(orders.values())
print(list(orders.values()))
```

You should get the following output:

```
dict_values([5, 3, 2])
[5, 3, 2]
```

The **values()** method in this code returns an iterable object. In order to use the values straight away, you can wrap them in a list directly.

3. Now, obtain a list of keys in a dictionary by using the **keys()** method:

```
print(list(orders.keys()))
```

You should get the following output:

```
['apple', 'orange', 'banana']
```

4. As you can't directly iterate a dictionary, you first convert it to a list of tuples using the **items()** method, then iterate the resulting list and access it. This is mentioned in the following code snippet:

```
for tuple in list(orders.items()):
  print(tuple)
```

You should get the following output:

```
('apple', 5)
('orange', 3)
('banana', 2)
```

In this exercise, you created a dictionary. In addition to this, you were able to list the keys mentioned in the dictionary, and later, in step 4, you were able to iterate the dictionary after converting the list to a tuple.

Tuples

A tuple object is similar to a list, but it cannot be changed. Tuples are immutable sequences, which means their values cannot be changed after initialization. You use a tuple to represent fixed collections of items:

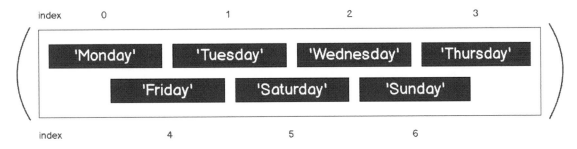

Figure 2.17: A representation of a Python tuple with a positive index

For instance, you can define the weekdays using a list, as follows:

```
weekdays_list = ['Monday', 'Tuesday', 'Wednesday','Thursday','Friday','Saturday',
'Sunday']
```

However, this does not guarantee that the values will remain unchanged throughout its lifetime because a list is **mutable**. What we can do is to define it using a tuple, as shown in the following code:

```
weekdays_tuple = ('Monday', 'Tuesday', 'Wednesday','Thursday','Friday','Saturday',
'Sunday')
```

As tuples are immutable you can be certain that the values are consistent throughout the entire program and will not be modified accidentally or unintentionally. In *Exercise 31, Exploring Tuple Properties in Our Shopping List*, we will explore the different properties tuples provide a Python developer.

Exercise 31: Exploring Tuple Properties in Our Shopping List

In this exercise, you will learn about the different properties of a tuple:

1. Open a Jupyter notebook.

2. Type the following code in a new cell to initialize a new tuple, **t**:

```
t = ('bread', 'milk', 'eggs')
print(len(t))
```

You should get the following output:

```
3
```

> **Note**
>
> Remember, a tuple is immutable; therefore, we are unable to use the **append** method to add a new item to an existing tuple. You can't change the value of any existing tuple's elements, either because both of the following statements will raise an error.

3. Now, as mentioned in the note, enter the following lines of code and observe the error:

```
t.append('apple')
t[2] = 'apple'
```

You should get the following output:

```
-----------------------------------------------------------------------
AttributeError                            Traceback (most recent call last)
<ipython-input-2-30ec3c1f0495> in <module>
----> 1 t.append('apple')
      2 #t[2]='apple'

AttributeError: 'tuple' object has no attribute 'append'
```

Figure 2.18: Errors occur when we try to modify the values of a tuple object

The only way to get around this is to create a new tuple by concatenating the existing tuple with other new items.

4. Now use the following code to add two items, **apple** and **orange**, to our tuple, **t**. This will give us a new tuple. Take note that the existing **t** tuple remains unchanged:

```
print(t + ('apple', 'orange'))
print(t)
```

You should get the following output:

```
('bread', 'milk', 'eggs', 'apple', 'orange')
('bread', 'milk', 'eggs')
```

Figure 2.19: A concatenated tuple with new items

5. Enter the following statements in a new cell and observe the output:

```
t_mixed = 'apple', True, 3
print(t_mixed)
t_shopping = ('apple',3), ('orange',2), ('banana',5)
print(t_shopping)
```

Tuples also support mixed types and nesting, just like lists and dictionaries. You can also declare a tuple without using parentheses, as shown in the code you entered in *Step* 5.

You should get the following output:

```
('apple', True, 3)
(('apple', 3), ('orange', 2), ('banana', 5))
```

Figure 2.20: Nested and mixed items in a tuple

A Survey of Sets

So far, in this chapter, you have covered lists, dictionaries, and tuples. You can now have a look at sets, which are another type of Python data structure.

Sets are a relatively new addition to the Python collection type. They are unordered collections of unique and immutable objects that support operations mimicking mathematical set theory. As sets do not allow multiple occurrences of the same element, they can be used to effectively prevent duplicate values.

A set is a collection of objects (called **members** or **elements**). For instance, you can define set A as even numbers between 1 to 10, and it will contain {2,4,6,8,10}, and set B can be odd numbers between 1 to 10, and it will contain {1,3,5,7,9}. In the following exercise, you will get our hands on sets in Python:

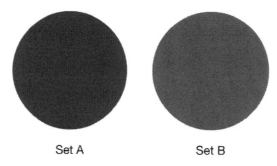

Set A   Set B

Figure 2.21: Set A and Set B – each set contains a unique, distinct value

Exercise 32: Using Sets in Python

In this exercise, you will gain an understanding of sets in Python. A set is a collection of objects:

1. Open a Jupyter notebook.

2. Initialize a set using the following code. You can pass in a list to initialize a set:

```
s1 = set([1,2,3,4,5,6])
print(s1)
s2 = set([1,2,2,3,4,4,5,6,6])
print(s2)
s3 = set([3,4,5,6,6,6,1,1,2])
print(s3)
```

You should get the following output:

```
{1, 2, 3, 4, 5, 6}
{1, 2, 3, 4, 5, 6}
{1, 2, 3, 4, 5, 6}
```

Figure 2.22: A set initialized using a list

You can see that the set is unique and unordered, so duplicate items and the original order are not preserved.

3. Enter the following code in a new cell:

```
s4 = {"apple", "orange", "banana"}
print(s4)
```

You can also initialize a set using curly brackets directly.

You should get the following output:

```
{'apple', 'orange', 'banana'}
```

4. Sets are mutable. Type the following code and see how we add a new item, **pineapple**, to an existing set, **s4**:

```
s4.add('pineapple')
print(s4)
```

You should get the following output:

```
{'apple', 'orange', 'pineapple', 'banana'}
```

In this exercise, you were introduced to sets in Python. In the next topic, you will dive in a bit deeper and understand the different set operations that Python has to offer you.

Set Operations

Sets support common operations such as unions and intersections. A **union** operation returns a single set that contains all the unique elements in both set A and B; an **intersect** operation returns a single set that contains unique elements that belong to set A and also belongs to set B at the same time:

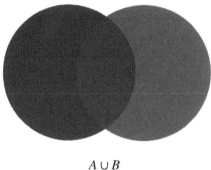

$$A \cup B$$

Figure 2.23: Set A in union with Set B

The following figure represents the intersect operation:

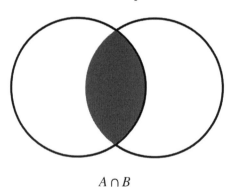

$$A \cap B$$

Figure 2.24: Set A intersects with Set B

Now you should look at how to implement these set operations in Python in the following exercise:

Exercise 33: Implementing Set Operations

In this exercise, we will be implementing and working with set operations:

1. Open a new Jupyter notebook.

2. In a new cell, type the following code to initialize two new sets:

```
s5 = {1,2,3,4}
s6 = {3,4,5,6}
```

3. Use the **|** operator or the **union** method for a union operation:

```
print(s5 | s6)
print(s5.union(s6))
```

You should get the following output:

```
{1, 2, 3, 4, 5, 6}
{1, 2, 3, 4, 5, 6}
```

Figure 2.25: Output with the union operator

4. Now use the **&** operator or the **intersection** method for an **intersection** operation:

```
print(s5 & s6)
print(s5.intersection(s6))
```

You should get the following output:

```
{3, 4}
{3, 4}
```

Figure 2.26: Output with the & operator

5. Use the **-** operator or the **difference** method to find the **difference** between two sets:

```
print(s5 - s6)
print(s5.difference(s6))
```

You should get the following output:

```
{1, 2}
{1, 2}
```

Figure 2.27: Output with the difference operator

6. Now enter the <= operator or the **issubset** method to check if one set is a subset of another:

```
print(s5 <= s6)
print(s5.issubset(s6))
s7 = {1,2,3}
s8 = {1,2,3,4,5}
print(s7 <= s8)
print(s7.issubset(s8))
```

You should get the following output:

```
False
False
True
True
```

Figure 2.28: Output with the issubset method

The first two statements will return **false** because **s5** is not a subset of **s6**. The last two statements will return **True** because **s5** is a subset of **s6**. Do take note that <= operator is a test for the subset. A proper subset is the same as a general subset, except that the sets cannot be identical. You can try it out in a new cell with the following code.

7. Check whether **s7** is a formal subset of **s8**, and check whether a set can be a proper subset of itself by entering the following code:

```
print(s7 < s8)
s9 = {1,2,3}
s10 = {1,2,3}
print(s9 < s10)
print(s9 < s9)
```

You should get the following output:

```
True
False
False
```

Figure 2.29: Output if s7 is a formal subset of s8

We can see that **s7** is a proper subset of **s8** because there are other elements in **s8** apart from all the elements of **s7**. But **s9** is not a subset of **s10** because they are identical. Therefore, a set is not a subset of itself.

8. Now use the **>=** operator or the **issuperset** method to check whether one set is the superset of another. Try it using the following code in another cell:

```
print(s8 >= s7)
print(s8.issuperset(s7))
print(s8 > s7)
print(s8 > s8)
```

You should get the following output:

```
True
True
True
False
```

Figure 2.30: Output with the >= operator checking whether the set is a superset of another

The first three statements will return **True** because **s8** is the superset of **s7** and is also a proper superset of **s7**. The last statement will return **false** because no set can be a proper superset of itself.

Having completed this exercise, you now know that Python sets are useful for efficiently preventing duplicate values and are suitable for common math operations such as unions and intersections.

> **Note**
>
> After all the topics covered so far, you may think that sets are similar to lists or dictionaries. However, sets are unordered and do not map keys to values, so they are neither a sequence or a mapping type; they are a type by themselves.

Choosing Types

By now, you have learned about most of the common data structures in Python. One of the challenges you might face is knowing when to use the various data types.

When choosing a collection type, it is useful to understand the unique properties of that type. For example, a list is for you to store multiple objects and to retain a sequence, a dictionary is for us to store unique key-value pair mappings, tuples are immutable, and sets only store unique elements. Choosing the right type for a particular dataset could mean an increase in efficiency or security.

Choosing an incorrect type for your data will lead to data loss, in most cases it leads to low efficiency while running our code, and in the worst case, we might lose our data.

Summary

To summarize, you need to remember that Python data structures include lists, tuples, dictionaries, and sets. Python provides these structures to enable you to code better as a developer. In this chapter, you have covered lists, which are one of the important data types in Python that store multiple objects, and also other data types, such as dictionaries, tuples, and sets. Each of these data types helps us to store and retrieve data effectively.

Data structures are an essential part of all programming languages. Most programming languages only provide basic data types to store different types of numbers, strings, and Booleans, as you learned in *Chapter 1, Vital Python - Math, Strings, Conditionals, and Loops*. They are an essential part of any program. In this chapter, you learned how to utilize advanced data structures such as nested lists and mixed data types, and lists with dictionaries – structures that you can use to store complex data.

Next up, we are going to learn how to use functions to write modular and understandable code that follows the **DRY (Don't Repeat Yourself)** principle.

3

Executing Python – Programs, Algorithms, and Functions

Overview

By the end of this chapter, you will be able to write and execute Python scripts from the command line; write and import Python modules; document your code with docstrings; implement basic algorithms in Python, including bubble sort and binary search; write functions utilizing iterative, recursive, and dynamic programming algorithms; modularize code to make it structured and readable and use helper functions and lambda functions.

This chapter will leave you empowered to write more powerful and concise code through an increased appreciation of well-written algorithms and an understanding of functions.

Introduction

Our experience with computers is a machine with a huge volume of carefully organized logic. No one piece of this logic is necessarily complex or can capture what drives the result. Rather, the entire system is organized such that it comes together to provide the output you expect.

In previous chapters, you focused on the basic Python idioms and data types. In this chapter, you will begin exploring more abstract concepts regarding how knowledge is formalized through logic in Python. You will explore a few fundamental algorithms that are used for solving typical problems in computer science, along with some simple logic.

For example, consider the problem of sorting a list of integers. Supermarkets use sorting techniques to sort through their customers to get an insight into the sales an individual customer provides. You may be surprised at the theoretical complexity behind writing such an algorithm in an efficient manner.

In this chapter, you will also learn about a few of the paradigms in Python for expressing our code in a concise but readable way. You will discuss the habits of a good programmer, and how to make sure you write code that is maintainable and does not repeat itself. In doing so, you can ensure yourself against needing to rework your code unnecessarily, as requirements change constantly in the IT world.

This chapter begins by moving away from running code in the Python shell and toward Python scripts and modules. This will allow us more flexibility to write clear, reusable, and powerful code.

Python Scripts and Modules

In previous chapters, you have been executing Python in an interactive Python console or a Jupyter Notebook. However, you may be aware that most Python code lives in text files with a **.py** extension. These files are simply plain text and can be edited with any text editor. Programmers typically edit these files using either a text editor such as Notepad++, or Integrated Development Environments (IDEs) such as Jupyter or PyCharm.

Typically, standalone **.py** files are either called **scripts** or **modules**. A script is a file that is designed to be executed, usually from the command line. On the other hand, a module is usually imported into another part of the code or an interactive shell to be executed. Note that this is not a hard distinction; modules can be executed, and scripts can be imported into other scripts/modules.

Exercise 34: Writing and Executing Our First Script

In this exercise, you will create a script called **my_script.py** and execute it on the command line. You will be then finding the sum of the factorials of three numbers:

1. Using your favorite text editor, create a new file called **my_script.py**. You can also use Jupyter (**New | Text File**).

2. Import the **math** library:

```
import math
```

3. Suppose that you had a list of numbers and you wanted to print the sum of the factorials of these numbers. Recall that a factorial is the product of all the integers up to and equal to a given number.

   For instance, the factorial of **5** is calculated as 5! = 5 * 4 * 3 * 2 * 1 = 120.

   In the following code snippet, you are going to find the sum of factorials of **5,7** and **11**.

```
numbers = [5, 7, 11]
```

4. Using the **math.factorial** function and list comprehension, compute and print **result**:

```
result = sum([math.factorial(n) for n in numbers])
print(result)
```

5. Save the file.

6. Open a Terminal or a Jupyter Notebook and ensure that your current directory is the same as the one with the **my_script.py** file. To check this, if you run **dir** in the Terminal, you should see **my_script.py** in the list of files. If not, navigate to the correct directory using the **cd** command.

7. Run **python my_script.py** to execute your script.

   You should get the following output:

```
39921960
```

In this exercise, you successfully created and executed a file by navigating to the correct directory from the Terminal or Jupyter Notebook.

Exercise 35: Writing and Importing Our First Module

In this exercise, as in *Exercise 34, Writing and Executing Our First Script*, you will be finding the factorials of three numbers. However, you will now create a module called **my_module.py**, and import it into a Python shell:

1. Using your favorite text editor, create a new file called **my_module.py**. You can also use Jupyter (**New | Text File**).

2. Add a function that prints the result of the computation in *Exercise 34, Writing and Executing Our First Script*. You will learn more about this function notation in the upcoming section on basic functions:

```python
import math
def compute(numbers):
    return([math.factorial(n) for n in numbers])
```

3. Save the file.

4. Open a Python shell or Jupyter Notebook and execute the following:

```python
from my_module import compute
compute([5, 7, 11])
```

You should get the following output:

```
[120, 5040, 39916800]
```

> **Note**
>
> Writing this code as a module is useful if you want to reuse our **welcome** function in another script or module. However, if you just want to execute the **print** statement once, and you don't want to have to import our function to a shell, the script is more convenient.

In this exercise, you created a module file called **my_module.py** and imported this module file to get the expected output on Jupyter or the Python shell.

Shebangs in Ubuntu

The first line of a Python script will often be:

```
#!/usr/bin/env python
```

As additional information, if you are using a Windows operating system, you can ignore this line. However, it is worth understanding its function. This path specifies the program that the computer should use to execute this file. In the previous example, you had to tell the Command Prompt to use Python to execute our **my_script.py** script. However, on UNIX systems (such as Ubuntu or macOS X), if your script has a shebang, you can execute it without specifying that the system should use Python. For example, using Ubuntu, you will simply write:

Figure 3.1: Executing a script with a shebang statement in a UNIX system

Docstrings

A docstring which was mentioned in the *Chapter 1, Vital Python: Math, Strings, Conditionals, and Loops* is a string appearing as the first statement in a script, function, or class. The docstring becomes a special attribute of the object, accessible with __ doc__. Docstrings are used to store **descriptive information** to explain to the user what the code is for, and some high-level information on how they should use it.

Exercise 36: Adding a Docstring to my_module.py

In this exercise, you extend our **my_module.py** module from *Exercise 35, Writing and Importing Our First Module*, by adding a docstring:

1. Open **my_module.py** in Jupyter or a text editor.

2. Add a docstring to the script (as the first line before beginning with your code as mentioned in the following code snippet):

    ```
    """ This script computes the sum of the factorial of a list of numbers"""
    ```

3. Open a Python console in the same directory as your **my_module.py** file.

4. Import the **my_module** module:

    ```
    import my_module
    ```

5. Call the **help** function on our **my_module** script to view the docstring. The **help** function can be used to obtain a summary of any available information regarding a module, function, or class in Python. You can also call it without an argument, that is, as **help()**, to start an interactive series of prompts:

```
help(my_module)
```

You should get the following output:

```
Help on module my_module:

NAME
    my_module - This script computes the factorial for a list of numbers

FUNCTIONS
    compute(numbers)

FILE
    c:\users\adrianc\desktop\python fundamental - trunk\code files\lesson03\python lesson03\python lesson03\exercise0
3\my_module.py
```

Figure 3.2: The output of the help function

6. View the **__doc__** property of **my_module** as a second way of viewing the docstring:

```
my_module.__doc__
```

You should get the following output:

```
'This script computes the factorial for a list of numbers'
```

Figure 3.3: Viewing the docstring

Docstrings can span one line, such as in the preceding example, or multiple lines. The following is an example of a Docstring:

```
"""
This script computes the sum of the factorial of a list of numbers.
"""
```

Imports

After the optional shebang statement and docstring, Python files typically import classes, modules, and functions from other libraries. For example, if you wanted to compute the value of **exp(2)**, you could import the **math** module from the standard library (you will learn more about the standard library in *Chapter 6, The Standard Library*):

```
import math
math.exp(2)
```

You should get the following output:

```
7.38905609893065
```

In the preceding example, you imported the **math** module and called an **exp** function that exists within the module. Alternatively, you could import the function itself from the **math** module:

```
from math import exp
exp(2)
```

You should get the following output:

```
7.38905609893065
```

Note that there is a third way of importing, which should generally be avoided unless necessary:

```
from math import *
exp(2)
```

You should get the following output:

```
7.38905609893065
```

The **import** * syntax simply imports everything in the module. It is considered undesirable primarily because you end up with references to too many objects, and there's a risk that the names of these objects will clash. It's also harder to see where certain objects are imported from if there are multiple **import** * statements.

You can also rename modules or imported objects in the **import** statement itself:

```
from math import exp as exponential
exponential(2)
```

You should get the following output:

```
7.38905609893065
```

This is sometimes useful if you simply find the name of the object to be unwieldy, making your code less readable. Or, it could be necessary where you want to use two modules that happen to have the same name.

Exercise 37: Finding the System Date

In this exercise, you write a script that prints the current system date to the console by importing the **datetime** module:

1. Create a new script called **today.py** in the Python Terminal.

2. Add a docstring to the script:

```
"""
This script prints the current system date.
"""
```

3. Import the **datetime** module:

```
import datetime
```

4. Print out the current date using the **now()** property of **datetime.date**:

```
print(datetime.date.today())
```

5. Run the script from the command line as shown in the *Figure 3.4*.

Figure 3.4: The command-line output

In this exercise, you were able to write a script that prints the date and time using the **datetime** module. Hence, you can see how modules can be helpful.

The if __name__ == "__main__" Statement

You will often see this cryptic statement in Python scripts. You won't cover this concept in-depth, but it's worth understanding. It is used when you want to be able to execute the script by itself, but also be able to import objects from the script as though it were a regular module.

For example, suppose you wanted to get the sum of the numbers from **1** to **10**. If you execute the function from the command line, you want the result printed to the console. However, you also want to be able to import the value to use it elsewhere in our code.

You may be tempted to write something like this:

```
result = 0
for n in range(1, 11):  # Recall that this loops through 1 to 10, not including 11
    result += n
print(result)
```

If you execute this program from the command line, it will print the output **55**, as expected. However, if you try importing the result in a Python console, it will print the result again. When importing the result, you just want the variable; you don't expect it to print to the console:

```
from sum_to_10 import result
```

You should get the following output:

```
55
```

To fix this, you only call the **print** function in the case where **__name__** == '**__main__**':

```
result = 0
for n in range(1, 11):  # Recall that this loops through 1 to 10, not including 11
    result += n
if __name__ == '__main__':
    print(result)
```

When executing from the command line, the Python interpreter sets the special **__name__** variable equal to the '**__main__**' string, such that when you get to the end of your script, the result is printed. However, when importing **result**, the **print** statement is never reached:

```
from sum_to_10 import result
result * 2
110
```

Activity 8: What's the Time?

You are asked to build a Python script that tells you the current time.

In this activity, you will use the **datetime** module to build the **current_time.py** script that outputs the current system time, and then you will import the **current_time.py** script into a Python console.

The steps to do this are as follows:

1. Create a new script called **current_time.py** in Jupyter or a text editor.

2. Add a **docstring** to the script to explain what it does.

3. Import the **datetime** module.

4. Get the current time using **datetime.now()**.

5. Print the result, but only if the script is to be executed.

6. Execute the script from Command Prompt to check it prints the time.

7. Import the time into a Python console and check if the console output does not print the time.

8. The output from the Command Prompt will be as follows:

```
(base) C:\Users\andrew.bird\Python-In-Demand\Lesson03\Activities>python current_time.py
16:48:22.416000

(base) C:\Users\andrew.bird\Python-In-Demand\Lesson03\Activities>
```

Figure 3.5: Printing the time to the command line

The output from a Python console should look like this:

```
from current_time import time
time
```

You should get the following output:

datetime.time(16, 44, 43, 699915)

Figure 3.6: The output in the datetime format

> **Note**
>
> The solution for this activity is available on page 529.

Python Algorithms

An algorithm is a series of instructions that can be executed to perform a certain task or computation. A recipe for a cake is an example of an algorithm. For example, preheat the oven, beat 125 g of sugar and 100 g of butter, and then add eggs and other ingredients. Similarly, simple computations in mathematics are algorithms. For example, when computing the perimeter of a circle, you multiply the radius by 2π. It's a short algorithm, but an algorithm, nonetheless.

Algorithms are often initially defined in **pseudocode**, which is a way of writing down the steps a computer program will make without coding in any specific language. A reader should not need a technical background in order to read the logic expressed in pseudocode. For example, if you had a list of positive numbers and wanted to find the maximum number of positive numbers in that list, an algorithm expressed in pseudocode could be as follows:

1. Set the `maximum` variable to `0`.

2. For each number in our list, check whether the number is bigger than the `maximum`.

   Set the `maximum` variable so that it is equal to that number.

3. `maximum` is now equal to the largest number in the list.

Pseudocode is useful because it allows us to show the logic of our code in a more universally accessible format than writing in a specific programming language. Programmers will often map out their thinking in pseudocode to explore the logic of their planned approach before writing the code itself.

In *Exercise 38*, *The Maximum Number*, you will be using this pseudocode to find the maximum number from a list of numbers.

Exercise 38: The Maximum Number

In this exercise, you will implement the pseudocode to find the maximum from a list of positive numbers:

1. Create a list of numbers:

```
l = [4, 2, 7, 3]
```

2. Set the `maximum` variable equal to `0`:

```
maximum = 0
```

3. Look through each number, and compare it to `maximum`:

```
for number in l:
    if number > maximum:
        maximum = number
```

4. Check the result:

```
print(maximum)
```

You should get the following output:

```
7
```

In this exercise, you successfully implemented the pseudocode given and found the maximum in a list of numbers.

Time Complexity

So far, in this book, we have become accustomed to our programs being executed at near-instantaneous speed. Computers are very fast, and the difference between performing 10 iterations in a loop and 1,000 iterations may seem immaterial to us. However, algorithms can quickly become inefficient as the problem grows. In measuring complexity, you are interested in knowing the time it takes to execute the algorithm changes as the size of the problem changes. If the problem is 10 times as large, does the algorithm take 10 times as long to execute, 100 times as long, or 1010 times as long? This relationship between the size of the problem and the steps taken is called the time complexity of an algorithm.

Of course, you could simply time our algorithm on problems of different sizes and observe the relationship on a graph. This technique is often useful when the algorithm is complex, and the theoretical relationship between size and time isn't computable. However, this isn't entirely satisfactory, as the actual time taken is also conditional on factors such as the memory that is available, the processor, the disk speed, and other processes consuming resources on the machine. It will only ever be an empirical approximation and may vary depending on the computer.

Instead, you simply count the number of operations required to execute the algorithm. The result of this counting is expressed with big-O notation. For example, O(*n*) means that, for a problem of size *n*, the number of steps taken is proportional to *n*. This means that the actual number of steps required can be expressed as $\alpha * n + \beta$, where alpha and beta are constants. Another way of thinking about this is that the steps required to execute the algorithm grow linearly with the problem size:

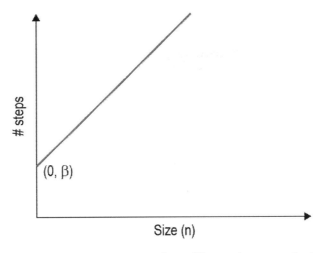

Figure 3.7: Visual representation of linear time complexity

Any such problem where the complexity can be expressed as a linear function, $\alpha * n + \beta$, has a time complexity of **O(n)**.

Other common time complexities include:

- **O(1): Constant time**. Here, the time taken is always the same, regardless of the problem size; for example, accessing an element of an array at a given index.

- **O(n^2): Quadratic time**. Here, the time taken is proportional to the square of the problem size; for example, the bubble sort algorithm (this is covered in *Exercise 39, Using Bubble Sort in Python*).

- **O(log n): Logarithmic time**. Here, the time taken is proportional to the natural logarithm of the problem size; for example, the binary search algorithm (this is covered in *Exercise 41, Binary Search in Python*).

Time Complexity for the Maximum Number Algorithm

In the previous exercise, you computed the maximum of a list of positive numbers. Here, you express the complexity of the algorithm using the big-O notation:

1. Our program starts by setting the `maximum = 0` variable. This is our first step: `total_steps = 1`.

2. For a list of size `n`, you are going to loop through each number and perform the following operations:

    (a) Check whether it's greater than the maximum variable.

    (b) If so, assign maximum to the number.

3. Sometimes, there will be one step executed for a number and, sometimes, there will be two steps (if that number happens to be the new maximum). You don't really care what this number is, so, let's take its average, which you'll call α. That is, for each number, there will be an average of α steps executed, where α is a number between 1 and 2.

4. So, `total_steps` $= 1 + \alpha * n$. This is a linear function, so the time complexity is `O(n)`.

Sorting Algorithms

The most commonly discussed family of algorithms in computer science courses are sorting algorithms. Sorting algorithms come to your aid when, say, you have a list of values, and you want to sort these into an ordered list. This problem is ever-present in our data-driven world; consider the following scenarios:

*   You have a database of contacts and want to see them listed alphabetically.

*   You want to retrieve the five best test results from a classroom of students.

*   You have a list of insurance policies and want to see which ones have the most recent claims.

The output of any sorting algorithm must satisfy two conditions:

1. It must be in non-decreasing order. That is, each element must be equal to or greater than the element that came before it.

2. It must be a permutation of the input. That is, the input elements must simply be rearranged and not altered.

Here is a simple example of what we want a sorting algorithm to accomplish:

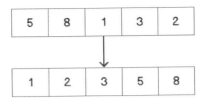

Figure 3.8: A simple problem for a sorting algorithm to solve

One such algorithm for performing this operation is called **bubble sort**. It is explained as follows:

1. Start with the first two elements of this list. If the first is larger than the second, then switch the positions of the numbers. In this case, you leave them as is, as 5 < 8:

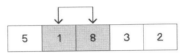

Figure 3.9: Step 1 for the bubble sort algorithm

2. Move onto the next two elements. Here, you switch the positions of 8 and 1:

Figure 3.10: Step 2 for the bubble sort algorithm

3. For the next pair, again, switch the positions, as 8 > 3:

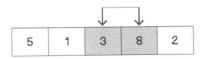

Figure 3.11: Step 3 for the bubble sort algorithm

4. For the final pair, switch the positions again, as 8 > 2:

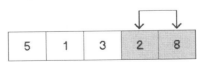

Figure 3.12: Step 4 for the bubble sort algorithm

5. Go back to the start of the list and repeat the preceding process.

6. Continue looping through the list until no further swaps are required.

Exercise 39: Using Bubble Sort in Python

In this exercise, you will implement the bubble sort algorithm in Python with a list of numbers:

1. Start with a list of numbers:

```
l = [5, 8, 1, 3, 2]
```

2. Create an indicator that will tell us when you can stop looping through the array:

```
still_swapping = True
```

3. Look through each number, and compare it to **maximum**:

```
while still_swapping:
    still_swapping = False
    for i in range(len(l) - 1):
        if l[i] > l[i+1]:
            l[i], l[i+1] = l[i+1], l[i]
            still_swapping = True
```

4. Check the result:

```
l
```

You should get the following output:

```
[1, 2, 3, 5, 8]
```

Bubble sort is a very simple but inefficient sorting algorithm. Its time complexity is $O(n^2)$, meaning that the number of steps required is proportional to the square of the size of the list.

Searching Algorithms

Another important family of algorithms is the searching algorithm. In a world where you are producing an exponentially increasing amount of data, these algorithms have a huge impact on our day-to-day lives. Simply considering the size of Google should give you an appreciation of the importance (and complexity) of these algorithms. Of course, you encounter the need for these algorithms just about every time you pick up a phone or open a laptop:

- Searching your contacts list to send a message
- Searching your computer for a specific application
- Searching for an email containing a flight itinerary

With any of these examples, you can apply the simplest form of search, that is, a linear search. This will involve simply looping through all possible results and checking whether they match the search criteria. For example, if you were searching your contacts list, you would look through each contact one by one, and check whether that contact met the search criteria. If so, return the position of the result. This is a simple but inefficient algorithm, with time complexity of **O(n)**.

Exercise 40: Linear Search in Python

In this exercise, you will implement the linear search algorithm in Python using a list of numbers:

1. Start with a list of numbers:

```
l = [5, 8, 1, 3, 2]
```

2. Specify a value to **search_for**:

```
search_for = 8
```

3. Create a **result** variable that has a default value of -1. If the search is unsuccessful, this value will remain -1 after the algorithm is executed:

```
result = -1
```

4. Loop through the list. If the value equals the search value, set the **result**, and exit the loop:

```
for i in range(len(l)):
    if search_for == l[i]:
        result = i
        break
```

5. Check the **result**:

```
print(result)
```

You should get the following output:

```
1
```

> **Note**
>
> This means that the search found the required value at position 1 in the list (which is the second item in the list, as indices start from 0 in Python).

Another common sorting algorithm is called a **binary search**. The binary search algorithm takes a sorted array and finds the position of the target value. Suppose that you were trying to find the position of the number 11 in the following list:

Figure 3.13: A simple problem for a search algorithm to solve

The binary search algorithm will be explained as follows:

1. Take the midpoint of the list. If this value is less than the target value, discard the left half of the list, and vice versa. In this case, our target value of 11 is greater than 8, so you know that you can restrict our search to the right side of the list (since you know the array is sorted):

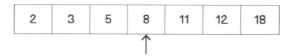

Figure 3.14: Splitting the list at the midpoint, 8

> **Note**
>
> If there is an even number of items on the list, simply take one of the two middle numbers, it doesn't matter which.

2. You repeat this process with the right side of the list, picking the midpoint of the remaining values. Since the target value, 11 is less than the midpoint 12, and you discard the right side of our sublist:

Figure 3.15: Splitting the list in the midpoint of the remaining list

3. This leaves you with the value that you were searching for:

Figure 3.16: Reaching the final result

Exercise 41: Binary Search in Python

In this exercise, you will implement the binary search algorithm in Python:

1. Start with a list of numbers:

```
l = [2, 3, 5, 8, 11, 12, 18]
```

2. Specify the value to **search_for**:

```
search_for = 11
```

3. Create two variables that will represent the start and end locations of the sublist you are interested in. Initially, it will represent the start and end indices for the entire list:

```
slice_start = 0
slice_end = len(l) - 1
```

4. Add a variable to indicate whether the search was successful:

```
found = False
```

5. Find the midpoint of the list, and check whether the value is greater or less than the search term. Depending on the outcome of the comparison, either finish the search or update the locations for the start/end of the sublist:

```
while slice_start <= slice_end and not found:
    location = (slice_start + slice_end) // 2
    if l[location] == search_for:
        found = True
    else:
        if search_for < l[location]:
            slice_end = location - 1
        else:
            slice_start = location + 1
```

6. Check the results:

```
print(found)
print(location)
```

You should get the following output:

```
True
4
```

In this exercise, you successfully implemented the binary search algorithm on a list of numbers.

Basic Functions

A function is a reusable piece of code that is only run when it is called. Functions can have inputs, and they usually return an output. For example, using a Python shell, you can define the following function that takes two inputs and returns the sum:

```
def add_up(x, y):
    return x + y
add_up(1, 3)
```

You should get the following output:

```
4
```

Exercise 42: Defining and Calling the Function in Shell

In this exercise, you create a function that will return the second element of a list if it exists:

1. In a Python shell, enter the function definition. Note that the tab spacing needs to match the following output:

```
def get_second_element(mylist):
    if len(mylist) > 1:
        return mylist[1]
    else:
        return 'List was too small'
```

Here you are calling **print** logs the parsed message to the standard output.

2. Try running the function on a small list of integers:

```
get_second_element([1, 2, 3])
```

You should get the following output:

```
2
```

3. Try running the function on a list with only one element:

```
get_second_element([1])
```

You should get the following output:

```
'List was too small'
```

Figure 3.17: We are unable to get the second item with a list length of 1

Defining functions in a shell can be difficult, as the shell isn't optimized for editing multiple lines of code blocks. Instead, it's preferable for our functions to live inside a Python script.

Exercise 43: Defining and Calling the Function in Python Script

In this exercise, you will define and call a function in a **multiply.py** Python script and execute it from Command Prompt:

1. Create a new file using a text editor called **multiply.py**:

```python
def list_product(my_list):
    result = 1
    for number in my_list:
        result = result * number
    return result
print(list_product([2, 3]))
print(list_product([2, 10, 15]))
```

2. Using Command Prompt, execute this script, ensuring that your Command Prompt is in the same folder as the **multiply.py** file:

Figure 3.18: Running from the command line

In this exercise, you worked on defining and calling a function within a Python script.

Exercise 44: Importing and Calling the Function from the Shell

In this exercise, you will import and call the **list_product** function you defined in **multiply.py**:

1. In a Python shell, import our **list_product** function:

```python
from multiply import list_product
```

You should get the following output:

```
6
300
```

One unintended consequence is that your **print** statements in **multiply.py** were also executed: **introduce __name__ == 'main'**.

2. Call the function with a new list of numbers:

```
list_product([-1, 2, 3])
```

You should get the following output:

```
-6
```

Now that you've completed this exercise, you have gained an understanding of how to import and call a function. You created the **multiply.py** file in *Exercise 43, Defining and Calling the Function in Python Script*, and imported and used this function in this exercise.

Positional Arguments

The preceding examples have all included positional arguments. In the following example, there are two positional arguments, **x** and **y**, respectively. When you call this function, the first value you pass in will be assigned to **x**, and the second value will be assigned to **y**:

```
def add_up(x, y):
    return x + y
```

You can also specify functions without any arguments:

```
from datetime import datetime
def get_the_time():
    return datetime.now()
print(get_the_time())
```

You should get the following output:

```
2019-04-23 21:33:02.041909
```

Figure 3.19: The current date and time

Keyword Arguments

Keyword arguments, also known as named arguments, are optional inputs to functions. These arguments have a default value that is taken when the function is called without the keyword argument specified.

Exercise 45: Defining the Function with Keyword Arguments

In this exercise, you will use the Python shell to define an **add_suffix** function that takes an optional keyword argument:

1. In a Python shell, define the **add_suffix** function:

```
def add_suffix(suffix='.com'):
    return 'google' + suffix
```

2. Call the **add_suffix** function without specifying the **suffix** argument:

```
add_suffix()
```

You should get the following output:

```
'google.com'
```

3. Call the function with a specific **suffix** argument:

```
add_suffix('.co.uk')
```

You should get the following output:

```
'google.co.uk'
```

Exercise 46: Defining the Function with Positional and Keyword Arguments

In this exercise, you use the Python shell to define a **convert_usd_to_aud** function that takes a positional argument and an optional keyword argument:

1. In a Python shell, define the **convert_usd_to_aud** function:

```
def convert_usd_to_aud(amount, rate=0.75):
    return amount / rate
```

2. Call the **convert_usd_to_aud** function without specifying the exchange rate argument:

```
convert_usd_to_aud(100)
```

You should get the following output:

```
133.33333333333334
```

3. Call the **convert_usd_to_aud** function with a specific exchange rate argument:

```
convert_usd_to_aud(100, rate=0.78)
```

You should get the following output:

```
128.2051282051282
```

The rule of thumb is to simply use positional arguments for required inputs that must be provided each time the function is called, and keyword arguments for optional inputs.

You will sometimes see functions that accept a mysterious-looking argument: **kwargs. This allows the function to accept any keyword arguments when it's called, and these can be accessed in a dictionary called "kwargs". Typically, this is used when you want to pass arguments through to another function.

Exercise 47: Using **kwargs

In this exercise, you will write a Python script to pass named arguments through a **convert_usd_to_aud** function:

1. Using a text editor, create a file called **conversion.py**.

2. Enter the **convert_usd_to_aud** function defined in the previous exercise:

```
def convert_usd_to_aud(amount, rate=0.75):
    return amount / rate
```

3. Create a new **convert_and_sum_list** function that will take a list of amounts, convert them to AUD, and return the sum:

```
def convert_and_sum_list(usd_list, rate=0.75):
    total = 0
    for amount in usd_list:
        total += convert_usd_to_aud(amount, rate=rate)
    return total
print(convert_and_sum_list([1, 3]))
```

4. Execute this script from Command Prompt:

Figure 3.20: Converting a list of USD amounts to AUD

Note that the **convert_and_sum_list** function didn't need the rate argument. It simply needed to pass it through to the **convert_usd_to_aud** function. Imagine that, instead of one argument, you had 10 that needed to be passed through. There will be a lot of unnecessary code. Instead, you will use the **kwargs** dictionary.

5. Add the following function to **conversion.py**:

```
def convert_and_sum_list_kwargs(usd_list, **kwargs):
    total = 0
    for amount in usd_list:
        total += convert_usd_to_aud(amount, **kwargs)
    return total
print(convert_and_sum_list_kwargs([1, 3], rate=0.8))
```

6. Execute this script from Command Prompt:

```
Anaconda Prompt                                      —    □    ×

(base) C:\Users\andrew.bird\Python-In-Demand\Lesson03>python conversion.py
5.0

(base) C:\Users\andrew.bird\Python-In-Demand\Lesson03>
```

Figure 3.21: Altering the result by specifying the kwarg rate

Activity 9: Formatting Customer Names

Suppose that you are building a **Customer Relationship Management (CRM)** system, and you want to display a user record in the following format: **John Smith (California)**. However, if you don't have a location in your system, you just want to see "John Smith."

Create a **format_customer** function that takes two required positional arguments, **first_name** and **last_name**, and one optional keyword argument, **location**. It should return a string in the required format.

The steps are as follows:

1. Create the **customer.py** file.

2. Define the **format_customer** function.

3. Open a Python shell and import your **format_customer** function.

4. Try running a few examples. The outputs should look like this:

```
from customer import format_customer
format_customer('John', 'Smith', location='California')
```

You should get the following output:

```
'John Smith (California)'
```

Figure 3.22: The formatted customer name

```
format_customer('Mareike', 'Schmidt')
```

You should get the following output:

```
'Mareike Schmidt'
```

Figure 3.23: Omitting the location

> **Note**
>
> The solution for this activity is available on page 530.

Iterative Functions

In the *For Loops* section in *Chapter 1, Vital Python – Math, Strings, Conditionals, and Loops*, you were introduced to the syntax for looping over objects in Python. As a refresher, here is an example where you perform five iterations and print the **i** variable in each loop:

```
for i in range(5):
    print(i)
```

You should get the following output:

```
0
1
2
3
4
```

For loops can also be placed within functions.

Exercise 48: A Simple Function with a for Loop

In this exercise, you create a **sum_first_n** function that sums up the first **n** integers. For example, if you pass the **n=3** function, it should return 1 + 2 + 3 = 6:

1. In a Python shell, enter the function definition. Note that the tab spacing needs to match the following output:

```
def sum_first_n(n):
    result = 0
    for i in range(n):
        result += i + 1
    return result
```

2. Test the **sum_first_n** function on an example:

```
sum_first_n(100)
```

You should get the following output:

```
5050
```

In this exercise, you successfully implemented a simple **sum_first_n** function with a **for** loop to find the total sum of **n** numbers.

Exiting Early

You can exit the function at any point during the iterations. For instance, you might want the function to return a value once a certain condition is met.

Exercise 49: Exiting the Function During the for Loop

In this exercise, you will create a function that (inefficiently) checks whether a certain number **x** is a prime. The function does this by looping through all the numbers from **2** to **x** and checks whether **x** is divisible by it. If it finds a number that **x** is divisible by, the iteration will stop and return **False**, as it has ascertained that **x** is not prime:

1. In a Python shell, enter the function definition. Note that the tab spacing needs to match the following output:

```
def is_prime(x):
    for i in range(2, x):
        if (x % i) == 0:
            return False
    return True
```

2. Test the function on a couple of examples:

```
is_prime(7)
```

You should get the following output:

```
True
```

Now, find out if 1000 is a prime number or not.

```
is_prime(1000)
```

You should get the following output:

```
False
```

In this exercise, you successfully implemented a code that checks whether the **x** variable is prime by looping through numbers. In the case that it is divisible, it will exit the loop and provide the output as **False**.

Activity 10: The Fibonacci Function with an Iteration

You work in an IT firm, and your colleague has realized that being able to quickly compute elements of the Fibonacci sequence will reduce the time taken to execute the testing suite on one of your internal applications. You will use an iterative approach to create a **fibonacci_iterative** function that returns the nth value in the Fibonacci sequence.

The steps are as follows:

1. Create a **fibonacci.py** file.

2. Define a **fibonacci_iterative** function that takes a single positional argument representing which number term in the sequence you want to return.

3. Run the following code:

```
from fibonacci import fibonacci_iterative
fibonacci_iterative(3)
```

You should get the following output:

```
2
```

Another example to test your code can be as mentioned in the following code snippet:

```
fibonacci_iterative(10)
```

You should get the following output:

```
55
```

Note

The solution for this activity is available on page 530.

Recursive Functions

When a function calls itself, it is known as a Recursive Function. This is like **for** loops. However, sometimes it allows you to write more elegant and terse functions than can be achieved with a loop.

You can imagine that a function that calls itself might end up in an infinite loop; it is true that you can write a recursive function that will keep running indefinitely:

```python
def print_the_next_number(start):
        print(start + 1)
        return print_the_next_number(start + 1)
print_the_next_number(5)
```

You should get the following output:

```
6
7
8
9
10
11
```

Note

The output mentioned above is truncated.

If you run this code in a Python shell, it will continue printing integers until you interrupt the interpreter (**Ctrl + C**). Take a look at the preceding code and ensure you understand why it behaves in this manner. The function executes the following steps:

- The function is called with **start = 5**.

- It prints **6** to the console, that is (**5 + 1 = 6**).

- It then calls itself, this time passing in the argument start = **6**.
- The function starts again, this time printing **7**, that is (**6 + 1 = 7**).

A Terminating Case

To avoid being stuck in an infinite loop, a recursive function will typically have a Terminating Case, such as a point where the chain of recursion is broken. In our previous example, you could make it stop once the **start** parameter is greater than or equal to **7**:

```
def print_the_next_number(start):
    print(start + 1)
    if start >= 7:
        return "I'm bored"
    return print_the_next_number(start + 1)
print_the_next_number(5)
```

You should get the following output:

```
6
7
8

"I'm bored"
```

Figure 3.24: Terminating the loop

Exercise 50: Recursive Countdown

In this exercise, you will create a **countdown** function that recursively counts down from integer **n** until we hit **0**:

1. In Jupyter Notebook, enter the function definition. Note that the tab spacing needs to match the output that follows:

```
def countdown(n):
    if n == 0:
        print('liftoff!')
    else:
        print(n)
        return countdown(n - 1)
```

2. Test the function:

```
countdown(3)
```

3. You should get the following output:

```
3
2
1
liftoff!
```

Figure 3.25: Counting down with recursion

In this exercise, you successfully implemented a termination statement after number 1, with the term **liftoff**. This shows us that the recursive countdown has ended.

Exercise 51: Factorials with Iteration and Recursion

In this exercise, you create a **factorial_iterative** function that takes an integer and returns the factorial using both an iterative and a recursive approach. Recall that a factorial is the product of all integers up to and equal to the number.

For instance, the factorial of 5 is calculated as $5! = 5 * 4 * 3 * 2 * 1 = 120$.

1. In a Jupyter Notebook, enter the following function to compute factorials using iteration:

```python
def factorial_iterative(n):
    result = 1
    for i in range(n):
        result *= i + 1
    return result
```

2. Test the function:

```python
factorial_iterative(5):
```

You should get the following output:

```
120
```

3. Note that you can express $n! = n * (n - 1)!$; for instance, $5! = 5 * 4!$. This means we can write the function with recursion as follows:

```python
def factorial_recursive(n):
    if n == 1:
        return 1
    else:
        return n * factorial_recursive(n - 1)
```

4. Test the function:

```python
factorial_recursive(5):
```

You should get the following output:

```
120
```

In this exercise, you successfully implemented and used both iteration and recursion to find the factorial of **n** numbers.

Activity 11: The Fibonacci Function with Recursion

Suppose that your colleague has told you that the iterative function you designed in *Activity 10, The Fibonacci Function with an Iteration,* is not elegant and should be written with fewer lines of code. Your colleague mentions that a recursive solution will be able to achieve this.

In this activity, you will use recursion to write a terse (but inefficient) function for computing the nth term of the Fibonacci sequence.

The steps are as follows:

1. Open the **fibonacci.py** file created in *Activity 10, The Fibonacci Function with an Iteration.*

2. Define a **fibonacci_recursive** function, which takes a single positional argument representing which number term in the sequence we want to return.

3. Try running a few examples in a Python shell:

```
from fibonacci import fibonacci_recursive
```

To find the fibonacci recursive for the value 3.

```
fibonacci_recursive(3)
```

You should get the following output:

```
2
```

You can run the following code and find the fibonacci recursive for the value 10.

```
fibonacci_recursive(10)
```

You should get the following output:

```
55
```

> **Note**
>
> The **fibonacci.py** file can be found on GitHub at https://packt.live/35yKulH.
>
> The solution for this activity is available on page 531.

Dynamic Programming

Our recursive algorithm for computing Fibonacci numbers may look elegant, but that doesn't mean it's efficient. For example, when computing the fourth term in the sequence, it calculates the value for both the second and third terms. Likewise, when calculating the value of the third term in the sequence, it calculates the value for the first and second terms. This isn't ideal, as the second term in the sequence was already being calculated in order to get the fourth term. Dynamic programming will help us to address this problem by ensuring you break down the problem into the appropriate subproblems, and never solve the same subproblem twice.

Exercise 52: Summing Integers

In this exercise, you write a **sum_to_n** function to sum integers up to **n**. You store the results in a dictionary, and the function will use the stored results to return the answer in fewer iterations. For example, if you already know the sum of integers up to 5 is 15, you should be able to use this answer when computing the sum of integers up to 6:

1. Create a new **dynamic.py** Python file.

2. Write a **sum_to_n** function that starts with **result = 0**, and an empty dictionary for saving results:

```
stored_results = {}
def sum_to_n(n):
    result = 0
```

3. Add in a loop that computes the sum, returns the result, and stores the result in our dictionary:

```
stored_results = {}
def sum_to_n(n):
    result = 0
    for i in reversed(range(n)):
        result += i + 1
    stored_results[n] = result
    return result
```

4. Finally, extend the function further by checking in each loop whether you already have a result for this number; if so, use the stored result and exit the loop:

```
stored_results = {}
def sum_to_n(n):
    result = 0
    for i in reversed(range(n)):
        if i + 1 in stored_results:
            print('Stopping sum at %s because we have previously computed it' %
str(i + 1))
            result += stored_results[i + 1]
            break
        else:
            result += i + 1
    stored_results[n] = result
    return result
```

5. Test the function in a Python shell to find the sum of integers up to 5:

```
sum_to_n(5)
```

You should get the following output:

```
15
```

Now, test the function once again to find the sum of integers up to 6.

```
sum_to_n(6)
```

You should get the following output:

```
Stopping sum at 5 because we have previously compu
ted it

21
```

Figure 3.26: Stopping early with saved results

In this exercise, you were able to reduce the number of steps in our code using dynamic programming to find the sum of integers up to **n**. The results were stored in a dictionary, and the function uses the stored result to output the answer in fewer iterations.

Timing Your Code

One measure of code efficiency is the actual time taken for your computer to execute it. In the examples given so far in this chapter, the code will execute too quickly to gauge any difference in the various algorithms. There are a few methods with which we can time programs in Python; you will focus on using the **time** module from the standard library.

Exercise 53: Timing Your Code

In this exercise, you will calculate the time taken to execute the function in the previous exercise:

1. Open the **dynamic.py** file created in the previous exercise.

    Add the following import at the top of the file:

    ```
    import time
    ```

2. Modify the function to calculate the time at the start, and print out the time elapsed at the end:

    ```
    stored_results = {}
    def sum_to_n(n):
        start_time = time.perf_counter()
        result = 0
        for i in reversed(range(n)):
            if i + 1 in stored_results:
                print('Stopping sum at %s because we have previously computed it' %
    str(i + 1))
                result += stored_results[i + 1]
                break
            else:
                result += i + 1
        stored_results[n] = result
        print(time.perf_counter() - start_time, "seconds")
    ```

3. Open a Python shell, import your new function, and try running an example with a large number:

    ```
    sum_to_n(1000000)
    ```

You should get the following output:

$$0.17615495599999775 \text{ seconds}$$

$$500000500000$$

Figure 3.27: Timing our code

4. Rerun the same code in the shell:

```
sum_to_n(1000000)
```

You should get the following output:

```
Stopping sum at 1000000 because we have previously
computed it
3.6922999981925386e-05 seconds
```

```
500000500000
```

Figure 3.28: Speeding up the execution with dynamic programming

> **Note**
>
> In the preceding example, the function returned the value faster by simply looking up the stored value in the dictionary.

Activity 12: The Fibonacci Function with Dynamic Programming

Your colleague has tried to use the code written in *Activity 11, The Fibonacci Function with Recursion*, and they notice that it is too slow when computing large Fibonacci numbers. They ask you to write a new function that can compute large Fibonacci numbers quickly.

In this activity, you will use dynamic programming to avoid the inefficient recursive loops that you implemented in *Activity 11, The Fibonacci Function with Recursion*.

The steps to do this are as follows:

1. Open the **fibonacci.py** file created in *Activity 10, The Fibonacci Function with Iteration*.

2. Define a **fibonacci_dynamic** function, which takes a single positional argument representing the number in the sequence that you want to return. Try starting with the **fibonacci_recursive** function from the previous activity and storing the results in a dictionary as the recursions are performed.

3. Try running a few examples in a Python shell:

```
from fibonacci import fibonacci_recursive
fibonacci_dynamic(3)
```

You should get the following output:

```
2
```

4. Note that if you try to use our recursive or iterative functions to compute the 100th Fibonacci number, they will be too slow and will never finish executing (unless you're willing to wait a few years).

> **Note**
>
> The solution for this activity is available on page 532.

Helper Functions

A helper function performs part of the computation of another function. It allows you to reuse common code without repeating ourselves. For instance, suppose you had a few lines of code that printed out the elapsed time at various points in a function:

```
import time
def do_things():
    start_time = time.perf_counter()
    for i in range(10):
        y = i ** 100
        print(time.perf_counter() - start_time, "seconds elapsed")
    x = 10**2
    print(time.perf_counter() - start_time, "seconds elapsed")
    return x

do_things()
```

You should get the following output:

```
2.4620000012021137e-06 seconds elapsed
6.0308000000189629e-05 seconds elapsed
8.65640000000667e-05 seconds elapsed
0.00010789800000310379 seconds elapsed
0.00012594900000095777 seconds elapsed
0.0002756930000025193 seconds elapsed
0.000301129000000034415 seconds elapsed
0.00032656500000172173 seconds elapsed
0.00034994900000002936 seconds elapsed
0.00037087300000138157 seconds elapsed
0.00039343700000031606 seconds elapsed

100
```

Figure 3.29: Timing our helper functions

The **print** statement is repeated twice in the preceding code, and will be better expressed as a helper function, as follows:

```
import time
def print_time_elapsed(start_time):
    print(time.perf_counter() - start_time, "seconds elapsed")
def do_things():
    start_time = time.perf_counter()
    for i in range(10):
        y = i ** 100
        print_time_elapsed(start_time)
    x = 10**2
    print_time_elapsed(start_time)
    return x
```

Don't Repeat Yourself

The preceding example encapsulates the Don't Repeat Yourself (DRY) programming principle. In other words, "*Every piece of knowledge or logic must have a single, unambiguous representation within a system.*" If you want to do the same thing multiple times in your code, it should be expressed as a function, and called wherever it is needed.

Exercise 54: Helper Currency Conversion

In this exercise, you will take a function that computes the total USD for a transaction and use a **helper** function to apply the DRY principle. You also want to add an optional margin into the currency conversion that should default to **0**:

```
def compute_usd_total(amount_in_aud=0, amount_in_gbp=0):
    total = 0
    total += amount_in_aud * 0.78
    total += amount_in_gbp * 1.29
    return total
compute_usd_total(amount_in_gbp=10)
```

You should get the following output:

```
12.9
```

1. Create a currency conversion function with an optional **margin**:

```
def convert_currency(amount, rate, margin=0):
    return amount * rate * (1 + margin)
```

2. Modify the original function to use the **helper** function:

```
def compute_usd_total(amount_in_aud=0, amount_in_gbp=0):
    total = 0
    total += convert_currency(amount_in_aud, 0.78)
    total += convert_currency(amount_in_gbp, 1.29)
    return total
```

3. Check the result:

```
compute_usd_total(amount_in_gbp=10)
```

You should get the following output:

```
12.9
```

4. Suppose that the business has decided to add a 1% margin for the conversion of the GBP component. Modify the function accordingly:

```
def compute_usd_total(amount_in_aud=0, amount_in_gbp=0):
    total = 0
    total += convert_currency(amount_in_aud, 0.78)
    total += convert_currency(amount_in_gbp, 1.29, 0.01)
    return total
```

5. Check the result:

```
compute_usd_total(amount_in_gbp=10)
```

You should get the following output:

```
13.029
```

Note that it's possible to get ahead of yourself when applying the DRY principle in writing reusable code. In the currency example, if our application really did just require converting currency once, then it probably shouldn't be written as a separate function. It may be tempting to think that generalizing our code is always good because it insures us against the possibility of needing to repeat the same code later; however, this attitude is not always optimal. You can end up spending a lot of time writing more abstract code than is necessary, and, often, this code can be less readable and may introduce unnecessary complexity to our codebase. Typically, the time to apply the DRY principle is when you find yourself writing the code for the second time.

Variable Scope

Variables are only available in the area where they are defined. This area is called the scope of the variable. Depending on how and where a variable is defined, it may or may not be accessible in certain parts of your code. Here, you will discuss what variables in Python represent, the difference in defining them inside or outside a function, and how the global and nonlocal keywords can be used to override these default behaviors.

Variables

A variable is a mapping between a name and an object at a certain location in the computer's memory. For example, if you set x = 5, then x is the variable's name, and the value 5 is stored in memory. Python keeps track of the mapping between the name x and the location of the value using namespaces. Namespaces can be thought of as dictionaries, with the names as the keys of the dictionary, and locations in memory as the values.

Note that when a variable is assigned to the value of another variable, this just means they are pointing to the same value, not that their equality will be maintained when one of the variables is updated:

```
x = 2
y = x
x = 4
print("x = " + str(x))
```

You should get the following output:

```
x = 4
print("y = " + str(y))
```

You should get the following output:

```
y = 2
```

In this example, both **x** and **y** are initially set to point to integer **2**. Note that the line **y** = **x** here is equivalent to writing **y** = **2**. When **x** is updated, it is updated to bind to a different location in memory, and **y** remains bound to the integer **2**.

Defining inside versus outside a Function

When you define a variable at the start of a script, it will be a global variable, accessible from anywhere in the script. This includes within the functions themselves:

```
x = 5
def do_things():
    print(x)
do_things()
```

With this code, you should get the following output:

```
5
```

However, if you define a variable within a function, it is only accessible within that function:

```
def my_func():
    y = 5
    return 2
my_func()
```

You should get the following output:

```
2
```

Now, enter the value y and observe the output

```
y
```

You should get the following output:

```
------------------------------------------------------------------
NameError                                    Traceback (most recent call last)
<ipython-input-2-80d732a03aaf> in <module>
      4
      5 my_func()
----> 6 y

NameError: name 'y' is not defined
```

Figure 3.30: We are unable to access the local variable y

Note that if you define a variable within a function that has already been defined globally, the value will change depending on where the variable is accessed. In the following example, **x** is defined globally as **3**. However, it is defined within the function as **5**, and when accessed within the function, you can see it takes the value of **5**.

```
x = 3
def my_func():
    x = 5
    print(x)

my_func()
```

You should get the following output:

```
5
```

However, when it is accessed outside of the function, it takes the global value, **3**.

This means you need to take care when updating global variables. For instance, can you see why the following fails to work? Take a look:

```
score = 0
def update_score(new_score):
    score = new_score
update_score(100)
print(score)
```

You should get the following output:

```
0
```

Within the function, the **score** variable is indeed updated to be equal to **100**. However, this variable is only local to the function, and outside the function the global score variable is still equal to **0**. However, you can get around this with the **global** keyword.

The Global Keyword

The **global** keyword simply tells Python to use the existing globally defined variable, where the default behavior will be to define it locally. You can do this using the same example as before:

```
score = 0
def update_score(new_score):
    global score
score = new_score
print(score)
```

You should get the following output:

```
0
```

Now, you update the score to 100 as shown in the following code snippet:

```
update_score(100)
```

Now, to print the scores

```
print(score)
```

You should get the following output:

```
100
```

The Nonlocal Keyword

The **nonlocal** keyword behaves in a similar way to the **global** keyword, in that it does not define the variable locally, and instead picks up the existing variable definition. However, it doesn't go straight to the global definition. It first looks at the closest enclosing scope; that is, it will look "one level up" in the code.

For example, consider the following:

```
x = 4
def myfunc():
    x = 3
    def inner():
        nonlocal x
        print(x)
    inner()
myfunc()
```

You should get the following output:

```
3
```

In this example, the **inner** function takes the variable definition's **x** from **myfunc**, and not the **global** keyword's **x**. If you instead write **global x**, then the integer **4** will be printed.

Lambda Functions

Lambda functions are small, anonymous functions that can be defined in a simple one-line syntax:

```
lambda arguments : expression
```

For example, take the following function that returns the sum of two values:

```
def add_up(x, y):
    return x + y
print(add_up(2, 5))
7
```

This function can equivalently be written using the lambda function syntax, as follows:

```
add_up = lambda x, y: x + y
print(add_up(2, 5))
```

You should get the following output:

```
7
```

Note that the main restriction of a lambda function is that it can only contain a single expression. That is, you need to be able to write the expression to return the value in a single line of code. This makes lambda functions convenient only in situations where the function is sufficiently simple such that it can be expressed in a single statement.

Exercise 55: The First Item in a List

In this exercise, you will write a lambda function, **first_item**, to select the first item in a list containing the items of the **cat**, **dog**, and **mouse**:

1. Create the **lambda** function:

```
first_item = lambda my_list: my_list[0]
```

2. Test the function:

```
first_item(['cat', 'dog', 'mouse'])
```

You should get the following output:

```
'cat'
```

Lambda functions can be particularly useful in passing custom functions to a map, as you can quickly define a function on the fly without assigning it to a variable name. The next two sections look at contexts where this is particularly useful.

Mapping with Lambda Functions

map is a special function in Python that applies a given function to all items in a list. For instance, suppose that you had a list of names and you wanted to get the average number of characters:

```
names = ['Magda', 'Jose', 'Anne']
```

For each name in the list, you want to apply the **len** function, which returns the number of characters in a string. One option will be to iterate manually over the names, and add the lengths to a list:

```
lengths = []
for name in names:
    lengths.append(len(name))
```

The alternative is to use the **map** function:

```
lengths = list(map(len, names))
```

The first argument is the function to be applied, and the second argument is an iterable (in this case, a list) of names. Note that the **map** function returns a generator object, not a list, so you convert it back to a list.

Finally, you take the average length of the list:

```
sum(lengths) / len(lengths)
4.33333333333
```

Exercise 56: Mapping with a Logistic Transform

In this exercise, you use **map** with a lambda function to apply the logistic function to a list of values.

The logistic function is often used in predictive modeling when dealing with binary response variables. It is defined as follows:

$$f(x) = \frac{1}{1 + e^{-x}}$$

Figure 3.31: The logistic function

1. Import the **math** module as needed for the exponential function:

```
import math
```

2. Create a list of values:

```
nums = [-3, -5, 1, 4]
```

3. Use a lambda function to map the list of values using a logistic transform:

```
list(map(lambda x: 1 / (1 + math.exp(-x)), nums))
```

You should get the following output:

```
[0.04742587317756678,
 0.0066928509242848554,
 0.7310585786300049,
 0.9820137900379085]
```

Figure 3.32: Applying the logistic function to a list

In this exercise, you used the **lambda** function to find the list of values by using **map**.

Filtering with Lambda Functions

The **filter** is another special function that, like **map**, takes a function and iterables (for example, a list) as inputs. It returns the elements for which the function returns **True**.

For example, suppose that you had a list of names and wanted to find those that were three letters long:

```
names = ['Karen', 'Jim', 'Kim']
list(filter(lambda name: len(name) == 3, names))
```

You should get the following output:

```
['Jim', 'Kim']
```

Figure 3.33: The filtered list

Exercise 57: Using the Filter Lambda

Consider a list of all-natural numbers below 10 that are multiples of 3 or 7. The multiples will be 3, 6, 7, and 9, and the sum of these when multiplied is 25.

In this exercise, you will be calculating the sum of all the multiples of 3 or 7 below 1,000:

1. Create a list of numbers from 0 to 999:

```
nums = list(range(1000))
```

2. Use a **lambda** function to filter the values that are divisible by 3 or 7:

```
filtered = filter(lambda x: x % 3 == 0 or x % 7 == 0, nums)
```

Recall that the **% (modulo)** operator returns the remainder from the division of the first argument by the second. So, **x % 3 == 0** is checking that the remainder of **x** divided by **3** is **0**.

3. **sum** the list to get the result:

```
sum(filtered)
```

You should get the following output:

```
214216
```

In this exercise, you successfully used filter lambdas that took a function as an input, in this case, **filtered**, and then returned the output as the sum of **filtered**.

Sorting with Lambda Functions

Another useful function that lambdas are often used with is **sorted**. This function takes an iterable, such as a list, and sorts them according to a function.

For example, suppose that you had a list of names, and wanted them sorted by length:

```
names = ['Ming', 'Jennifer', 'Andrew', 'Boris']
sorted(names, key=lambda x : len(x))
```

You should get the following output:

```
['Ming', 'Boris', 'Andrew', 'Jennifer']
```

Figure 3.34: Sorting using the lambda function

Recall that the **%** (**modulo**) operator returns the remainder from the division of the first list.

Summary

In this chapter, you were introduced to a few of the fundamental tools in Python for formalizing your knowledge. You learned how to write scripts and modules instead of using the interactive shell. You were introduced to functions and several different popular ways of writing functions. Additionally, common algorithms that are discussed in basic computer science were presented, including bubble sort and binary search. You also learned about the importance of the DRY principle. You learned how functions help us to adhere to this principle, and how helper functions allow us to express the logical components of our code succinctly.

In the next chapter, you will turn to the practical tools that you will need in your Python toolkit, such as how to read and write files, and how to plot visual graphs of data.

Extending Python, Files, Errors, and Graphs

Overview

By the end of this chapter, you will be able to read and write to files using Python; use defensive programming techniques, such as assertions, to debug your code; use exceptions, assertions, and tests with a defensive mindset and plot, draw and create graphs as outputs using Python.

We will cover the basic input/output (I/O) operations for Python and how to use the matplotlib and seaborn libraries to create visualizations.

Introduction

In *Chapter 3, Executing Python – Programs, Algorithms, and Functions*, you covered the basics of Python programs and learned how to write algorithms, functions, and programs. Now, you will learn how to make your programs more relevant and usable in the IT world.

First, in this chapter, you are going to look at file operations. File operations are essential for scripting for a Python developer, especially when you need to process and analyze a large number of files, like in data science. In companies that deal with data science, you often do not have direct access to a database, stored on a local server or a cloud server. Rather, we receive files in text format. These include **CSV** files for column data, and txt files for unstructured data (such as patient logs, news articles, user comments, etc.).

In this chapter, you will also cover error handling. This prevents your programs from crashing and also does its best to behave elegantly when encountering unexpected situations. You will also learn about exceptions, the special objects used in programming languages to manage runtime errors. Exception handling deals with situations and problems that can cause your programs to crash, which makes our programs more robust when they encounter either bad data or unexpected user behavior.

Reading Files

While databases such as MySQL and Postgres are popular and are widely used in many web applications, there is still a large amount of data that is stored and exchanged using text file formats. Popular formats like **comma-separated values (CSV)**, **JavaScript Object Notation (JSON)**, and **plain text** are used to store information such as weather data, traffic data, and sensor readings. You should take a look at the following exercise to read text from a file using Python.

Exercise 58: Reading a Text File Using Python

In this exercise, you will be downloading a sample data file online and reading data as the output:

1. Open a new Jupyter Notebook.

2. Now, copy the **text** file from the URL (https://packt.live/2MIHzhO), save it to a local folder as **pg37431.txt**, and remember where it is located.

3. Upload the file to your Jupyter Notebook by clicking on the **Upload** button in the top-right corner. Select the **pg37431.txt** file from your local folder, and then click on the **Upload** button again to store it in the same folder where your Jupyter Notebook runs:

Figure 4.1: The Upload button on the Jupyter Notebook

4. Now, you should extract the content of the file using Python code. Open a new Jupyter notebook file and type the following code into a new cell. You will be using the **open()** function in this step; don't worry too much about this, as you will be explained about this in more detail later:

```
f = open('pg37431.txt')
text = f.read()
print(text)
```

You should get the following output:

```
_PRIDE AND PREJUDICE_

_A PLAY_

[Illustration: "_Mr. Darcy, I have never desired your good opinion, and
you have certainly bestowed it most unwillingly._"]




_PRIDE AND PREJUDICE_

_A PLAY_

_FOUNDED ON JANE AUSTEN'S
NOVEL_
```

Figure 4.2: Output showing the extracted content from the file

Note that you can scroll within the cell and check the entire content.

5. Now, in a new cell, type **text** only, without the **print** command, and you will get the following output:

```
text
```

```
Out[6]: '\ufeffThe Project Gutenberg EBook of Pride and Prejudice, a play, by \nMary Keith Medbery Mackaye\n\nThis eBook is f
or the use of anyone anywhere at no cost and with\nalmost no restrictions whatsoever.  You may copy it, give it away
or\nre-use it under the terms of the Project Gutenberg License included\nwith this eBook or online at www.gutenberg.o
rg\n\nTitle: Pride and Prejudice, a play\n\nAuthor: Mary Keith Medbery Mackaye\n\nRelease Date: September 15, 2011
[EBook #37431]\n\nLanguage: English\n\n\n*** START OF THIS PROJECT GUTENBERG EBOOK PRIDE AND PREJUDICE, A PLAY ***\n
\n\n\nProduced by Chuck Greif and the Online Distributed\nProofreading Team at http://www.pgdp.net (This book was\n
produced from scanned images of public domain material\nfrom the Internet Archive.)\n\n\n\n\n\n\n\n_PRIDE AND PREJU
DICE_\n\n_A PLAY_\n\n[Illustration: "_Mr. Darcy, I have never desired your good opinion, and\nyou have certainly best
owed it most unwillingly._"]\n\n\n\n_PRIDE AND PREJUDICE_\n\n_A PLAY_\n\n_FOUNDED ON JANE AUSTEN\'S\nNOVEL_\n\n_BY_
\n\n_MRS. STEELE MACKAYE_\n\n[Illustration: colophon]\n\n_NEW YORK_\n\n_DUFFIELD AND COMPANY_\n\n_1906_\n\n\n
COPYRIGHT, 1906, BY DUFFIELD & COMPANY.\n\n                              Published September, 1906.\n\n
------\n\n               SPECIAL COPYRIGHT NOTICE.\n\n      This play is fully protected by copyright, all r
equirements of the\n     law having been complied with. Performances may be given only with\n    the written permiss
ion of Duffield & Company, agents for Mrs.\n     Steele Mackaye, owner of the acting rights.\n\n      Extract from the
law relating to copyright:\n\n      "SEC. 4996. Any person publicly performing or representing any\n    dramatic or m
usical composition for which a copyright has been\n     obtained, without the consent of the proprietor of said drama
tic or\n    musical composition or his heirs or assigns, shall be liable for\n    damages therefor, such damages in
all cases to be assessed at such\n     sum not less than one hundred dollars for the first and fifty\n     dollars fo
r every subsequent performance as to the Court shall\n     appear just. If the unlawful performance and representatio
```

Figure 4.3: Output with the text-only command

The difference in the output between this cell and the previous cell, shown in *Figures 4.2* and *4.3*, is the presence of control characters. Using the **print** command helps us to render the control characters while calling **text** shows the actual content and does not render as the output.

In this exercise, you have learned how to read the content of the entire data sample file.

Moving ahead, you will take a look at the **open()** function that you used in this exercise. It opens the file to let us access it. The **open()** function requires the name of the file you want to open as the argument. If you provide a filename without the full path, Python will look for the file in the same directory where it is currently running. In your case, it looks for the **text** file under the same folder where our **ipynb** file is, and where the Jupyter Notebook started. The **open()** function returns an object, which you store as **f** (which represents "**file**"), and you use the **read()** function to extract its content.

You may also be wondering whether you need to close the file. The answer is that it depends. Usually, when you call a **read()** function, you can assume that Python will close the file automatically, either during garbage collection or at the program exit. However, your program might end prematurely, and the file may never close. Files that have not been closed properly can cause data to be lost or corrupted. However, calling **close()** too early in our program will also lead to more errors. It's not always easy to know exactly when you should close a file. However, with the structure shown here, Python will figure that out for you. All you have to do is open the file and work with it as desired, trusting that Python will close it automatically when the time is right.

Although most of the data in the real world today is in the form of databases, and content such as videos, audio, and images is stored using respective proprietary formats, the use of text files is still important. They can be exchanged and opened in all operating systems without requiring any special parser. In practical use cases, you use a text file to record ongoing information, such as server logs in the IT world.

But what if you are dealing with a large file or you only need to access parts of the content or read the file line by line? You should check this out in the next exercise.

Exercise 59: Reading Partial Content from a Text File

In this exercise, you will be using the same sample data file from *Exercise 58, Reading a Text File Using Python*. Here, however, you will only be partially reading the content from the text file:

1. Open a new Jupyter Notebook.

2. Copy the **pg37431.txt** text file that you used in *Exercise 58* and save it in a separate folder that will be used to execute this exercise.

3. Write the following code in a new cell to read the first **5** characters:

```
with open("pg37431.txt") as f:
    print(f.read(5))
```

You should get the following output:

```
The P
```

In this way, you include an argument to tell Python to read the first **5** characters each time.

Notice that you use a **with** statement here. The **with** statement is a control flow structure of Python. It guarantees that the preceding file object, **f**, will close automatically after the code block exits, no matter how the nested block exits.

If an exception occurs before the end of the block, it will still close the file before the exception is caught. Of course, it will close the file even if the nested block runs successfully.

4. Now, access the **text** file by reading it line by line using the **.readline** function for which you need to enter the following code in a new cell on your notebook:

```
with open("pg37431.txt") as f:
    print(f.readline())
```

You should get the following output of the very first line in the text file:

```
The Project Gutenberg EBook of Pride and Prejudice, a play, by
```

Figure 4.4: Output accessing the text line by line

By completing this exercise, you have learned the use of the control structure that is used in Python to close a code block automatically. Doing so, you were able to access the raw data text file and read it one line at a time.

Writing Files

Now that you have learned how to read the content of a file, you are going to learn how to write content to a file. Writing content to a file is the easiest way for us to store content in our database storage, save our data by writing it to a particular file, and save data on our hard disk. This way, the output will still be available for us after you close the terminal or terminate the notebook that contains our program output. This will allow us to reuse the content later with the **read()** method that was covered in the previous section, *Reading Files*.

You will still be using the **open()** method to write to a file, except when it requires an extra argument to indicate how you want to access and write to the file.

For instance, consider the following:

```
f = open("log.txt","w+")
```

The preceding code snippet allows us to open a file in **w+**, a mode that supports both **reading** and **writing**, that is updating the file. Other modes in Python include the following:

- **R**: The default mode. This opens a file for reading.

- **W**: The write mode. This opens a file for writing, creates a new file if the file does not exist, and overwrites the content if the file already exists.

- **X**: This creates a new file. The operation fails if the file exists.

- **A**: This opens a file in **append** mode, and creates a new file if a file does not exist.

- **B**: This opens a file in **binary** mode.

Now, you should take a look at the following exercise to write content to a file:

Exercise 60: Creating and Writing Content to Files to Record the Date and Time in a Text File

In this exercise, you will be writing content to a file. We are going to create a **log** file, which records the value of our counter every second:

1. Open a new Jupyter Notebook.

2. In a new cell, type the following code:

```
f = open('log.txt', 'w')
```

From the code mentioned in this step of this exercise, you open the **log.txt** file in **write** mode, which you will be using to write our values.

3. Now, in the next cell of your notebook, type the following code:

```
from datetime import datetime
import time
for i in range(0,10):
    print(datetime.now().strftime('%Y%m%d_%H:%M:%S - '),i)
    f.write(datetime.now().strftime('%Y%m%d_%H:%M:%S - '))
    time.sleep(1)
    f.write(str(i))
    f.write("\n")
f.close()
```

In this code block, you are importing the **datetime** and **time** modules that Python provides us with. You are also using a **for** loop to print the year, month, and day, as well as the hour, minutes, and seconds. You are using the **write()** function here to add on to the previous condition; that is, every time the loop exits, the **write** command prints a number in place of **i**.

You should get the following output:

```
20190420_23:47:08 -  0
20190420_23:47:09 -  1
20190420_23:47:10 -  2
20190420_23:47:11 -  3
20190420_23:47:12 -  4
20190420_23:47:13 -  5
20190420_23:47:14 -  6
20190420_23:47:15 -  7
20190420_23:47:16 -  8
20190420_23:47:17 -  9
```

Figure 4.5: Output with the write() function in use

4. Now, go back to the main page of your Jupyter Notebook, or browse to your Jupyter Notebook folder using **Windows Explorer** or **Finder** (if you are using a Mac). You will see the newly created **log.txt** file present:

.ipynb_checkpoints	7/26/2019 9:00 AM	File folder	
Exercise03.ipynb	7/26/2019 9:01 AM	IPYNB File	1 KB
log	7/26/2019 9:03 AM	Text Document	1 KB

Figure 4.6: The log file is created

5. Open the file inside Jupyter Notebook or your favorite text editor (for example, Visual Studio Code or Notepad), and you should see content that is similar to the following:

```
 1  20190420_23:47:08 - 0
 2  20190420_23:47:09 - 1
 3  20190420_23:47:10 - 2
 4  20190420_23:47:11 - 3
 5  20190420_23:47:12 - 4
 6  20190420_23:47:13 - 5
 7  20190420_23:47:14 - 6
 8  20190420_23:47:15 - 7
 9  20190420_23:47:16 - 8
10  20190420_23:47:17 - 9
11
```

Figure 4.7: Content added to the log.txt file

You have now created your first **text** file. The example shown in this exercise is very common in most data science processing tasks; for instance, recording the readings of sensors and the progress of a long-running process.

The **close()** method at the very end makes sure that the file is closed properly and that all content in the buffer is written to the file.

Preparing for Debugging (Defensive Code)

In the programming world, a bug refers to defects or problems that prevent code or programs from running normally or as expected. Debugging is the process of finding and resolving those defects. Debugging methods include interactive debugging, unit testing, integration testing, and other types of monitoring and profiling practices.

Defensive programming is a form of debugging approach that ensures the continuing function of a piece of a program under unforeseen circumstances. Defensive programming is particularly useful when you require our programs to have high reliability. In general, you practice defensive programming to improve the quality of software and source code, and to write code that is both readable and understandable.

By making our software behave in a predictable manner, you can use exceptions to handle unexpected inputs or user actions that can potentially reduce the risk of crashing our programs.

Writing Assertions

The first thing you need to learn about writing defensive code is how to write an assertion. Python provides a built-in **assert** statement to use the **assertion** condition in the program. The **assert** statement assumes the condition always to be true. It halts the program and raises an **AssertionError** message if it is false.

The simplest code to showcase **assert** is mentioned in the following code snippet:

```
x = 2
assert x < 1, "Invalid value"
```

Here, since **2** is not smaller than **1**, and the statement is false, it raises an **AssertionError** message as follows:

```
AssertionError                          Traceback (most recent call last)
<ipython-input-14-3a9a99a5e24a> in <module>
      1 x = 2
----> 2 assert x < 1, "Invalid value"

AssertionError: Invalid value
```

Figure 4.8: Output showing AssertionError

> **Note**
>
> You can also write the **assert** function without the optional error message.

Next, you will take a look at how to use **assert** in a practical example.

Say that you want to calculate the average marks of a student in a semester. You need to write a function to calculate the average, and you want to make sure that the user who calls the function actually passes in the marks. You will explore how you can implement this in the following exercise.

Exercise 61: Working with Incorrect Parameters to Find the Average Using Assert with Functions

In this exercise, you will be using the assertion error with functions to check the error message when you enter incorrect parameters to calculate the average marks of students:

1. Continue in the previous Jupyter notebook.

2. Type the following code into a new cell:

```python
def avg(marks):
    assert len(marks) != 0
    return round(sum(marks)/len(marks), 2)
```

Here, you created an **avg** function that calculates the average from a given list, and you have used the **assert** statement to check for any incorrect data that will throw the assert error output.

3. In a new cell, type the following code:

```python
sem1_marks = [62, 65, 75]
print("Average marks for semester 1:",avg(sem1_marks))
```

In this code snippet, you provide a list and calculate the average marks using the **avg** function.

You should get the following output:

```
Average marks for semester 1: 67.33
```

4. Next, test whether the **assert** statement is working by providing an empty list. In a new cell, type the following code:

```python
ranks = []
print("Average of marks for semester 1:",avg(ranks))
```

You should get the following output:

```
----------------------------------------------------------------------
AssertionError                              Traceback (most recent call last)
<ipython-input-21-cec864bd4977> in <module>
      1 ranks = []
----> 2 print("Average of mark1:",avg(ranks))
      3

<ipython-input-18-5b6c83fe5ee4> in avg(marks)
      1 def avg(marks):
----> 2     assert len(marks) != 0
      3     return round(sum(marks)/len(marks), 2)

AssertionError:
```

Figure 4.9: Assertion fails when we pass in an empty list

In the cell with the code where you provide 3 scores, the **len(marks) !=0** statement returns **true**, and therefore no **AssertionError** will be raised. However, in the next cell, you did not provide any marks, and therefore it raises an **AssertionError** message

In this exercise, you have used the **AssertionError** message to throw the output in case it is incorrect or if missing data is provided. This has proved to be useful when, in the real world, data can be of the incorrect format, and you can then use this to debug the incorrect data.

Note that although **assert** behaves like a check or data validation tool, it is not. Asserts in Python can be disabled globally to nullify all of the assert statements. Do not use **assert** to check whether a function argument contains an invalid or unexpected value, as this can quickly lead to bugs and security holes. The baseline is to treat Python's assert statement like a debugging tool and not to use it for handling runtime errors. The goal of using assertions is to let us detect a bug more quickly. An **AssertionError** message should never happen unless there's a bug in your program. In the next section, you will look at plotting functions to provide you with a visual output using Python.

Plotting Techniques

Unlike machines, humans are terrible at understanding data without graphics. Various visualization techniques have been invented to make humans understand different datasets. There are various types of graphs that you can plot, each with its own strengths and weakness.

Each type of chart is only suitable for a certain scenario, and they shouldn't be mixed up. For instance, to present dropped-out customer details for marketing scatter plots is a good example. A scatter plot is suitable for visualizing a categorical dataset with numeric values, and you will be exploring this further in the following exercise.

For the best presentation of your data, you should choose the right graph for the right data. In the following exercises, you will be introduced to various graph types and their suitability for different scenarios. You will also demonstrate how to avoid plotting misleading charts.

You will plot each of these graphs in the following exercises and observe the changes in these graphs.

> **Note**
>
> These exercises require external libraries such as **seaborn** and **matplotlib**. Please refer to the Preface section of this chapter to find out how to install these libraries.
>
> In some installations of Jupyter, graphs do not show automatically. Use the **%matplotlib inline** command at the beginning of your notebook to get around this.

Exercise 62: Drawing a Scatter Plot to Study the Data between Ice Cream Sales versus Temperature

In this exercise, you will be aiming to get scatter plots as the output using sample data from the ice cream company to study the growth in the sale of ice cream against varying temperature data:

1. Begin by opening a new Jupyter Notebook file.

2. Enter the following code to import the **matplotlib**, **seaborn**, and **numpy** libraries with the following alias:

```
import matplotlib.pyplot as plt
import seaborn as sns
import numpy as np
```

You should take a look at the following example. Imagine you are assigned to analyze the sales of a particular ice cream outlet with a view to studying the effect of temperature on ice cream sales.

3. Prepare the dataset, as specified in the following code snippet:

```
temperature = [14.2, 16.4, 11.9, 12.5, 18.9, 22.1, 19.4, 23.1, 25.4, 18.1, 22.6,
17.2]
sales = [215.20, 325.00, 185.20, 330.20, 418.60, 520.25, 412.20, 614.60, 544.80,
421.40, 445.50, 408.10]
```

4. Plot the lists using the **scatter** plot:

```
plt.scatter(temperature, sales, color='red')
plt.show()
```

You should get the following output:

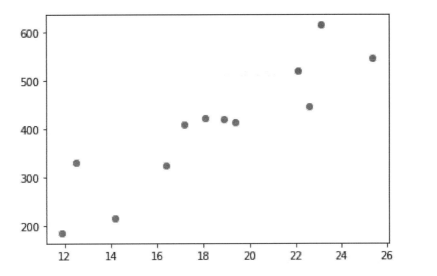

Figure 4.10: Output as the scatterplot with the data of the ice cream temperature and sales data

Our plot looks fine, but only to our eyes. Anyone who has just seen the chart will not have the context and will not understand what the chart is trying to tell them. Before we go on to introduce other plots, it is useful for you to learn how to edit your plots and include additional information that will help your readers to understand it.

5. Add a **title** command to your plot, as well as the x-axis (horizontal) and y-axis (vertical) labels. Then, add the following lines before the **plt.show()** command:

```
plt.title('Ice-cream sales versus Temperature')
plt.xlabel('Sales')
plt.ylabel('Temperature')
plt.scatter(temperature, sales, color='red')
plt.show()
```

You should get the following output:

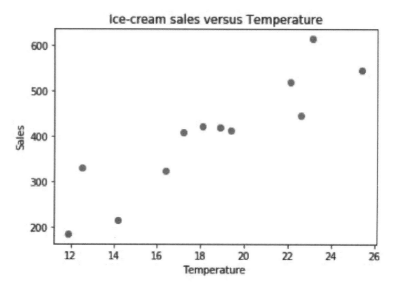

Figure 4.11: Updated scatter plot of ice cream sales versus temperature

Our chart is now easier to understand. In this exercise, you used the sample ice cream sales versus temperature dataset and used the data to create a scatter plot that will be easier to understand for another user.

However, what if your dataset is a time-based dataset? In that case, you will usually use a line plot. Some examples of a line plot include the plotting of heart rate, the visualization of population growth against time, or even the stock market. By creating a line plot, you are able to understand the trend and seasonality of data.

In the following exercise, you will be outputting the line chart, which corresponds to the time (that is, the number of days) and the price. For this, you will be plotting out stock prices.

Exercise 63: Drawing a Line Chart to Find the Growth in Stock Prices

In this exercise, you will be plotting the stock prices of a well-known company. You will be plotting this as a line chart that will be plotted as the number of days against the growth in price.

1. Open a new Jupyter Notebook.

2. Enter the following code in a new cell to initialize our data as a list:

```
stock_price = [190.64, 190.09, 192.25, 191.79, 194.45, 196.45, 196.45, 196.42,
200.32, 200.32, 200.85, 199.2, 199.2, 199.2, 199.46, 201.46, 197.54, 201.12, 203.12,
203.12, 203.12, 202.83, 202.83, 203.36, 206.83, 204.9, 204.9, 204.9, 204.4, 204.06]
```

3. Now, use the following code to plot the chart, configure the chart title, and configure the titles of the axes:

```python
import matplotlib.pyplot as plt
plt.plot(stock_price)
plt.title('Opening Stock Prices')
plt.xlabel('Days')
plt.ylabel('$ USD')
plt.show()
```

In the preceding code snippet, you are adding a title to the graph, and adding the number of days to the x axis and the price to the y axis.

Execute the cell **twice**, and you should see the following chart as the output:

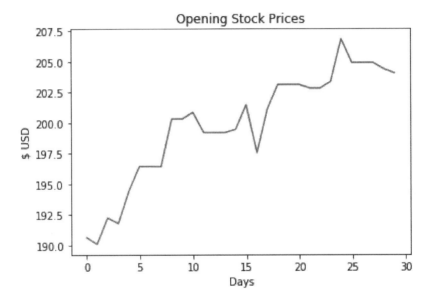

Figure 4.12: Line chart for opening stock prices

If you've noticed that the number of days in our line plot starts at **0**, you have sharp eyes. Usually, you start your axes at **0**, but in this case, it represents the day, so you have to start from **1** instead. You can fix these issues.

4. You can fix this by creating a list that starts with **1** to **31**, representing the days in March:

```python
t = list(range(1, 31))
```

5. Plot this together with the data. You can also define the numbers on the x axis using **xticks**:

```
plt.plot(t, stock_price, marker='.', color='red')
plt.xticks([1, 8, 15, 22, 28])
```

The complete code with the underlined changes is shown here:

```
stock_price = [190.64, 190.09, 192.25, 191.79, 194.45, 196.45, 196.45, 196.42,
200.32, 200.32, 200.85, 199.2, 199.2, 199.2, 199.46, 201.46, 197.54, 201.12, 203.12,
203.12, 203.12, 202.83, 202.83, 203.36, 206.83, 204.9, 204.9, 204.9, 204.4, 204.06]
t = list(range(1, 31))

import matplotlib.pyplot as plt
plt.title('Opening Stock Prices')
plt.xlabel('Days')
plt.ylabel('$ USD')

plt.plot(t, stock_price, marker='.', color='red')
plt.xticks([1, 8, 15, 22, 28])
plt.show()
```

You should get the following output:

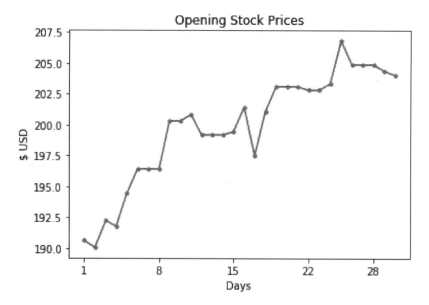

Figure 4.13: Updated line chart with customized line color, marker, and date range

In this exercise, you learned how to generate a line graph that displays the output based on time. In the next exercise, you will learn how to plot bar graphs, which is another useful visualization for displaying categorical data.

Exercise 64: Plotting Bar Plots to Grade Students

A bar plot is a straightforward chart type. It is great for visualizing the count of items in different categories. When you get the final output for this exercise, you may think that histograms and bar plots look the same. But that's not the case. The main difference between a histogram and a bar plot is that there is no space between the adjacent columns in a histogram. You will take a look at how to plot a bar graph.

In this exercise, you will draw bar charts to display the data of students and corresponding bar plots as a visual output.

1. Open a new Jupyter Notebook file.

2. Type the following code into a new cell, to initialize the dataset:

```
grades = ['A', 'B', 'C', 'D', 'E', 'F']
students_count = [20, 30, 10, 5, 8, 2]
```

3. Plot the bar chart with our dataset and customize the **color** command:

```
import matplotlib.pyplot as plt
plt.bar(grades, students_count, color=['green', 'gray', 'gray', 'gray', 'gray',
'red'])
```

Execute the cell **twice**, and you should get the following output:

Out[5]: <BarContainer object of 6 artists>

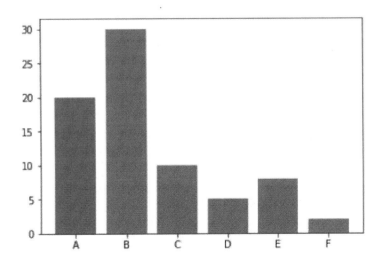

Figure 4.14: Output showing the number of students without any labels on the plot

Here, you define two lists: the **grades** list stores the grades, which you use as the x-axis, and the **students_count** list stores the number of students who score a respective grade. Then, you use the **plt** plotting engine and the **bar** command to draw a bar chart.

4. Enter the following code to add the main title and the axis titles to our chart for better understanding. Again, you use the **show()** command to display the rendered chart:

```
plt.title('Grades Bar Plot for Biology Class')
plt.xlabel('Grade')
plt.ylabel('Num Students')
plt.bar(grades, students_count, color=['green', 'gray', 'gray', 'gray', 'gray',
'red'])
plt.show()
```

Execute the cell, and you will get the following chart as the output:

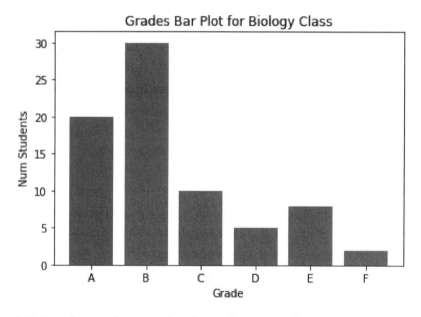

Figure 4.15: Bar plot graph outputting the grade and number of students with labels

Sometimes, it is easier to use horizontal bars to represent relationships. What you have to do is to change the bar function to **.barh**.

5. Enter the following code in a new cell and observe the output:

```
plt.barh(grades, students_count, color=['green', 'gray', 'gray', 'gray', 'gray',
'red'])
```

You should get the following output:

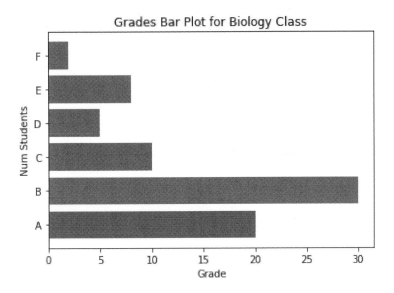

Figure 4.16: Horizontal bar plots

In this exercise, you implemented a sample list of data and outputting data as bar graphs; these bar graphs were shown as vertical bars and horizontal bars as well. This could vary depending on your usage.

In the next exercise, you will be implementing pie charts that many organizations use to pictorially classify their data. Pie charts are good for visualizing percentages and fractional data; for instance, the percentage of people who agree or disagree on some opinions, the fractional budget allocation for a certain project, or the results of an election.

However, a pie chart is often regarded as not a very good practice by many analysts and data scientists for the following reasons:

- Pie charts are often overused. Many people use pie charts without understanding why they should use them.

- A pie chart is not effective for comparison purposes when there are many categories.

- It is easier not to use a pie chart when the data can simply be presented using tables or even written words.

Exercise 65: Creating a Pie Chart to Visualize the Number of Votes in a School

In this exercise, you will plot a pie chart on the number of votes for each of the three candidates in an election for club president:

1. Open a new Jupyter Notebook.

2. Type the following code into a new cell by setting up our data:

```
# Plotting
labels = ['Monica', 'Adrian', 'Jared']
num = [230, 100, 98] # Note that this does not need to be percentages
```

3. Draw a pie chart by using the **pie()** method, and then set up **colors**:

```
import matplotlib.pyplot as plt
plt.pie(num, labels=labels, autopct='%1.1f%%', colors=['lightblue', 'lightgreen', 'yellow'])
```

4. Add **title** and display the chart:

```
plt.title('Voting Results: Club President', fontdict={'fontsize': 20})
plt.pie(num, labels=labels, autopct='%1.1f%%', colors=['lightblue', 'lightgreen', 'yellow'])
plt.show()
```

You should get the following output:

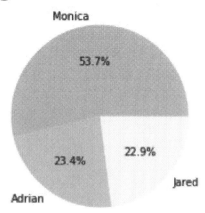

Figure 4.17: Pie chart with three categories

Having completed this exercise, you are now able to generate data as a pie chart. This type of representation is the best visual aid that many organizations use when sorting out data.

In the next exercise, you will be implementing a **heatmap** visualization. Heatmaps are useful for showing the relationship between two categorical properties; for instance, the number of students who passed exams in three different classes. Now you will follow an exercise and learn how to draw a **heatmap** visualization.

Exercise 66: Generating a Heatmap to Visualize the Grades of Students

In this exercise, you will be generating a heatmap:

1. Open a new Jupyter Notebook.

2. Now, type in the following code snippet to define a **heatmap** function. First, you prepare the plot:

```
def heatmap(data, row_labels, col_labels, ax=None, cbar_kw={}, cbarlabel="",
**kwargs):
    if not ax:
        ax = plt.gca()
    im = ax.imshow(data, **kwargs)
```

3. Define the color bar as **colorbar**, as mentioned in the following code snippet:

```
cbar = ax.figure.colorbar(im, ax=ax, **cbar_kw)
cbar.ax.set_ylabel(cbarlabel, rotation=-90, va="bottom")
```

4. Show all **ticks** and label them with their respective list entries:

```
ax.set_xticks(np.arange(data.shape[1]))
ax.set_yticks(np.arange(data.shape[0]))
ax.set_xticklabels(col_labels)
ax.set_yticklabels(row_labels)
```

5. Configure the horizontal axes for the labels to appear on top of the plot:

```
ax.tick_params(top=True, bottom=False,
               labeltop=True, labelbottom=False)
```

6. Rotate the tick labels and set their alignments:

```
plt.setp(ax.get_xticklabels(), rotation=-30, ha="right",
         rotation_mode="anchor")
```

7. Turn off **spine** and create a white grid for the plot, as mentioned in the following code snippet:

```
for edge, spine in ax.spines.items():
    spine.set_visible(False)

ax.set_xticks(np.arange(data.shape[1]+1)-.5, minor=True)
ax.set_yticks(np.arange(data.shape[0]+1)-.5, minor=True)
ax.grid(which="minor", color="w", linestyle='-', linewidth=3)
ax.tick_params(which="minor", bottom=False, left=False)
```

8. Return the heatmap:

```
return im, cbar
```

This is the code you obtain directly from the **matplotlib** documentation. The heatmap functions help to generate a heatmap.

9. Execute the cell, and, in the next cell, enter and execute the following code. You define a **numpy** array to store our data and plot the heatmap using the functions defined previously:

```
import numpy as np
import matplotlib.pyplot as plt
data = np.array([
    [30, 20, 10,],
    [10, 40, 15],
    [12, 10, 20]
])
im, cbar = heatmap(data, ['Class-1', 'Class-2', 'Class-3'], ['A', 'B', 'C'],
cmap='YlGn', cbarlabel='Number of Students')
```

You can see that the heatmap is quite plain without any textual information to help our readers understand the plot. You will now continue the exercise and add another function that will help us to annotate our **heatmap** visualization.

10. Type and execute the following code in a new cell:

Exercise66.ipynb

```
def annotate_heatmap(im, data=None, valfmt="{x:.2f}",
                     textcolors=["black", "white"],
                     threshold=None, **textkw):
    import matplotlib
    if not isinstance(data, (list, np.ndarray)):
        data = im.get_array()
    if threshold is not None:
        threshold = im.norm(threshold)
    else:
        threshold = im.norm(data.max())/2.
    kw = dict(horizontalalignment="center",
              verticalalignment="center")
    kw.update(textkw)
    if isinstance(valfmt, str):
        valfmt = matplotlib.ticker.StrMethodFormatter(valfmt)
```

https://packt.live/2ps1byv

> **Note**
>
> If the above link does not render, use https://nbviewer.jupyter.org/

11. In the new cell, type and execute the following code:

```
im, cbar = heatmap(data, ['Class-1', 'Class-2', 'Class-3'], ['A', 'B', 'C'],
cmap='YlGn', cbarlabel='Number of Students')
texts = annotate_heatmap(im, valfmt="{x}")
```

This will annotate the heatmap and give us the following output:

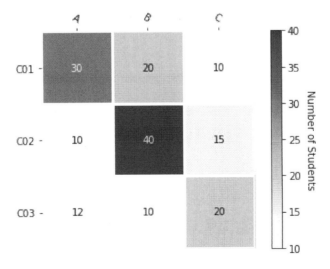

Figure 4.18: Heatmap output from the sample data

Note that you put our data in a **numpy** array (**np.array**). This is because the methods you are going to call expect a **numpy** array.

Next, you plotted our heatmap using the **heatmap** method. You passed in our **data**, the **row** labels, **['Class-1', 'Class-2', 'Class-3']**, and then our **column** labels, **['A', 'B', 'C']**. You also pass in **YlGn** as **cmap**, which means you want to use the color yellow for small values, and the color green for big values. You pass in **cbarlabel** as **Number of Students** to denote that the values we are plotting represent the number of students. Lastly, you annotate our heatmap with the data (**30, 20, 10**...).

So far, you have learned how to visualize discrete categorical variables using heatmaps and bar plots. But what if you want to visualize a continuous variable? For example, instead of the grades of students, you want to plot the distribution of scores. For this type of data, you should use a density distribution plot, which you will look at in the next exercise.

Exercise 67: Generating a Density Plot to Visualize the Score of Students

In this exercise, you will be generating a density plot from a list of sample data:

1. Begin by continuing from the previous Jupyter Notebook file.

2. Enter the following code into a new cell, set up the data, and initialize the plot:

```
import seaborn as sns
data = [90, 80, 50, 42, 89, 78, 34, 70, 67, 73, 74, 80, 60, 90, 90]
sns.distplot(data)
```

You have imported the **seaborn** module, which is explained later in this exercise, and then created a list as data. **sns.displot** is used to plot the data as a density plot.

3. Configure the **title** and axes labels:

```
import matplotlib.pyplot as plt
plt.title('Density Plot')
plt.xlabel('Score')
plt.ylabel('Density')
sns.distplot(data)
plt.show()
```

You should get the following output:

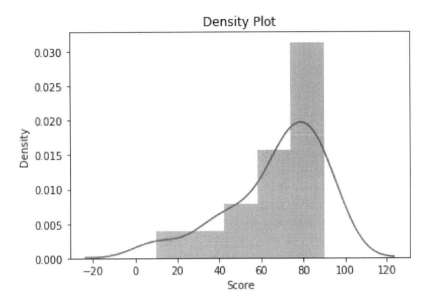

Figure 4.19: Density plot output from the sample data

So far, in this exercise, you have used the **seaborn** library, which is a data visualization library based on **matplotlib**. It provides a high-level interface for drawing appealing visual graphs and supports chart types that do not come with **matplotlib**. For example, you use the **seaborn** library for density plots simply because it is not available in **matplotlib**.

In this exercise, you were able to implement and output the density plot graph, as shown in *Figure 4.19*, from the list sample data we inputted.

If you were to do it using **matplotlib**, you would need to write a separate function that calculates the density. To make things easier and create density plots using **seaborn**. The line in the chart is drawn using **kernel density estimation (KDE)**. KDE estimates the probability density function of a random variable, which, in this case, is the score of students.

In the next exercise, you will be implementing contour plots. Contour plots are suitable for visualizing large and continuous datasets. A contour plot is like a density plot with two features. In the following exercise, you will examine how to plot a contour plot using sample weight data.

Exercise 68: Creating a Contour Plot

In this exercise, you will be using the sample dataset of the different weights of people to output a contour plot:

1. Open a new Jupyter Notebook.

2. Initialize the **weight** recording data using the following code in a new cell:

```
weight=[85.08,79.25,85.38,82.64,80.51,77.48,79.25,78.75,77.21,73.11,82.03,82.54,74.6
2,79.82,79.78,77.94,83.43,73.71,80.23,78.27,78.25,80.00,76.21,86.65,78.22,78.51,79.6
0,83.88,77.68,78.92,79.06,85.30,82.41,79.70,80.16,81.11,79.58,77.42,75.82,74.09,78.3
1,83.17,75.20,76.14]
```

3. Now, draw the plot using the following code. Execute the cell twice:

```
import seaborn as sns
sns.kdeplot(list(range(1,45)),weight, kind='kde', cmap="Reds", )
```

4. Add **legend**, **title**, and **axis** labels to the plot:

```
import matplotlib.pyplot as plt
plt.legend(labels=['a', 'b'])
plt.title('Weight Dataset - Contour Plot')
plt.ylabel('height (cm)')
plt.xlabel('width (cm)')
sns.kdeplot(list(range(1,45)),weight, kind='kde', cmap="Reds", )
```

5. Execute the code and you will see the following output:

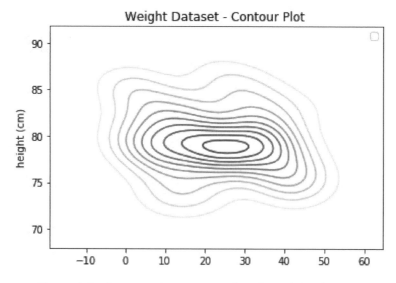

Figure 4.20: Contour plot output using the weight dataset

By the end of this exercise, you learned to output a contour graph from a dataset.

Compare this with the scatter plot that we have implemented before in *Exercise 62, Drawing a Scatter Plot*. Which chart type do you think is easier for us to visualize the data?

Extending Graphs

Sometimes, you will need to show multiple charts in the same figure for comparison purposes, or to extend the depth of the story that you are telling. For instance, in an election, you want one chart that shows the percentage, and another chart that shows the actual votes. You will now take a look at how you can use subplots in **matplotlib** in the following example.

Note that the following code is shown in multiple plots.

> **Note**
>
> You will use **ax1** and **ax2** to plot our charts now, instead of **plt**.

To initialize the figure and two axis objects, execute the following command:

```
import matplotlib.pyplot as plt
# Split the figure into 2 subplots
fig = plt.figure(figsize=(8,4))
ax1 = fig.add_subplot(121) # 121 means split into 1 row , 2 columns, and put in 1st part.
ax2 = fig.add_subplot(122) # 122 means split into 1 row , 2 columns, and put in 2nd part.
```

The following code plots the first subplot, which is a pie chart:

```
labels = ['Adrian', 'Monica', 'Jared']
num = [230, 100, 98]
ax1.pie(num, labels=labels, autopct='%1.1f%%', colors=['lightblue', 'lightgreen', 'yellow'])
ax1.set_title('Pie Chart (Subplot 1)')
```

Now, plot the second subplot, which is a bar chart:

```
# Plot Bar Chart (Subplot 2)
labels = ['Adrian', 'Monica', 'Jared']
num = [230, 100, 98]
plt.bar(labels, num, color=['lightblue', 'lightgreen', 'yellow'])
ax2.set_title('Bar Chart (Subplot 2)')
ax2.set_xlabel('Candidate')
ax2.set_ylabel('Votes')
fig.suptitle('Voting Results', size=14)
```

This will produce the following output:

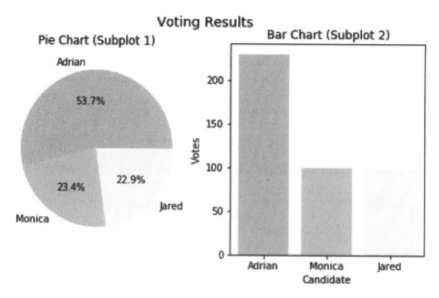

Figure 4.21: Output showing a pie chart and a bar chart with the same data next to each other

> **Note**
>
> If you want to try out the previously mentioned code example, be sure to put all the code in a single input field in your Jupyter Notebook in order for both the outputs to be shown next to one another.

In the following exercise, you will be using **matplotlib** to output 3D plots.

Exercise 69: Generating 3D plots to Plot a Sine Wave

Matplotlib supports 3D plots. In this exercise, you will plot a 3D sine wave using sample data:

1. Open a new Jupyter Notebook file.

2. Now, type the following code into a new cell and execute the code:

```
from mpl_toolkits.mplot3d import Axes3D
import numpy as np
import matplotlib.pyplot as plt
import seaborn as sns
X = np.linspace(0, 10, 50)
Y = np.linspace(0, 10, 50)
X, Y = np.meshgrid(X, Y)
Z = (np.sin(X))

# Setup axis
fig = plt.figure(figsize=(7,5))
ax = fig.add_subplot(111, projection='3d')
```

First, you import the **mplot3d** package. The **mplot3d** package adds 3D plotting capabilities by supplying an axis object that can create a 2D projection of a 3D scene. Next, you will be initializing data and setting up our drawing axis.

3. You will use the **plot_surface()** function to plot the 3D surface chart and configure the title and axes labels:

```
ax.plot_surface(X, Y, Z)

# Add title and axes labels
ax.set_title("Demo of 3D Plot", size=13)
ax.set_xlabel('X')
ax.set_ylabel('Y')
ax.set_zlabel('Z')
```

> **Note**
>
> Enter the preceding code in a single input field in your Jupyter Notebook, as shown in *Figure 4.22*.

Execute the cell twice, and you should get the following output:

```
In [10]:  from mpl_toolkits.mplot3d import Axes3D
          import numpy as np
          import matplotlib.pyplot as plt
          import seaborn as sns
          X = np.linspace(0, 10, 50)
          Y = np.linspace(0, 10, 50)
          X, Y = np.meshgrid(X, Y)
          Z = (np.sin(X))

          # Setup axis
          fig = plt.figure(figsize=(7,5))
          ax = fig.add_subplot(111, projection='3d')
          ax.plot_surface(X, Y, Z)

          # Add title and axes labels
          ax.set_title("Demo of 3D Plot", size=13)
          ax.set_xlabel('X')
          ax.set_ylabel('Y')
          ax.set_zlabel('Z')
```

```
Out[10]:  Text(0.5, 0, 'Z')
```

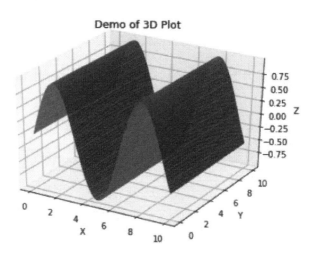

Figure 4.22: 3D plot of demo data using matplotlib

In this exercise, you were successfully able to implement a very interesting feature provided by `matplotlib`; that is, the 3D plot, which is an added feature in Python visualizations.

The Don'ts of Plotting Graphs

In newspapers, blogs, or social media there are a lot of misleading graphs that make people misunderstand the actual data. You will be going through some of these examples and learn how to avoid them.

Manipulating the Axis

Imagine you have three students with three different scores from an exam. Now, you have to plot their scores on a bar chart. There are two ways to do this: the misleading way, and the right way:

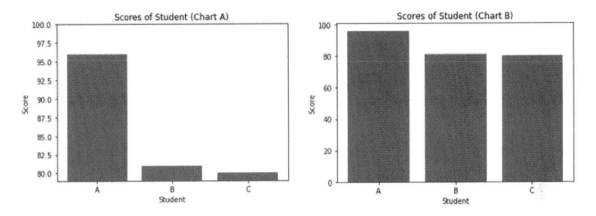

Figure 4.23: Chart A (starts from 80) and Chart B (starts from 0)

Looking at **Chart A**, it will be interpreted that the score of student **A** is about 10 times higher than student **B** and student **C**. However, that is not the case. The scores for the students are 96, 81, and 80, respectively. **Chart A** is misleading because the y-axis ranges from 80 to 100. The correct y-axis should range from 0 to 100, as in **Chart B**. This is simply because the minimum score a student can get is 0, and the maximum score a student can get is 100. The scores of students **B** and **C** are actually just slightly lower compared to student **A**.

Cherry Picking Data

Now, you will have a look at the opening stock prices:

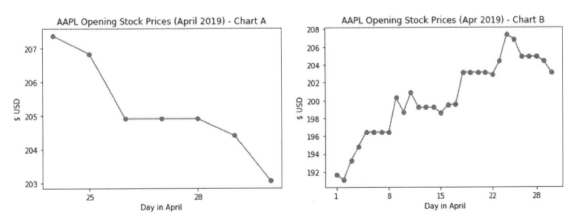

Figure 4.24: Chart A (shows only 7 days) and Chart B (shows the entire month)

Chart A, with the title **AAPL Opening Stock Prices (April 2019)**, shows a declining trend on Apple® stock prices. However, the chart is only showing the last 7 days of April. The title of the chart is mismatched with the chart. **Chart B** is the correct chart, as it shows a whole month of stock prices. As you can see, cherry-picking the data can give people a different perception of the reality of the data.

Wrong Graph, Wrong Context

You can have a look at two graphs that show a survey to demolish an old teaching building:

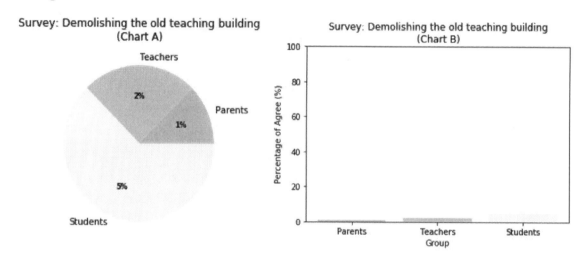

Figure 4.25: A pie chart versus a column chart

Using the wrong graph can give readers the wrong context to understand the data. Here, **Chart A** uses a pie chart to make readers think that the students want to demolish the old teaching building. However, as you can see in **Chart B**, the majority (95%) of the students voted to not demolish the old teaching building. The pie chart should only be used when every piece of the pie adds up to 100%. In this case, a bar chart is better at visualizing the data.

Activity 13: Visualizing the Titanic Dataset Using a Pie Chart and Bar Plots

Charts are not only a useful visualization device in presentations and reports; they also play a crucial role in Exploratory Data Analysis (EDA). In this activity, you will learn how to explore a dataset using visualizations.

In this activity, you will be using the famous Titanic dataset. Here, you will focus on plotting the expected data. The steps to load the dataset will be covered in the later chapters of this book. For this activity, the steps that you need to complete are as follows.

> **Note**
>
> In this activity, we will be using the Titanic dataset. This **titanic_train.csv** dataset **CSV** file is uploaded to our GitHub repository and can be found at https://packt.live/31egRmb.

Follow these steps to complete this activity:

1. Load the **CSV** file.

   To load the CSV file, add in the code, as mentioned in the following code snippet:

```python
import csv
lines = []
with open('titanic_train.csv') as csv_file:
    csv_reader = csv.reader(csv_file, delimiter=',')
    for line in csv_reader:
        lines.append(line)
```

2. Prepare a data object that stores all the **passengers** details using the following variables:

```python
data = lines[1:]
passengers = []
headers = lines[0]
```

3. Now, create a simple **for** loop for the **d** variable in **data**, which will store the values in a list.

4. Extract the following fields into their respective lists: **survived**, **pclass**, **age**, and **gender** for the passengers who survived:

```
survived = [p['Survived'] for p in passengers]
pclass = [p['Pclass'] for p in passengers]
age = [float(p['Age']) for p in passengers if p['Age'] != '']
gender_survived = [p['Sex'] for p in passengers if int(p['Survived']) == 1]
```

5. Based on this, your main goal and output will be to generate plots according to the requirements mentioned here:

- Visualize the proportion of passengers that survived the incident (in a pie chart).

   You should get the following output:

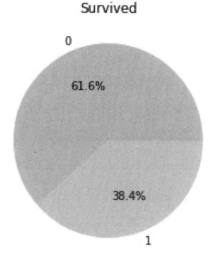

Figure 4.26: A pie chart showing the survival rate of the passengers

- Compare the gender of passengers who survived the incident (in a bar plot).

You should get the following output:

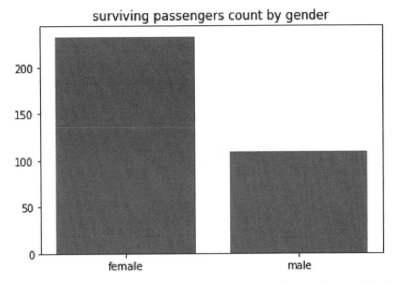

Figure 4.27: A bar plot showing the variation in the gender of those who survived the incident

> **Note**
>
> The solution to this activity is available on page 533.

Summary

In this chapter, you looked at how to read and write to a text file using Python, followed by using assertions in defensive programming, which is a way of debugging your code. Finally, you explored different types of graphs and charts to plot data. You discussed the suitability of each plot for different scenarios and datasets, giving suitable examples along the way. You also discussed how to avoid plotting charts that could be misleading.

In the next chapter, you will learn how to use Python to write **Object-Oriented Programming (OOP)** codes. This includes creating classes, instances, and using `write` subclasses that inherit the property of the parent class and extending functionalities using methods and properties.

5

Constructing Python – Classes and Methods

Overview

By the end of this chapter, you will be able to Use class and instance attributes to distinguish between attributes; use instance methods to perform calculations based on the instance attributes of an object; use static methods to write small utility functions to refactor code in a class to avoid repetition; use property setters to handle the assignment of values to computed properties and perform validation and create classes that inherit methods and attributes from other classes.

Introduction

In *Chapter 4*, *Extending Python, Files, Errors, and Graphs*, you began to move beyond the basic and fundamental, into writing defensive code and anticipating potential issues. In this chapter, you are introduced to one of the cornerstones of object-oriented programming (OOP): classes. Classes contain the definition of the objects we work with. All objects you work with in OOP are defined by a class, either in your code, or in a python library. So far in this course we have been using this, but we have not discussed how to extend and customize the behavior of objects. In this chapter you start with objects you are familiar with and build on these by introducing the concept of classes.

Perhaps you have been working with a string object in Python. What exactly is a string? What sort of things can you do with strings? Are there things you'd like to be able to do with strings that Python's string object doesn't allow? Can you customize the behavior of this object somehow? This chapter will answer these questions by exploring classes. Writing classes will unlock a world of possibilities, in which you'll be able to elegantly modify and combine code from external sources to fit your requirements.

For example, say you find a third-party library for managing calendars that you want to incorporate into your organization's internal application. You will want to inherit classes from the library and override methods/properties in order to use the code as per your particular context. So, you can see how methods can come in handy.

Your code will become increasingly more intuitive and readable, and your logic will be more elegantly encapsulated according to the **Do Not Repeat Yourself (DRY)** principle, which will be explained later in the chapter.

Classes and Objects

Classes are fundamental to object-oriented programming languages such as Python. A class is simply a template for creating objects. Classes define an object's various properties and specify the things you can do with that object. So far in this book, you have been relying on classes defined in the Python standard library or built into the Python programming language itself. For example, in *Exercise 37*, *Finding the System Date* of *Chapter 3*, *Executing Python – Programs, Algorithms, and Functions*, you used the `datetime` class to retrieve the current date. You will start off by exploring some more of the classes you've already been using. This can be performed in a Python shell or Jupyter Notebook.

Create a new integer object called **x** in a Python console:

```
>>> x = 10
>>> x
10
```

You can see the class that **x** was created from by calling the **type** function:

```
>>> type(x)
<class 'int'>
```

The integer class doesn't just let you store a single number – our **x** object has other properties, too:

```
>>> x.bit_length()
4
```

This method computes the number of binary digits needed to represent **x** as a binary number (1010).

As you learned in *Chapter 3, Executing Python – Programs, Algorithms, and Functions*, you can also view the docstring to read about this object and its class:

```
>>> print(x.__doc__)
int([x]) -> integer
int(x, base=10) -> integer
```

Convert a number or string to an integer, or return 0 if no arguments are given. If **x** is a number, return **x.__int__()**. For floating point numbers, this truncates towards zero.

So, you can see that even the simplest objects in Python, such as strings, have many interesting properties and methods that can be used to retrieve information about the object or perform some computation with the object. When you reach a point in your programming where you want to customize the behavior of these methods, or perhaps create a new type of object entirely, you will need to start writing your own classes. For example, perhaps instead of a string object, you want a **name** object that has a string as its main property and also contains methods that allow you to translate the name into other languages.

Exercise 70: Exploring Strings

Many of our examples and exercises so far have involved strings. In this exercise, you go beyond the text that a string object can store and look at the other properties and methods available in this class.

The aim of the exercise is to demonstrate that the string objects you are already familiar with have many other methods and properties that you might not have been aware of. This exercise can be performed in a Jupyter Notebook:

1. Define a new string:

```
my_str = 'hello World!'
```

2. Check what class our object has:

```
type(my_str)
```

You should get the following output:

```
str
```

3. View the docstring of the **str** class:

```
print(my_str.__doc__)
```

You should get the following output:

```
str(object='') -> str
str(bytes_or_buffer[, encoding[, errors]]) -> str

Create a new string object from the given object. If encoding or
errors is specified, then the object must expose a data buffer
that will be decoded using the given encoding and error handler.
Otherwise, returns the result of object.__str__() (if defined)
or repr(object).
encoding defaults to sys.getdefaultencoding().
errors defaults to 'strict'.
```

Figure 5.1: The docstring of the str class

4. View the full list of properties and methods of **my_str**:

```
my_str.__dir__()
```

You should get the following output:

```
['__repr__',
 '__hash__',
 '__str__',
 '__getattribute__',
 '__lt__',
 '__le__',
 '__eq__',
 '__ne__',
 '__gt__',
 '__ge__',
 '__iter__',
 '__mod__',
 '__rmod__',
 '__len__',
 '__getitem__',
 '__add__',
 '__mul__',
 '__rmul__',
 '__contains__',
 '__new__',
 'encode',
 'replace',
 'split',
 'rsplit',
 'join',
 'capitalize',
```

Figure 5.2: Complete list of the properties and methods of my_str

Note

The output in the preceding figure is truncated.

5. You will see the results of a few of the preceding methods:

```
my_str.capitalize()
```

You should get the following output:

```
'Hello world!'
```

Now to get the output in the uppercase:

```
my_str.upper()
```

You should get the following output:

```
'HELLO WORLD!'
```

Now to get the output in the lowercase without any spacing:

```
my_str.replace(' ', '')
```

You should get the following output:

```
'helloworld!'
```

In this exercise, you explored the various properties of a string object in Python. The purpose here was to illustrate that you are already working with objects that don't just represent simple data types but have more complex definitions. You will now turn to creating templates to build our own custom objects using classes.

Defining Classes

Built-in classes and classes imported from Python packages are sometimes sufficient for our requirements. However, often you want to invent a new type of object because there isn't an object in the standard libraries that has the properties/methods that you require. Recall that a class is like a template for creating a new object.

For example, create a new class called **Australian**:

```
>>> class Australian():
    is_human = True
    enjoys_sport = True
```

You now have a new template for creating **Australian** objects (or people, if you prefer). Our code assumes that all new Australians will be human and enjoy sport.

You will firstly create a new Australian:

```
>>> john = Australian()
```

Check the class of our Australian:

```
>>> type(john)
<class '__main__.Australian'>
```

You will also view some of John's attributes:

```
>>> john.is_human
True
>>> john.enjoys_sport
True
```

The `is_human` and `enjoys_sport` attributes are called class attributes. **Class attributes** do not change between objects of the same class. For example, let's create another Australian:

```
>>> ming = Australian()
```

Ming is also human and enjoys sport. We will soon learn about instance attributes, which can vary between objects created by a class.

Exercise 71: Creating a Pet Class

The aim of this exercise is to create our first class. You will create a new class called **Pet** with class attributes and a docstring. You will also create instances of this class:

1. Define a **Pet** class with two class attributes and a docstring:

```
class Pet():
    """
    A class to capture useful information regarding my pets, just incase
    I lose track of them.
    """
    is_human = False
    owner = 'Michael Smith'
```

2. Create an instance of this class:

```
chubbles = Pet()
```

3. Check the **is_human** properties of our new pet, **chubbles**:

```
chubbles.is_human
```

You should get the following output:

```
False
```

4. Check the owner:

```
chubbles.owner
print(chubbles.__doc__)
```

You should get the following output:

```
'Michael Smith'
```

```
A class to capture useful information regarding my pets, just incase
I lose track of them.
```

Figure 5.3: Output showing Chubbles is owned by Michael Smith and the output of a class to capture useful information

In this exercise, you created our first class and examined the properties of an object created with our new class.

The __init__ method

In *Exercise 71, Creating a Pet Class*, you used our **Pet** class to create a **Pet** object called **chubbles** in the following manner:

```
chubbles = Pet()
```

Here, you'll explore more about what happens when you create objects from a class in this manner.

Python has a special method called **__init__**, which is called when you initialize an object from one of our class **templates**. For example, building on the previous exercise, suppose you wanted to specify the height of our **Pet**. We would add an **__init__** method as follows:

```
class Pet():
    """
    A class to capture useful information regarding my pets, just incase
    I lose track of them.
    """

    def __init__(self, height):
        self.height = height

    is_human = False
    owner = 'Michael Smith'
```

The **init** method takes the height value and assigns it as an attribute of our new object. You can test this as follows:

```
chubbles = Pet(height=5)
chubbles.height
out: 5
```

Exercise 72: Creating a Circle Class

The aim of this exercise is to use the **init** method. You create a new class called **Circle** with an **init** method that allows us to specify the radius and color of a new **Circle** object. You then use this class to create two circles:

1. Create a **Circle** class with a class attribute called **is_shape**:

```
class Circle():
    is_shape = True
```

2. Add an **init** method to our class, allowing us to specify the radius and color of the specific circle:

```
class Circle():
    is_shape = True


    def __init__(self, radius, color):
        self.radius = radius
        self.color = color
```

3. Initialize two new **Circle** objects with different radii and colors:

```
first_circle = Circle(2, 'blue')
second_circle = Circle(3, 'red')
```

You should have a look at some of the attributes of the **Circle** objects:

```
first_circle.color
```

```
'blue'
```

```
second_circle.color
```

```
'red'
```

```
first_circle.is_shape
```

```
True
```

Figure 5.4: Checking the attributes of our circles

In this exercise, you learned how to use the **init** method to set instance attributes.

> **Note**
>
> Any **Circle** objects created from our **Circle** class will always have **is_shape** =
> **True**, but may have different radii and colors. This is because **is_shape** is a class
> attribute defined outside of the **init** method, and **radius** and **color** are instance
> attributes set in the **init** method.

Keyword Arguments

As we learned in *Chapter 3, Executing Python – Programs, Algorithms, and Functions,*
in the *Basic Functions* section, there are two types of arguments that can go into
functions: **positional** arguments and **keyword** arguments (kwarg). Recall that positional
arguments are listed first, and must be specified when calling the function, whereas
keyword arguments are optional:

```
def function_name (thing, thang = 4)
                      ↓         ↓
                     arg     kwarg
```

Figure 5.5: Args and Kwargs

The examples so far in this chapter have just contained positional arguments. However,
you may want to provide a default value for an instance attribute. For example, you can
take your previous example and add a default value for **color**:

```
class Circle():
    is_shape = True

    def __init__(self, radius, color='red'):
        self.radius = radius
        self.color = color
```

Now, if you initialize a circle without specifying a color, it will default to red:

```
my_circle = Circle(23)
my_circle.color
```

You should get the following output:

```
'red'
```

Exercise 73: The Country Class with Keyword Arguments

The aim of this exercise is to use keyword arguments to allow optional instance attribute inputs to be specified in the **init** function.

You create a class called **Country**, where there are three optional attributes that can be passed in the **init** method:

1. Create the **Country** class with three keyword arguments to capture details about the **Country** object:

```
class Country():
    def __init__(self, name='Unspecified', population=None, size_kmsq=None):
        self.name = name
        self.population = population
        self.size_kmsq = size_kmsq
```

2. Initialize a new **Country**, noting that the order of parameters does not matter because you are using named arguments:

```
usa = Country(name='United States of America', size_kmsq=9.8e6)
```

> **Note**
>
> Here 'e' is shorthand for '10 to the power of'. For instance, $2e4 == 2 * 10 \wedge 4 == 20000$

3. Use the **__dict__** method to view a list of the attributes of the **usa** object:

```
usa.__dict__
```

You should get the following output:

```
{'name': 'United States of America',
 'population': None,
 'size_kmsq': 9800000.0}
```

Figure 5.6: Dictionary output of our usa object

In this exercise, you learned how keyword arguments can be used when initializing an object with a class.

Methods

You have already come across one special method, the **init** method. However, the power of classes will start to become more obvious to you as you begin writing our own custom methods. There are three types of methods you will explore in the following sections:

- Instance methods
- Static methods
- Class methods

Instance Methods

Instance methods are the most common type of method you will need to use. They always take self as the first positional argument. The **__init__** method discussed in the previous section is an example of an instance method.

Here is another example of an instance method, extending our **Circle** class from *Exercise 72, Creating a Circle Class*:

```python
import math
class Circle():
    is_shape = True

    def __init__(self, radius, color='red'):
        self.radius = radius
        self.color = color

    def area(self):
        return math.pi * self.radius ** 2
```

The **area** method will use the **radius** attribute of the circle to compute the area of the circle using the following formula, which you may recall from math classes:

$$Area = \pi * r^2$$

Figure 5.7: Formula to calculate the area of a circle

You can now test the **area** method:

```python
circle = Circle(3)
circle.area()
```

You should get the following output:

```
28.274333882308138
```

As you may have realized by now, **self** represents the instance (that is, the object) within the method. This is always the first positional argument of an instance method, and Python passes it to the function without you needing to do anything. So, in the preceding example, when you call the **area** function, behind the scenes, Python passes the circle object through as the first argument.

This is necessary because it allows you to access other attributes and methods of our **Circle** object within the method.

Note the elegance of being able to change the radius of our circle without needing to worry about updating the area.

For example, taking our previously defined **circle** object, let's change the radius from **3** to **2**:

```
circle.radius = 2
circle.area()
```

You should get the following output:

```
12.566370614359172
```

If you had set **area** as an attribute of **Circle**, you would need to update it each time the radius changed. However, writing it as a method where it is expressed as a function of the radius makes your code more maintainable.

Exercise 74: Adding an Instance Method to Our Pet Class

The aim of this exercise is to add our first instance method to a class in order to determine whether or not our pet should be considered tall.

You will continue and add an instance method to the **Pet** class created in *Exercise 71, Creating a Pet Class*:

1. Start with your previous definition of **Pet**:

```
class Pet():
    def __init__(self, height):
        self.height = height

    is_human = False
    owner = 'Michael Smith'
```

2. Add a new method that allows you to check whether your pet is tall or not, where your definition of tall is where **Pet** has a height of at least **50**:

```python
class Pet():
    def __init__(self, height):
        self.height = height

    is_human = False
    owner = 'Michael Smith'

    def is_tall(self):
        return self.height >= 50
```

3. Now, create a **Pet** and check whether he is tall:

```python
bowser = Pet(40)
bowser.is_tall()
```

You should get the following output:

```
False
```

4. Now suppose that Bowser grows. Then you need to update his height and check again whether he is tall:

```python
bowser.height = 60
bowser.is_tall()
```

You should get the following output:

```
True
```

Adding Arguments to Instance Methods

The preceding example showed an instance method that took only the positional **self** parameter. Often, you need to specify other inputs to compute our methods. For instance, in *Exercise 74, Adding an Instance Method to Our Pet Class*, you hardcoded the definition of "tall" as any pet with a height greater than or equal to 50. Instead, you could allow that definition to be passed in via the method in the following manner:

```python
class Pet():
    def __init__(self, height):
        self.height = height

    is_human = False
```

```
    owner = 'Michael Smith'

    def is_tall(self, tall_if_at_least):
        return self.height >= tall_if_at_least
```

You can then create a pet and check whether its height exceeds some arbitrary benchmark that you specify:

```
bowser = Pet(40)
bowser.is_tall(30)
```

You should get the following output:

```
True
```

Now changing the height to 50 as mention below:

```
bowser.is_tall(50)
```

You should get the following output:

```
False
```

Exercise 75: Computing the Size of Our Country

The aim of this exercise is to use a keyword argument in the context of an instance method.

You create a **Country** class and add a method to calculate the area of the country in square miles:

1. Start with the following definition of **Country**, which allows the name, population, and size in square kilometers to be specified:

```
class Country():
    def __init__(self, name='Unspecified', population=None, size_kmsq=None):
        self.name = name
        self.population = population
        self.size_kmsq = size_kmsq
```

2. There are 0.621371 miles in a kilometer. Use this constant to write a method that returns the size in square miles. The class should now look like this:

```python
class Country():
    def __init__(self, name='Unspecified', population=None, size_kmsq=None):
        self.name = name
        self.population = population
        self.size_kmsq = size_kmsq

    def size_miles_sq(self, conversion_rate=0.621371):
        return self.size_kmsq * conversion_rate ** 2
```

3. Create a new **Country** and check the conversion:

```python
algeria = Country(name='Algeria', size_kmsq=2.382e6)
algeria.size_miles_sq()
919694.772584862
```

4. Suppose someone told you the conversion rate was incorrect, and that there are 0.6 miles in a kilometer. Without changing the default parameter, recalculate the size of Algeria in square miles using the new rate:

```python
algeria.size_miles_sq(conversion_rate=0.6)
```

You should get the following output:

```
857520.0
```

In this exercise, you learned how to allow optional keyword arguments to be passed into instance methods to alter the calculation performed.

The __str__ method

Like __init__, the __str__ method is another special instance method that you need to know about. This is the method that is called whenever the object is rendered as a string.

For example, it is what is displayed when you print the object to the console. You can explore this in the context of our **Pet** class. Suppose you have a **Pet** class in which you can assign a height and name to the **Pet** instance:

```
class Pet():
    def __init__(self, height, name):
        self.height = height
        self.name = name

    is_human = False
    owner = 'Michael Smith'
```

Now you create a pet and print it to the console:

```
my_pet = Pet(30, 'Chubster')
print(my_pet)
```

You should get the following output:

```
<__main__.Pet object at 0x0000018E1BBA5630>
```

Figure 5.8: An unhelpful string representation of the Pet object

This is not a very helpful representation of our pet. So, we need to add an **__str__** method:

```
class Pet():
    def __init__(self, height, name):
        self.height = height
        self.name = name

    is_human = False
    owner = 'Michael Smith'

    def __str__(self):
        return '%s (height: %s cm)' % (self.name, self.height)
```

Like any instance method, our **__str__** method takes **self** as the first argument in order to access attributes and other methods of the **Pet** object. You can create another pet:

```
my_other_pet = Pet(40, 'Rudolf')
print(my_other_pet)
```

You should get the following output:

```
Rudolf (height: 40 cm)
```

Figure 5.9: A much nicer string representation of the object

This is a much nicer representation of our **Pet** object and makes it easier to quickly inspect objects without diving into the individual attributes. It also makes it easier for someone to import your code into their work and be able to understand what the various objects represent.

Exercise 76: Adding an __str__ Method to the Country Class

The aim of this exercise is to learn how to add string methods in order to give more helpful string representations of objects when printed to the console.

You extend the **Country** class from *Exercise 75, Computing the Size of Our Country* by adding an **__str__** method to customize how the object is rendered as a string:

1. Start with our previous definition of **Country**:

```python
class Country():
    def __init__(self, name='Unspecified', population=None, size_kmsq=None):
        self.name = name
        self.population = population
        self.size_kmsq = size_kmsq
```

2. Add a simple string method that returns the name of the country:

```python
def __str__(self):
    return self.name
```

3. Create a new country and test the string method:

```python
chad = Country(name='Chad')
print(chad)
```

You should get the following output:

```
Chad
```

4. You now try adding more complex string method that displays the other information regarding our country, but only if that information is available:

```
def __str__(self):
    label = self.name
    if self.population:
        label = '%s, population: %s' % (label, self.population)
    if self.size_kmsq:
        label = '%s, size_kmsq: %s' % (label, self.size_kmsq)
    return label
```

5. Create a new country and test the string method:

```
chad = Country(name='Chad', population=100)
print(chad)
```

You should get the following output:

```
Chad, population: 100
```

In this exercise, you learned how to add a string method to improve the string representation of objects when printed to the console.

Static Methods

Static methods are similar to instance methods, except that they do not implicitly pass the positional **self** argument. Static methods aren't used as frequently as instance methods, so they only warrant a brief mention here. Static methods are defined by using the **@staticmethod** decorator. Decorators allow us to alter the behavior of functions and classes.

Here is an example of a static method added to our **Pet** class:

```
class Pet():
    def __init__(self, height):
        self.height = height

    is_human = False
    owner = 'Michael Smith'
```

```
    @staticmethod
    def owned_by_smith_family():
        return 'Smith' in Pet.owner
nibbles = Pet(100)
nibbles.owned_by_smith_family()
```

You should get the following output:

```
True
```

The **@staticmethod** notation is how decorators are added to functions in Python. Technically, this is actually passing the **owned_by_smith_family** function to a higher-order function that alters its behavior. However, for now, just think of it as allowing us to avoid having the positional **self** argument. This method should not be written as an instance method, because it does not rely on any instance attributes of the **Pet** object. That is, the result will be the same for all pets created from the class. Of course, you could alternatively write this as a class attribute, that is, **owned_by_smith_family = True**.

However, generally, you prefer to avoid writing code that needs to be updated in two places when one piece of underlying information changes. If you changed the pet owner to **Ming Xu**, you would also need to remember to update the **owned_by_smith_**family attribute to **False**. The preceding implementation avoids this problem, as the **owned_by_smith_family** static method is a function of the current owner.

Exercise 77: Refactoring Instance Methods Using a Static Method

Static methods are used to store utilities related to a class. In this exercise, you create a **Diary** class and show how you can use a static method to apply the **Do Not Repeat Yourself (DRY)** principle (refer to *Chapter 3, Executing Python – Programs, Algorithms, and Functions* which discussed *helper functions*) to refactor our code:

1. Create a simple **Diary** class that stores two dates:

```
import datetime
class Diary():
    def __init__(self, birthday, christmas):
        self.birthday = birthday
        self.christmas = christmas
```

2. Suppose you want to be able to view the dates in a custom date format. Add two instance methods that print out the dates in **dd-mm-yy** format:

```python
def show_birthday(self):
    return self.birthday.strftime('%d-%b-%y')
def show_christmas(self):
    return self.christmas.strftime('%d-%b-%y')
```

3. Create a new **Diary** object and test one of the methods:

```python
my_diary = Diary(datetime.date(2020, 5, 14), datetime.date(2020, 12, 25))
my_diary.show_birthday()
```

You should get the following output:

```python
'14-May-20'
```

4. Imagine you had a more complex **Diary** class, where you needed to format dates in this custom manner throughout our code. You would have the line **strftime('%d-%b-%y')** appearing many times in our code. If someone came to you and asked you to update the display format throughout the entire code base, you would need to change the code in lots of places. Instead, you could create a **format_date** static method utility to store this logic once:

```python
class Diary():
    def __init__(self, birthday, christmas):
        self.birthday = birthday
        self.christmas = christmas

    @staticmethod
    def format_date(date):
        return date.strftime('%d-%b-%y')

    def show_birthday(self):
        return self.format_date(self.birthday)
    def show_christmas(self):
        return self.format_date(self.christmas)
```

Now, if someone asks you to update the date format, there is a single location in the code that is your source of truth.

Class Methods

The third type of method you will explore is class methods. Class methods are like instance methods, except that instead of the instance of an object being passed as the first positional **self** argument, the class itself is passed as the first argument. As with static methods, you use a decorator to designate a class method. For example, you can take our **Australian** class and add a class method:

```python
class Australian():
    is_human = True
    enjoys_sport = True

    @classmethod
    def is_sporty_human(cls):
        return cls.is_human and cls.enjoys_sport
```

Note the first positional argument of this method is **cls**, not **self**. You can call this method on the class itself:

```python
Australian.is_sporty_human()
```

You should get the following output:

```
True
```

Alternatively, you can also call it on an instance of the class:

```python
aussie = Australian()
aussie.is_sporty_human()
```

You should get the following output:

```
True
```

Another way class methods are used is to provide nice utilities for creating new instances.

For example, you should take our **Country** class, as defined earlier:

```python
class Country():
    def __init__(self, name='Unspecified', population=None, size_kmsq=None):
        self.name = name
        self.population = population
        self.size_kmsq = size_kmsq
```

Suppose you want to avoid a situation where you create a country where people can specify the size in square miles rather than square kilometers. You could use a class method that takes the square mile input from the user and converts it to square kilometers, before initializing an instance of the class:

```
@classmethod
def create_with_msq(cls, name, population, size_msq):
    size_kmsq = size_msq / 0.621371 ** 2
    return cls(name, population, size_kmsq)
```

Now suppose you want to create a **mexico** object, and you know it has an area of 760,000 square miles:

```
mexico = Country.create_with_msq('Mexico', 150e6, 760000)
mexico.size_kmsq
```

You should get the following output:

```
1968392.1818017708
```

Exercise 78: Extending Our Pet Class with Class Methods

In this exercise, you show two common uses of class methods in the context of our **Pet** class:

1. Start with the following definition of the **Pet** class:

```
class Pet():
    def __init__(self, height):
        self.height = height


    is_human = False
    owner = 'Michael Smith'
```

2. Add a class method that returns whether the pet is owned by a member of the **Smith** family:

```
@classmethod
def owned_by_smith_family(cls):
    return 'Smith' in cls.owner
```

3. Now suppose that you want a way of producing pets with various random heights. Perhaps you're performing some simulations regarding buying 100 pets, and you want to see what the average height might be. Firstly, import the **random** module:

```
import random
```

4. Next, add a class method that picks a random number from **0** to **100**, and assigns it to the **height** property of a new pet:

```
@classmethod
def create_random_height_pet(cls):
    height = random.randrange(0, 100)
    return cls(height)
```

5. Lastly, you create **5** new pets and see what their heights are:

```
for i in range(5):
    pet = Pet.create_random_height_pet()
    print(pet.height)
```

You should get the following output:

```
99
61
26
92
53
```

In this exercise, you learned how class methods can be used to customize the creation of new objects and how to perform a basic calculation based on a class attribute.

> **Note**
>
> Your output may look different because these are random numbers between 0 and 100.

Properties

Properties are used to manage the attributes of objects. They are an important and powerful aspect of object-oriented programming but can be challenging to grasp at first. For example, suppose you have an object that has a **height** attribute and a **width** attribute. You might also want such an object to have an **area** property, which is simply the product of the **height** and **width** attributes. You would prefer not to save the area as an attribute of the shape because the area should update whenever the height or width changes. In this sort of scenario, you will want to use a property.

You will start by exploring the property decorator and then discuss the getter/setter paradigm.

The Property Decorator

The property decorator looks similar to the static methods and class methods that you have already encountered. It simply allows a method to be accessed as an attribute of an object rather than needing to call it like a function with ().

To understand the need for this decorator, consider the following class, which stores information about the temperature:

```
class Temperature():
    def __init__(self, celsius, fahrenheit):
        self.celsius = celsius
        self.fahrenheit = fahrenheit
```

Let's create a new temperature and check the **fahrenheit** attribute:

```
freezing = Temperature(0, 32)
freezing.fahrenheit
```

You should get the following output:

```
32
```

Now, suppose you decide it would be better to just store the temperature in Celsius, and convert to Fahrenheit when needed:

```
class Temperature():
    def __init__(self, celsius):
        self.celsius = celsius

    def fahrenheit(self):
        return self.celsius * 9 / 5 + 32
```

This is nicer because if the value of the temperature in Celsius is updated, you won't need to worry about updating **fahrenheit** as well:

```
my_temp = Temperature(0)
print(my_temp.fahrenheit())
my_temp.celsius = -10
print(my_temp.fahrenheit())
```

You should get the following output:

```
32.0
14.0
```

In the preceding code, you can see you need to call the **fahrenheit** instance method with (), whereas when you were accessing the attribute before, no parentheses were necessary.

This could be a problem if the previous version of this code was being used elsewhere or by other people. All references to **fahrenheit** would have to have parentheses appended. Instead, you could turn **fahrenheit** into a property, which allows us to access it like an attribute, despite it being a method of the class. To do this, you simply add the property decorator:

```python
class Temperature():
    def __init__(self, celsius):
        self.celsius = celsius


    @property
    def fahrenheit(self):
        return self.celsius * 9 / 5 + 32
```

You can now access the **fahrenheit** property in the following manner:

```python
freezing = Temperature(100)
freezing.fahrenheit
```

You should get the following output:

```
212.0
```

Exercise 79: The Full Name Property

The aim of this exercise is to use the property decorator to add object properties.

In this exercise, you create a **Person** class and show how to use a property to display their full name:

1. Create a **Person** class with two instance attributes, the first and last names:

```python
class Person():
    def __init__(self, first_name, last_name):
        self.first_name = first_name
        self.last_name = last_name
```

2. Add a **full_name** property with the **@property** decorator:

```python
    @property
    def full_name(self):
        return '%s %s' % (self.first_name, self.last_name)
```

3. Create a **customer** object and test the **full_name** property:

```python
customer = Person('Mary', 'Lou')
customer.full_name
```

You should get the following output:

```
'Mary Lou'
```

4. Suppose someone was using your code and decided to update the name of this customer in the following manner:

```
customer.full_name = 'Mary Schmidt'
```

They would see the following error:

```
--------------------------------------------------------------------
AttributeError                              Traceback (most recent call last)
<ipython-input-222-fef40f29f19e> in <module>
----> 1 customer.full_name = 'Mary Schmidt'

AttributeError: can't set attribute
```

Figure 5.10: Trying to set a value of a property that doesn't support attribute setting

The following section introduces the concept of setters, which allows you to customize how the input is handled when you try to assign attributes in this way.

The Setter Method

The setter method will be called whenever a user assigns a value to a property. This will allow us to write code where the user doesn't need to think about which attributes of an object are stored as instance attributes rather than computed by functions. Here is an example of what *Exercise 79, Full Name Property*, would look like if we added a full name setter:

```python
class Person():
    def __init__(self, first_name, last_name):
        self.first_name = first_name
        self.last_name = last_name


    @property
    def full_name(self):
        return '%s %s' % (self.first_name, self.last_name)


    @full_name.setter
    def full_name(self, name):
        first, last = name.split(' ')
        self.first_name = first
        self.last_name = last
```

Note the following conventions:

- The decorator should be the method name, followed by .setter.

- It should take the value being assigned as a single argument (after self).

- The name of the setter method should be the same as the name of the property.

Now you can create the same customer, but this time you can update their first and last names simultaneously by assigning a new value to the full_name property:

```
customer = Person('Mary', 'Lou')
customer.full_name = 'Mary Schmidt'
customer.last_name
```

You should get the following output:

```
'Schmidt'
```

Exercise 80: Writing a Setter Method

The aim of this exercise is to use a setter method to customize the way values are assigned to properties.

You extend our **Temperature** class by allowing the user to assign a new value for **fahrenheit** directly to the property:

1. Start with our **Temperature** class from earlier:

```
class Temperature():
    def __init__(self, celsius):
        self.celsius = celsius

    @property
    def fahrenheit(self):
        return self.celsius * 9 / 5 + 32
```

2. Add a **@fahrenheit.setter** function that converts the **fahrenheit** value to Celsius and stores it in the **celsius** instance attribute:

```
@fahrenheit.setter
def fahrenheit(self, value):
    self.celsius = (value - 32) * 5 / 9
```

3. Create a new temperature and check the **fahrenheit** property:

```
temp = Temperature(5)
temp.fahrenheit
```

You should get the following output:

```
41.0
```

4. Update the **fahrenheit** property and check the **celsius** attribute:

```
temp.fahrenheit = 32
temp.celsius
```

You should get the following output:

```
0.0
```

In this exercise, you wrote our first setter method, allowing you to customize how values are set to properties.

Validation via the Setter Method

Another common use of the setter method is to prevent the user from setting values that shouldn't be allowed. If you consider our previous example with the **Temperature** class, the minimum temperature theoretically possible is approximately –460 degrees Fahrenheit. It seems prudent that you prevent people from creating temperatures that are lower than this value. You can update the setter method from the previous exercise as follows:

```
@fahrenheit.setter
def fahrenheit(self, value):
    if value < -460:
        raise ValueError('Temperatures less than -460F are not possible')
    self.celsius = (value - 32) * 5 / 9
```

Now if the user attempts to update the temperature to an impossible value, the code will throw an exception:

```
temp = Temperature(5)
temp.fahrenheit = -500
```

You should get the following output:

```
--------------------------------------------------------------------------
ValueError                                Traceback (most recent call last)
<ipython-input-112-a59047203345> in <module>
      1 temp = Temperature(5)
----> 2 temp.fahrenheit = -500

<ipython-input-108-256b69371a35> in fahrenheit(self, value)
     10      def fahrenheit(self, value):
     11          if value < -460:
---> 12              raise ValueError('Temperatures less than -460F are not poss
ible')
     13          self.celcius = (value - 32) * 5 / 9

ValueError: Temperatures less than -460F are not possible
```

Figure 5.11: Demonstrating validation as part of the setter property

Inheritance

Class inheritance allows attributes and methods to be passed from one class to another. For example, suppose there is already a class available in a Python package that does almost everything you want. However, you just wish it had one extra method or attribute that would make it right for your purpose. Instead of rewriting the entire class, you could inherit the class and add additional properties, or change existing properties.

The DRY Principle Revisited

Recall the DRY principle: "*Every piece of knowledge or logic must have a single, unambiguous representation within a system.*" So far in this chapter, we have seen how classes allow us to more elegantly encapsulate logic about what objects represent. This has already moved us further along the path to writing clean, modularized code. Inheritance is the next step in this journey. Suppose we wanted to create two classes, one representing cats and the other, dogs.

Our **Cat** class may look like this:

```
class Cat():
    is_feline = True

    def __init__(self, name, weight):
        self.name = name
        self.weight = weight
```

Similarly, our **Dog** class would look the same, except that it would have a different value for the **is_feline** class attribute:

```
class Dog():
    is_feline = False

    def __init__(self, name, weight):
        self.name = name
        self.weight = weight
```

You can probably already see that this is a violation of the DRY principle. A lot of the preceding code is identical in the two classes. However, suppose that, in our program, cats and dogs are sufficiently different to require separate class definitions. You need a way to capture the common information about cats and dogs, without repeating it in both class definitions – enter inheritance.

Single Inheritance

Single inheritance, also known as sub-classing, involves creating a child class that inherits the attributes and methods of a single parent class. Taking the preceding example of cats and dogs, we can instead create a **Pet** class that represents all the common parts of the **Cat** and **Dog** classes:

```
class Pet():
    def __init__(self, name, weight):
        self.name = name
        self.weight = weight
```

The **Cat** and **Dog** classes can now be created by sub-classing the parent class, **Pet**:

```
class Cat(Pet):
    is_feline = True

class Dog(Pet):
    is_feline = False
```

You can check whether this is working as expected:

```
my_cat = Cat('Kibbles', 8)
my_cat.name
```

You should get the following output:

```
'Kibbles'
```

Now the logic in the **init** method is specified only once, and our **Cat** and **Dog** classes simply inherit it from the parent class, **Pet**. Now, if you decide to change the logic in the **init** method, you don't need to change it in two places, making our code easier to maintain. Likewise, it will be easier in the future to create different types of **Pet** classes. Additionally, you could create further subclasses of the **Dog** class if you wanted to create different types of **Dog** classes depending on breed. You can show the structure of our classes as a hierarchy, much like a family tree:

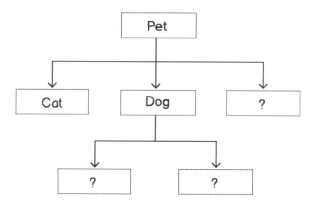

Figure 5.12: Class inheritance

Exercise 81: Inheriting from the Person Class

The goal of this exercise is to see how methods and attributes are inherited by child classes from parent classes.

In this exercise, you will create a **Baby** class and an **Adult** class, which will both inherit from a common **Person** class:

1. Start with the following **Person** class definition, which takes a first and last name as inputs in the **init** function:

```
class Person():
    def __init__(self, first_name, last_name):
        self.first_name = first_name
        self.last_name = last_name
```

2. Create a **Baby** class that inherits from **Person**, and add a **speak** instance method:

```
class Baby(Person):
    def speak(self):
        print('Blah blah blah')
```

3. Do the same for an **Adult** class:

```
class Adult(Person):
    def speak(self):
        print('Hello, my name is %s' % self.first_name)
```

4. Create a **Baby** and an **Adult** object, and make them speak:

```
jess = Baby('Jessie', 'Mcdonald')
tom = Adult('Thomas', 'Smith')
jess.speak()
tom.speak()
```

You should get the following output:

```
Blah blah blah
Hello, my name is Thomas
```

Figure 5.13: Our baby and adult speaking

In this exercise, you learned how to inherit attributes and methods between classes.

Sub-Classing Classes from Python Packages

In our examples so far, you have written the parent class ourselves. However, often, the reason for sub-classing is that a class already exists in a third-party package, and you just want to extend the functionality of that class with a few custom methods.

For example, suppose you wanted to have an integer object where you could check whether it was divisible by another number. You could create our own integer class and add a custom instance method as follows:

```
class MyInt(int):
    def is_divisible_by(self, x):
        return self % x == 0
```

You could then use this class to create integer objects that have this useful method:

```
a = MyInt(8)
a.is_divisible_by(2)
```

You should get the following output:

```
True
```

Exercise 82: Sub-Classing the datetime.date Class

The aim of this exercise is to show how you can inherit from classes in external libraries.

In this exercise, you create our own custom date class by inheriting from the **datetime** module. You add our own custom method that allows us to increment the date by a given number of days:

1. Import the **datetime** module:

```
import datetime
```

2. Create a **MyDate** class that inherits from **datetime.date**. Create an **add_days** instance method that uses a **timedelta** object to increment the date:

```
class MyDate(datetime.date):
    def add_days(self, n):
        return self + datetime.timedelta(n)
```

3. Create a new object using the **MyDate** class, and try out your custom **add_days** method:

```
d = MyDate(2019, 12, 1)
print(d.add_days(40))
print(d.add_days(400))
```

You should get the following output:

```
2020-01-10
2021-01-04
```

Figure 5.14: Adding days to a date

In this exercise, you learned how to inherit from classes in external libraries. This will often be useful, as external libraries may get you 90% of the way to solving the problem, but they're rarely built exactly for your own use case.

Overriding Methods

When inheriting classes, you often do so in order to change the behavior of the class, not just to extend the behavior. The custom methods or attributes you create on a child class can be used to override the method or attribute that was inherited from the parent.

For example, suppose the following **Person** class was provided by a third-party library:

```python
class Person():
    def __init__(self, first_name, last_name):
        self.first_name = first_name
        self.last_name = last_name


    @property
    def full_name(self):
        return '%s %s' % (self.first_name, self.last_name)


    @full_name.setter
    def full_name(self, name):
        first, last = name.split(' ')
        self.first_name = first
        self.last_name = last
```

Perhaps you are using this class, but you have problems when setting the names of people whose full name consists of three parts:

```python
my_person = Person('Mary', 'Smith')
my_person.full_name = 'Mary Anne Smith'
```

You should get the following output:

```
------------------------------------------------------------------
ValueError                               Traceback (most recent call last)
<ipython-input-146-9604ddbc3006> in <module>
      1 my_person = Person('Mary', 'Smith')
----> 2 my_person.full_name = 'Mary Anne Smith'

<ipython-input-142-a8f3417079a7> in full_name(self, name)
     10         @full_name.setter
     11         def full_name(self, name):
---> 12             first, last = name.split(' ')
     13             self.first_name = first
     14             self.last_name = last

ValueError: too many values to unpack (expected 2)
```

Figure 5.15: Failing to set a property

Suppose that in cases where there are three or more names that make up the full name, you want to assign the first part of the name to the **first_name** attribute, and the rest of the names to the **last_name** attribute. You could subclass **Person** and override the method as follows:

1. Start by creating a **BetterPerson** class that inherits from **Person**:

```
class BetterPerson(Person):
```

2. Add a full name property that combines the first and last names:

```
@property
def full_name(self):
    return '%s %s' % (self.first_name, self.last_name)
```

3. Add **full_name.setter** to firstly split the full name into its components, then set the first name equal to the first part of the name and set the last name equal to the second part of the name. The code also deals with cases where there are more than two components to the name, and it puts everything except the first name into the last name:

```
@full_name.setter
def full_name(self, name):
    names = name.split(' ')
    self.first_name = names[0]
    if len(names) > 2:
        self.last_name = ' '.join(names[1:])
    elif len(names) == 2:
        self.last_name = names[1]
```

4. Now create a **BetterPerson** instance and see it in action:

```
my_person = BetterPerson('Mary', 'Smith')
my_person.full_name = 'Mary Anne Smith'
print(my_person.first_name)
print(my_person.last_name)
```

You should get the following output:

```
Mary
Anne Smith
```

Calling the Parent Method with super()

Suppose the parent class has a method that is almost what you want it to be, but you need to make a small alteration to the logic. If you override the method as you did previously, you'll need to specify the entire logic of the method again, which may become a violation of the DRY principle. When building an application, you often require code from third-party libraries, and some of this code can be quite complex. If a certain method has 100 lines of code, you wouldn't want to include all that code in your repository in order to simply change one of those lines.

For example, suppose you have the following **Person** class:

```python
class Person():
    def __init__(self, first_name, last_name):
        self.first_name = first_name
        self.last_name = last_name


    def speak(self):
        print('Hello, my name is %s' % self.first_name)
```

Now, suppose you want to create a sub-class to make the person say more things in the **speak** method. One option would be to do so as follows:

```python
class TalkativePerson(Person):
    def speak(self):
        print('Hello, my name is %s' % self.first_name)
        print('It is a pleasure to meet you!')
john = TalkativePerson('John', 'Tomic')
john.speak()
```

You should get the following output:

```
Hello, my name is John
It is a pleasure to meet you!
```

Figure 5.16: Our talkative person speaking

This implementation is okay, though it isn't ideal that you've copied the "Hello, my name is John" line from the **Person** class. All you wanted to do was add additional things for **TalkativePerson** to say; you didn't need to change the way they say their name. Perhaps the **Person** class will be updated in the future to say something slightly different, and you want our **TalkativePerson** class to also reflect those changes. This is where the **super()** method comes in handy. **super()** allows you to access the parent class without explicitly referring to it by name. In the preceding example, you can use **super()** as follows:

```python
class TalkativePerson(Person):
    def speak(self):
        super().speak()
        print('It is a pleasure to meet you!')
john = TalkativePerson('John', 'Tomic')
john.speak()
```

You should get the following output:

```
Hello, my name is John
It is a pleasure to meet you!
```

Figure 5.17: Using the super() method to write cleaner code

The **super()** method allows you to access the parent class, **Person**, and call the corresponding **speak** method. Now, if any updates were made to the **Person** class's **speak** method, it would be reflected in what our **TalkativePerson** says as well.

Exercise 83: Overriding Methods Using super()

The aim of this exercise is to learn how to override methods using the **super** function. You subclass our previously created **Diary** class and show how **super** can be used to modify the behavior of a class without unnecessarily repeating code:

1. Import the **datetime** module:

```python
import datetime
```

2. Start with the **Diary** class, as defined previously:

```python
class Diary():
    def __init__(self, birthday, christmas):
        self.birthday = birthday
        self.christmas = christmas
```

```
@staticmethod
def format_date(date):
return date.strftime('%d-%b-%y')


def show_birthday(self):
    return self.format_date(self.birthday)
def show_christmas(self):
    return self.format_date(self.christmas)
```

3. Suppose you're unhappy with the fact that the hardcoded datetime format is in the **format_date** method, and you would prefer that a custom format can be specified for each **diary** object separately. One temptation would be to simply copy the whole class and start making modifications. However, when dealing with more complex classes, this is almost never a good option. Instead, let's subclass **Diary** and start by allowing it to be initialized with a custom **date_format** string:

```
class CustomDiary(Diary):
    def __init__(self, birthday, christmas, date_format):
        self.date_format = date_format
        super().__init__(birthday, christmas)
```

4. You also want to override the **format_date** method to use your new **date_format** attribute:

```
def format_date(self, date):
    return date.strftime(self.date_format)
```

5. Now when you create **diary** objects, each object can have a different string representation of the dates:

```
first_diary = CustomDiary(datetime.date(2018,1,1), datetime.date(2018,3,3), '%d-%b-
%Y')
second_diary = CustomDiary(datetime.date(2018,1,1), datetime.date(2018,3,3),
'%d/%m/%Y')
print(first_diary.show_birthday())
print(second_diary.show_christmas())
```

You should get the following output:

```
01-Jan-2018
03/03/2018
```

Figure 5.18: Viewing our diary dates

In this exercise, you learned how to override methods using the super function. This allows you to more carefully override methods in the parent classes you inherit from.

Multiple Inheritance

You often think of inheritance as allowing us to reuse common methods and attributes between related child classes. For example, a typical class structure could look like this:

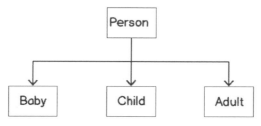

Figure 5.19: Single inheritance

Each child class is inheriting from a single parent class, **Person**.

However, it's also possible to inherit from more than one parent class. Often, there are elements of multiple classes that you want to combine to create a new class. For example, you might combine an **Adult** class with a **Calendar** class to make an **OrganizedAdult** class:

Figure 5.20: Multiple inheritance

Exercise 84: Creating a Consultation Appointment System

Suppose you are running a hospital and building a consultation appointment system. You want to be able to schedule appointments for various types of patients.

In this exercise, you start with our previously defined **Adult** and **Baby** classes and create **OrganizedAdult** and **OrganizedBaby** classes by inheriting from a second parent class, **Calendar**:

1. Import the **datetime** module:

```
import datetime
```

2. Start with the **Baby** and **Adult** classes, as defined previously:

```python
class Person():
    def __init__(self, first_name, last_name):
        self.first_name = first_name
        self.last_name = last_name
class Baby(Person):
    def speak(self):
        print('Blah blah blah')
class Adult(Person):
    def speak(self):
        print('Hello, my name is %s' % self.first_name)
```

3. Create a **Calendar** class that you can use to help our adults and babies become more organized:

```python
class Calendar():
    def book_appointment(self, date):
        print('Booking appointment for date %s' % date)
```

4. Create **OrganizedBaby** and **OrganizedAdult** classes that inherit from multiple parent classes:

```python
class OrganizedAdult(Adult, Calendar):
    pass
class OrganizedBaby(Baby, Calendar):
    pass
```

> **Note**
>
> If you want to define a class without adding or customizing its methods/attributes, you simply write **pass**.

5. Create some objects from your new classes and test their methods:

```python
andres = OrganizedAdult('Andres', 'Gomez')
boris = OrganizedBaby('Boris', 'Bumblebutton')
andres.speak()
boris.speak()
boris.book_appointment(datetime.date(2018,1,1))
```

You should get the following output:

```
Hello, my name is Andres
Blah blah blah
Booking appointment for date 2018-01-01
```

Figure 5.21: Booking an appointment

6. Suppose you wanted to warn the user when they try to book an appointment with a baby. You could override the **book_appointment** method, using the **super()** method to run the **book_appointment** method on the **Calendar** class:

```python
class OrganizedBaby(Baby, Calendar):
    def book_appointment(self, date):
        print('Note that you are booking an appointment with a baby.')
        super().book_appointment(date)
```

7. Now test whether it works:

```python
boris = OrganizedBaby('Boris', 'Bumblebutton')
boris.book_appointment(datetime.date(2018,1,1))
```

You should get the following output:

```
Note that you are booking an appointment with a baby.
Booking appointment for date 2018-01-01
```

Figure 5.22: Booking an appointment with a baby

Note that it's not always necessary to use inheritance when building your classes. If you only have one child class, having a parent class is often unnecessary. In fact, your code may be more readable if it's all stored in one class. Sometimes, the job of a good programmer is to consider the future and answer the question, "Will it become useful at some point to have built this with multiple inherited classes?" Answering this question simply becomes easier with experience.

Method Resolution Order

Suppose you were inheriting from two parent classes, both of which have a method of the same name. Which would be used when calling the method on the child class? Which would be used when calling it via **super()**? You should find this out through an example. Suppose you have **Dog** and **Cat** classes, and you combine them to make a monstrosity, **DogCat**:

```python
class Dog():
    def make_sound(self):
        print('Woof!')
```

```
class Cat():
    def make_sound(self):
        print('Miaw!')
class DogCat(Dog, Cat):
    pass
```

What sort of sounds would such a creature make?

```
my_pet = DogCat()
my_pet.make_sound()
```

You should get the following output:

```
Woof!
```

So, you can see that Python first checks for the existence of the **make_sound** method on the **Dog** class, and since it is implemented, you don't end up calling the **make_sound** method of the **Cat** class. Simply, Python reads from left to right in the list of classes. If you switched the order of **Dog** and **Cat**, our DogCat would miow:

```
class DogCat(Cat, Dog):
    pass


my_pet = DogCat()
my_pet.make_sound()
```

You should get the following output:

```
Miaw!
```

Suppose you wanted to override the method on **DogCat** and use the **super()** method. The same method resolution order would apply:

```
class DogCat(Dog, Cat):
    def make_sound(self):
        for i in range(3):
            super().make_sound()


my_pet = DogCat()
my_pet.make_sound()
```

You should get the following output:

```
Woof!
Woof!
Woof!
```

Activity 14: Creating Classes and Inheriting from a Parent Class

Suppose you are writing a computer game where the graphics are made up of various types of shapes. Each shape has certain properties, such as the number of edges, area, color, and so on. The shapes also behave in different ways. You want to be able to customize the way each shape behaves independently, while also not duplicating any code between the definition of each shape.

The aim of this activity is to create classes that can be used to represent a rectangle and a square. These two classes will inherit from a parent class called **Polygon**. The **Rectangle** and **Square** classes will have a property for computing the number of sides, perimeter, and area of the shape:

1. Add a **num_sides** property to the **Polygon** class that returns the number of sides.

2. Add a **perimeter** property to the **Polygon** class.

3. Add a **docstring** to the **Polygon** class.

4. Add a **__str__** method to the **Polygon** class that represents the polygon as "Polygon with X sides", where **X** is the actual number of sides of the **Polygon** instance.

5. Create a child class called **Rectangle**, which accepts two arguments from the user in the **init** method: **height** and **width**.

6. Add an area property to **Rectangle**.

7. Create a **Rectangle** object and check the computation of the area and perimeter.

   You should get the following output:

   ```
   (5, 12)
   ```

8. Create a child class called **Square** that inherits from **Rectangle**. You should only take one argument from the user when initializing a square.

9. Create a **Square** object and check the computation of the area and perimeter. You should get the following output:

   ```
   (25, 20)
   ```

   > **Note**
   >
   > The solution for this activity is available on page 536.

Summary

In this chapter, you have begun our journey into a cornerstone of object-oriented programming: classes. You have learned how classes allow you to write more elegant, reusable, and DRY code. You learned about the importance of and distinction between class and instance attributes, and how to set them in the class definition. You also explored various types of methods and when to use them. You explored the concept of a property and the Pythonic implementation of getters and setters. Lastly, you learned how to share methods and attributes between classes via single and multiple inheritance.

In the next chapter, you will explore the Python standard library and the various tools you can avail yourself of before needing to turn to third-party modules.

The Standard Library

Overview

By the end of this chapter, you will be able to utilize Python's standard library to write efficient code; use multiple standard libraries to write code; create and manipulate files by interacting with the OS filesystem; evaluate dates and times efficiently without falling into the most common mistakes and set up applications with logs to facilitate future troubleshooting.

Introduction

In the previous chapters, you saw how we can create our own classes incorporating logic and data. Yet, you often don't need to do that – you can rely on the standard library's functions and classes to do most of the work.

The Python standard library consists of modules that are available on all implementations of the language. Every installation of Python will have access to these without the need for any further steps for the modules defined in the standard library

While other famous languages don't have a standard library (such as JavaScript, which, as of 2019, is looking at implementing one), others have what seems to be an extensive set of tooling and functionality. Python goes a step further by including a vast number of basic utilities and protocol implementations as part of the default installation of the interpreter.

Standard libraries are useful and perform tasks such as unzipping files, speaking with other processes and the OS on your computer, processing HTML, and even printing graphics on the screen. A program that sorts a list of music files according to their artists can be written in a few lines when you use the correct modules of the standard library.

In this chapter, you will look at the importance of the standard library and how it can be used in our code to write faster and better Python with fewer keystrokes. You will walk through a subset of the modules, covering them in detail on a user level.

The Importance of the Standard Library

Python is often described as coming with "*batteries included*," which is usually a reference to its standard library. The Python standard library is vast, unlike any other language in the tech world. The Python standard library includes modules to connect to a socket; that is, one to send emails, one to connect to SQLite, one to work with the locale module, or one to encode and decode JSON and XML.

It is also renowned for including such modules as **turtle** and **tkinter**, graphical interfaces that most users probably don't use anymore, but they have proven useful when Python is taught at schools and universities.

It even includes **IDLE**, a Python-integrated development environment, it is not widely used as there are either other packages within the standard library that are used more often or external tools to substitute them. These libraries are divided into high-level modules and lower-level modules:

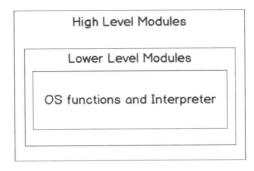

Figure 6.1: Graphical representation of the types of standard libraries

High-Level Modules

The Python standard library is truly vast and diverse, providing a *toolbelt* for the user that can be used to write most of their trivial programs. You can open an interpreter and run the following code snippet to print graphics on the screen. This can be executed on the Python terminal. The code mentioned here is with the >>> symbol:

```
>>> from turtle import Turtle, done
>>> turtle = Turtle()
>>> turtle.right(180)
>>> turtle.forward(100)
>>> turtle.right(90)
>>> turtle.forward(50)
>>> done()
```

This code uses the **turtle** module which can be used to print the output on the screen, as shown in *Figure 6.2*. This output will look like the trail of a turtle that follows when the cursor is moved. The **turtle** module allows the user to interact with the cursor and leave a trail as it keeps moving. It has functions to move around the screen and print as it advances.

Here is a detailed explanation of the **turtle** module code snippet:

1. It creates a turtle in the middle of the screen.

2. It then rotates it 180 degrees to the right.

3. It moves forward 100 pixels, painting as it walks.

4. It then rotates to the right once again, this time by 90 degrees.

5. It then moves forward 50 pixels once again.

6. It ends the program using **done()**.

The code mentioned earlier in this section will result in the following output:

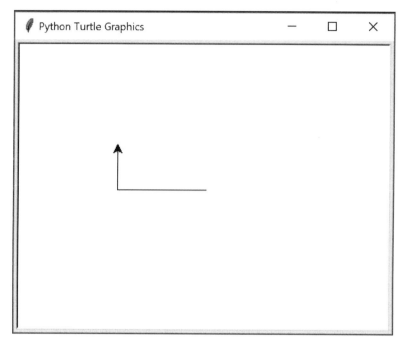

Figure 6.2: Example of output screen when using turtle

You can go ahead and explore and input different values, playing around a bit with the **turtle** module and checking the different outputs you get, before you dive further into this chapter.

The **turtle** module you worked on is an example of one of the high-level modules that the standard library offers.

Other examples of high-level modules include:

- Difflib: To check the differences line by line across two blocks of text.

- Re: For regular expressions, which will be covered in *Chapter 7, Being Pythonic*.

- Sqlite3: To create and interact with SQLite databases.

- Multiple data compressing and archiving modules, such as **gzip**, **zipfile**, and **tarfile**.

- XML, JSON, CSV, and config parser: For working with multiple file formats.

- Sched: To schedule events in the standard library.

- Argparse: For the straightforward creation of command-line interfaces.

Now, you will use another high-level module **argparse** as an example and see how it can be used to create a command-line interface that echoes words passed in and, optionally, capitalizes them in a few lines of code. This can be executed in the Python terminal:

```
>>> import argparse
>>> parser = argparse.ArgumentParser()
>>> parser.add_argument("message", help="Message to be echoed")
>>> parser.add_argument("-c", "--capitalize", action="store_true")
>>> args = parser.parse_args()
>>> if args.capitalize:
        print(args.message.capitalize())
    else:
        print(args.message)
```

This code example creates an instance of the **ArgumentParser** class, which helps you to create command-line interface applications.

It then defines two arguments in lines 3 and 4: **message** and **capitalize**.

Note that **capitalize** can also be referred to as **-c**, and we make it a Boolean flag option by changing the default action to **store_true**. At that point, you can just call **parse_args**, which will take the arguments passed in the command line, validate them, and expose them as attributes of **args**.

The code then takes the input message and chooses whether to capitalize it based on the flag.

You can now interact with this file, named **echo.py**, as shown in output *Figure 6.3*:

```
mcorcherojim at PF11AY8S in ~
$ python3.7 echo.py --help
usage: echo.py [-h] [-c] message

positional arguments:
  message              Message to be echoed

optional arguments:
  -h, --help           show this help message and exit
  -c, --capitalize
mcorcherojim at PF11AY8S in ~
$ python3.7 echo.py hello --capitalize
Hello
```

Figure 6.3: Example help message of an argparse script

Note

We will be using this capitalize tool in *Exercise 86, Extending the echo.py Example*.

Lower-Level Modules

The standard library also contains multiple lower-level modules that users rarely interact with. These lower-level modules are outside that of the standard library. Good examples are the different internet protocol modules, text formatting and templating, interacting with C code, testing, serving HTTP sites, and so on. The standard library comes with low-level modules to satisfy the needs of users in many of those scenarios, but you will usually see Python developers relying on libraries such as `jinja2`, `requests`, `flask`, `cython`, and `cffi` that are built on top of the low-level standard library module as they provide a nicer, simpler, more powerful interface. It is not that you cannot create an extension with the C API or ctypes, but cython allows you to remove a lot of the boilerplate, whereas the standard library requires you to write and optimize the most common scenarios.

Finally, there is another type of low-level module, which extends or simplifies the language. Notable examples of these are the following:

- Asyncio: To write asynchronous code

- Typing: To type hinting

- Contextvar: To save state based on the context

- Contextlib: To help with the creation of context managers

- Doctest: To verify code examples in documentation and docstrings

- Pdb and bdb: To access debugging tools

There are also modules such as `dis`, `ast`, and `code` that allow the developer to inspect, interact, and manipulate the Python interpreter and the runtime environment, but those aren't required by most beginner and intermediate developers.

Knowing How to Navigate in the Standard Library

Getting to know the standard library is key for any intermediate/advanced developer, even if you don't know how to use all the modules. Knowing what the library contains and when modules can be used provides any developer with a boost in speed and quality when developing Python applications.

> **Note**
>
> Python beginners are usually encouraged to take the standard library tour in the Python documentation (link: https://docs.python.org/3/tutorial/stdlib.html) once they master the basic syntax of the language.

While developers from other languages may try to implement everything on their own from scratch, experienced Python programmers will always first ask themselves "*how can I do this with the standard library?*" since using the code in the standard library brings multiple benefits, which will be explained later in the chapter.

The standard library makes code simpler and easier to understand. By using modules such as **dataclasses**, you can write code that would otherwise take hundreds of lines to create by ourselves and would most likely include bugs.

The **dataclass** module allows you to create value semantic types with fewer keystrokes by providing a decorator that can be used in a class, which will generate all the required boilerplate to have a class with the most common methods.

> **Note**
>
> Value semantic types represent the classes of the data that they hold. Objects can be easily copied by attributes and printed, and can then be compared using these attributes.

Exercise 85: Using the dataclass Module

In this exercise, you will create a class to hold data for a geographical point. This is a simple structure with two coordinates, **x** and **y**.

These coordinate points, **x** and **y**, are used by other developers who need to store geographical information. They will be working daily with these points, so they need to be able to create them with an easy constructor and be able to print them and see their values – converting them into a dictionary to save them into their database and share it with other people.

This exercise can be performed in the Jupyter notebook:

1. Import the **dataclass** module:

    ```
    import dataclasses
    ```

    This line brings the **dataclasses** module to the local namespace, allowing us to use it.

2. Define a **dataclass**:

    ```
    @dataclasses.dataclass
    class Point:
        x: int
        y: int
    ```

With these four lines, you have defined a **dataclass** by its most common methods. You can now see how it behaves differently from a standard class.

3. Create an instance, which is the data for a geographical point:

```
p = Point(x=10, y=20)
print(p)
```

The output will be as follows:

```
Point(x=10, y=20)
```

4. Now, compare the data points with another **Point** object:

```
p2 = Point(x=10, y=20)
p == p2
```

The output will be as follows:

```
True
```

5. Serialize the data:

```
dataclasses.asdict(p)
```

The output will be as follows:

```
{'x': 10, 'y': 20}
```

You now know how to use data classes to create value semantic types!

> **Note**
>
> Even if developers might be tempted to implement methods by themselves because they seem trivial, there are many edge cases that modules such as **dataclass** already takes account of, such as what happens if **__eq__** receives an object of a different type or a subclass of it.

The **dataclasses** module is part of the standard library, so most experienced users will understand how a class decorated with a **dataclass** decorator will behave compared to a custom implementation of those methods. This would require either further documentation to be written, or for users to fully understand all the code in all classes that are manually crafting those methods.

Moreover, using a battle-tested code that the standard library provides is also key to writing an efficient and robust application. Functions such as **sort** in Python use a custom sorting algorithm known as **timsort**. This is a hybrid stable sorting algorithm derived from **merge** sort and **insertion** sort, and will usually result in better performance results and fewer bugs than any algorithm that a user could implement in a limited amount of time.

Exercise 86: Extending the echo.py Example

> **Note**
>
> In this exercise, you will be using the previously mentioned **capitalize** tool with help messages and a variable number of arguments.

After the creation of the **capitalize** tool that you saw earlier in this topic, you can implement an enhanced version of the **echo** tool in Linux, which is used in some embedded systems that have Python. You will, use the previous code for **capitalize** and enhance it to have a nicer description. This will allow the echo comman to repeat the word passed in and to take more than one word.

When you execute the code, it should generate the following **help** message:

```
mariocj89 at DESKTOP-9B6VH3A in ~/workspace
$ python3.7 echo.py -h
usage: echo.py [-h] [-c] [--repeat REPEAT] message [message ...]

Prints out the words passed in, capitalizes them if required and repeat them
in as many lines as requested.

positional arguments:
  message               Messages to be echoed

optional arguments:
  -h, --help            show this help message and exit
  -c, --capitalize
  --repeat REPEAT
```

Figure 6.4: Expected output from the Exercise 86 help command

It should produce the following output when running with these arguments:

```
mariocj89 at DESKTOP-9B6VH3A in ~/workspace
$ python3.7 echo.py hello packt reader --repeat=3 -c
Hello Packt Reader
Hello Packt Reader
Hello Packt Reader
```

Figure 6.5: Expected output of running the Exercise 86 script

1. Add a description to the **echo** command.

   Start by adding a description to the **echo.py** script command. You can do so by passing it as an argument to the **ArgumentParser** class:

   ```
   parser = argparse.ArgumentParser(description="""
   Prints out the words passed in, capitalizes them if required
   and repeats them in as many lines as requested.
   """)
   ```

   The description passed in as an argument of the **ArgumentParser** class will be used as the help message when the user either runs the tools incorrectly or asks for help on how to use the tool.

   > **Note**
   >
   > Notice how you can split the description into multiple lines to easily format our code, but the output appears as if all lines were together.

2. Configure an argument to take multiple messages.

   The next step is to allow multiple messages rather than a single message. You can do so by using the **nargs** keyword argument when adding a positional parameter:

   ```
   parser.add_argument("message", help="Messages to be echoed", nargs="+")
   ```

   By passing **nargs="+"**, you tell **argparse** that we require at least one **message** to be passed in. Other options include ? for optional, and * for 0 or more. You can also use any natural number to require a specific number of parameters.

3. Add a **repeat** flag with a **default** value.

   Finally, you need to add a new option with a default value to control the number of times the message is repeated:

   ```
   parser.add_argument("--repeat", type=int, default=1)
   ```

   This adds a new option, **repeat**, which allows us to pass an integer that defaults to one, and that will control the number of times the words are repeated.

   > **Note**
   >
   > Notice how you pass a type, which is just a callable. This will be used to transform and validate the argument passed in, and you indicate what the default value is if a user does not specify the option. Alternatively, you could have marked it as **required=True** to force the user to always pass a value.

Altogether, the code and implementation will be as shown in the following code snippet:

```python
import argparse
parser = argparse.ArgumentParser(description="""
Prints out the words passed in, capitalizes them if required
and repeat them in as many lines as requested.
""")
parser.add_argument("message", help="Messages to be echoed", nargs="+")
parser.add_argument("-c", "--capitalize", action="store_true")
parser.add_argument("--repeat", type=int, default=1)
args = parser.parse_args()
if args.capitalize:
    messages = [m.capitalize() for m in args.message]
else:
    messages = args.message
for _ in range(args.repeat):
    print(" ".join(messages))
```

You just created a CLI application that allows you to echo messages with an intuitive interface. You can now use the **argparse** module to create any other CLI application.

Quite often, the standard library in Python has answers to developers' most common questions. By having a general knowledge of the different modules in Python and always questioning what can be used from the standard library, you will write better Python code that uses easy-to-read, well-tested, and efficient utilities.

Dates and Times

Many programs will need to deal with dates and times, and Python comes with multiple modules to help you handle those effectively. The most common module is the **datetime** module. The **datetime** module comes with three types that can be used to represent dates, times, and timestamps. There are also other modules, such as the **time** module, or the **calendar** module, which can be used for some other use cases.

datetime.date can be used to represent any date between the years 1 and 9999. For any date/time outside of this range, you would need to use more specialized libraries, such as the **astropy** library.

You can create a **datetime.date** by passing the year, month, and day, or get today by just calling **datetime.date.today()**:

```python
import datetime
datetime.date.today()
```

The output is as follows:

```
datetime.date(2019, 4, 20)
```

Figure 6.6: Representation of a date object

The output format for time is similar; it takes hour, minute, second, and microsecond. All of them are optional and are initialized at 0 if not provided. This can also be created with **tzinfo**, but you will see more about that attribute in the **datetime.datetime** section.

Within the **datetime** module, you have what is probably the most frequently used class, the **datetime.datetime** class. It can represent a combination of a date and a time, and it actually inherits from **datetime.date**. But before you start to explore the **datetime** class within the **datetime** module, you need to better understand the concept of time and how you represent it.

There are usually two kinds of **time** that you need to represent. They are commonly referred to as timestamps and wall time.

The first, timestamps, can be seen as a unique point in time independent from any human interpretation of it. It is an absolute point in the line of time that is not relative to any geographical location or country. This is used for astronomical events, log records, and the synchronization of machines, among other things.

The second, wall time, refers to the time *on the wall* at a specific location. This is the time humans use, and you synchronize your time using it. This time is the "legal" time as it is dictated by the country and is related to a time zone. This is used for meetings, flight schedules, working hours, and so on. The interval of time can change at any point due to legislation. As an example, think of countries that observe daylight saving time (DST) and change their standard clock accordingly.

> **Note**
>
> If you need to work extensively with time, it is important to read about UTC and the history of how you measure time to avoid more complex issues, but you will go through a quick overview of good practices when handling time in this topic to avoid the most common mistakes.

When you are working with wall time, you just need to treat **datetime.datetime** objects as a mere combination of a date and a time at a location. But you should usually attach a time zone to it to be more precise and get proper semantics for time comparison and basic arithmetic. The two most commonly used libraries to handle time zones are **pytz** and **dateutil**.

You must use **dateutil** when using wall times; **pytz** has a time model that will lead the inexperienced user to make mistakes more often than not. To create a **datetime** with a time zone, you just need to pass it through the **tzinfo** argument:

```
import datetime
from dateutil import tz
datetime.datetime(1989, 4, 24, 10, 11,
                  tzinfo=tz.gettz("Europe/Madrid"))
```

This creates a **datetime** with that time zone information attached.

Exercise 87: Comparing datetime across Time Zones

The goal of this exercise is to create two different **datetime** and compare them when they are in different time zones:

1. Import the **datetime** and **tz** modules from **dateutil**:

```
import datetime
from dateutil import tz
```

> **Note**
>
> **Dateutil** is not a module from the standard library, though it is the one recommended by the standard library.

2. Create the first **datetime** for **Madrid**:

```
d1 = datetime.datetime(1989, 4, 24, hour=11,
                       tzinfo=tz.gettz("Europe/Madrid"))
```

With this line, you create a **datetime** for April 24, 1989, at 11 a.m. in Madrid.

3. Create the second **datetime** for **Los_Angeles**:

```
d2 = datetime.datetime(1989, 4, 24, hour=8,
                       tzinfo=tz.gettz("America/Los_Angeles"))
```

This creates a **datetime** object that seems to have a difference of 3 hours less and a different time zone.

4. Now, compare them:

```
print(d1.hour > d2.hour)
print(d1 > d2)
```

The output is as follows:

True
False

Figure 6.7: Output when comparing the conditions for the time zones

When you compare the two **datetime** objects, you can see that even though the first **datetime** has a higher hour than the second (that is, the first is at 11 and the second is at 8), the first is not greater, and is, therefore later than the second, as the time zone is different, and 8 in Los Angeles happens after 11 in Madrid.

5. Now, convert the **datetime** object to a different time zone.

   You can convert a **datetime** from one time zone to another. You should do that to see what time the second **datetime** would show if it was in Madrid:

```
d2_madrid = d2.astimezone(tz.gettz("Europe/Madrid"))
print(d2_madrid.hour)
```

The output is as follows:

```
17
```

It is 5 p.m. Now, it is obvious that the second **datetime** is later than the first.

At other times, you might work just with timestamps, with time not related to any location. The easiest way to do this is to use UTC, with 0 as the offset. UTC is Coordinated Universal Time and is a system that provides a universal way of coordinating time across locations – you have most likely already used it. It is *the most common standard* for the time. The time zones you saw in the previous exercises define offsets from UTC that allow the library to identify what time corresponds to time from one location to another.

To create a **datetime** with an offset of 0, also known as a **datetime** in UTC, you can use **datetime.timezone.utc** as the **tzinfo** argument. This will then represent an absolute point in the line of time. You can safely add, subtract, and compare **datetimes** without any issue when using UTC. On the other hand, if you use any specific time zone, you should be aware that nations might change the time at any point, which could make any of your calculations invalid.

You now know how to create datetimes, compare them, and convert them across time zones. This is a common exercise when developing applications that deal with time.

In the next exercise, you'll look at the time delta between two **datetime** objects. Here, the delta is the difference.

Exercise 88: Calculating the Time Delta between Two datetime Objects

In this exercise, you will subtract two **datetime** objects to calculate the delta between the two timestamps.

Quite often, when you work with **datetime**, what really matters is the difference between them; that is, the delta in time between two specific dates. Here, you will find out the difference in seconds between two important events that happened in your company, one on February 25, 2019, at 10:50, and the other on February 26 at 11:20. Both these times are in UTC. This exercise can be performed in a Jupyter notebook:

1. Import the **datetime** module:

```
import datetime as dt
```

Quite often, developers import the **datetime** module through an alias, **dt**. This is done in many codebases to differentiate the **datetime** module from the **datetime** class.

2. Create two **datetime** objects.

You now create two dates:

```
d1 = dt.datetime(2019, 2, 25, 10, 50,
                 tzinfo=dt.timezone.utc)
d2 = dt.datetime(2019, 2, 26, 11, 20,
                 tzinfo=dt.timezone.utc)
```

We created two **datetime** objects as **dt.datetime**, and you now have two **datetime** objects.

3. Subtract **d1** from **d2**.

You can subtract two **datetime** to get a time delta back or add a time delta to a **datetime**.

Adding two **datetime** makes no sense, and the operation will, therefore, output an error with an exception. Hence, you subtract the two **datetime** to get the delta:

```
d2 - d1
```

The output is as follows:

```
datetime.timedelta(days=1, seconds=1800)
```

Figure 6.8: Output with the delta between 2 days and seconds

4. You can see that the delta between the two **datetime** is 1 day and 1,800 seconds, which can be translated to the total number of seconds by calling **total_seconds** in the time delta object that the subtraction returns:

```
td = d2 - d1
td.total_seconds()
```

The output is as follows:

```
88200.0
```

5. It happens quite often that you need to send **datetime** objects in formats such as JSON or others that do not support native datetimes. A common way to serialize **datetime** is by encoding them in a string using the ISO 8601 standard.

This can be done by using **isoformat**, which will output a string, and parsing them with the **fromisoformat** method, which takes a **datetime** serialized to a string with **isoformat** and transforms it back to a **datetime**:

```
d1 = dt.datetime.now(dt.timezone.utc)
d1.isoformat()
```

The output is as follows:

```
'2019-04-21T12:38:49.117769+00:00'
```

Figure 6.9: Output with the datetime serialized to a string with isoformat and back to datetime

Another module that you use when dealing with time is the **time** module. In the **time** module, you can get the Unix time through **time.time**. This will return the number of seconds since the Unix epoch is without leap seconds. This is known as **Unix time** or **POXIS time**.

You are encouraged to read about leap seconds if you need to develop highly time-sensitive applications, but Python offers no time support for them. The **time** and **datetime** modules just use the system clock, which will not count leap seconds.

But what happens in an instance where a leap second occurs is up to the OS admin. Some companies slow down time around leap seconds, while others just skip them by making a second take two seconds in the real world. If you need to figure this out in your workplace, you will need to check with your OS admin how the NTP servers are configured to act in leap seconds. Luckily, you know well in advance when the next leap second will happen, as the International Earth Rotation and Reference Systems Service (https://packt.live/2oKYtUR) publishes leap seconds at least 8 weeks in advance.

You now understand the basics of time arithmetic and know how to calculate the time delta between two timestamps.

Exercise 89: Calculating the Unix Epoch Time

In this exercise, you will use the **datetime** and **time** modules to calculate Unix Epoch time.

If you can just look it up, you can also calculate the Unix epoch. As **time.time** gives us the number of seconds since the epoch, you can create a time delta with it and subtract it from a **datetime** you've created. You will see how to perform that in this exercise.

This exercise can be performed in a Jupyter notebook:

1. Import the **time** and **datetime** modules and get them to the current namespace:

```
import datetime as dt
import time
```

2. Get the current time. You use both **datetime** and **time** to do this:

```
time_now = time.time()
datetime_now = dt.datetime.now(dt.timezone.utc)
```

> **Note**
>
> You use the UTC time zone when getting time with **datetime**. This is necessary because **time.time** returns Unix time, which uses an **epoch** that is in UTC.

3. You can now calculate the epoch by subtracting **datetime** and a time delta, which you get from the current time since you said that these are the number of seconds since the **epoch**:

```
epoch = datetime_now - dt.timedelta(seconds=time_now)
print(epoch)
```

The output is as follows:

```
1970-01-01 00:00:00.000052+00:00
```

Figure 6.10: Calculating the epoch

The result is the Unix epoch – January 1, 1970.

Having completed this exercise, you know how to use the **time** and **datetime** modules to get the output as the Unix **epoch** time, as shown in *Figure 6.10*, and to use **timedelta** to represent intervals.

There is one more module that it is sometimes used in combination with **datetime**, which is the **calendar** module. The **calendar** module provides additional information about calendar years; that is, how many days there are in a month. This can also be used to output calendars such as the Unix function.

Now have a look at an example where you create a calendar and get all of the days in a month as follows:

```
import calendar
c = calendar.Calendar()
list(c.itermonthdates(2019, 2))
```

The output is as follows:

```
datetime.date(2019, 1, 28),
datetime.date(2019, 1, 29),
datetime.date(2019, 1, 30),
datetime.date(2019, 1, 31),
datetime.date(2019, 2, 1),
datetime.date(2019, 2, 2),
```

Figure 6.11: Output showing month 1 and its days as a calendar

> **Note**
>
> Though the function returns all date instances for all the weeks in the month, if you want to get only the days that belong to the specific month, you need to filter them.

```
list(d for d in c.itermonthdates(2019, 2)
        if d.month == 2)
```

You should get the following output:

```
datetime.date(2019, 2, 1),
datetime.date(2019, 2, 2),
datetime.date(2019, 2, 3),
datetime.date(2019, 2, 4),
datetime.date(2019, 2, 5),
```

Figure 6.12: Output showing month 2 and it's days as a calendar

Note

Bear in mind in mind that when working with **datetimes**, there are some basic assumptions that you might make that will cause bugs in your code. For instance, assuming a year will have 365 days will cause problems for 29 February, or assuming that a day has 24 hours when any international traveler can tell you that this isn't the case. A detailed table on the wrong assumptions of time and its reasoning is mentioned in the appendix of this book on *Page 541*.

If you need to work with dates and times, make sure to always use well-tested libraries such as **dateutil** from the standard library, and consider using a good testing library such as **freezegun** to validate your assumptions. You'd be surprised to discover the endless number of bugs that computer systems have when exposed to time quirks.

To know more about time, you first need to understand how the system clock works. For example, your computer clock is not like a clock on the wall; it uses the **Network Time Protocol** (NTP) to coordinate with other connected computers. NTP is one of the oldest internet protocols that is still in use. Time is really hard to measure, and the most efficient way to do so is by using atomic clocks. The NTP creates a hierarchy of clocks and synchronizes them periodically. A good exercise is to disable the NTP sync on your computer for a day and check how your system clock deviates from the internet by running the NTP manually.

Handling dates and times properly is extremely difficult. For simple applications, you should be fine with a basic level of understanding, but otherwise, further reading and more specialized libraries will be needed. In Python, we have the **datetime** module as the key to handling date and time, which also contains the **timezone.utc** time zone. There are also **time** and **calendar** modules, which can be used when we need to measure with UNIX time and to get calendar information, respectively.

Activity 15: Calculating the Time Elapsed to Run a Loop

You are part of an IT department, and you are asked to inspect an application that outputs random numbers but with a delay. In order to investigate this delayed output, you check the code as there have been updates to the application where the development team has added a new line of code to get a list of random numbers. You are asked to confirm this by checking the time it takes to run that line of code using the **time** module.

> **Note**
>
> To perform this activity, you can just record the time by using **time.time** to compute the difference in time since, before, and after the function. If you want to be more precise and use the time in nanoseconds, you can use **time_ns**.

You will see in the topic about profiling in a later chapter how to measure performance in a more precise way.

This was the line of code that was added in by the development team:

```
l = [random.randint(1, 999) for _ in range(10 * 3)]
```

While it is possible to run the code and use **time.time** to calculate the elapsed time, is there any better function in the time module to do this?

Steps:

1. Record the time before running the code mentioned above in a hint with the **time.time** function.

2. Record the time after running the code mentioned above in a hint with the **time.time** function.

3. Find the difference between the two.

4. Repeat the steps using **time.time_ns**.

   You should get the following output:

   ```
   187500
   ```

> **Note**
>
> The solution for this activity is available on page 538.

Interacting with the OS

One of the most common uses of Python is to write code that interacts with the OS and its filesystem. Whether you are working with files or you just need some basic information about the OS, this topic will cover the essentials of how to do it in a multiplatform way through the **os**, **sys**, **platform**, and **pathlib** modules of the standard library.

OS Information

There are three key modules that are used to inspect the runtime environment and the OS. The **os** module enables miscellaneous interfaces with the OS. You can use it to inspect environment variables or to get other user and process-related information. This, combined with the **platform** module, which contains information about the interpreter and the machine where the process is running, and the **sys** module, which provides you with helpful system-specific information, will usually provide you with all the information that you need about the runtime environment.

Exercise 90: Inspecting the Current Process Information

The goal of this exercise is to use the standard library to report information about the running process and the platform on your system:

1. Import the **os**, **platform**, and **sys** modules:

```
import platform
import os
import sys
```

2. Get basic process information:

    To obtain information such as the **Process id**, **Parent id** you can use the **os** module:

```
print("Process id:", os.getpid())
print("Parent process id:", os.getppid())
```

The output is as follows:

```
Process id: 13244
Parent process id: 8792
```

Figure 6.13: The expected output showing the process ID and the parent process ID of the system

This gives us the process ID and the parent process ID. This constitutes a basic step when you try to perform any interaction with the OS that involves your process and is the best way to uniquely identify the running process. You can try restarting the kernel or the interpreter and see how the **pid** changes, as a new process ID is always assigned to a running process in the system.

3. Now, get the **platform** and Python interpreter information:

```
print("Machine network name:", platform.node())
print("Python version:", platform.python_version())
print("System:", platform.system())
```

The output is as follows:

```
Machine network name: PF11AY8S
Python version: 3.7.0
System: Windows
```

Figure 6.14: The expected output showing the network name, Python version, and the system type

These functions of the module platform can be used to ascertain the information of the computer where your Python code is running, which is useful when you are writing code that might be specific to the machine or system information.

4. Get the Python path and the arguments passed to the interpreter:

```
print("Python module lookup path:", sys.path)
print("Command to run Python:", sys.argv)
```

This will give us a list of paths where Python will look for modules and the command line that was used to start the interpreter as a list of arguments.

5. Get the username through an environment variable.

```
print("USERNAME environment variable:", os.environ["USERNAME"])
```

The output is as follows:

```
USERNAME environment variable: CorcheroMario
```

Figure 6.15: The expected output showing the username environment variable

The **environ** attribute of the **os** module is a **dict** that maps the **environment** variable name to its values. The keys are the name of the environment variables, and the value is the one that it was set to initially. It can be used to read and set environment variables, and it has the methods that you would expect a **dict**. You can use **os.environ. get(varname, default)** to provide a default value if a variable was not set, and **pop** to remove items or just assign a new value. There are also two other methods, **getenv** and **putenv**, which can be used to get and set environment variables, but, using the **os.environ** as a **dict** is more readable.

This is just a small peek into these three modules and some of the attributes and functions that they provide. Further and more specialized information can be found in the modules, and you are encouraged to explore the module when any specific runtime information is needed.

Having completed this exercise, you learned how to use multiple modules such as **os** and **platform** to query information about the environment that can be used to create programs that interact with it.

Using pathlib

Another useful module is **pathlib**. Even though many of the actions that are performed with pathlib can be done with **os.path**, the **pathlib** library offers a much better experience, which you'll go into more detail about later.

The **pathlib** module provides a way to represent and interact with filesystem paths.

A **path** object of the module, which is the basic **util** of the module, can just be created with its default argument to start a relative path to the current working directory:

```
import pathlib
path = pathlib.Path()
print(repr(path))
```

You should get the following output:

```
WindowsPath('.')
```

> **Note**
>
> You can get and change the current working directory with **os.getcwd()** and **os.chdir()**, respectively.

You will get either a **PosixPath** or a **WindowsPath** function of the platform you are running on.

You can use the string representation of a path at any time to be used in the functions that accept a string as a path; this can be done by calling **str(path)**.

path objects can be joined with just a forward slash (/), which feels really natural and easy to read, as shown in the following code snippet:

```
import pathlib
path = pathlib.Path(".")
new_path = path / "folder" / "folder" / "example.py"
```

You can now perform multiple operations on those path objects. One of the most common ones is to call resolve in the resulting object, which will make the path absolute and resolve all .. references. As an example, paths such as **./my_path/** will be resolved to paths such as **/current/workspace/my_path**, which start with the root filesystem.

Some of the most common operations to perform on a path are the following:

- **exists**: Checks whether the path exists in the filesystem and whether it is a file or a directory.
- **is_dir**: Checks whether the path is a directory.
- **is_file**: Checks whether the path is a file.
- **iterdir**: Returns an iterator with path objects to all the files and directories contained within the **path** object.
- **mkdir**: Creates a directory in the path indicated by the **path** object.
- **open**: Opens a file in the current path, similar to running **open** and passing the string representation of the path. It returns a **file** object that can be operated like any other.
- **read_text**: Returns the content of the file as a Unicode string. If the file is in binary format, the **read_bytes** method should be used instead.

Finally, a key function of Path objects is **glob**. Glob allows you to specify a set of filenames by using wildcards. The main character used to do so is *, which matches any character in the path level. ** matches any name but crossing directories. This means that **"/path/*"** will match any file in **"path" whilst "/path/**"** and will match any file within its path and any of its directories.

You will look at this in the next exercise.

Exercise 91: Using the glob Pattern to List Files within a Directory

In this exercise, you will learn how to list the files of an existing source tree. This is a key part of developing any application that works with a filesystem.

You are given the following file and folder structure, which you have in the GitHub repository:

```
.
|____file_a.txt
|____folder_1
| |____file_b.txt
| |____file_c.py
|____folder_2
| |____folder_3
| | |____file_d.txt
```

Figure 6.16: Initial folder structure

1. Create a path object for the current **path**:

```
import pathlib
p = pathlib.Path("")
```

> **Note**
>
> You could also use **pathlib.Path.cwd()** and get an absolute path directly.

2. Find all files in the directory with the **txt** extension.

   You can start by listing all files with the **txt** extension by using the following **glob**:

```
txt_files = p.glob("*.txt")
print("*.txt:", list(txt_files))
```

The output is as follows:

```
*.txt: [WindowsPath('path-exercise/file_a.txt')]
```

Figure 6.17: Output showing the file with the .txt extension

This lists all the files in the current location that end with **txt**, which, in this case, is the only **file_a.txt**. Folders within other directories are not listed, as the single star, *, does not cross directories and if there was another file not ending in **txt**, it would not be included either.

Note how you need to transform **txt_files** into a list. This is needed as **glob** returns an iterator and you want to print the list. This is useful since, when you are listing files, there might be an endless number of files.

If you wanted to list all of the text files in any folder within the path, no matter the number of subdirectories, you could use the double star syntax, **:

```
print("**/*.txt:", list(p.glob("**/*.txt")))
```

The output is as follows:

```
**/*.txt: [WindowsPath('path-exercise/file_a.txt'), WindowsP
ath('path-exercise/folder_1/file_b.txt'), WindowsPath('path-
exercise/folder_2/folder_3/file_d.txt')]
```

Figure 6.18: Output showing all the files in all the folders

This lists all files that end with .txt within any folder in the current path described by the path object, **p**.

This lists **folder_1/file_b.txt** and **folder_2/folder_3/file_d.txt**, but also **file_a.txt**, which is not within any folder, as ** matches within any number of nested folders, including 0.

> **Note**
>
> **folder_1/file_c.py** won't be listed, however, as it does not match the ending we provided in the **glob**.

3. List all files one level deep that are within the subdirectory.

    If you wanted to list all files one level deep within a subdirectory only, you could use the following **glob** pattern:

```
print("*/*:", list(p.glob("*/*")))
```

The output is as follows:

```
*/*: [WindowsPath('path-exercise/folder_1/file_b.txt'), Wind
owsPath('path-exercise/folder_1/file_c.py'), WindowsPath('pa
th-exercise/folder_2/folder_3')]
```

Figure 6.19: Output showing the files within a subdirectory

This will list both files within **folder_1 and the folder "folder_2/folder_3**, which is also a path. If you wanted to get only files, you could filter each of the paths by checking the **is_file** method, as mentioned previously:

```
print("Files in */*:", [f for f in p.glob("*/*") if f.is_file()])
```

The output is as follows:

```
Files in */*: [WindowsPath('path-exercise/folder_1/file_b.tx
t'), WindowsPath('path-exercise/folder_1/file_c.py')]
```

Figure 6.20: Output showing the files within folder_1, folder_2, and folder_3

This will not include paths that are no longer a file.

> **Note**
>
> There is also another module that is worth mentioning, which contains high-level functions for file and folder operations, **shutil**. With **shutil**, it is possible to recursively copy, move, or delete files.

You now know how to list files within a tree based on their attributes or extensions.

Listing All Hidden Files in Your Home Directory

In Unix, *hidden* files are those that start with a **dot**. Usually, those files are not listed when you list files with tools such as **ls** unless you explicitly ask for them. You will now use the **pathlib** module to list all hidden files in your home directory. The code snippet indicated here will show exactly how to list these hidden files:

```python
import pathlib
p = pathlib.Path.home()
print(list(p.glob(".*")))
```

The **pathlib** docs find the function that gives us the home directory, and then we use the **glob** pattern to match any file starting with a dot. In the next topic, we will be using the subprocess module.

Using the subprocess Module

Python is really useful in situations where we need to start and communicate with other programs on the OS.

The **subprocess** module allows us to start a new process and communicate with it, bringing to Python all the available tools installed on your OS through an easy-to-use API. The **subprocess** module can be seen by calling any other program from your shell.

This module has gone through some work to modernize and simplify its API, and you might see code using subprocess in ways different from those shown in this topic.

The **subprocess** module has two main APIs: the **subprocess.run** call, which manages everything from you passing the right arguments; and **subprocess.Popen**, a lower-level API that is available for more advanced use cases. You are going to cover only the high-level API, **subprocess.run**, but if you need to write an application that requires something more complex, as we have previously seen with the standard library, go through the documentation and explore the APIs for more complex use cases.

> **Note**
>
> The following examples have been run on a Linux system, but **subprocess** can be used on Windows as well; it will just need to call Windows programs. You can use **dir** instead of **ls**, for example.

Now you will see how you can call the Linux system **ls** by using **subprocess** and listing all the files:

```
import subprocess
subprocess.run(["ls"])
```

This will just create a process and run the **ls** command. If the **ls** command is not found (in Windows, for example), running this command will fail and raise an exception.

> **Note**
>
> The return value is an instance of **CompletedProcess**, but the output of the command is sent to standard output in the console.

If you want to be able to capture and see the output that our process produced, you need to pass the **capture_output** argument. This will capture **stdout** and **stderr** and make it available in the **completedProcess** instance returned by **run**:

```
result = subprocess .run(["ls"], capture_output=True)
print("stdout: ", result.stdout)
print("stderr: ", result.stderr)
```

The output is as follows:

```
stdout:   b'subprocess-examples.ipynb\n'
stderr:   b''
```

Figure 6.21: Output showing the subprocess module

> **Note**
>
> The **stdout** and **stderr** result is a byte string. If you know that the result is text, you can pass the **text** argument to have it decoded.

Now, Let's omit **stderr** from the output as you know it is empty as shown in the Figure 6.21.

```
result = subprocess .run(
        ["ls"],
        capture_output=True, text=True
    )
print("stdout: \n", result.stdout)
```

The output is as follows:

```
stdout:
    subprocess-examples.ipynb
```

Figure 6.22: Output showing the subprocesses using stdout

You can also pass more arguments, such as **-1**, to have the files listed with details:

```
result = subprocess.run(
        ["ls", "-l"],
        capture_output=True, text=True
    )
print("stdout: \n", result.stdout)
```

The output is as follows:

```
stdout:
 total 4
-rwxrwxrwx 1 mcorcherojim mcorcherojim 1957 Apr 19 17:14 subprocess-examples.ipynb
```

Figure 6.23: Output showing the files listed in detail using -l

The first thing that usually surprises users when using **suprocess.run** is that the command that needs to be passed in to run is a list of strings. This is for convenience and security. Many users will jump into using the shell argument, which will make passing the command arguments as a string work but there are security concerns. When doing so, you are basically asking Python to run our command in the system shell, and you are therefore responsible for escaping the characters as needed. Imagine for a moment that you accept user input, and you are going to pass it to the **echo** command. A user would then be able to pass **hacked; rm -rf /** as the argument for echo.

Note

Do not run this command: **hacked; rm -rf /**.

By using the semicolon, the user can mark the end of a shell command and start their own, which will delete all of your root! Additionally, when your arguments have spaces or any other shell character, you have to escape them accordingly. The simplest and safest way to use **subprocess.run** is to pass all tokens one by one as a list of strings, as shown in the examples here.

In some situations, you might want to inspect the return code that our return process has returned. In those situations, you can just check the **returncode** attribute in the returning instance of **subprocess.run**:

```
result = subprocess.run(["ls", "non_existing_file"])
print("rc: ", result.returncode)
```

The output is as follows:

```
rc: 2
```

If you wanted to make sure that our command succeeded without always having to check that the return code was **0** after running, you could use the **check=True** argument. This will raise errors if the program reported any:

```
result = subprocess.run(
    ["ls", "non_existing_file"],
    check=True
)
print("rc: ", result.returncode)
```

The output is as follows:

```
------------------------------------------------------------
CalledProcessError                    Traceback (most recent call last)
<ipython-input-31-36d3d0f47957> in <module>()
----> 1 result = subprocess .run(["ls", "non_existing_file"], check=True)
      2 print("rc: ", result.returncode)

/usr/local/lib/python3.7/subprocess.py in run(input, capture_output, timeout, check, *popenargs, **kwargs)
    479         if check and retcode:
    480             raise CalledProcessError(retcode, process.args,
--> 481                                     output=stdout, stderr=stderr)
    482     return CompletedProcess(process.args, retcode, stdout, stderr)
    483

CalledProcessError: Command '['ls', 'non_existing_file']' returned non-zero exit status 2.
```

Figure 6.24: The result of running subprocess on a failed command

This is a great way to call other programs in which we just want them to be executed to have a look at the error, such as calling batch processing scripts or programs. The exceptions raised in those situations contain information such as the command that was run, the output if it was captured, and the return code.

The **subprocess.run** function also has some other interesting arguments that are helpful in some more special situations. As an example, if you are using **subprocess.call** with a program that expects any input through **stdin**, you can pass such input via the **stdin** argument. You can also pass a timeout for how many seconds you should wait for the program to finish. If the program does not return by that time, it will be terminated and, once finished, a timeout exception will be raised to inform us of the failure.

Processes created with the **subprocess.run** method will inherit the environment variables from the current process.

sys.executable is a string giving the absolute path of the executable binary for the Python interpreter on systems. If Python, is unable to retrieve the real path to its executable process, **sys.executable** will be an empty string or **None**.

> **Note**
>
> The **-c** option on the Python interpreter is for running code inline. You will be using this option in *Activity 16: Testing Python Code*.

You will see how you can customize child processes in the following exercise.

Exercise 92: Customizing Child Processes with env vars

As part of an auditing tool, you are asked to print our environment variables by using the **subprocess** module, without relying on the Python **os.environ** variable. However, you have to do so concealing our server name, as our manager does not want to show this information to our clients.

In this exercise, you will call other apps in the OS while changing the environment variables of the parent process. You will see how you can change environment variables when using **subprocess**:

1. Import subprocess.

   Bring the **subprocess** module into the current namespace:

   ```
   import subprocess
   ```

   You can also bring just the **run** command by running **subprocess** by importing **run**, but by importing this module itself, we can see the module name when we are calling **run**. Otherwise, you wouldn't know where the **run** was coming from. Additionally, **subprocess** defines some constants that are used for some arguments on the advanced use of **Popen**. By importing **subprocess**, you have all those available.

2. Run **env** to print the environment variables.

   You can run the **env** Unix command, which will list the process environment variables in **stdout**:

   ```
   result = subprocess.run(
       ["env"],
       capture_output=True,
       text=True
   )
   print(result.stdout)
   ```

   You pass **capture_output** and **text** to be able to read the **stdout** result in a Unicode string. You can confirm that the process indeed has a list of environment variables already set; those match the ones of the parent process:

   ```
   SHELL_TITLE=PF11AY8S | Started: 2019-04-19T04:44:27 UTC
   TERM=xterm-color
   SHELL=/bin/bash
   HISTSIZE=100000
   SERVER=PF11AY8S
   DOCKER_HOST=localhost:2375
   ```

   Figure 6.25: Output showing the environment variables using env

3. Use a different set of environment variables.

If you wanted to customize the environment variables that our subprocess has, you could use the **env** keyword of the **subprocess.run** method:

```
result = subprocess.run(
    ["env"],
    capture_output=True,
    text=True,
    env={"SERVER": "OTHER_SERVER"}
)
print(result.stdout)
```

The output is as follows:

SERVER=OTHER_SERVER

Figure 6.26: Output showing a different set of environment variables

4. Now, modify the default set of variables.

Most of the time, you just want to modify or add one variable, not just replace them all. Therefore what we did in the previous step is too radical, as tools might require environment variables that are always present in the OS.

To do so, you will have to take the current process environment and modify it to match the expected result. We can access the current process environment variables via **os.environ** and copy it via the **copy** module. Though you can also use the **dict** expansion syntax with the keys that you want to change to modify it, as shown in the following example:

```
import os
result = subprocess.run(
    ["env"],
    capture_output=True,
    text=True,
    env={**os.environ, "SERVER": "OTHER_SERVER"}
)
print(result.stdout)
```

The output is as follows:

```
SHELL_TITLE=PF11AY8S | Started: 2019-04-19T04:44:27 UTC
TERM=xterm-color
SHELL=/bin/bash
HISTSIZE=100000
SERVER=OTHER_SERVER
DOCKER_HOST=localhost:2375
```

Figure 6.27: Modifying the default set of environment variables

You can see that you now have the same environments in the process created with **subprocess** as those in the current process, but that you have modified **SERVER**.

You can use the **subprocess** module to create and interact with other programs installed on our OS. The **subprocess.run** function and its different arguments make it easy to interact with different kinds of programs, check their output, and validate their results. There are also more advanced APIs available through the **subprocess.Popen** call if they are needed.

Activity 16: Testing Python Code

A company that receives small Python code snippets from its clients with basic mathematical and string operations has realized that some of the operations crash their platform. There is some asked for code requested by clients that cause the Python interpreter to abort as it cannot compute it.

This is an example:

```
compile("1" + "+1" * 10 ** 6, "string", "exec")
```

You are therefore asked to create a small program that can run the requested code and check whether it will crash without breaking the current process. This can be done by running the same code with **subprocess** and the same interpreter version that is currently running the code.

To get this code, you need to:

1. Find out the executable of our interpreter by using the **sys** module.

2. Use **subprocess** to run the code with the interpreter that you used in the previous step.

3. Use the **-c** option of the interpreter to run code inline.

4. Check whether the result code is **-11**, which corresponds to an abort in the program.

> **Note**
>
> The solution for this activity is available on page 539.

In the following topic, you will be using logging, which plays a major part in the life of a developer.

Logging

Setting up an application or a library to log is not just good practice; it is a key task of a responsible developer. It is as important as writing documentation or tests. Many people consider logging the "runtime documentation"; the same way developers read the documentation when interacting with the DevOps source code, and other developers will use the log traces when the application is running.

Hardcore logging advocates state that debuggers are extremely overused, and people should rely more on logging, using both info and trace logs to troubleshoot their code in development.

The idea is that if you are not able to troubleshoot your code with the highest level of verbosity in development, then you may have issues in production that you won't be able to figure out the root issue of.

Using Logging

Logging is the best way to let the users of the running application know which state the process is in, and how it is processing its work. It can also be used for auditing or troubleshooting client issues. There is nothing more frustrating than trying to figure out how your application behaved last week and having no information at all about what happened when it faced an issue.

You should also be careful about what information we log. Many companies will require users to never log information such as credit cards or any sensitive user data. Whilst it is possible to conceal such data after it is logged, it is better to be mindful when we log it.

You might wonder what is wrong with just using **print** statements, but when you start to write large-scale applications or libraries, you realize that just using **print** does nothing to instrument an application. By using the **logging** module, you also get the following:

- Multithreading support: The logging module is designed to work in multithreaded environments. This is needed when using multiple threads as, otherwise, the data that you log will get interleaved, as can happen with **print**.

- Categorization through multiple levels of logging: When using **print**, there is no way to transmit the importance of the log trace being emitted. By using logging, we can choose the category that we want to log under to transmit the importance of it.

- Separation of concerns between instrumentation and configuration: There are two different users of the logging library – users who just emit and those who configure the logging stack. The logging library separates those nicely, allowing libraries and applications to just instrument their code with logs at different levels, and the final user to configure the logging stack at will.

- Flexibility and configurability: The logging stack is easily extensible and configurable. There are many types of handlers, and it is trivial to create new classes that extend its functionality. There is even a cookbook on how to extend the logging stack in the standard library documentation.

The main class you interact with when using the logging library is **logger**. can be used to emit logs in any category. You usually create loggers by getting them through the **logging.getLogger(<logger name>)** factory method.

Once you have a **logger** object, you can call the different logging methods that match the different default categories that you are able to log in:

- **debug**: Fine-grained messages that are helpful for debugging and troubleshooting applications, usually enabled in development. As an example, a web server will log the input payload when receiving a request at this level.

- **info**: Coarse-grained informational messages that highlight the progress of an application. As an example, a web server will emit the requests being handled at this level without details of the data being received.

- **warning**: Messages that inform the user of a potentially harmful situation in the application or library. In our example of a web server, this will happen if you fail to decode an input JSON payload because it is corrupted. Note that while it might feel like an error and it might be for the whole system, if you own the frontend as well, the issue is not in the application handling the request; it is in the process sending it. Therefore, a warning might help notify the user of such an issue, but it is not an error. The error should be reported to the client as an error response, and the client should handle it as appropriate.

- **error**: Used for situations where an error has taken place, but the application can continue to function properly. Logging an error usually means there is an action that needs to be carried out by a developer in the source code that logged it. Logging errors commonly happen when you capture an exception, and you have no way of handling it effectively. It is quite common to set up alerts in connection with errors to inform the DevOps or developer that an error situation took place. In our web server application, this might happen if you fail to encode a response or an exception is raised that was not expected when handling the request.

- **fatal**: Fatal logs indicate that there has been an error situation that compromises the current stability of the program, and, quite often, the process is restarted after a fatal message is logged. A fatal log means that the application needs an operator to take action urgently, compared to an error that a developer is expected to handle. A common situation is when the connection to a database is lost, or any other resource that is key for the application is no longer reachable.

Logger Object

Loggers have a hierarchy of names split by a dot. For example, if you ask for a logger named **my.logger**, you are creating a **logger** that is a child of **my**, which is a child of the **root** logger. All top-level loggers "inherit" from the root logger.

You can get the root logger by calling **getLogger** without arguments or by logging directly with the logging module. A common practice is to use **__name__** as the logger module. This makes your logging hierarchy follow your source code hierarchy. Unless you have a strong reason not to do that, use **__name__** when developing libraries and applications.

Exercise 93: Using a logger Object

The goal of this exercise is to create a **logger** object and use four different methods that allow us to log in the categories mentioned in the Logging section:

1. Import the **logging** module:

```
import logging
```

2. Create a **logger**.

    We can now get a logger through the factory method **getLogger**:

```
logger = logging.getLogger("logger_name")
```

This **logger** object will be the same everywhere, and you call it with the same name.

3. Log with different categories:

```
logger.debug("Logging at debug")
logger.info("Logging at info")
logger.warning("Logging at warning")
logger.error("Logging at error")
logger.fatal("Logging at fatal")
```

The output is as follows:

```
Logging at warning
Logging at error
Logging at fatal
```

Figure 6.28: The output of running logging

By default, the logging stack will be configured to log warnings and above, which explains why you only see those levels being printed to the console. You will see later how to configure the logging stack to include other levels, such as info. Use files or a different format to include further information.

4. Include information when logging:

```
system = "moon"
for number in range(3):
    logger.warning("%d errors reported in %s", number, system)
```

Usually, when you log, you don't pass just a string, but also some variable or information that helps us with the current state of the application:

```
0 errors reported in moon
1 errors reported in moon
2 errors reported in moon
```

Figure 6.29: The output of running warning logs

> **Note**
>
> You use Python standard string interpolation, and you pass the remainder of the variables as attributes. **%d** is used to format numbers, while **%s** is used for strings. The string interpolation format also has syntax to customize the formatting of numbers or to use the **repr** of an object.

After this exercise, you now know how to use the different **logger** methods to log in different categories depending on the situation. This will allow you to properly group and handle your application messages.

Logging in warning, error, and fatal Categories

You should be mindful when you log in warning, error, and fatal. If there is something worse than an error, it is two errors. Logging an error is a way of informing the system of a situation that needs to be handled, and if you decide to log an error and raise an exception, you are basically duplicating the information. As a rule of thumb, following these two pieces of advice is key to an application or library that logs errors effectively:

- Never ignore an exception that transmits an error silently. If you handle an exception that notifies you of an error, log that error.

- Never raise and log an error. If you are raising an exception, the caller has the ability to decide whether it is truly an error situation, or whether they were expecting the issue to occur. They can then decide whether to log it following the previous rule, to handle it, or to re-raise it.

A good example of where the user might be tempted to log an error or warning is in the library of a database when a constraint is violated. From the library perspective, this might look like an error situation, but the user might be trying to insert it without checking whether the key was already in the table. The user can therefore just try to insert and ignore the exception, but if the library code logs a warning when such a situation happens, the warning or error will just spew the log files without a valid reason. Usually, a library will rarely log an error unless it has no way of transmitting the error through an exception.

When you are handling exceptions, it is quite common to log them and the information they come with. If you want to include the exception and trace back the full information, you can use the **exc_info** argument in any of the methods that we saw before:

```
try:
    int("nope")
except Exception:
    logging.error("Something bad happened", exc_info=True)
```

The output is as follows:

```
ERROR:root:Something bad happened
Traceback (most recent call last):
  File "<ipython-input-8-adcdec9cc60b>", line 2, in <module>
    int("nope")
ValueError: invalid literal for int() with base 10: 'nope'
```

Figure 6.30: Example output when logging an exception with exc_info.

The error information now includes the message you passed in, but also the exception that was being handled with the traceback. This is so useful and common that there is a shortcut for it. You can call the **exception** method to achieve the same as using **error** with **exc_info**:

```
try:
    int("nope")
except Exception:
    logging.exception("Something bad happened")
```

The output is as follows:

```
ERROR:root:Something bad happened
Traceback (most recent call last):
  File "<ipython-input-9-39a74a45c693>", line 2, in <module>
    int("nope")
ValueError: invalid literal for int() with base 10: 'nope'
```

Figure 6.31: Example output when logging an exception with the exception method

Now, you will review two common bad practices with the **logging** module.

The first one is a greedy string formatting. You might see some linters complain about formatting a string by the user, rather than relying on the **logging** module's string interpolation. This means that **logging.info("string template %s", variable)** is preferred over **logging.info("string template {}".format(variable))**. This is the case since, if you perform the string interpolation with the format, you will be doing it no matter how we configure the logging stack. If the user who configures the application decides that they don't need to print out the logs in the information level, you will have to perform interpolation, when it wasn't necessary:

```
# prefer
logging.info("string template %s", variable)
# to
logging.info("string template {}".format(variable))
```

> **Note**
>
> Linters are programs that detect code style violations, errors, and suggestions for the user.

The other, more important, bad practice is capturing and formatting exceptions when it's not really needed. Often, you see developers capturing broad exceptions and formatting them manually as part of a log message. This is not only boilerplate but also less explicit. Compare the following two approaches:

```
d = dict()

# Prefer
try:
    d["missing_key"] += 1
except Exception:
    logging.error("Something bad happened", exc_info=True)

# to
try:
    d["missing_key"] += 1
except Exception as e:
    logging.error("Something bad happened: %s", e)
```

The output is as follows:

```
ERROR:root:Something bad happened
Traceback (most recent call last):
  File "<ipython-input-18-997c7c2a8b8d>", line 5, in <module>
    d["missing_key"] += 1
KeyError: 'missing_key'
ERROR:root:Something bad happened: 'missing_key'
```

Figure 6.32: Example output difference of exc_info versus logging an exception string

The output in the second approach will only print the text of the exception, without further information. We don't know if it was a key error, nor where the issue appeared. If the exception was raised without a message, we would just get an empty message. Additionally, if logging an error, use an exception, and you won't need to pass **exc_info**.

Configuring the Logging Stack

Another part of the **logging** library is the functions to configure it, but before diving into how to configure the logging stack, you should understand its different parts and the role they play.

You've already seen **logger** objects, which are used to define the logging messages that need to be generated. There are also the following classes, which take care of the process of processing and emitting a log:

- Log Records: This is the object that is generated by the logger and contains all the information about the log, including the line where it was logged, the level, the template, and arguments, among others.

- Formatters: These take log records and transform them into strings that can be used by handlers that output to streams.

- Handlers: These are the ones that actually emit the records. They frequently use a formatter to transform records into strings. The standard library comes with multiple handlers to emit log records into **stdout**, **stderr**, **files**, **sockets**, and so on.

- Filters: Tools to fine-tune log record mechanisms. They can be added to both handlers and loggers.

If the functionality that is already provided by the standard library is not enough, you can always create our own kind of classes that customize how the logging process is performed.

> **Note**
>
> The logging library is truly flexible. If you are interested in doing so, read through the logging cookbook in the Python official documentation to see some examples at https://docs.python.org/3/howto/logging-cookbook.html.

Armed with this knowledge, there are multiple ways to configure all of the elements of the logging stack. You can do so by plugging together all the classes manually with code, passing a **dict** via **logging.config.dictConfig**, or through an **ini** file with **logging. config.iniConfig**.

Exercise 94: Configuring the Logging Stack

In this exercise, you will learn how to configure the logging stack through multiple methods to output log messages to **stdout**.

You want to configure the logging stack to output logs to the console, which should look like this:

```
INFO: Hello logging world
```

Figure 6.33: Outputting logs to the console

> **Note**
>
> The background is white, which means the output went to **stdout** and not **stderr**, as in the previous examples. Make sure to restart the kernel or interpreter every time prior to configuring the logging stack.

You will see how you can configure it with code, with a dictionary, with **basicConfig**, and with a **config** file:

1. Open a new Jupyter notebook.

2. Start with configuring the code.

   The first way to configure the stack is by manually creating all the objects and plugging them together:

```
import logging
import sys
root_logger = logging.getLogger()
handler = logging.StreamHandler(sys.stdout)
formatter = logging.Formatter("%(levelname)s: %(message)s")
handler.setFormatter(formatter)
root_logger.addHandler(handler)
root_logger.setLevel("INFO")
logging.info("Hello logging world")
```

   The output will be as follows:

```
INFO: Hello logging world
```

   In this code, you get a handle of the root logger in the third line by calling **getLogger** without any arguments. You then create a stream handler, which will output to **sys. stdout** (the console) and a formatter to configure how we want the logs to look. Finally, you just need to bind them together by setting the formatter in the handler and the handler in the logger. You set the level in the logger, though you could also configure it in the handler.

3. Restart the kernel on Jupyter and now use **dictConfig** to achieve the same configuration:

Exercise94.ipynb

```
import logging
from logging.config import dictConfig

dictConfig({
    "version": 1,
    "formatters": {
        "short":{
            "format": "%(levelname)s: %(message)s",
        }
    },
    "handlers": {
        "console": {
            "class": "logging.StreamHandler",
            "formatter": "short",
            "stream": "ext://sys.stdout",
```

https://packt.live/33U0z3D

> **Note**
>
> If the above link does not render, use https://nbviewer.jupyter.org/

The output will be as follows:

```
INFO: Hello logging world
```

The dictionary configuring the logging stack is identical to the code in step 1. Many of the configuration parameters that are passed in as strings can also be passed as Python objects. For example, you can use **sys.stdout** instead of the string passed to the **stream** option or **logging.INFO** rather than **INFO**.

> **Note**
>
> The code in *Step 3* is identical to the code in *Step 2*; it just configures it in a declarative way through a dictionary.

4. Now, again, restart the kernel on Jupyter and use **basicConfig** as mentioned in the following code snippet:

```
import sys
import logging
logging.basicConfig(
```

```
        level="INFO",
        format="%(levelname)s: %(message)s",
        stream=sys.stdout
    )
    logging.info("Hello there!")
```

The output will be as follows:

```
INFO: Hello there!
```

The logging stack comes with a utility function, **basicConfig**, which can be used to perform some basic configurations, such as the one we're performing here, as mentioned in the code snippet that follows.

5. Using an **ini** file.

    Another way to configure the logging stack is by using an **ini** file. We require an **ini** file, as follows:

logging-config.ini

```
[loggers]
keys=root

[handlers]
keys=console_handler

[formatters]
keys=short

[logger_root]
level=INFO
handlers=console_handler

[handler_console_handler]
class=StreamHandler
```

https://packt.live/32727X3

> **Note**
>
> If the above link does not render, use https://nbviewer.jupyter.org/

You can then load it with the following code:

```
import logging
from logging.config import fileConfig
fileConfig("logging-config.ini")
logging.info("Hello there!")
```

The output will be as follows:

```
INFO: Hello there!
```

All applications should configure the logging stack only once, ideally at startup. Some functions, such as **basicConfig**, will not run if the logging stack has already been configured.

You now know all of the different ways to configure an application's logging stack. This is one of the key parts of creating an application.

In the next topic, you will learn about collections.

Collections

You read about built-in collections in *Chapter 2*, *Python Structures*. You saw **list**, **dict**, **tuple**, and **set**, but sometimes, those collections are not enough. The Python standard library comes with modules and collections that provide a number of advanced structures that can greatly simplify our code in common situations. Now, you will explore how you can use **counters**, **defauldict**, and **chainmap**.

Counters

A **counter** is a class that allows us to count **hashable** objects. It has **keys** and **values** as a dictionary (it actually inherits from **dict**) to store objects as keys and the number of occurrences in values. A **counter** object can be created either with the list of objects that you want to count or with a dictionary that already contains the mapping of objects to their count. Once you have a counter instance created, you can get information about the count of objects, such as getting the most common ones or the count of a specific object.

Exercise 95: Counting Words in a Text Document

In this exercise, you will use a counter to count the occurrences of words in the text document https://packt.live/2OOaXWs:

1. Get the list of words from https://packt.live/2OOaXWs, which is our source data:

```
import urllib.request
url = 'https://www.w3.org/TR/PNG/iso_8859-1.txt'
response = urllib.request.urlopen(url)
words = response.read().decode().split()
len(words)  # 858
```

Here, you are using **urllib**, another module within the standard library, to get the contents of the URL of https://packt.live/2OOaXWs. You can then read the content and split it based on spaces and break lines. You will be using words to play with the counter.

2. Now, create a counter:

```
import collections
word_counter = collections.Counter(words)
```

This creates a counter with the list of words passed in through the words list. You can now perform the operations you want on the counter.

> **Note**
>
> As this is a subclass of the **dictionary**, you can perform all the operations that you can also perform on the **dictionary**.

3. Get the five most common words:

```
for word, count in word_counter.most_common(5):
    print(word, "-", count)
```

You can use the **most_common** method on the counter to get a list of tuples with all the words and the number of occurrences. You can also pass a limit as an argument that limits the number of results:

```
LETTER - 114
SMALL - 58
CAPITAL - 56
WITH - 55
SIGN - 21
```

Figure 6.34: Getting the five common words as output

4. Now, explore occurrences of some words, as shown in the following code snippet:

```
print("QUESTION", "-", word_counter["QUESTION"])
print("CIRCUMFLEX", "-", word_counter["CIRCUMFLEX"])
print("DIGIT", "-", word_counter["DIGIT"])
print("PYTHON", "-", word_counter["PYTHON"])
```

You can use the counter to explore the occurrences of specific words by just checking them with a key. Now check for **QUESTION**, **CIRCUMFLEX**, **DIGIT**, and **PYTHON**:

```
QUESTION - 2
CIRCUMFLEX - 11
DIGIT - 10
PYTHON - 0
```

Figure 6.35: Output exploring the occurrences of some words

Note how you can just query the counter with a key to get the number of occurrences. Something else interesting to note is that when you query for a word that does not exist, you get **0**. Some users might have expected a KeyError.

In this exercise, you just learned how to get a text file from the internet and perform some basic processing operations, such as counting the number of words.

defaultdict

Another class that is considered to create simpler-to-read code is the **defaultdict** class. This class behaves like a **dict** but allows you to provide a factory method to be used when a key is missing. This is extremely useful in multiple scenarios where you edit values, and especially if you know how to generate the first value, such as when you are building a cache or counting objects.

In Python, whenever you see code like the following code snippet, you can use defaultdict to improve the code quality:

```
d = {}
def function(x):
    if x not in d:
        d[x] = 0 # or any other initialization
    else:
        d[x] += 1 # or any other manipulation
```

Some people will try to make this more Pythonic by using **EAFP** over **LBYL**, which handles the failure rather than checking whether it will succeed:

```
d = {}
def function(x):
    try:
        d[x] += 1
    except KeyError:
        d[x] = 1
```

While this is indeed the preferred way to handle this code according to Python developers as it better conveys the information that the main part of the logic is the successful case, the correct solution for this kind of code is **defaultdict**. Intermediate to advanced Python developers will immediately think of transforming that code into a default **dict** and then comparing how it looks:

```
import collections
d = collections.defaultdict(int)
def function(x):
    d[x] += 1
```

The code becomes trivial, and it is identical to what you saw in the two previous examples. **defaultdict** is created with a factory method that will just call **int()** if the key is missing, which returns **0** and is incremented by one. It is a simply beautiful piece of code. But note that **defaultdict** can be used in other ways; the function passed to its constructor is a callable **factory** method. You use **int** not as a **type**, but as a function that is called. In the same way, you could pass **list**, **set**, or any callable you want to create.

Exercise 96: Refactoring Code with defaultdict

In this exercise, you will learn how to refactor code and simplify it by using **defaultdict**:

```
_audit = {}

def add_audit(area, action):
    if area in _audit:
        _audit[area].append(action)
    else:
        _audit[area] = [action]

def report_audit():
    for area, actions in _audit.items():
        print(f"{area} audit:")
        for action in actions:
            print(f"- {action}")
        print()
```

> **Note**
>
> The aforementioned code can be found on GitHub: https://packt.live/31ccJ6k.

The code template mentioned earlier in this exercise keeps an audit of all the actions that are performed in a company. They are split by area and the dictionary that was used. You can clearly see in the **add_audit** function the pattern we spoke about before. You will see how you can transform that into simpler code by using **defaultdict** and how it could be later extended in a simpler way:

1. Run the code that keeps an audit of all the actions, as mentioned previously.

   First, run the code to see how it behaves. Before doing any refactoring, you should understand what you are trying to change, and ideally, have tests for it

```
add_audit("HR", "Hired Sam")
add_audit("Finance", "Used 1000£")
add_audit("HR", "Hired Tom")
report_audit()
```

   You should get the following output:

```
                    HR audit:
                    - Hired Sam
                    - Hired Tom

                    Finance audit:
                    - Used 1000£
```

   Figure 6.36: Output showing the code keeping an audit of the changes

   You can see that this works as expected, and you can add items to the audit and report them.

2. Introduce a default **dict**.

   You can change **dict** for **defaultdict** and just create a **list** whenever you try to access a key that does not exist. This will need to be done only in the **add_audit** function. As **report_audit** uses the object as a dictionary and **defaultdict** is a dictionary, you don't need to change anything in that function. You will see how it will look in the following code snippet:

```
import collections
_audit = collections.defaultdict(list)
def add_audit(area, action):
    _audit[area].append(action)


def report_audit():
    for area, actions in _audit.items():
        print(f"{area} audit:")
        for action in actions:
```

```
        print(f"- {action}")
    print()
```

> **Note**
>
> The **add_audit** function has become a single line. It just appends an action to an area.

When a key is not found in the **_audit** object, our **defaultdict** just calls the **list** method, which returns an empty list. The code could not be any simpler.

What about if you are asked to log the creation of an area in the audit? Basically, whenever a new area is created in our **audit** object, to have an element present. The developer that initially wrote the code claims that it was easier to change with the old layout, without using **defaultdict**.

3. Use the **add_audit** function to create the first element.

   The code without **defaultdict** for **add_audit** will be as follows:

```
def add_audit(area, action):
    if area not in _audit:
        _audit[area] = ["Area created"]
    _audit[area].append(action)
```

The code change performed in **add_audit** is much more complex than the one you will have to perform in your function with **defaultdict**.

With **defaultdict**, you just need to change the factory method from being a list to being a list with the initial string:

```
import collections
_audit = collections.defaultdict(lambda: ["Area created"])
def add_audit(area, action):
    _audit[area].append(action)

def report_audit():
    for area, actions in _audit.items():
        print(f"{area} audit:")
        for action in actions:
            print(f"- {action}")
        print()
```

And it is still simpler than without **defaultdict**:

```
add_audit("HR", "Hired Sam")
add_audit("Finance", "Used 1000£")
add_audit("HR", "Hired Tom")
report_audit()
```

You should get the following output:

```
HR audit:
- Area created
- Hired Sam
- Hired Tom

Finance audit:
- Area created
- Used 1000£
```

Figure 6.37: Output with a function to create the first element

At the end of this exercise, you now know how to use **defaultdict** with multiple different factory methods. This is useful when writing **Pythonic** code and simplifying existing code bases.

ChainMap

Another interesting class in the collection's module is **ChainMap**. **ChainMap** is a structure that allows you to combine lookups for multiple mapping objects, usually dictionaries. It can be seen as a multi-level object; the user can see the front of it with all the keys and all the mappings, but the keys that map on the frontend hide the mappings on the backend.

Say you want to create a function that returns the menu our users will have at a restaurant; the function just returns a dictionary with the different types of elements of the lunch and the value of them. You want to allow our users to customize any part of the lunch, but you also want to provide some defaults. This can easily be done with ChainMap:

```
import collections
_defaults = {
    "apetisers": "Hummus",
    "main": "Pizza",
    "desert": "Chocolate cake",
```

```
        "drink": "Water",
}
def prepare_menu(customizations):
    return collections.ChainMap(customizations, _defaults)
def print_menu(menu):
    for key, value in menu.items():
        print(f"As {key}: {value}.")
```

> **Note**
>
> You have a dictionary that provides you with the defaults, and you are combining
> it with the user's customizations by using **ChainMap**. The order is important, as it
> makes the user's dictionary values appear before the defaults and, if desired, you
> can also have more than two dictionaries, which might be useful for other use
> cases.

You will now see how `chainmap` behaves when you pass in different values:

```
menu1 = prepare_menu({})
print_menu(menu1)
```

The output is as follows:

```
As appetizers: Hummus.
As main: Pizza.
As desert: Chocolate cake.
As drink: Water.
```

Figure 6.38: Chainmap outputting different values

If the user passes in no customization, you get the default menu. All keys and values are
taken from the **_default** dictionary that we provided:

```
menu3 = prepare_menu({"side": "French fries"})
print_menu(menu3)
```

The output is as follows:

```
As appetizers: Hummus.
As main: Pizza.
As desert: Chocolate cake.
As drink: Water.
As side: French fries.
```

Figure 6.39: Output with no customization; that is, the default menu

When a user passes a dictionary that changes one of the keys that is present in the **_default** dictionary, the value of the second dictionary is shadowed by the first one. You can see how the drink is now **Red Wine** rather than **Water**:

```
menu2 = prepare_menu({"drink": "Red Wine"})
print_menu(menu2)
```

The output is as follows:

```
As appetizers: Hummus.
As main: Pizza.
As desert: Chocolate cake.
As drink: Red Wine.
```

Figure 6.40: Value of the dictionary changed, changing the drink to red wine

Users can also pass in new keys, which will be reflected in **ChainMap**.

You might be tempted to think that this is just an over-complication of using the dictionary constructor and that the same could be achieved with an implementation like the following one:

```
def prepare_menu(customizations):
    return {**customizations, **_defaults}
```

But the semantics are different. That implementation would create a new dictionary, which would not allow changes to the user's customizations or the defaults. Say you wanted to change the defaults after you have created some menus, we can do this with the **ChainMap** implementation since the returned object is just a view of multiple dictionaries:

```
_defaults["main"] = "Pasta"
print_menu(menu3)
```

The output is as follows:

```
As appetizers: Hummus.
As main: Pasta.
As desert: Chocolate cake.
As drink: Water.
As side: French fries.
```

Figure 6.41: Output with changed default values

> **Note**
>
> You were able to change the main dish. Changes in any of the **dict** that is part of **chainmap** are visible when interacting with it.

The different classes in the collection modules allow the developer to write better code by using more appropriate structures. With the knowledge you have gained in this topic, try to explore others, such as deque or basic skeletons, to build your own containers. Using these classes effectively in many situations is what differentiates an experienced Python programmer from a beginner.

Functools

The final module of the standard library you are going to look at allows constructs with a minimal amount of code. In this topic, you are going to see how to use **lru_cache** and **partial**.

Caching with functools.lru_cache

Often, you have a function that is heavy to compute, in which you just want to cache results. Many developers will create their own caching implementation by using a dictionary, but that is error-prone and adds unnecessary code to our project. The **functools** module comes with a **decorator** – that is, **functools.lru_cache**, which is provided exactly for these situations. It is a recently used cache, with a **max_size** that is provided when the code is constructed. This means that you can specify a number of input values that you want to cache as a maximum, to limit the memory this function can take, or it can grow indefinitely. Once you reach the maximum number of different inputs that we want to cache, the input that was the least recently used will be thrown away in favor of a new call.

Additionally, the decorator provides some new methods in the function that can be used to interact with the cache. We can use **cache_clear** to remove all of the previous hits saved in **cache** or **cache_info** to get information about the **hits** and **misses**, so as to allow us to tune it if needed. The original function information is also offered for inspection, as with any properly decorated function, through the **__wrapped__** decorator.

It is important to keep in mind that the LRU cache should be used only in functions. This is useful if we just want to reuse existing values or the side effect will not happen. As an example, we should not use the cache on a function that writes something into a file or sends a package to an endpoint, as those actions will not be performed once the function is called again with the same input, which is the main purpose of the cache.

Lastly, for the cache to be usable in a function, all objects being passed need to be hashable. This means that **integers**, **frozensets**, **tuples**, and so on are allowed, but not modifiable objects, such as **dicts**, **sets**, or **lists**.

Exercise 97: Using lru_cache to Speed Up Our Code

In this exercise, you will see how to configure a function to use cache with functools and to reuse the results from previous calls to speed up the overall process.

You use the **lru** cache function of the **functools** module to reuse values that a function has already returned without having to execute them again.

We will start with a function that is mentioned in the following code snippet, which simulates taking a long time to compute, and we will see how we can improve this:

```python
import time
def func(x):
    time.sleep(1)
    print(f"Heavy operation for {x}")
    return x * 10
```

If we call this function twice with the same arguments, we will be executing the code twice to get the same result:

```python
print("Func returned:", func(1))
print("Func returned:", func(1))
```

The output is as follows:

```
Heavy operation for 1
Func returned: 10
Heavy operation for 1
Func returned: 10
```

Figure 6.42: Output showing the same arguments by calling the function twice

We can see this in the output and the print within the function, which happens twice. This is a clear improvement in performance as, once the function is executed, future executions are practically free. Now, we will improve the performance in the steps that follow:

1. Add the **lru** cache decorator to the **func** function:

    The first step is to use the decorator on our function:

    ```python
    import functools
    import time
    @functools.lru_cache()
    def func(x):
        time.sleep(1)
        print(f"Heavy operation for {x}")
        return x * 10
    ```

    When we execute the function for the same input, we now see that the code is executed only once, but we still get the same output from the function:

    ```python
    print("Func returned:", func(1))
    print("Func returned:", func(1))
    print("Func returned:", func(2))
    ```

    The output is as follows:

    ```
    Heavy operation for 1
    Func returned: 10
    Func returned: 10
    Heavy operation for 2
    Func returned: 20
    ```

    Figure 6.43: Output showing the code being executed once but with the same output

    > **Note**
    >
    > The **Heavy operation** only happens once for **1**. We are also calling **2** here to show that the value is different based on its input, and, since **2** was not cached before, it has to execute the code for it.

    This is extremely useful; with just one line of code, we have at hand a fully working implementation of an LRU cache.

2. Change the cache size using the **maxsize** argument.

The cache comes with a default size of 128 elements, but this can be changed if needed, through the **maxsize** argument:

```python
import functools
import time
@functools.lru_cache(maxsize=2)
def func(x):
    time.sleep(1)
    print(f"Heavy operation for {x}")
    return x * 10
```

By setting it to **2**, we are sure that only two different inputs will be saved. We can see this by using three different inputs and calling them in reverse order later:

```python
print("Func returned:", func(1))
print("Func returned:", func(2))
print("Func returned:", func(3))
print("Func returned:", func(3))
print("Func returned:", func(2))
print("Func returned:", func(1))
```

The output is as follows:

```
Heavy operation for 1
Func returned: 10
Heavy operation for 2
Func returned: 20
Heavy operation for 3
Func returned: 30
Func returned: 30
Func returned: 20
Heavy operation for 1
Func returned: 10
```

Figure 6.44: Output with a changed cache size

The cache successfully returned the previous values for the second call of **2** and **3**, but the result for **1** was destroyed once **3** arrived, since we limited the size to two elements only.

3. Now, use it in other functions, such as **lru_cache**.

Sometimes, the functions you want to cache are not in our control to change. If you want to keep both versions, that is, a cached and an uncached one, we can achieve this by using the **lru_cache** function just as a function and not as a **decorator**, as decorators are just functions that take another function as an argument:

```python
import functools
import time
def func(x):
    time.sleep(1)
    print(f"Heavy operation for {x}")
    return x * 10
cached_func = functools.lru_cache()(func)
```

Now, we can use either **func** or its cached version, **cached_func**:

```python
print("Cached func returned:", cached_func(1))
print("Cached func returned:", cached_func(1))
print("Func returned:", func(1))
print("Func returned:", func(1))
```

The output is as follows:

```
Heavy operation for 1
Cached func returned: 10
Cached func returned: 10
Heavy operation for 1
Func returned: 10
Heavy operation for 1
Func returned: 10
```

Figure 6.45: Output with the lru_cache function

We can see how the cached version of the function did not execute the code in the second call, but the uncached version did.

You just learned how to use **functools** to cache the values of a function. This is a really quick way to improve the performance of your application when applicable.

Partial

Another often used function in **functools** is **partial**. **partial** allows us to adapt existing functions by providing values for some of their arguments. It is like binding arguments in other languages, such as C++ or JavaScript, but this is what you would expect from a Python function. **partial** can be used to remove the need for specifying positional or keyword arguments, which makes it useful when we need to pass a function that takes arguments as a function that does not take them. Have look at some examples:

You will use a function that just takes three arguments and prints them:

```
def func(x, y, z):
    print("x:", x)
    print("y:", y)
    print("z:", z)
func(1, 2, 3)
```

The output is as follows:

```
x: 1
y: 2
z: 3
```

Figure 6.46: The output, which simply prints the arguments

You can use **partial** to transform this function to take fewer arguments. This can be done in two ways, mainly, bypassing the arguments as a keyword, which is more expressive; or through positional arguments:

```
import functools
new_func = functools.partial(func, z='Wops')
new_func(1, 2)
```

The output is as follows:

```
x: 1
y: 2
z: Wops
```

Figure 6.47: Using partial to transform the output

You can call **new_func** without passing the **z** argument, as you have provided a value through the **partial** function. The **z** argument will always be set to the value provided when the function was created through the partial call.

If you decide to use **positional** only, the number of arguments you pass will bind from left to right, which means that if you only pass one argument, the **x** argument should no longer be provided:

```
import functools
new_func = functools.partial(func, 'Wops')
new_func(1, 2)
```

The output is as follows:

```
x: Wops
y: 1
z: 2
```

Figure 6.48: Output with positional arguments

Exercise 98: Creating a print Function That Writes to stderr

By using **partial**, you can also rebind the optional arguments to a different default, allowing us to change the default value that the function has. You will see how you can repurpose the **print** function to create a **print_stderr** function that just writes to **stderr**.

In this exercise, you will create a function that acts like **print**, but the output is **stderr** rather than **stdout**:

1. Explore the **print** argument.

    To start, you need to explore the arguments that **print** takes are. You will call **help** on **print** to see what the documentation offers:

    ```
    help(print)
    ```

    The output is as follows:

    ```
    Help on built-in function print in module builtins:

    print(...)
        print(value, ..., sep=' ', end='\n', file=sys.stdout, flush=False)

        Prints the values to a stream, or to sys.stdout by default.
        Optional keyword arguments:
        file:  a file-like object (stream); defaults to the current sys.stdout.
        sep:   string inserted between values, default a space.
        end:   string appended after the last value, default a newline.
        flush: whether to forcibly flush the stream.
    ```

    Figure 6.49: Output with print arguments

The argument that you are interested in is the **file**, which allows us to specify the stream you want to write to.

2. Print to **stderr**.

   Now, print the default value for the optional argument file, which is **sysstdout**, but you can pass **sys.stderr** to get the behavior you are looking for:

   ```
   import sys
   print("Hello stderr", file=sys.stderr)
   ```

   The output is as follows:

   Hello stderr

   Figure 6.50: Print to stderr output

   As you are printing to **stderr**, the output appears in red as expected.

3. Use partial to change the default.

   You can use **partial** to specify arguments to be passed and create a new function. You will bind **file** to **stderr** and see the output:

   ```
   import functools
   print_stderr = functools.partial(print, file=sys.stderr)
   print_stderr("Hello stderr")
   ```

   The output is as follows:

   Hello stderr

   Figure 6.51: Print to stderr output through partial

Great – this works as expected; we now have a function that has changed the default value for the optional **file** argument.

Activity 17: Using partial on class Methods

Even though **partial** is an extremely useful and versatile function of the **functools** module, it seems to fail when we try to apply it to a **class** method.

To begin with, you are working in a company that models superheroes. You are asked to fix the following code snippet, as the previous developer attempted to use **functools.partial** to create the **reset_name** function but it does not seem to work well. Explore **functools** to make the following code snippet work without errors by creating **partial** on a **class** method.

In this activity, you will explore the **partial** module to see how **partial** can be used in more advanced use cases. This activity can be performed on the Jupyter notebook:

```python
import functools
if __name__ == "__main__":
    class Hero:
        DEFAULT_NAME = "Superman"
        def __init__(self):
            self.name = Hero.DEFAULT_NAME

        def rename(self, new_name):
            self.name = new_name

        reset_name = functools.partial(rename, DEFAULT_NAME)

        def __repr__(self):
            return f"Hero({self.name!r})"
```

When we try to use **partial** in this class, to create the **reset_name** method, something seems to not work. Make the following succeed by modifying the way we used **partial** previously:

```python
if __name__ == "__main__":
    hero = Hero()
    assert hero.name == "Superman"
    hero.rename("Batman")
    assert hero.name == "Batman"
    hero.reset_name()
    assert hero.name == "Superman"
```

> **Note**
>
> The aforementioned code can be found on GitHub: https://packt.live/33AxfPs

Steps:

1. Run the code and see what error it outputs.

2. Check for alternatives for **functools.partial** by running **help (functools)**.

3. Use **functools.partialmethod** to implement the new class.

> **Note**
>
> The solution for this activity is available on page 540.

Summary

You have looked at multiple modules in the standard library and how they help you write well-tested and easier-to-read code. However, there are still many more modules to explore and understand in order to use them effectively, though. We have learned that Python comes with *batteries included*, through its vast standard library, and that, in many situations, the utilities it provides are extended through an advanced API. By having the mindset of checking how things can be solved with the standard library before trying to write our own code, you can become better Python programmers.

Now that you have some knowledge of the standard library, you will start to look more deeply into how to make our code easier to read for Python programmers, usually known as Pythonic code. While using the standard library as much as possible is a good start, there are some other tips and tricks that we will look at in *Chapter 7, Becoming Pythonic.*

7

Becoming Pythonic

Overview

By the end of this chapter, you will be able to, write succinct, readable expressions for creating lists; use Python comprehensions with lists, dictionaries, and sets; use **collections.defaultdict** to avoid exceptions when using dictionaries; write iterators to enable Pythonic access to your own data types; explain how generator functions are related to iterators, and write them in order to defer complex calculations; use the **itertools** module to succinctly express complex sequences of data and use the **re** module to work with regular expressions in Python.

Introduction

Python is not just a programming language – it is made up of a community of programmers who use, maintain, and enjoy the Python programming language. As with any community, its members have a shared culture and shared values. The values of the Python community are well summarized in Tim Peter's document *The Zen of Python* (PEP 20), which includes this statement, among others:

"There should be one – and preferably only one – obvious way to do it."

The Python community has a long history of friendly rivalry with another community of programmers centered around the Perl programming language. Perl was designed around the idea that *There Is More Than One Way To Do It* (TIMTOWTDI, which is pronounced "Tim Toady"). While Tim Peter's line in *PEP 20* is a dig at Perl, it also introduces the idea of pythonicity.

Code is pythonic if it clearly and obviously works the way that a Python programmer would expect it to work. Sometimes, writing Pythonic code is easy and entails doing the simplest thing that could possibly work. However, if you are writing a class, data structure, or module that will be used by other programmers, then sometimes you must go the extra mile so that they will be able to do the simplest thing that could possibly work. Hopefully, your module will have more users than writers, and this is the correct trade-off to make.

In the previous chapter, you were introduced to the different standard libraries, and you also learned how logging could be useful when it comes to handling data. This chapter introduces a few of the Python language and library features that are particularly Pythonic. You already explored how collections worked in the previous chapter. Now you will add to this knowledge by exploring collection comprehensions that work with lists, sets, and dictionaries. Iterators and generators allow you to add list-like behavior to your own code so that it can be used in a more Pythonic way. You will also examine some of the types and functions in Python's standard library that make advanced use of collections easier to write, and easier to understand.

Having these tools at your disposal will make it easier for you to read, write, and understand Python code. In the current world of open-source software, and with data scientists sharing their code through Jupyter notebooks, Pythonic code is your gateway to membership of the global Python community.

Using List Comprehensions

List comprehensions are a flexible, expressive way of writing Python expressions to create sequences of values. They make iterating over the input and building the resulting list implicit so that program authors and readers can focus on the important features of what the list represents. It is this concision that makes list comprehensions a Pythonic way of working with lists or sequences.

List comprehensions are built out of bits of Python syntax we have already seen. They are surrounded by square brackets ([]), which signify Python symbols for a literal list. They contain **for** elements in a list, which is how Python iterates over members of a collection. Optionally, they can filter elements out of a list using the familiar syntax of the **if** expression.

Exercise 99: Introducing List Comprehensions

In this exercise, you will be writing a program that creates a list of the cubes of whole numbers from 1 to 5. This example is trivial because we're focusing more on how you can build a list than on the specific operations that are done to each member of the list.

Nonetheless, you may need to do this sort of thing in the real world. For instance, if you were to write a program to teach students about functions by graphing those functions. That application might require a list of **x** coordinates and generated a list of **y** coordinates so that it could plot a graph of the function. First, you will explore what this program looks like using the Python features you have already seen:

1. Open a Jupyter notebook and type in the following code:

```
cubes = []
for x in [1,2,3,4,5]:
        cubes.append(x**3)
print(cubes)
```

You should get the following output:

```
cubes = []
for x in [1,2,3,4,5]:
    cubes.append(x**3)
print(cubes)
```

```
[1, 8, 27, 64, 125]
```

Figure 7.1: The output showing the cubes of whole numbers from 1 to 5

Understanding this code involves keeping track of the state of the cube's variable, which starts as an empty list, and of the **x** variable, which is used as a cursor to keep track of the program's position in the list. This is all irrelevant to the task at hand, which is to list the cubes of each of these numbers. It will be better – more Pythonic, even – to remove all the irrelevant details. Luckily, list comprehensions allow us to do that.

2. Now write the following code, which replaces the previous loop with a list comprehension:

```
cubes = [x**3 for x in [1,2,3,4,5]]
print(cubes)
```

You should get the following output:

```
cubes = [x**3 for x in [1,2,3,4,5]]
print(cubes)
```

```
[1, 8, 27, 64, 125]
```

Figure 7.2: The output with the replaced loop showing the cubes of whole numbers from 1 to 5

This says, "For each member in the **[1,2,3,4,5]** list, call it **x**, calculate the **x**∗∗**3** expression, and put that in the list cubes." The list used can be any list-like object; for example, a range.

3. Now you can make this example even simpler by writing the following:

```
cubes = [x**3 for x in range(1,6)]
print(cubes)
```

You should get the following output:

```
In [4]: cubes = [x**3 for x in range(1,6)]
        print(cubes)
```

```
[1, 8, 27, 64, 125]
```

Figure 7.3: The output with the optimized style of writing code

Now the code is as short and succinct as it can be. Rather than telling you the recipe that the computer follows to build a list of the cubes of the numbers 1, 2, 3, 4, and 5, it tells you that it calculates the cube of **x** for every **x** starting from 1 and smaller than 6. This, then, is the essence of Pythonic coding: reducing the gap between what you say and what you mean when you tell the computer what it should do.

A list comprehension can also filter its inputs when building a list. To do this, you add an **if** expression to the end of the comprehension, where the expression can be any test of an input value that returns **True** or **False**. This is useful when you want to transform some of the values in a list while ignoring others. As an example, you could build a photo gallery of social media posts by making a list of thumbnail images from photos found in each post, but only when the posts are pictures, not text status updates.

4. You want to get Python to shout the names of the Monty Python cast, but only those whose name begins with **"T"**. Enter the following Python code into a notebook:

```
names = ["Graham Chapman", "John Cleese", "Terry Gilliam", "Eric Idle", "Terry Jones"]
```

5. Those are the names you are going to use. Enter this list comprehension to filter only those that start with **"T"** and operate on them:

```
print([name.upper() for name in names if name.startswith("T")
```

You should get the following output:

```
In [7]:  names = ["Graham Chapman", "John Cleese", "Terry Gilliam", "Eric Idle", "Terry Jones"]
         print([name.upper() for name in names if name.startswith("T")])

         ['TERRY GILLIAM', 'TERRY JONES']
```

Figure 7.4: The output with the optimized style of writing code

By completing this exercise, we have created a filter list using list comprehension.

Exercise 100: Using Multiple Input Lists

All the examples you have seen so far build one list out of another by performing an expression on each member of the list. You can define a comprehension over multiple lists, by defining a different element name for each of the lists.

> **Note**
>
> Monty Python is the name of an Anglo-American comedy group known for their TV show "Monty Python's Flying Circus" (BBC, 1969), as well as films such as "Monty Python and the Holy Grail" (1975), stage shows, and albums. The group has achieved international popularity, especially among the computer science community. The Python language was named after the group. The term spam, now used for unsolicited email and other unwanted digital communications, also comes from a Monty Python sketch in which a café humorously insists on serving tinned meat (or spam) with everything. Other jokes, scenarios, and names taken from the group are often found in examples and even official Python documentation. So, if you ever encounter strange names or odd situations when going through tutorials, now you know why.

To show how this works, in this exercise, you will be multiplying the elements of two lists together. The Spam Café in *Monty Python's Flying Circus (refer to the preceding note)* famously served a narrow range of foodstuffs mostly centered around a processed meat product. You will use ingredients from its menu to explore multiple-list comprehension:

1. Enter this code into a Jupyter notebook:

```
print([x*y for x in ['spam', 'eggs', 'chips'] for y in [1,2,3]])
```

You should get the following output:

```
In [8]:  print([x*y for x in ['spam', 'eggs', 'chips'] for y in [1,2,3]])

         ['spam', 'spamspam', 'spamspamspam', 'eggs', 'eggseggs', 'eggseggseggs', 'chips', 'chipschips', 'chipschipschips']
```

Figure 7.5: The output printing the elements of two lists together

Inspecting the result shows that the collections are iterated in a nested fashion, with the rightmost collection on the inside of the nest and the leftmost on the outside. Here, if x is set to **spam**, then **x*y** is calculated with **y** being equal to each of the values of **1**, **2**, and then **3** before **x** is set to **eggs**, and so on.

2. Reverse the order of the lists:

```
print([x*y for x in [1,2,3] for y in ['spam', 'eggs', 'chips']])
```

You should get the following output:

```
In [9]: print([x*y for x in [1,2,3] for y in ['spam', 'eggs', 'chips']])
        ['spam', 'eggs', 'chips', 'spamspam', 'eggseggs', 'chipschips', 'spamspamspam', 'eggseggseggs', 'chipschipschips']
```

Figure 7.6: The output with the reverse order of the list

Swapping the order of the lists changes the order of the results in the comprehension. Now, **x** is initially set to **1**, then **y** to each of **spam**, **eggs**, and **chips**, before **x** is set to **2**, and so on. While the result of anyone multiplication does not depend on its order (for instance, the results of **'spam'***2 and 2***'spam'** are the same, namely, **spamspam**), the fact that the lists are iterated in a different order means that the same results are computed in a different sequence.

For instance, the same list could be iterated multiple times in a list comprehension – the lists for **x** and **y** do not have to be different:

```
numbers = [1,2,3]
print([x**y for x in numbers for y in numbers])
```

You should get the following output:

```
[1, 1, 1, 2, 4, 8, 3, 9, 27]
```

Figure 7.7: The output iterating lists multiple times

In the following activity, we will be creating fixtures for a chess tournament among four players. We will be using list comprehension and filters to find the best fixture.

Activity 18: Building a Chess Tournament

In this activity, you will use a list comprehension to create the fixtures for a chess tournament. Fixtures are strings of the form "player 1 versus player 2." Because there is a slight advantage to playing as white, you also want to generate the "player 2 versus player 1" fixture so that the tournament is fair. But you do not want people playing against themselves, so you should also filter out fixtures such as "player 1 versus player 1."

You need to complete this activity with the following steps:

1. Open a Jupyter notebook.

2. Define the list of player names: **Magnus Carlsen**, **Fabiano Caruana**, **Yifan Hou**, and **Wenjun Ju**.

3. Create a list comprehension that uses this list of names twice to create tournament fixtures in the correct format.

4. Add a filter to the comprehension so that no player is pitted against themselves.

5. Print the list of tournament fixtures.

You should get the following output:

```
In [1]:  names = ["Magnus Carlsen", "Fabiano Caruana", "Yifan Hou", "Wenjun Ju"]
         fixtures = [f"{p1} vs. {p2}" for p1 in names for p2 in names if p1 != p2]
         print(fixtures)

         ['Magnus Carlsen vs. Fabiano Caruana', 'Magnus Carlsen vs. Yifan Hou', 'Magnus Carlsen vs. Wenjun Ju', 'Fabiano Caruana vs.
         Magnus Carlsen', 'Fabiano Caruana vs. Yifan Hou', 'Fabiano Caruana vs. Wenjun Ju', 'Yifan Hou vs. Magnus Carlsen', 'Yifan H
         ou vs. Fabiano Caruana', 'Yifan Hou vs. Wenjun Ju', 'Wenjun Ju vs. Magnus Carlsen', 'Wenjun Ju vs. Fabiano Caruana', 'Wenju
         n Ju vs. Yifan Hou']
```

Figure 7.8: The expected output showing the tournament fixtures

> **Note**
>
> The solution for this activity is available on page 542.

Set and Dictionary Comprehensions

List comprehensions are handy ways in which to concisely build sequences of values in Python. Other forms of comprehensions are also available, which you can use to build other collection types. A set is an unordered collection: you can see what elements are in a set, but you cannot index into a set nor insert an object at a particular location in the set because the elements are not ordered. An element can only be present in a set once, whereas it could appear in a list multiple times.

Sets are frequently useful in situations where you want to quickly test whether an object is in a collection but do not need to track the order of the objects in the collection. For example, a web service might keep track of all of the active session tokens in a set, so that when it receives a request, it can test whether the session token corresponds to an active session.

A dictionary is a collection of pairs of objects, where one object in the pair is called the key, and the other is called the value. In this case, you associate a value with a particular key, and then you can ask the dictionary for the value associated with that key. Each key may only be present in a dictionary once, but multiple keys may be associated with the same value. While the name "dictionary" suggests a connection between terms and their definitions, dictionaries are commonly used as indices (and, therefore, a dictionary comprehension is often used to build an index). Going back to your web service example, different users of the service could have different permissions, thus limiting the actions that they can perform. The web service could construct a dictionary in which the keys are session tokens, and the values represent user permissions. This is so that it can quickly tell whether a request associated with a given session is permissible.

The syntax for both set and dictionary comprehensions looks very similar to list comprehension, with the square brackets (`[]`) simply replaced by curly braces (`{}`). The difference between the two is how the elements are described. For a set, you need to indicate a single element, for example, `{ x for x in … }`. For a dictionary, you need to indicate a pair containing the key and the value, for example, `{ key:value for key in… }`.

Exercise 101: Using Set Comprehensions

The difference between a list and a set is that the elements in a list have an order, and those in a set do not. This means that a set cannot contain duplicate entries: an object is either in a set or not.

In this exercise, you will be changing a set comprehension into a set:

1. Enter the following comprehension code into a notebook to create a list:

```
print([a + b for a in [0,1,2,3] for b in [4,3,2,1]])
```

You should get the following output:

```
In [1]:   [a + b for a in [0,1,2,3] for b in [4,3,2,1]]

Out[1]:   [4, 3, 2, 1, 5, 4, 3, 2, 6, 5, 4, 3, 7, 6, 5, 4]
```

Figure 7.9: The result of the set

2. Now change the result into a set.

   Change the outer square brackets in the comprehension to curly braces:

   ```
   print({a+b for a in [0,1,2,3] for b in [4,3,2,1]})
   ```

   You should get the following output:

   ```
   In [2]:  {a+b for a in [0,1,2,3] for b in [4,3,2,1]}

   Out[2]:  {1, 2, 3, 4, 5, 6, 7}
   ```

   Figure 7.10: A set without duplicate entries

Notice that the set created in *step 2* is much shorter than the list created in *step 1*. The reason for this is that the set does not contain duplicate entries – try counting how many times the number **4** appears in each collection. It's in the list four times (because $0 + 4 = 4, 1 + 3 = 4, 2 + 2 = 4$, and $3 + 1 = 4$), but sets don't retain duplicates, so there's only one instance of the number **4** in the set. If you just removed the duplicates from the list produced in *step 1*, you'd have a list of [4, 3, 2, 1, 5, 6, 7]. Sets don't preserve the order of their elements either, so the numbers appear in a different order in the set created in *step 2*. The fact that the numbers in the set appear in numerical order is due to the implementation of the **set** type in Python.

Exercise 102: Using Dictionary Comprehensions

Curly-brace comprehension can also be used to create a dictionary. The expression on the left-hand side of the **for** keyword in the comprehension should contain a comprehension. You write the expression that will generate the dictionary keys to the left of the colon and the expression that will generate the values to the right. Note that a key can only appear once in a dictionary.

In this exercise, you will create a lookup dictionary of the lengths of the names in a list and print the length of each name:

1. Enter this list of names of Monty Python stars in a notebook:

   ```
   names = ["Eric", "Graham", "Terry", "John", "Terry"]
   ```

2. Use a comprehension to create a lookup dictionary of the lengths of the names:

   ```
   print({k:len(k) for k in ["Eric", "Graham", "Terry", "John", "Terry"]})
   ```

You should get the following output:

```
In [1]:  names = ["Eric", "Graham", "Terry", "John", "Terry"]
         print({k:len(k) for k in ["Eric", "Graham", "Terry", "John", "Terry"]})

         {'Eric': 4, 'Graham': 6, 'Terry': 5, 'John': 4}
```

Figure 7.11: A lookup dictionary equaling the length of the names in the list

Notice that the entry for **Terry** only appears once, because dictionaries cannot contain duplicate keys. You have created an index of the length of each name, keyed by name. An index like this could be useful in a game, where it could work out how to layout the score table for each player without repeatedly having to recalculate the length of each player's name.

Activity 19: Building a Scorecard Using Dictionary Comprehensions and Multiple Lists

You are the backend developer for a renowned college. The management has asked you to build a demo scorecard for their students based on the marks they have achieved in their exams.

Your goal in this activity is to use dictionary comprehension and lists in Python to build a demo scorecard for four students in the college.

Let's do this with the following steps:

1. Create two separate lists: one for the names of the students and the other for their scores.

2. Create a dictionary comprehension that iterates over the numbers in a range of the same length as the lists of names and scores. The comprehension should create a dictionary where, for the **i**th number in the range, the key is the ith name, and the value is the ith score.

3. Print out the resulting dictionary to make sure it's correct.

You should get the following output:

```
In [6]: print(scores)
        {'Vivian': 70, 'Racheal': 82, 'Tom': 80, 'Adrian': 79}
```

Figure 7.12: A dictionary indicating names and scores as a key-value pair

> **Note**
>
> The solution for this activity is available on page 543.

Default Dictionary

The built-in dictionary type considers it to be an error when you try to access the value for a key that doesn't exist. It will raise a **KeyError**, which you have to handle or your program crashes. Often, that's a good idea. If the programmer doesn't get the key correct, it could indicate a typo or a misunderstanding of how the dictionary is used.

It's often a good idea, but not always. Sometimes, it's reasonable that a programmer doesn't know what the dictionary contains; whether it's created from a file supplied by the user or the content of a network request, for example. In situations like this, any of the keys the programmer expects could be missing, but handling **KeyError** instances everywhere will be tedious, repetitive, and make the intent of the code harder to see.

For these situations, Python provides the **collections.defaultdict** type. It works like a regular dictionary, except that you can give it a function that creates a default value to use when a key is missing. Rather than raise an error, it calls that function and returns the result.

Exercise 103: Adopting a Default Dict

In this exercise, you will be using a regular dictionary that raises a **KeyError** when you try to access a missing key:

1. Create a dictionary for **john**:

```
john = { 'first_name': 'John', 'surname': 'Cleese' }
```

Attempt to use a **middle_name** key that was not defined in the dictionary:

```
john['middle_name']
```

You should get the following output:

```
In [1]: john = { 'first_name': 'John', 'surname': 'Cleese' }
        john['middle_name']

        ---------------------------------------------------------------------
        KeyError                                Traceback (most recent call last)
        <ipython-input-1-63d140c09c07> in <module>
            1 john = { 'first_name': 'John', 'surname': 'Cleese' }
        ----> 2 john['middle_name']

        KeyError: 'middle_name'
```

Figure 7.13: The output showing KeyError: 'middle_name'

2. Now, import the **defaultdict** from **collections** and wrap the dictionary in a **defaultdict**:

```
from collections import defaultdict
safe_john = defaultdict(str, john)
```

The first argument is the type constructor for a string, so missing keys will appear to have the empty string as their value.

3. Attempt to use a key that was not defined via the wrapped dictionary:

```
print(safe_john['middle_name'])
```

You should get the following output:

```
In [2]: from collections import defaultdict
        safe_john = defaultdict(str, john)
        safe_john['middle_name']

Out[2]: ''
```

Figure 7.14: Using the wrapped dictionary does not throw an error when undefined keys are used

No exception is triggered at this stage; instead, an empty string is returned. The first argument to the constructor of **defaultdict**, called **default_factory**, can be any callable (that is, function-like) object. You can use this to compute a value based on the key or return a default value that is relevant to your domain.

4. Create a **defaultdict** that uses a lambda as its **default_factory**:

```
from collections import defaultdict
courses = defaultdict(lambda: 'No!')
courses['Java'] = 'This is Java'
```

This dictionary will return the value from the **lambda** on any unknown key.

5. Access the value at an unknown key in this new dictionary:

```
print(courses['Python'])
 'No!'
```

You should get the following output:

```
In [4]:  from collections import defaultdict
         courses = defaultdict(lambda: 'No!')
         courses['Java'] = 'This is Java'

In [5]:  print(courses['Python'])

         No!
```

Figure 7.15: The returned value from the lambda on an unknown key

6. Access the value at a known key in this new dictionary:

```
print(courses['Java'])
```

The output is as follows:

```
In [6]:  print(courses['Java'])

         This is Java
```

Figure 7.16: The print value for the Java list

The benefit of the default dictionary is that in situations where you know it is likely that expected keys will be missing from a dictionary, you can work with default values and not have to sprinkle your code with exception-handling blocks. This is another example of Pythonicity: if what you mean is "use the value for the "foo" key, but if that doesn't exist, then use "bar" as the value," then you should write that, rather than "use the value for the "foo" key, but if you get an exception and the exception is **KeyError**, then use "bar" as the value."

Default dicts are great for working with untrusted input, such as a file chosen by the user or an object received over the network. A network service shouldn't expect any input it gets from a client to be well formatted. If it treats the data, it receives in a request as a JSON object. It should be ready for the data to not be in JSON format. If the data is really JSON, the program should not expect all of the keys defined by the API to have been supplied by the client. The default dict gives you a really concise way to work with such under-specified data.

Iterators

The Pythonic secret that enables comprehensions to find all of the entries in a list, range, or other collection is an iterator. Supporting iterators in your own classes opens them up for use in comprehensions, **for..in** loops, and anywhere that Python works with collections. Your collection must implement a method called **__iter__()**, which returns the iterator.

The iterator itself is also a Python object with a simple contract. It must provide a single method, **__next__()**. Each time **__next__()** is called, the iterator returns the next value in the collection. When the iterator reaches the end of the collection, **__next__()** raises **StopIteration** to signal that the iteration should terminate.

If you've used exceptions in other programming languages, you may be surprised by this use of an exception to signal a fairly commonplace situation. After all, plenty of loops reach an end, so it's not exactly an exceptional circumstance. Python is not so dogmatic about exceptions, favoring simplicity and expressiveness over universal rules-lawyering.

Once you've learned the techniques to build iterators, the applications are limitless. Your own collections or collection-like classes can supply iterators so that programmers can work with them using Pythonic collection techniques such as comprehensions. For example, an application that stores its data model in a database can use an iterator to retrieve each row that matches a query as a separate object in a loop or comprehension. A programmer can say, "For each row in the database, do this to the row," and treat it like a list of rows, when your data model object is secretly running a database query each time the iterator's **__next__()** method is called.

Exercise 104: The Simplest Iterator

The easiest way to provide an iterator for your class is to use one from another object. If you are designing a class that controls access to its own collection, then it might be a good idea to let programmers iterate over your object using the collection's iterator. In this case, just have **__iter__()** return the appropriate iterator.

In this exercise, you will be coding an **Interrogator** who asks awkward questions to people on a quest. It takes a list of questions in its constructor. You will write this program that prints these questions as follows:

1. Enter the constructor into a notebook:

```
class Interrogator:
    def __init__(self, questions):
        self.questions = questions
```

Using an **Interrogator** in a loop probably means asking each of its questions in sequence. The easiest iterator that can achieve this is the iterator for the collection of questions. Therefore to implement the **__iter__()** method to return that object.

2. Add the **__iter__()** method:

```
def __iter__(self):
    return self.questions.__iter__()
```

Now you can create a list of questions, give them to an **Interrogator**, and use that object in a loop.

3. Create a list of questions:

```
questions = ["What is your name?", "What is your quest?", "What is the average
airspeed velocity of an unladen swallow?"]
```

4. Create an **Interrogator**:

```
awkward_person = Interrogator(questions)
```

5. Now use the **Interrogator** in a **for** loop:

```
for question in awkward_person:
    print(question)
```

You should get the following output:

```
for question in awkward_person:
    print(question)



What is your name?
What is your quest?
What is the average airspeed velocity of an unladen swallow?
```

Figure 7.17: The list of questions asked through the use of Interrogator

On the face of it, you've done nothing more than adding a level of interaction between the **Interrogator** class and the collection of questions. From an implementation perspective, that's exactly right. However, from a design perspective, what you've done is much more powerful. You've designed an **Interrogator** class that programmers can ask to iterate over its questions, without having to tell the programmer anything about how the **Interrogator** stores its questions. While it's just forwarding a method call to a list object today, you could change that tomorrow to use a SQLite3 database or a web service call, and programmers using the **Interrogator** class will not need to change anything.

For a more complicated case, you need to write your own iterator. The iterator is required to implement a __next__() method, which returns the next element in the collection or raises StopIteration when it gets to the end.

Exercise 105: A Custom Iterator

In this exercise, you'll implement a classical-era algorithm called the Sieve of Eratosthenes. To find prime numbers between 2 and an upper bound value, n, first, list all of the numbers in that range. Now, 2 is a prime, so return that. Then, remove 2 from the list, and all multiples of 2, and return the new lowest number (which will be 3). Continue until there are no more numbers left in the collection. Every number that gets returned using this method is a successively higher prime. It works because any number you find in the collection to return did not get removed at an earlier step, so has no lower prime factors other than itself.

First, build the architecture of the class. Its constructor needs to take the upper bound value and generate the list of possible primes. The object can be its own iterator, so its __iter__() method will return itself:

1. Define the PrimesBelow class and its initializer:

```
class PrimesBelow:
    def __init__(self, bound):
        self.candidate_numbers = list(range(2,bound))
```

2. Implement the __iter__() method to return itself:

```
def __iter__(self):
    return self
```

The main body of the algorithm is in the __next__() method. With each iteration, it finds the next lowest prime. If there isn't one, it raises StopIteration. If there is one, it sieves that prime number and its multiples from the collection and then returns the prime number.

3. Define the __next__() method and the exit condition. If there are no remaining numbers in the collection, then the iteration can stop:

```
def __next__(self):
    if len(self.candidate_numbers) == 0:
        raise StopIteration
```

4. Complete the implementation of **__next__()** by selecting the lowest number in the collection as the value for **next_prime** and removing any multiples of that number before returning the new prime:

```
            next_prime = self.candidate_numbers[0]
            self.candidate_numbers = [x for x in self.candidate_numbers if x % next_
    prime != 0]
            return next_prime
            return next_prime
```

5. Use an instance of this class to find all the prime numbers below 100:

```
    primes_to_a_hundred = [prime for prime in PrimesBelow(100)]
    print(primes_to_a_hundred)
```

You should get the following output:

```
In [2]: primes_to_a_hundred = [prime for prime in PrimesBelow(100)]
        print(primes_to_a_hundred)
```
```
        [2, 3, 5, 7, 11, 13, 17, 19, 23, 29, 31, 37, 41, 43, 47, 53, 59, 61, 67, 71, 73, 79, 83, 89, 97]
```

Figure 7.18: The output indicating all prime numbers below 100

This exercise demonstrates that by implementing an iterative algorithm as a Python iterator, you can treat it like a collection. In fact, the program does not actually build the collection of all of the prime numbers: you did that yourself in *step* 5 by using the **PrimesBelow** class, but otherwise, **PrimesBelow** was generating one number at a time, whenever you called the **__next()__** method. This is a great way to hide the implementation details of an algorithm from a programmer. Whether you actually give them a collection of objects to iterate over or an iterator that computes each value as it is requested, programmers can use the results in exactly the same way.

Exercise 106: Controlling the Iteration

You do not have to use an iterator in a loop or comprehension. You can use the **iter()** function to get its argument's iterator object, and then pass that to the **next()** function to return successive values from the iterator. These functions call through to the **__iter__()** and **__next__()** methods, respectively. You can use them to add custom behavior to an iteration or to gain more control over the iteration.

In this exercise, you will print the prime numbers below 5. An error should be raised when the object runs out of prime numbers. To do this, you will use the **PrimesBelow** class created in the previous exercise:

1. Get the iterator for a **PrimesBelow** instance. **PrimesBelow** is the class you created in *Exercise 105, A Custom Iterator*, so if you still have the notebook you created for that exercise, you can enter this code in a cell at the end of that notebook:

```
primes_under_five = iter(PrimesBelow(5))
```

2. Repeatedly use **next()** with this object to generate successive prime numbers:

```
next(primes_under_five)
```

You should get the following output:

```
2
```

Now, run this code once again.

```
next(primes_under_five)
```

You should get the following output:

```
3
```

3. When the object runs out of prime numbers, the subsequent use of **next()** raises the **StopIteration** error:

```
next(primes_under_five)
```

You should get the following output:

```
In [1]:  primes_under_five = iter(PrimesBelow(5))
         next(primes_under_five)
         2
         next(primes_under_five)
         3
         next(primes_under_five)
```

```
---------------------------------------------------------------------------
NameError                                 Traceback (most recent call last)
<ipython-input-1-c81778c59ded> in <module>
----> 1 primes_under_five = iter(PrimesBelow(5))
      2 next(primes_under_five)
      3 2
      4 next(primes_under_five)
      5 3

NameError: name 'PrimesBelow' is not defined
```

Figure 7.19: The StopIteration error is thrown when the object runs out of prime numbers

Being able to step through an iteration manually is incredibly useful in programs that are driven by a sequence of inputs, including a command interpreter. You can treat the input stream as an iteration over a list of strings, where each string represents a command. Call **next()** to get the next command, work out what to do, and then execute it. Then, print the result, and go back to **next()** to await the subsequent command. When **StopIteration** is raised, the user has no more commands for your program, and it can exit.

Itertools

Iterators are useful for describing sequences, such as Python lists and ranges, and sequence-like collections, such as your own data types, that provide ordered access to their contents. Iterators make it easy to work with these types in a Pythonic way. Python's library includes the **itertools** module, which has a selection of helpful functions for combining, manipulating, and otherwise working with iterators. In this section, you will use a couple of helpful tools from the module. There are plenty more available, so be sure to check out the official documentation for **itertools**.

One of the important uses of **itertools** is in dealing with infinite sequences. There are plenty of situations in which a sequence does not have an end: everything from infinite series in mathematics to the event loop in a graphical application. A graphical user interface is usually built around an event loop in which the program waits for an event (such as a keypress, a mouse click, a timer expiring, or something else) and then reacts to it. The stream of events can be treated as a potentially infinite list of event objects, with the program taking the next event object from the sequence and doing its reaction work. Iterating over such a sequence with either a Python **for..in** loop or a comprehension will never terminate. There are functions in **itertools** for providing a window onto an infinite sequence, and the following exercise will look at one of those.

Exercise 107: Using Infinite Sequences and takewhile

An alternative algorithm to the Sieve of Eratosthenes for generating prime numbers is to test each number in sequence – to see whether it has any divisors other than itself. This algorithm uses a lot more time than the Sieve in return for a lot less space.

In this exercise, you will be implementing a better algorithm that uses less space than the Sieve for generating prime numbers:

1. Enter this iterator algorithm into a notebook:

Exercise107.ipynb

```
class Primes:
    def __init__(self):
        self.current = 2
    def __iter__(self):
        return self
    def __next__(self):
        while True:
            current = self.current
            square_root = int(current ** 0.5)
            is_prime = True
```

https://packt.live/32Ebiiw

> **Note**
>
> If the above-mentioned link does not render, please enter the URL here - https://nbviewer.jupyter.org/

> **Note**
>
> The class you just entered is an iterator, but the **__next__()** method never raises a **StopIteration** error. That means it never exits. Even though you know that each prime number it returns is bigger than the previous one, a comprehension doesn't know that so you can't simply filter out large values.

2. Enter the following code to get a list of primes that are lower than 100:

```
[p for p in Primes() if p < 100]
```

Because the iterator never raises **StopIteration**, this program will never finish. You'll have to force it to exit.

3. Click on the **Stop** button in the Jupyter notebook.

You should get the following output:

```
-------------------------------------------------------------------------
KeyboardInterrupt                           Traceback (most recent call last)
<ipython-input-23-afd3c871a33d> in <module>()
----> 1 [p for p in Primes() if p < 100]

<ipython-input-23-afd3c871a33d> in <listcomp>(.0)
----> 1 [p for p in Primes() if p < 100]

<ipython-input-22-c1ad65bf0095> in __next__(self)
     11             if square_root >= 2:
     12                 for i in range(2, square_root + 1):
---> 13                     if current % i == 0:
     14                         is_prime = False
     15                         break

KeyboardInterrupt:
```

Figure 7.20: Iterator forced exit

To work with this iterator, **itertools** provides the **takewhile()** function, which wraps the iterator in another iterator. You also supply **takewhile()** with a Boolean function, and its iteration will take values from the supplied iterator until the function returns **False**, at which time it raises **StopIteration** and stops. This makes it possible to find the prime numbers below 100 from the infinite sequence entered previously.

4. Use **takewhile()** to turn the infinite sequence into a finite one:

```
import itertools
print([p for p in itertools.takewhile(lambda x: x<100, Primes())])
```

You should get the following output:

```
[2, 3, 5, 7, 11, 13, 17, 19, 23, 29, 31, 37, 41, 43, 47, 53, 59, 61, 67, 71, 73, 79, 83, 89, 97]
```

Figure 7.21: Using the takewhile function to produce a finite sequence

Surprisingly, it's also useful to be able to turn a finite sequence into an infinite one.

Exercise 108: Turning a Finite Sequence into an Infinite One, and Back Again

In this exercise, consider a turn-based game, such as chess. The person playing white makes the first move. Then, the person playing black takes their turn. Then white. Then black. Then white, black, white, and so on until the game ends. If you had an infinite list of white, black, white, black, white, and so on, then you could always look at the next element to decide whose turn it is:

1. Enter the list of players into a notebook:

```
import itertools
players = ['White', 'Black']
```

2. Use the **itertools** function **cycle** to generate an infinite sequence of turns:

```
turns = itertools.cycle(players)
```

   To demonstrate that this has the expected behavior, you'll want to turn it back into a finite sequence so that you can view the first few members of the **turns** iterator. You can use **takewhile()** for that, and, here, combine it with the **count()** function from **itertools**, which produces an infinite sequence of numbers.

3. List the players who take the first 10 turns in a chess game:

```
countdown = itertools.count(10, -1)
print([turn for turn in itertools.takewhile(lambda x:next(countdown)>0, turns)])
```

   You should get the following output:

```
['White', 'Black', 'White', 'Black', 'White', 'Black', 'White', 'Black', 'White', 'Black']
```

Figure 7.22: Using the takewhile function to list the players who take the first 10 turns in the chess game

This is the "round-robin" algorithm for allocating actions (in this case, making a chess move) to resources (in this case, the players), and has many more applications than board games. A simple way to do load balancing between multiple servers in a web service or database application is to build an infinite sequence of the available servers and choose one in turn for each incoming request.

Generators

A function that returns a value does all of its computation and gives up control to its caller, which supplies that value. This is not the only possible behavior for a function. It can instead yield a value, which passes control (and the value) back to the caller but leaves the function's state intact. Later, it can yield another value, or finally return to indicate that it is done. A function that yields is called a generator.

Generators are useful because they allow a program to defer or postpone calculating a result until it's required. Finding the successive digits of π, for example, is hard work, and it gets harder as the number of digits increases. If you wrote a program to display the digits of π, you might calculate the first 1,000 digits. Much of that effort will be wasted if the user only asks to see the first 10 digits. Using a generator, you can put off the expensive work until your program actually requires the results.

A real-world example of a situation where generators can help is when dealing with I/O. A stream of data coming from a network service can be represented by a generator that yields the available data until the stream is closed when it returns the remaining data. Using a generator allows the program to pass control back and forth between the I/O stream when data is available, and the caller where the data can be processed.

Python internally turns generator functions into objects that use the iterator protocol (such as __iter__, __next__, and the StopIteration error), so the work you put into understanding iterations in the previous section means you already know what generators are doing. There is nothing you can write for a generator that could not be replaced with an equivalent iterator object. However, sometimes, a generator is easier to write or understand. Writing code that is easier to understand is the definition of Pythonicity.

Exercise 109: Generating a Sieve

In this exercise, you will be rewriting the Sieve of Eratosthenes as a generator function and comparing it with the result of the iterator version:

1. Rewrite the Sieve of Eratosthenes as a generator function that yields its values:

```
def primes_below(bound):
    candidates = list(range(2,bound))
    while(len(candidates) > 0):
        yield candidates[0]
        candidates = [c for c in candidates if c % candidates[0] != 0]
```

2. Confirm that the result is the same as the iterator version:

```
[prime for prime in primes_below(100)]
```

You should get the following output:

```
In [2]: print([prime for prime in primes_below(100)])
        [2, 3, 5, 7, 11, 13, 17, 19, 23, 29, 31, 37, 41, 43, 47, 53, 59, 61, 67, 71, 73, 79, 83, 89, 97]
```

Figure 7.23: The output indicating all prime numbers below 100

That's really all there is to generators – they're just a different way of expressing an iterator. They do, however, communicate a different design intention; namely, that the flow of control is going to pass back and forth between the generator and its caller.

The answer to *Why does Python provide both the iterator and the generator?* is found at the end of *Exercise 109, Generating a Sieve*. They do the same thing, but they expose different design intentions. The PEP in which generators were introduced (https://www.python.org/dev/peps/pep-0255/) contains more, in the "motivations" and "Q&A" sections, for students who would like to dig deeper.

Activity 20: Using Random Numbers to Find the Value of Pi

The Monte Carlo method is a technique that is used for approximating a numerical solution using random numbers. Named after the famous casino, chance is at the core of Monte Carlo methods. They use random sampling to obtain information about a function that will be difficult to calculate deterministically. Monte Carlo methods are frequently used in scientific computation to explore probability distributions, and in other fields including quantum physics and computational biology. They're also used in economics to explore the behavior of financial instruments under different market conditions. There are many applications for the Monte Carlo principle.

In this activity, you'll use a Monte Carlo method to find an approximate value for π. Here's how it works: two random numbers, **(x,y)**, somewhere between **(0,0)** and **(1,1)**, represent a random point in a square positioned at **(0,0)** with sides of length **1**:

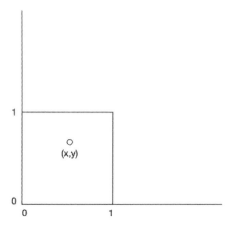

Figure 7.24: A random point in a square having its side as unit 1

Using Pythagoras' Theorem, if the value of $$\sqrt{x^2 + y^2}$$ is less than 1, then the point is also in the top-right corner of a circle centered at (0,0) with a radius of -1:

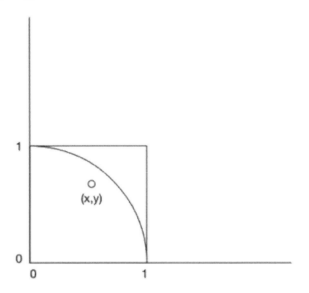

Figure 7.25: Applying Pythagoras' Theorem to locate the point with respect to the circle segment

Generate lots of points, count how many are within the circle segment, and divide the number of points within the circle by the total number of points generated. This gives you an approximation of the area of the circle segment, which should be $\pi/4$. Multiply by 4, and you have an approximate value of π. Data scientists often use this technique to find the area under more complex curves that represent probability distributions.

Write a generator to yield successive estimates of π. The steps are as follows:

1. Define your generator function.

2. Set the total number of points, and the number within the circle segment, to 0.

3. Do the following substeps 10,000 times:

   Generate two numbers between 0 and 1, using Python's **random.random()** function.

   Add 1 to the total number of points.

   Use **math.sqrt()** to find out how far the point represented by the numbers is from (0,0).

If the distance is less than 1; add 1 to the number of points within the circle.

Calculate your estimate for π: 4 * (points within the circle) / (total points generated).

If you have generated a multiple of 1,000 points, yield the approximate value for π. If you have generated 10,000 points, return the value.

4. Inspect the successive estimates of π and check how close they are to the true value (`math.pi`).

    Note that because this activity uses random numbers, you may not get the exact results shown here:

```
print(estimates)
print(errors)

[3.236, 3.232, 3.2106666666666666, 3.206, 3.1824, 3.1633333333333336, 3.1582857142857144, 3.1645, 3.1577777777777776]
[0.0944073464102071, 0.09040734641020709, 0.06907401307687344, 0.06440734641020684, 0.04080734641020678, 0.0217406797435404
36, 0.016693060695921247, 0.022907346410206753, 0.016185124187984457]
```

Figure 7.26: A generator yielding successive estimates of π

> **Note**
>
> The solution for this activity is available on page 544.

Regular Expressions

Regular expressions (or regexes) are a domain-specific programming language, defining a grammar for expressing efficient and flexible string comparisons. Introduced in 1951 by Stephen Cole Kleene, regular expressions have become a popular tool for searching and manipulating text. As an example, if you're writing a text editor and you want to highlight all web links in a document and make them clickable, you might search for strings that start with HTTP or HTTPS, then those that contain `://`, and then those that contain some collection of printable characters, until you stop finding printable characters (such as a space, newline, or the end of the text), and highlight everything up to the end. With standard Python syntax, this will be possible, but you will end up with a very complex loop that will be difficult to get right. Using regexes, you match against `https?://\S+`.

This section will not teach you the full regular expression syntax – there are better resources for doing that. For example, check out *Mastering Python Regular Expressions* (https://packt.live/2ISz4zs) by Félix López and Victor Romero. This section will teach you how to use Python's **re** module to work with the regular expressions in Python. That said, some small amount of regex syntax will be useful, so let's examine the features used in regular expressions as seen in the preceding URL:

- Most characters match their own identities, so "**h**" in a regex means "match exactly the letter **h**."

- Enclosing characters in square brackets can mean choosing between alternates, so if we thought a web link might be capitalized, we could start with "[Hh]" to mean "match either H or h." In the body of the URL, we want to match against any non-whitespace characters, and rather than write them all out. We use the **\S** character class. Other character classes include **\w** (word characters), **\W** (non-word characters), and **\d** (digits).

- Two quantifiers are used: ? means "0 or 1 time," so "s?" means "match if the text does not have s at this point or has it exactly once." The quantifier, +, means "1 or more times," so "\S+" says "one or more non-whitespace characters." There is also a quantifier *, meaning "0 or more times."

  Additional regex features that you will use in this chapter are listed here:

- Parentheses () introduce a numbered sub-expression, sometimes called a "capture group." They are numbered from 1, in the order that they appear in the expression.

- A backslash followed by a number refers to a numbered sub-expression, described previously. As an example, **\1** refers to the first sub-expression. These can be used when replacing text that matches the regex or to store part of a regex to use later in the same expression. Because of the way that backslashes are interpreted by Python strings, this is written as **\\1** in a Python regex.

Regular expressions have various uses throughout software development, as so much software deals with text. Validating user input in a web application, searching for and replacing entries in text files, and finding interesting events in application log files are all uses that regular expressions can be put to in a Python program.

Exercise 110: Matching Text with Regular Expressions

In this exercise, you'll use the Python **re** module to find instances of repeated letters in a string.

The regex you will use is **(\w)\\1+**."**(\w)** searches for a single character from a word (that is, any letter or the underscore character, _) and stores that in a numbered sub-expression, **\1**. Then, **\\1+** uses a quantifier to find one or more occurrences of the same character. The steps for using this regex are as follows:

1. Import the **re** module:

```
import re
```

2. Define the string that you will search for, and the pattern by which to search:

```
title = "And now for something completely different"
pattern = "(\w)\\1+"
```

3. Search for the pattern and print the result:

```
print(re.search(pattern, title))
```

You should get the following output:

```
In [1]:  import re
         title = "And now for something completely different"
         pattern = "(\w)\\1+"
         print(re.search(pattern, title))

         <re.Match object; span=(35, 37), match='ff'>
```

Figure 7.27: Searching for a string using the re module

The **re.search()** function finds matches anywhere in the string: if it doesn't find any matches, it will return **None**. If you were only interested in whether the beginning of the string matched the pattern, you could use **re.match()**. Similarly, modifying the search pattern to start with the beginning-of-line marker (^) achieves the same aim as **re.search("^(\w)\\1+", title)**.

Exercise 111: Using Regular Expressions to Replace Text

In this exercise, you'll use a regular expression to replace occurrences of a pattern in a string with a different pattern. The steps are as follows:

1. Define the text to search:

```
import re
description = "The Norwegian Blue is a wonderful parrot. This parrot is notable for
its exquisite plumage."
```

2. Define the pattern to search for, and its replacement:

```
pattern = "(parrot)"
replacement = "ex-\\1"
```

3. Substitute the replacement for the search pattern, using the **re.sub()** function:

```
print(re.sub(pattern, replacement, description))
```

You should get the following output:

```
In [1]: import re
        description = "The Norwegian Blue is a wonderful parrot. This parrot is notable for its exquisite plumage."
        pattern = "(parrot)"
        replacement = "ex-\\1"
        print(re.sub(pattern, replacement, description))

        The Norwegian Blue is a wonderful ex-parrot. This ex-parrot is notable for its exquisite plumage.
```

Figure 7.28: Replacing occurrences of a repeating pattern in the string

The replacement refers to the capture group, **"\1"**, which is the first expression in the search pattern to be surrounded by parentheses. In this case, the capture group is the whole word **parrot**. This lets you refer to the word **parrot** in the replacement without having to type it out again.

Activity 21: Regular Expressions

At your online retail company, your manager has had an idea for a promotion. There is a whole load of old "The X-Files" DVDs in the warehouse, and she has decided to give one away for free to any customer whose name contains the letter x.

In this activity, you will be using Python's **re** module to find winning customers. The x could be capitalized if it's their initial, or lower case if it's in the middle of their name, so use the regular expression [Xx] to search for both cases:

1. Create a list of customer names. The customers are **Xander Harris**, **Jennifer Smith**, **Timothy Jones**, **Amy Alexandrescu**, **Peter Price**, and **Weifung Xu**.

2. Create a list comprehension using the list of names. Use the comprehension to filter only names where a search for the [Xx] regex is successful.

3. Print the list of matching names. The result should look like this:

```
['Xander Harris', 'Amy Alexandrescu', 'Weifung Xu']
```

You should get the following output:

```
print(winners)
```

```
['Xander Harris', 'Amy Alexandrescu', 'Weifung Xu']
```

Figure 7.29: The winner's list, indicating the presence of "Xx" in a customer name

> **Note**
>
> The solution for this activity is available on page 546.

Summary

In this chapter, you've learned how even though there is often more than one way to do something in Python, there is often a "Pythonic" way. The Pythonic way is succinct and easy to understand, leaving out boilerplate code and extraneous information to focus on the task at hand. Comprehensions are a Pythonic tool for manipulating collections, including lists, sets, and dictionaries. Comprehensions are powered by iterators, which can be written as classes or as generator functions that yield the iterated values. The Python library includes useful functions for working with iterators, including infinite sequences expressed as iterators.

In the next chapter, you'll move past the details of the Python language and into how to work as a professional Python programmer. You'll see how to debug your Python code, write unit tests, and document, package, and share your Python code with other coders.

8

Software Development

Overview

By the end of this chapter, you will be able to, troubleshoot issues in Python applications; explain why testing in software development is important; write test scenarios in Python to validate code; create a Python package that can be published to PyPI; write and publish documentation on the web and create a Git repository and manage your source code versions.

Introduction

Software development goes beyond writing code. In previous *Chapter 7, Becoming Pythonic* you were introduced to the idea of being Pythonic. When you write software as professionals, we expect the code to be up to a certain standard and to be able to manage and distribute that code in a way that can be easily consumed by other developers.

In this chapter, you will go through the various concepts and tools that allow you to elevate the level of your source code and applications. You will examine Python tools that every Python developer uses for testing, writing documentation, packaging their code, and version control, as well as learning about techniques that allow us to debug issues that occur in existing code. Additionally, you will write tests to validate our assumptions and implementations of our code. These are all concepts and tools that are key to any successful developer in any company, as they allow developers to develop and collaborate effectively. Finally, you will cover some basics about using Git to manage your source code versions.

Debugging

Sooner or later in your development, you will reach a point where you see our program behave differently than you initially expected. In situations like these, you usually look back at the source code and try to understand what is different between your expectations and the code or inputs that are being used. To facilitate that process, there are multiple methods (in general, and some that are specific to Python) that you can use to try to "debug" or "troubleshoot" the issue.

Usually, the first action of an experienced developer, when frustration arises from unexpected results in their code, is to look at the logs or any other output that the application produces. A good starting point is trying to increase the logging verbosity, as discussed in *Chapter 6, Standard Library*. If you are not able to troubleshoot the problem with just logs, it usually means that you should look back at how we are instructing our application to log its state and activity producing what are known as traces, as there might be a good opportunity to improve it.

The next step of verifying the inputs and outputs of the program is to receive and verify the log. The usual next step in Python is to use the Python debugger, **pdb**.

The **pdb** module and its command line interface which is a `cli` tool allows you to navigate through the code as it runs and ask questions about the state of the program, its variables, and the flow of execution. It is similar to other tools, such as **gdb**, but it is at a higher level and is designed for Python.

There are two main ways to start **pdb**. You can just run the tool and feed it with a file or use the **breakpoint** command.

As an example, take a look at the following file:

```
# This is a comment
this = "is the first line to execute"
def secret_sauce(number):
    if number <= 10:
        return number + 10
    else:
        return number - 10
def magic_operation(x, y):
    res = x + y
    res *= y
    res /= x
    res = secret_sauce(res)
    return res
print(magic_operation(2, 10))
```

When you begin executing the script with **pdb**, it works as follows:

```
python3.7 -m pdb magic_operation.py
> [...]Lesson08/1.debugging/magic_operation.py(3)<module>()
-> this = "is the first line to execute"
(Pdb)
```

It will stop on the first line of the Python code to execute and give us a prompt to interact with **pdb**.

The first line shows us which current file you are in at the moment, while the final line shows us the **pdb** prompt **(pdb)**, which tells us which debugger you are running and that it is waiting for input from the user.

Another way to start **pdb** is to change the source code to do this. At any point in the code, we can write **"import pdb;pdb.set_trace()"** for earlier versions of Python to tell the Python interpreter that you want to start a debugging session at that point. If you are using Python 3.7 or a later version, you can use **breakpoint()**.

If you execute the **magic_operation_with_breakpoint.py** file attached in the GitHub repository, which has **breakpoint()** in one of its lines, you will see that the debugger starts for you where you requested it.

> **Note**
>
> The previously mentioned **magic_operation_with_breakpoint.py** file can be found on GitHub at https://packt.live/2VNsSxP.

When you are running things in an IDE or code in a large application you could achieve the same effect by using the operations that we will demonstrate later, but just dropping that line in the file is by far the simplest and fastest way:

```
$ python3.7 magic_operation_with_breakpoint.py
> [...]/Lesson08/1.debugging/magic_operation_with_breakpoint.py(7)secret_sauce()
-> if number <= 10:
(Pdb)
```

At this point, you can get a list of all the commands by running **help**, or you can get more information about a specific command by running the **help** command. The most commonly used commands are as follows:

- **break filename:linenumber**: This sets a breakpoint in the specified line. It ensures that you will stop the code at that point when other commands are running by continuing the execution. Breakpoints can be set in any file included in the standard library. If we want to set a breakpoint in a file that is part of a module, you can do so by just using its full path within the Python path. For example, to stop the debugger in the parser module, which is part of the HTML package of the standard library, you would perform **b html/parser:50** to stop the code on line 50 of the file.

- **break** function: You can request to stop the code when a specific function is called. If the function is in the current file, you can pass the function name. If the function is imported from another module, you will have to pass the full function specification, for example, **html.parser. HTMLParser.reset**, to stop at the **reset** function of the **HTMLParser** class of **html.parser**.

- **break without arguments**: This lists all the current breakpoints that are set in the current state of the program.

- **continue**: This continues the execution until a breakpoint is found. This is quite useful when you start a program, set breakpoints in all the lines of code or functions you want to inspect, and then just let it run until it stops at any of those.

- **where**: This prints a stack trace with the current line of execution where the debugger stopped. It is useful to know what called this function or to be able to move around the stack.

- **down** and **up**: These two commands allow us to move around in the stack. If we are in a function call, we can use **up** to move to the caller of the function and inspect the state in that frame, or you can use **down** to go deeper in the stack after we have moved up.

- **list**: This displays 11 lines of code from the point where the execution stopped for the first time to when it is called. Successive calls to **list** will display the following lines in batches of 11. To start again from where the execution stopped, use **list**.

- **longlist**: This shows the source code of the current function in the current frame that is being executed.

- **next**: This executes the line and moves to the following one.

- **step**: This executes the current line and stops at the first opportunity within the function being executed. This is useful when you don't want to just execute a function, but we want to step through it.

- **p**: This prints the value of an expression. It is useful for checking the content of variables.

- **pp**: This allows you to pretty print an expression. It is useful for when we are trying to print long structures.

- **run/restart**: This restarts the program keeping all the breakpoints still set. It is useful if you have passed an event you expected to see.

Many functions have shortcuts; for example, you can use **b** instead of **break**, **c** or **cont** instead of **continue**, **l** instead of a **list**, **ll** for **longlist**, and so on.

There are other functions not covered here, **pdb** comes with a broad toolbox. Use **help** to learn about all the different functions and how to use them.

Exercise 112: Debugging a Salary Calculator

In this exercise, you will use the skills you learned to use **pdb** to debug an application that is not working as expected.

This is a salary calculator. Our company is using this to calculate the salary increase that will be given to our employees year after year, and a manager has reported that she is getting a 20% raise when the rulebook seems to suggest that she should be getting a 30% raise.

You are just told that the manager's name is **Rose**, and you will find that the code for the salary raise calculation is the following:

Exercise112.py

```
3 def _manager_adjust(salary, rise):
4     if rise < 0.10:
5         # We need to keep managers happy.
6         return 0.10
7
8     if salary >= 1_000_000:
9         # They are making enough already.
10         return rise - 0.10
11
12
13 def calculate_new_salary(salary, promised_pct, is_manager, is_good_year):
14     rise = promised_pct
15     # remove 10% if it was a bad year
16     if not is_good_year:
```

https://packt.live/2MIFaoF

> **Note**
>
> If you read this code on GitHub, it is quite convoluted and difficult to read, but it applies different raises depending on factors such as whether the person is a manager, whether it was a good year and the person's current salary. The aim here is to provide you with a complex code structure so that you can debug it by following the steps mentioned in this exercise. This could be very helpful in your everyday developer life as well when you are provided with a bunch of code, and you need to find a way to debug it.

The following steps will help you complete this exercise:

1. Understand the problem by asking the right questions.

   The first step is to fully understand the issue, evaluate whether there is an issue with the source code, and to get all the possible data. You need to ask the user who reported the error, and ourselves, common questions such as the following indent question list:

   What version of the software were they using?

   When did the error happen for the first time?

   Has it worked before?

   Is it an intermittent failure, or can the user consistently reproduce it?

   What was the input of the program when the issue manifested?

What is the output and what would be the expected output?

Do we have any logs or any other information to help us debug the issue?

In this instance, you get to know that this happened with the last version of our script and the person who reported it could reproduce it. It seems to be happening only to **Rose**, but that might be related to the arguments she is providing.

For instance, she reported that her current salary is $1,000,000. She was told she would get a 30% raise, and even if she is aware that managers earning that much get a penalty of 10%, as the company had a good year and she was a high earner, she was expecting a 10% bonus, which should amount to 30%. But she saw that her new salary was $1,200,000, rather than $1,300,000.

You can translate this into the following `arguments`:

`salary`: 1,000,000.

`promised_pct`: 0.30.

`is_manager`: True

`is_good_year`: True

The expected output was 1,300,000, and the output she reported was 1,200,000.

We don't have any logs about the execution, as the code was not instrumented with this.

2. Reproduce the issue by running the **`calculate_new_salary`** function and the known arguments.

   The next step in our debugging investigation is to confirm that you can reproduce the issue. If you are not able to reproduce it, then it means that some of the input or assumptions that either we or the user made were incorrect, and you should go back to step 1 for clarification.

   In this scenario, trying to reproduce the issue is easy—you need to run the function with the known arguments:

```
rose_salary = calculate_new_salary(1_000_000, 0.30, True, True)
print("Rose's salary will be:", rose_salary)
```

   The output will be as follows:

```
1200000
```

This effectively returns **1200000** rather than 1,300,000, and you know from the HR guidelines that she should be getting the latter. Indeed, something starts to look suspicious.

3. Run the code with the other current inputs, such as 1,000,000 and 2,000,000, to see the difference.

In some situations, it is helpful to try with other inputs to see how the program behaves before even running the debugger. This can give you some extra information. You know that there are special rules for people that earn a million dollars or more, so what happens if you raise that number to, say, $2,000,000?

Consider the following:

```
rose_salary = calculate_new_salary(2_000_000, 0.30, True, True)
print("Rose's salary will be:", rose_salary)
```

You see that, now, the output is 2,400,000. The raise was 20% rather than 30%. There is something wrong in the code.

You can also try changing the percentage, so let's try that with a promised initial raise of 40%:

```
rose_salary = calculate_new_salary(1_000_000, 0.40, True, True)
print("Rose's salary will be:", rose_salary)
```

The output will be as follows:

```
Rose's salary will be: 1400000
```

Interestingly, she would get a **40%** raise because there is no penalty applied.

From just trying out different inputs, you have seen what is special about Rose's situation, it is her 30% increase. When you start to debug things in the following step, you will see that you should keep an eye on the code that interacts with the promised percentage, as the initial salary change did not make a difference.

4. Start the debugger by firing up **pdb** and set up a breakpoint in your **calculate_new_salary** function:

```
$ python3.7 -m pdb salary_calculator.py
> /Lesson08/1.debugging/salary_calculator.py(1)<module>()
-> """Adjusts the salary rise of an employ"""
(Pdb) b calculate_new_salary
Breakpoint 1 at /Lesson08/1.debugging/salary_calculator.py:13
(Pdb)
```

5. Now run **continue** or **c** to ask the interpreter to run until the function is executed:

```
(Pdb) c
```

The output will be as follows:

```
> /Lesson08/1.debugging/salary_calculator.py(14)calculate_new_salary()
-> rise = promised_pct
(Pdb)
```

6. Run the **where** command in order to get information about how you got to this point:

```
(Pdb) where
```

The output will be as follows:

```
  /usr/local/lib/python3.7/bdb.py(585)run()
-> exec(cmd, globals, locals)
  <string>(1)<module>()
  /Lesson08/1.debugging/salary_calculator.py(34)<module>()
-> rose_salary = calculate_new_salary(1_000_000, 0.30, True, True)
> /Lesson08/1.debugging/salary_calculator.py(14)calculate_new_salary()
-> rise = promised_pct
(Pdb)
```

See how **pdb** tells you that you are on line 14 of the **salary_calculator** file and this function was executed as it was called from line 34 with the arguments that are displayed on the screen.

> **Note**
>
> You can use **up** here if you want to go to the stack frame where the function was executed. This is the line of code with the state that the program was in when the function was called.

When you can pinpoint the issue to a part of the program, you can go step by step, running the code and checking whether your expectations match what the result of running that line gives us.

An important step here is to think about what you expect to happen before you run the line. This might seem to make it take longer to debug the program, but it will pay off, because if there is a result that appears to be correct, but it is not, it will be easier to detect whether you expected the result rather than just confirming whether it was right a posteriori. Let's do this in your program.

7. Run the **l** command to confirm where we are in the program and **args** to print the arguments of the function:

> **Note**
>
> The output from the debugger and the input that we provide is mentioned next.

```
(Pdb) l
```

You should get the following output:

```
(Pdb) l
  9                 # They are making enough already.
 10                 return rise - 0.10
 11
 12
 13 B   def calculate_new_salary(salary, promised_pct, is_manager, is_good_year):
 14 ->       rise = promised_pct
 15
 16             # remove 10% if it was a bad year
 17             if not is_good_year:
 18                 rise -= 0.01
 19             else:
```

Figure 8.1: Listing the pdb output

To use **args** to print the arguments of the function:

```
(Pdb) args
```

You should get the following output:

```
(Pdb) args
salary = 1000000
promised_pct = 0.3
is_manager = True
is_good_year = True
```

Figure 8.2: The args output (continued)

You are effectively on the first line of the code, and the arguments are what you expected. We could also run **ll** to get the whole function printed.

8. Advance the lines of code by using **n** to move one line at a time:

```
(Pdb) n
```

You should get the following output:

```
> /Lesson08/1.debugging/salary_calculator.py(17)calculate_new_salary()
```

```
-> if not is_good_year:
(Pdb) n
> /Lesson08/1.debugging/salary_calculator.py(23)calculate_new_salary()
-> if is_manager:
(Pdb) n
> /Lesson08/1.debugging/salary_calculator.py(24)calculate_new_salary()
-> rise = _manager_adjust(salary, rise)
```

You next check on whether it was a good year. As the variable is **True**, it does not get into the branch and jumps to line 23. As Rose is a manager, this does get into that branch, where it will perform the manager adjustment.

9. Print the value of the raise before and after the **_manager_adjust** function is called by running **p rise**.

You can run **step** to get into the function, but the error is unlikely to be there, so you can print the current raise before and after executing the function. You know that, as she is earning a million dollars, her pay should be adjusted, and, therefore, the rise should be **0.2** after executing it:

```
(Pdb) p rise
0.3
(Pdb) n
> /Lesson08/1.debugging/salary_calculator.py(27)calculate_new_salary()
-> if rise >= 0.20:
(Pdb) p rise
0.19999999999999998
```

The adjusted raise is **0.199999999999999998** rather than **0.20**, so what is going on here? There is clearly an issue within the **_manager_adjust** function. You will have to restart the debugging and investigate it.

10. You can then continue to the second execution and print the lines and arguments at that point, by running "c", "c", "ll" and "args" as follows:

```
(Pdb) b _manager_adjust
Breakpoint 2 at /Lesson08/1.debugging/salary_calculator.py:3
(Pdb) restart
```

The output will be as follows:

```
Restarting salary_calculator.py with arguments:
        salary_calculator.py
> /Lesson08/1.debugging/salary_calculator.py(1)<module>()
-> """Adjusts the salary rise of an employ"""
(Pdb) c
```

```
> /Lesson08/1.debugging/salary_calculator.py(14)calculate_new_salary()
-> rise = promised_pct
(Pdb) c
> /Lesson08/1.debugging/salary_calculator.py(4)_manager_adjust()
-> if rise < 0.10:
(Pdb) ll
  3 B   def _manager_adjust(salary, rise):
  4 ->      if rise < 0.10:
  5             # We need to keep managers happy.
  6             return 0.10
  7
  8         if salary >= 1_000_000:
  9             # They are making enough already.
 10             return rise - 0.10
(Pdb) args
salary = 1000000
rise = 0.3
(Pdb)
```

You see the input is what you expected (**0.3**), but you know the output is not. Rather than **0.2**, you are getting **0.19999999999999998**. Let's walk through this function code to understand what is happening. By running "n" three times until the end of the function, you can then use "**rv**" to see the returned value as follows:

```
(Pdb) n
> /Lesson08/1.debugging/salary_calculator.py(8)_manager_adjust()
-> if salary >= 1_000_000:
(Pdb) n
> /Lesson08/1.debugging/salary_calculator.py(10)_manager_adjust()
-> return rise - 0.10
(Pdb) n
--Return--
> /Lesson08/1.debugging/salary_calculator.py(10)_manager_adjust()-
>0.19999999999999998
-> return rise - 0.10
(Pdb) rv
0.19999999999999998
```

You found the error: when we are subtracting **0.10** from **0.30**, the result is not **0.20** as you might have expected. It is that weird number, **0.19999999999999998**, due to the loose precision of float numbers. This is a well-known issue in computer science. We should not rely on floats for equality comparison if you need fraction numbers, we should use the decimal module instead, as we have seen in previous chapters.

In this exercise, you have learned how to identify errors when you perform debugging. You can now start to think about how to fix these errors and propose solutions to our colleagues.

Now, let's take a look at an activity to debug a Python code application.

Activity 22: Debugging Sample Python Code for an Application

Consider the following scenario: you have a program that creates a picnic basket for you. The baskets are created in a function that depends on whether the user wants a healthy meal and whether they are hungry. You provide a set of initial items in the basket, but users can also customize this via a parameter.

A user reported that they got more strawberries than expected when creating multiple baskets. When asked for more information, they said that they tried to create a healthy basket for a non-hungry person first, and a non-healthy basket for a hungry person with just "tea" in the initial basket. Those two baskets were created correctly, but when the third basket was created for a healthy person who was also hungry, the basket appeared with one more strawberry than expected.

In this activity, you need to run the reproducers mentioned on GitHub and check for the error in the third basket. Once you have found the error with the basket, you need to debug the code and fix the error.

> **Note**
>
> The code file for this activity, along with the reproducers, is mentioned on GitHub: https://packt.live/2MhvHnU.

The following table is a summary of the preceding scenario:

Health?	Hungry?	Initial Basket	Output
True	False	-	['orange', 'apple', 'strawberry']
False	True	["tea"]	['tea', 'jam', 'sandwich']
True	True	-	['orange', 'apple', 'strawberry', 'strawberry', 'sandwich']

Figure 8.3: A summary table of the problem

There is a reproducer in the code example, so continue the debugging from there, and figure out where the issue is in the code.

Take a look at the following steps:

1. First, write test cases with the inputs provided in the preceding table.

2. Next, confirm whether the error report is genuine.

3. Then, run the reproducers in the code file and confirm the error in the code.

4. Finally, fix the code with the simple logic of **if and else**.

   You should get the following output:

```
In [6]:  print("First basket:", create_picnic_basket(True, False))

         First basket: ['orange', 'apple', 'strawberry']

In [7]:  print("Second basket:", create_picnic_basket(False, True, ["tea"]))

         Second basket: ['tea', 'jam', 'sandwich']

In [8]:  print("Third basket:", create_picnic_basket(True, True))

         Third basket: ['orange', 'apple', 'strawberry', 'sandwich']
```

Figure 8.4: The expected output from the basket

> **Note**
>
> The solution for this activity is available on page 547.

In the next topic, you will be learning about automated testing

Automated Testing

Even though you explored and learned how to debug applications when errors are reported, you would prefer not having to find errors in our applications. To increase the chances of having a bug-free code base, most developers rely on automated testing.

At the beginning of their careers, most developers will just manually test their code as they develop it. By just providing a set of inputs and verifying the output of the program, you can get a basic level of confidence that our code "works." But this quickly becomes tedious and does not scale as the code base grows and evolves. Automated testing allows you to record a series of steps and stimuli that you perform in our code and have a series of expected output recorded.

This is extremely efficient to reduce the number of bugs in our code base, because not only are we verifying the code, but we are also implementing it, and you keep a record of all those verifications for future modifications of the codebase.

The amount of test lines that you write for each line of code really depends on each application. There are notorious cases, such as SQLite, where orders of magnitude more lines of tests are needed than lines of code, which greatly improves confidence in the software and allows quick release of new versions as features are added without needing the extensive quality assurance (QA) that other systems might require.

Automated testing is similar to the QA process that we see in other engineering fields. It is a key step of all software development and should be taken into account when developing a system.

Additionally, having automated tests also helps you to troubleshoot, as we have a set of test scenarios that you can adapt to simulate the user's input and environment and keep what is known as a regression test. This is a test that is added when an issue is detected, to ensure that the issue never happens again.

Test Categorization

One of the first things to think about when writing an automated test is "*What are we verifying?*". And that would depend on the "*level*" of testing that you are doing. There is a lot of literature about how to categorize different test scenarios in the functions that they validate and the corresponding dependencies they have. It is not the same to write a test that just validates a simple Python function in our source code, as it is to write something that validates an accounting system that connects to the internet and sends emails. To validate large systems, it is common to create different types of tests. They are usually known as the following:

- **Unit tests**: These are tests that just validate a small part of your code. Usually, they just validate a function with specific inputs within one of your files and only depend on code that has already been validated with other unit tests.

- **Integration tests**: These are more coarse-grained tests that will either validate interactions between different components of your codebase (known as integration tests without environment) or the interactions between your code and other systems and the environment (known as integration tests with the environment).

- **Functional or end-to-end tests**: These are usually really high-level tests that depend on the environment and often on external systems that validate the solution with inputs as the user provides them.

Say that you were to test the workings of Twitter, using the tests you are familiar with:

- A unit test would verify one of the functions, which will check whether a tweet body is shorter than a specific length.

- An integration test would validate that, when a tweet is injected into the system, the trigger to other users is called.

- An end-to-end test is one that ensures that, when a user writes a tweet and clicks **Send**, they can then see it on their home page.

Software developers tend to prefer unit tests as they don't have external dependencies and are more stable and faster to run. The further we go into more coarse-grained tests, the more we'll come across what the user will perform, but both integration and end-to-end tests usually take much longer to run, as the dependencies need to be set up and they are usually flakier because, for example, the email server might not be working on that day, meaning we would be unable to run our tests.

> **Note**
>
> This categorization is a simplification of many experts working in the field. If you are interested in the different levels of testing and getting the right balance of tests, then a good place to start is the famous Testing Pyramid.

Test Coverage

Something that generates debate across the community is test coverage. When you write tests for our code, you start to exercise it and begin to hit different code paths. As you write more tests, we cover more and more of the code that you are testing. The percentage of code that you test is known as **test coverage**, and developers will argue that different percentages are "the right amount." Getting to 100% coverage might seem an unnecessary task, but it proves to be quite useful in large codebases that need to perform tasks such as migrating from Python 2 to Python 3. However, this all depends on how much you are willing to invest in testing your application, and each developer might target a different number for each of the projects that they run.

Moreover, something important to remember is that 100% coverage does not mean that your code does not have bugs. You can write tests that exercise your code but do not properly validate it, so be mindful of falling into the trap of just writing tests to hit the coverage target. Tests should be written to exercise the code with inputs that will be provided by users and try to find edge cases that can uncover issues with the assumptions that you made at the time that you wrote it, and not just to hit a number.

Writing Tests in Python with Unit Testing

The Python standard library comes with a module, **unittest**, to write test scenarios and validate your code. Usually, when you are creating tests, we create a file for the test to validate the source code of another file. In that file, you can create a class that inherits from **unittest.TestCase** and has method names that contain the word **test** to be run on execution. You can record expectations through functions such as **assertEquals** and **assertTrue**, which are part of the base class, and you can, therefore, access them.

Exercise 113: Checking Sample Code with Unit Testing

In this exercise, you will write and run tests for a function that checks whether a number is divisible by another. This will help you to validate the implementation and potentially find any existing bugs:

1. Create a function, **is_divisible**, which checks whether a number is divisible by another. Save this function in a file named **sample_code**.

   This function is also provided in the **sample_code.py** file. The file just has a single function that checks whether a number is divisible by another:

```python
def is_divisible(x, y):
    if x % y == 0:
        return True
    else:
        return False
```

2. Create a **test** file that will include the test cases for our function. Then, add the skeleton for a test case:

```python
import unittest
from sample_code import is_divisible
class TestIsDivisible(unittest.TestCase):
    def test_divisible_numbers(self):
        pass
if __name__ == '__main__':
    unittest.main()
```

   This code imports the function to test, **is_divisible**, and the **unittest** module. It then creates the common boilerplate to start writing tests: a class that inherits from **unittest.TestCase** and two final lines that allow us to run the code and execute the tests.

3. Now, write the test code:

```
def test_divisible_numbers(self):
    self.assertTrue(is_divisible(10, 2))
    self.assertTrue(is_divisible(10, 10))
    self.assertTrue(is_divisible(1000, 1))

def test_not_divisible_numbers(self):
    self.assertFalse(is_divisible(5, 3))
    self.assertFalse(is_divisible(5, 6))
    self.assertFalse(is_divisible(10, 3))
```

You now write the code for Your tests by using the **self.assertX** methods. There are different kinds of methods for different kinds of asserts. For example, **self. assertEqual** will check whether the two arguments are equal or fail otherwise. You will use **self.assertTrue** and **self.assertFalse**. With this, you can create the preceding tests.

4. Run the test:

```
python3.7 test_unittest.py  -v
```

Run the test by executing it with a Python interpreter. By using **-v**, you get extra information about the test names as the tests are running.

You should get the following output:

```
test_divisible_numbers (__main__.TestIsDivisible) ... ok
test_not_divisible_numbers (__main__.TestIsDivisible) ... ok

----------------------------------------------------------------------
Ran 2 tests in 0.016s

OK
```

Figure 8.5: The unit test run output

5. Now, add more complex tests:

```
def test_dividing_by_0(self):
    with self.assertRaises(ZeroDivisionError):
        is_divisible(1, 0)
```

By adding a test when you pass **0**, you want to check whether it will raise an exception.

The **assertRaises** context manager will validate that the function raises the exception passed in within the context.

So, there you go: you have a test suite with the standard library **unittest** module.

Unit testing is a great tool for writing automated tests, but the community seems to generally prefer to use a third-party tool named **Pytest**. Pytest allows the user to write tests by just having plain functions in their function and by using Python **assert**.

This means that rather than using **self.assertEquals(a, b)**, you can just do **assert a == b**. Additionally, pytest comes with some enhancements, such as capturing output, modular fixtures, or user-defined plugins. If you plan to develop any test suite that is bigger than a few tests, consider checking for pytest.

Writing a Test with pytest

Even if a unit test is part of the standard library, it is more common to see developers use pytest to run and write the test. You can refer to the **pytest** package for more information about how to write and run tests with pytest: https://docs.pytest.org/en/latest/

```
from sample_code import is_divisible
import pytest
def test_divisible_numbers():
    assert is_divisible(10, 2) is True
    assert is_divisible(10, 10) is True
    assert is_divisible(1000, 1) is True

def test_not_divisible_numbers():
    assert is_divisible(5, 3) is False
    assert is_divisible(5, 6) is False
    assert is_divisible(10, 3) is False
def test_dividing_by_0():
    with pytest.raises(ZeroDivisionError):
        is_divisible(1, 0)
```

This code creates three test cases by using **pytest**. The main difference is that having a class that has **assert** methods within it, you can create free functions and use the **assert** keyword of Python itself. This also gives us more explicit error reports when they fail.

In the next section, let's take a look at creating PIP packages.

Creating a PIP Package

When you are working with Python code, you need to differentiate between the **source code tree**, the **source distributions (sdist)**, and a **binary distribution** (wheels for example which is explained ahead). The folder where you work on the code is known as the source code tree, which is essentially how it is presented in the folder. This also contains Git files, configuration files, and others. The source distribution is a way to package our code so that it can be executed and installed on any machine— it just contains all the source code without any development-related files. A binary distribution is similar to source distribution, but it comes with the files ready to be installed on the system—there is no execution needed in the client host. Wheels are a particular standard for binary distributions that replace the old format, Python eggs. When we consume Python wheels we just get a file that is ready to be installed without the need of any compilation or build step, just ready to be consumed. This is especially useful for Python packages with C extensions.

When you want to distribute our code to users, you need to create source or binary distributions and then upload them to a repository. The most common Python repository is **PyPI**, which allows users to install packages by using **pip**.

The **Python Packaging Index (PyPI)**, is an official package repository maintained by the Python Software Foundation that contains Python packages. Anyone can publish packages to it, and many Python tools usually default to consume packages from it. The most common way to consume from **PyPI** is through **pip**, which is the **Python Packaging Authority (PyPA)**. This is the recommended tool for consuming Python packages.

The most common tool to package our source code is **setuptools**. With **setuptools**, you can create a **setup.py** file that contains all the information about how to create and install the package. **Setuptools** comes with a method named **setup**, which should be called with all the **metadata** that we want to create a package with.

Here's some example boilerplate code that could be copied and pasted when creating a package:

```python
import setuptools
setuptools.setup(
    name="packt-sample-package",
    version="1.0.0",
    author="Author Name",
    author_email="author@email.com",
    description="packt example package",
    long_description="This is the longer description and will appear in the
        web.",
    py_modules=["packt"],
```

```
    classifiers=[
        "Programming Language :: Python :: 3",
        "Operating System :: OS Independent",
    ],
)
```

Take special note of the following parameters:

- **Name**: The name of the package in PyPA. It is a good practice to have it match your library or file import name.

- **Version**: A string that identifies the version of the package.

- **Py_modules**: A list of Python files to package. You can also use the **package** keyword to target full Python packages– you will explore how to do this in the next exercise.

You can now create the source distribution by running the following:

```
python3.7 setup.py sdist
```

This will generate a file in the **dist** folder, which is ready to be distributed to PyPI.

If you have the **wheel** package installed, you can also run the following to create a **wheel**:

```
python3.7 setup.py bdist_wheel
```

Once you have this file generated, you can install Twine, which is the tool recommended by the PyPA for uploading packages to PyPI. With twine installed, you just need to run the following:

```
twine upload dist/*
```

You can test our package by installing any of the artifacts in the **dist** folder.

Usually, you won't just have a single file to distribute, but a whole set of files within a folder, which makes a Python package. In those situations, there is no need to write all the files within the folder one by one–you can just use the following line instead of the **py_module** option:

```
packages=setuptools.find_packages(),
```

This will find and include all the packages in the directory where the **setup.py** file is.

Exercise 114: Creating a Distribution That Includes Multiple Files within a Package

In this exercise, you are going to create our own package that can contain multiple files and upload them to the test version of PyPI:

1. Create a virtual environment and install **twine** and **setuptools**.

    Start by creating a virtual environment with all the dependencies that you need.

    Make sure you are in an **empty** folder to start:

    ```
    python3.7 -m venv venv
    . venv/bin/activate
    python3.7 -m pip install twine setuptools
    ```

    You now have all the dependencies we need to create and distribute our package.

2. Create the actual package source code.

    You will create a Python package named **john_doe_package**.

    Note, please change this to your first and last name:

    ```
    mkdir john_doe_package
    touch john_doe_package/__init__.py
    echo "print('Package imported')" > john_doe_package/code.py
    ```

    The second line will create a Python file, which you will package within the Python package.

    This is a basic Python package that just contains an **init** file and another file named **code**—we can add as many files as desired. The '**__init__**' file marks the folder as a Python package.

3. Add the **setup.py** file.

    You need to add a **setup.py** file at the top of our source tree to indicate how our code should be packaged. Add a **setup.py** file like the following:

    ```
    import setuptools
    setuptools.setup(
        name="john_doe_package",
        version="1.0.0",
        author="Author Name",
        author_email="author@email.com",
    ```

```
        description="packt example package",
        long_description="This is the longer description and will appear in
            the web.",
        packages=setuptools.find_packages(),
        classifiers=[
            "Programming Language :: Python :: 3",
            "Operating System :: OS Independent",
        ],
    )
```

The previously mentioned code is a function call where you pass all the metadata.

Be sure to change **john_doe_package** to the name of your own package.

4. Create the distribution by calling the **setup.py** file:

```
python3.7 setup.py sdist
```

This will create a source distribution. You can test it out by installing it locally:

```
cd dist && python3.7 -m pip install *
```

5. Upload to the **PyPI** test:

```
twine upload --repository-url=https://test.pypi.org/legacy/ dist/*
```

The last step is to upload the file to the test version of **PyPI**.

To run this step, you need an account in Test **PyPI**. Go to https://test.pypi.org/account/register/ to create one.

Once created, you can run the following command to upload the package to the web:

```
$ twine upload --repository-url=https://test.pypi.org/legacy/ dist/*
Uploading distributions to https://test.pypi.org/legacy/
Enter your username: mariocj89
Enter your password:
Uploading john_doe_package-1.0.0.tar.gz
100%|||||||||||||||||||||||||||||||||||||||||||||||||||||||||||||
```

Figure 8.6: Uploading with the twine output

This will prompt you for the user and password that you used to create your account. Once this is uploaded, you can go to https://packt.live/2qj1o7N, click on your **project**, and you should be able to see the following on the **PyPI** web:

Figure 8.7: Sample uploaded package website

You just published your first package. In this exercise, you learned how to create a Python package, package it, and upload it to **PyPI**.

Adding More Information to Your Package

So, you have seen how to create a really simple package. When you create a package, you should also include a **README** file that can be used to generate a description of the project and is part of the source distribution. This file gets packaged by default.

Consider exploring the different attributes that can be used with **setuptools.setup**. By having a look through documentation, you can find a lot of useful metadata that might be appropriate for your package.

Additionally, to facilitate testing, many people consider it to be good practice to place all the source code of your package within an **src** directory. This is done to prevent the Python interpreter from automatically finding your package, as it is part of the current working directory, as Python adds the current working directory to the Python path. If your package contains any logic about the data files that are packaged with your code, you should really use the **src** directory, as it will force you to work against the installed version of your package, rather than the source directory tree.

PyPA has recently created a guide on how to package projects, which contains further details than those discussed in this book.

> **Note**
>
> If you need to package multiple applications, consider having a look through https://packaging.python.org/tutorials/packaging-projects/.

Creating Documentation the Easy Way

A critical part of all software that is distributed across the world is documentation. Documentation allows the users of your code to be able to understand calling the different functions that we provide without having to read the code. There are multiple levels of documentation that you are going to explore in this topic. You will see how to write documentation that can be consumed in the console and on the web. In the purpose and size of our project, you should consider how broad our documentation should be and what kind of instructions and information it should contain.

Docstrings

In Python, documentation is part of the language. When you declare a function, you can use docstrings to document its interface and behavior. Docstrings can be created by having a triple-quoted string block just after the function signature. This content is not only available to the reader but also to the user of the API, as it is part of a __doc__ attribute of the function, class, or module. It is the content that will be provided if we call the help function in the object passed. As an example, take a look at the contents of the __doc__ attribute of the print function:

```
print(print.__doc__)
```

```
print(value, ..., sep=' ', end='\n', file=sys.stdout, flush=False)

Prints the values to a stream, or to sys.stdout by default.
Optional keyword arguments:
file:  a file-like object (stream); defaults to the current sys.stdout.
sep:   string inserted between values, default a space.
end:   string appended after the last value, default a newline.
flush: whether to forcibly flush the stream.
```

Figure 8.8: Print documentation

It is the same content as calling **help(print)**. You can create your own function with a __doc__ attribute, as follows:

```
>>>def example():
    """Prints the example text"""
    print("Example")
>>>example.__doc__
'Prints the example text'
```

You can now use **help** in your function, by executing the "help(example)" which will result in the following text:

```
Help on function example in module __main__:

example()
    Prints the example text
```

Figure 8.9: The Help content in the example module

Docstrings usually contain a title with a short description of the function and a body with further information about what it does in detail. Additionally, you can also document all the parameters the function takes, including its types, the return type, and whether it raises any exceptions. This is all really useful information for your users and even for ourselves when you have to use the code at a later time.

Using Sphinx

Using docstrings to document APIs is useful, but quite often you need something more. You want to generate a website with guides and other information about your library. In Python, the most common way to do this is via **Sphinx**. Sphinx allows you to generate documentation in multiple formats, such as **PDF**, **epub**, or **html**, easily from **RST** with some markup. Sphinx also comes with multiple plugins, and some of them are useful for Python, such as generating API documentation from docstrings or allowing you to view code behind the API implementation.

Once installed via **pip**, it comes with two main CLI scripts, which the user interacts with: **sphinx-build and sphinx-quickstart**. The first is used to build the documentation on an existing project with Sphinx configuration, while the second can be used to quickly bootstrap a project.

When you bootstrap a project, Sphinx will generate multiple files for you, and the most important ones are as follows:

- **Conf.py**: This contains all the user configuration for generating the documentation. This is the most common place to look for configuration parameters when you want to customize something from the Sphinx output.

- **Makefile**: An easy-to-use **makefile** that can be used to generate the documentation with a simple "make html." There are other targets that can be useful, such as the one to run **doctests**.

- **Index.rst**: The main entry point for our documentation.

Usually, most projects create a folder named **docs** within their source tree root to contain everything related to the documentation and Sphinx. This folder can then refer to the source code by either installing it or by adding it to the path in their configuration file.

If you are not familiar with **RST**, it is best to have a quick look through https://www.sphinx-doc.org/en/master/usage/restructuredtext/basics.html. It has a short explanation of the different special syntaxes you can find in **RST** that will be translated into special HTML tags such as **links**, **anchors**, **tables**, **images**, and others.

On top of this, Sphinx is easily extendible via plugins. Some of them are part of the default distribution when you install sphinx. Plugins allow you to extend the functionality to do things such as automatically create documentation for your modules, classes, and functions by just writing a single directive.

Finally, there are multiple themes available when you generate documentation with Sphinx—these are all configurable in conf.py. Quite often, you can find more Sphinx themes available on **PyPI**, which can be just installed easily via **pip**.

Exercise 115: Documenting a Divisible Code File

In this exercise, you are going to document the module that you created in the testing topic, **divisible.py**, from *Exercise 113, Checking Sample Code with Unit Testing* using **sphinx**:

1. Create a folder structure.

    First, create an empty folder with just the **divisible.py** module and another empty folder named **docs**. The **divisible.py** module should contain the following code:

    ```
    def is_divisible(x, y):
        if x % y == 0:
            return True
        else:
            return False
    ```

2. Run the **sphinx** quick-start tool:

    Make sure you have Sphinx installed (otherwise, run **python3.7 -m pip install sphinx -user**) and run **sphinx-quickstart** within the **docs** folder. You can leave all the functions with the default value by pressing return when prompted, except for the following:

    Project name: **divisible**.

Author name: Write your name here.

Project Release: 1.0.0.

Autodoc: y.

Intersphinx: y.

With these options, you are ready to start a project that can be easily documented and generate HTML output with Sphinx. Additionally, you have enabled two of the most common plugins: **autodoc**, which we will use to generate documentation out of the code; and **intersphinx**, which allows you to reference other sphinx projects, such as the Python standard library.

3. Build the documentation for the first time.

    Building the documentation is easy—just run make html within the docs directory to generate the HTML output of your documentation. You can now open the **index. html** file in your browser within the **docs/build/html** folder.

    You should get the following output:

Figure 8.10: The first documentation output with Sphinx

It's not a lot of content, but it's quite impressive for the amount of code you have written.

4. Configure Sphinx to find our code.

    The next step is to generate and include documentation from your Python source code. The first thing that you will have to do to be able to do that is to edit the **conf.py** file within the docs folder and uncomment these three lines:

```
# import os
# import sys
# sys.path.insert(0, os.path.abspath('.'))
```

Once uncommented, the last line should be changed to this since you have our divisible source code one level above our code:

```
sys.path.insert(0, os.path.abspath('..'))
```

A better alternative to this would be to make sure your package is installed when running Sphinx—this is a more extended method, but a simpler solution.

Last but not least, you are going to use another plugin, called **Napoleon**. This allows you to format your functions by using the **Napoleon** syntax. To do so, add the following line in the list of extensions within the **conf.py** file, within the extensions variable, after 'sphinx.ext.autodoc':

```
'sphinx.ext.napoleon',
```

You can read https://www.sphinx-doc.org/en/master/usage/extensions/napoleon.html for more information about the **Napoleon** syntax for Sphinx.

5. Generate documentation from the source code.

Adding the documentation from a module to Sphinx is really simple—you can just add the following two lines to your **index.rst**:

```
automodule:: divisible
   :members:
```

Once those two lines are added, run **make html** again and check whether an error is generated. If no error appears, then you are all set. You have configured Sphinx to bring the documentation from docstrings to your **rst** file.

6. Add docstrings.

To give Sphinx something to work with, add a docstring at the module level and one docstring for the function that you defined.

Our **divisible.py** file should now look like the following:

```
"""Functions to work with divisibles"""
def is_divisible(x, y):
    """Checks if a number is divisible by another
    Arguments:
        x (int): Divisor of the operation.
        y (int): Dividend of the operation.
    Returns:
        True if x can be divided by y without reminder,
        False otherwise.
```

```
    Raises:
        :obj:'ZeroDivisionError' if y is 0.
    """

    if x % y == 0:
        return True
    else:
        return False
```

You are using the **napoleon** style syntax to define the different arguments that our function takes, what it can return, and the exception it raises.

Note that you we use a special syntax to reference the exception that it raises. This will generate a link to the definition of the object.

If you run **make html** again, you should get the following output:

Figure 8.11: HTML documentation output with docstring

You can now distribute our documentation to our users. Note that it will always be up to date as you are generating it from the source code.

More Complex Documentation

In the previous exercise, you examined simple documentation for a really small module. Most libraries also include tutorials and guides along with their API documentation. Check **Django**, **flask**, or **CPython** as examples, as they are all generated with Sphinx.

Note that if you intend our library to be used extensively and successfully, then documentation will be a key part of it. When you want to document how an API behaves, you should use just the plain API documentation that you generated before. However, there is also room to create small guides for specific features or tutorials to walk users through the most common steps to start a project.

Additionally, there are tools such as Read the Docs, which greatly simplifies the generation and hosting of documentation. You can take the project that we just generated and connect it to **readthedocs** through their UI to have our documentation hosted on the web and automatically regenerated every time you update the master branch of our project.

> **Note**
>
> You can go to https://readthedocs.org/ to create an account and set up your repositories in GitHub to automatically generate documentation.

Source Management

When you work with code, you need a way in which to keep a picture of how your code evolves and how changes are being applied to different files. For instance, say that, by mistake, you make changes to your code that suddenly breaks it, or you start to make changes and just want to go back to the previous version. Many people start with just copying their source code into different folders and naming them with a timestamp based on checkpoints they make on different phases of the project. This is the most rudimentary approach to version control.

Version control is the system by which you keep control of code as it evolves over time. Developers have been suffering for long enough to create a piece of software that can do this job efficiently, and one of the most popular tools to do this is a Git. **Git** is a **Distributed Version Control System** that allows developers to manage their code locally as it evolves, look at the history, and easily collaborate with other developers. Git is used to manage some of the biggest projects around the world, such as the Windows kernel, CPython, Linux, or Git itself; however, at the same time, git is really useful and versatile for small projects as well.

Repository

A repository is an isolated workspace where you can work with your changes and have git record them and track the history of them. One repository can contain as many files and folders as you want, with all of them tracked by git.

There are two ways to create a repository: you can either clone an existing repository by using `git clone <url of the repository>`, which will bring a local copy of a repository into your current path, or you can create a repository from an existing folder with `git init`, which will just mark the folder as a repository by creating the necessary files.

Once you have a repository locally created, you can start to work with our version control system by issuing different commands to indicate whether you want to add changes, check previous versions, or more.

Commit

A `commit` object is the history of our repository. Each repository has many commits: one for every time we use `git commit`. Each of those commits will contain the commit title, the person who added the commit to the repository, the author of the changes, the dates when the commit and the changes were made, an ID that is represented by a hash, and the hash of the parent commit. With this, you can create a tree of all the commits within the repository, which allows us to see the history of our source code. You can see the content of any commit by running `git show <commit sha>`.

When you run `git commit`, we create a commit from all the changes that you have in the staging area. An editor will open, which includes some meta-information such as the title and the commit body.

Figure 8.12: Git commands showing how they interact with the repository and the Staging area

> **Note**
>
> A good guide on how to write good commit messages can be found here: https://packt.live/33zARRV. You suggest that you take a look after finishing this book.

Staging Area

When you are working locally, making changes to our files and source code, git will report that those changes happened, and they are not saved. By running **git status**, you can see what files were modified. If you decide that we want to save those changes in the staging area in preparation for a commit, you can add them with the **git add <path>** command. It can be used in files or folders to add all the files within that folder. Once they are added to the staging area, the next **git commit** command will save the changes in the repository through a commit object.

Sometimes, you don't want to add all the contents of a file to the staging area, just part of them. For this use case, both **git commit** and **git add** have an option to guide you through the different changes in the file and allow you to select which ones you want to add. This is through the **-p** option, which will ask you for each of the changed chunks within your code, which ones you do want to add.

Undoing Local Changes

When you are working on a file, you can run **git diff** to see all the changes that have been made locally but are not yet part of the staging area or a commit. Sometimes, you realize we want to undo our changes and come back to the version you have saved in the staging area or in the last commit. You can do this by checking out the file by running **git checkout <path>**. This applies to both files and folders.

If instead, you want to revert our repository back to a previous commit in history, you can do this by running **git reset <commit sha>**.

History

As you mentioned before, the repository has a commit history. This includes all the commits that have been performed before. You can see them by running **git log**, which will present you with the title, body, and some other information. The most important part of each of these entries is the **sha** of the commit, which uniquely represents each of the commits.

Ignoring Files

When you work with our source code, we may find that, by running our program or any other action, you have files in your repository that you don't want git to track. In that scenario, you can use a special file that has to be placed at the top of the directory and named **.gitignore**, which can list all the files in glob patterns that you don't want git to track. This is especially handy for adding things such as IDE-generated files, compiled Python files, and more.

Exercise 116: Making a Change in CPython Using git

In this exercise, you are going to change a file in the local **CPython** repository by cloning the repository and working on our local copy. For the sake of the exercise, you will just add our name to the list of authors of the project.

> **Note**
>
> The repository will be on your local PC, so no one will see the changes – don't worry.

You begin by first installing **git**. That is the first step to installing the tool itself. You can install it on Windows via https://git-scm.com/download/win, or in Unix by following the instructions here: https://git-scm.com/book/en/v2/Getting-Started-Installing-Git.

If you are running on Windows, follow this exercise by using the **git-shell** for Windows. On Unix, just use your preferred Terminal:

1. Now, begin by cloning the **cpython** repository.

    As you mentioned before, you can create a repository by simply cloning it. You can clone the **cpython** source code by running the following:

    ```
    git clone https://github.com/python/cpython.git
    ```

    This will create a folder named **cpython** in the current workspace. Don't worry; it is normal for it to take a few minutes, as CPython has a lot of code and long history:

    ```
    $ git clone https://github.com/python/cpython.git
    Cloning into 'cpython'...
    remote: Enumerating objects: 1, done.
    remote: Counting objects: 100% (1/1), done.
    remote: Total 745673 (delta 0), reused 0 (delta 0), pack-reused 745672
    Receiving objects: 100% (745673/745673), 277.17 MiB | 2.38 MiB/s, done.
    Resolving deltas: 100% (599013/599013), done.
    Checking connectivity... done.
    Checking out files: 100% (4134/4134), done.
    ```

    Figure 8.13: The git clone output of CPython

2. Edit the **Misc/ACKS** file and confirm the changes.

You can now add your name to the **Misc/ACKS** file. To do this, just open the file in that path and add your name in alphabetical and your surname.

Check the changes by running **git status**. This command will show you whether there are any changed files:

```
$ git status
On branch master
Your branch is up-to-date with 'origin/master'.
Changes not staged for commit:
  (use "git add <file>..." to update what will be committed)
  (use "git checkout -- <file>..." to discard changes in working directory)

        modified:   Misc/ACKS

no changes added to commit (use "git add" and/or "git commit -a")
```

Figure 8.14: The git status output

Note how it gives you instructions on how to proceed if you want to add the changes to the staging area in preparation for a commit or to reset them. Let's check the content of the changes by running **git diff**:

```
$ git diff
diff --git a/Misc/ACKS b/Misc/ACKS
index ec5b017..f38f40b 100644
--- a/Misc/ACKS
+++ b/Misc/ACKS
@@ -326,6 +326,7 @@ David M. Cooke
 Jason R. Coombs
 Garrett Cooper
 Greg Copeland
+Mario Corchero
 Ian Cordasco
 Aldo Cortesi
 Mircea Cosbuc
```

Figure 8.15: The git diff output

This provides you with a nice output that indicates the changes in the lines. Green with a plus sign means that a line was added, while red with a minus sign means a line was removed.

3. Now `commit` the changes.

Now that you are happy with the changes that you have made let's add those to the staging area by running **git add Misc/ACKS**, which will move the file into the staging area, allowing us to then commit them at any time by running **git commit**. When you run **git commit**, an editor will open to create the commit. Add a title and body (separated by an empty line):

```
Add Mario Corchero to Misc/ACKS file

Adds my name as I am experimenting how to user git
# Please enter the commit message for your changes. Lines starting
# with '#' will be ignored, and an empty message aborts the commit.
# On branch master
# Your branch is up-to-date with 'origin/master'.
#
# Changes to be committed:
#       modified:   Misc/ACKS
#
```

Figure 8.16: A commit message output example

When you close the editor and save, the commit should be created:

```
$ git commit
[master 6bdb37c] Add Mario Corchero to Misc/ACKS file
 1 file changed, 1 insertion(+)
```

Figure 8.17: The git commit output

You have created your first commit. You can check the contents of it by running **git show**:

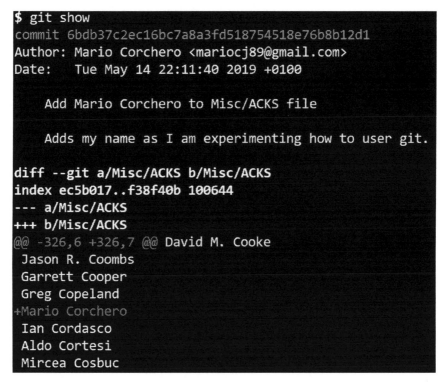

```
$ git show
commit 6bdb37c2ec16bc7a8a3fd518754518e76b8b12d1
Author: Mario Corchero <mariocj89@gmail.com>
Date:   Tue May 14 22:11:40 2019 +0100

    Add Mario Corchero to Misc/ACKS file

    Adds my name as I am experimenting how to user git.

diff --git a/Misc/ACKS b/Misc/ACKS
index ec5b017..f38f40b 100644
--- a/Misc/ACKS
+++ b/Misc/ACKS
@@ -326,6 +326,7 @@ David M. Cooke
 Jason R. Coombs
 Garrett Cooper
 Greg Copeland
+Mario Corchero
 Ian Cordasco
 Aldo Cortesi
 Mircea Cosbuc
```

Figure 8.18: Git showing the output

Note

This was an introduction to Git. If you plan to use Git daily, check out the Git pro book. This is a free book that will guide you on how to use git: https://packt.live/35EoBS5

Summary

In this chapter, you have seen that software development is more than just writing code in Python. When you want to elevate your code further than a simple script on our computer, you need to know how to troubleshoot it, distribute it, document it, and test it. The Python ecosystem provides us with tools to do all of these things. You have learned how to troubleshoot code using **pdb** and steps on how to identify and narrow down a problem by inspecting logs and the input. You have also learned how to write automated tests and the importance of them.

You saw how you can package our code to be distributed across the internet, how we can also document those packages to make them easier to use and consume by your final users, and finally, how to use git to manage changes as your code evolves.

In the next chapter, you we will touch on some more advanced topics; some of them build on top of what you just learned. You will explore things such as how to take the code we just wrote and have it processed from package to production, how to use git to collaborate with other members of the team through GitHub, and how to profile your code when you suspect that it is not as fast as it could be.

Practical Python – Advanced Topics

Overview

By the end of this chapter, you will be able to, write Python collaboratively as a member of a team; use conda to document and set up the dependencies for your Python programs; use Docker to create reproducible Python environments to run your code; write programs that take advantage of multiple cores in modern computers; write scripts that can be configured from the command line and explain the performance characteristics of your Python programs, and use tools to make your programs faster.

Introduction

In this chapter, you'll continue the move which started in *Chapter 8, Software Development*, away from your individual focus on learning the syntax of the Python language toward becoming a contributing member of a Python development team. Large projects solving complex problems need expertise from multiple contributors, so it's very common to work on code with one or more colleagues as a developer community. Having already seen how to use **git** version control in *Chapter 8, Software Development*, you'll apply that knowledge in this chapter to working with teams. You'll be using GitHub, branches, and **pull** requests in order to keep your project in sync.

Moving on, in the IT world, when you deliver a certain project, at some point, you'll want to deliver your code to your customers or stakeholders. An important part of the deployment process is making sure that the customer's system has the libraries and modules that your software needs, and also the same versions that you were developing against. For this, you'll learn how to use **conda** to create baseline Python environments with particular libraries present, and how to replicate those environments on another system.

Next, you will look at Docker, which is a popular way to deploy software to internet servers and cloud infrastructure. You'll learn how to create a container that includes your **conda** environment and your Python software, and how to run the containerized software within Docker.

Finally, you'll learn some useful techniques for developing real-world Python software. These include learning how to take advantage of parallel programming, how to parse command-line arguments, and how to profile your Python to discover and fix performance problems.

Developing Collaboratively

In *Chapter 8, Software Development*, you used **git** to keep track of the changes you made to your Python project. At its heart, membership of a programming team involves multiple people sharing their changes through **git** and ensuring that you are incorporating everybody else's changes when doing your own work.

There are many ways for people to work together using **git**. The developers of the Linux kernel each maintain their own repository and share potential changes over email, which they each choose whether to incorporate or not. Large companies, including Facebook and Google, use *trunk-based development*, in which all changes must be made on the main branch, usually called the "*master*."

A common workflow popularized by support in the GitHub user interface is the **pull** request.

In the **pull** request workflow, you maintain your repository as a **fork** in GitHub of the canonical version from which software releases are made, often referred to as **upstream** or **origin**. You make a small collection of related changes, each representing progress toward a single bug fix or new feature, in a named branch on your own repository, which you push to your hosted repository with **git push**. When you are ready, you submit a **pull** request to the upstream repository. The team reviews these changes together in the **pull** request, and you add any further work needed to the branch. When the team is happy with the **pull** request, a supervisor or another developer merges it upstream, and the changes are "pulled" into the canonical version of the software.

The advantage of the **pull** request workflow is that it's made easy by the user interface in applications such as Bitbucket, GitHub, and GitLab. The disadvantage comes from keeping those branches around while the **pull** request is being created and is under review. It's easy to fall behind as other work goes into the upstream repository, leaving your branch out of date and introducing the possibility that your change will conflict with some other changes, and those conflicts will need a resolution.

To deal with fresh changes and conflicts as they arise, rather than as a huge headache when it comes time to merge the **pull** request, you use **git** to fetch changes from the upstream repository, and either merge them into your branch or rebase your branch on the up-to-date upstream revision. Merging combines the history of commits on two branches and rebasing reapplies commits such that they start at the tip of the branch you are rebasing against. Your team should decide which of these approaches they prefer.

Exercise 117: Writing Python on GitHub as a Team

In this exercise, you will learn how to host code on GitHub, make a **pull** request, and then approve changes to the code. To make this exercise more effective, you can collaborate with a friend.

1. If you don't have an account already, create one on github.com.

2. Log into https://github.com/ and create a new repository by clicking on **New**:

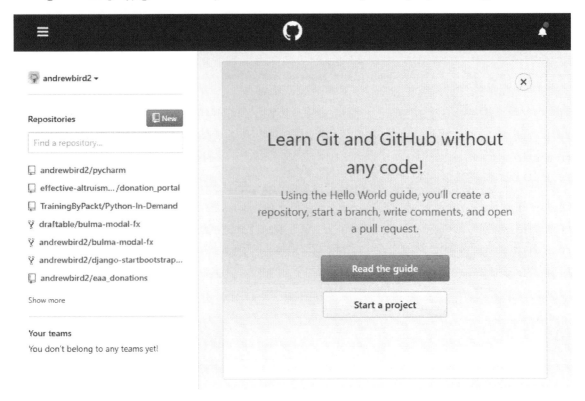

Figure 9.1: The GitHub home page

3. Give the repository an appropriate name, such as **python-demo**, and click on **Create**.

4. Now click on **Clone or download,** and you will be able to see the HTTPS URL; however, note that we will need the SSH URL. Hence, you will see **Use SSH** on the same tab, which you need to click on:

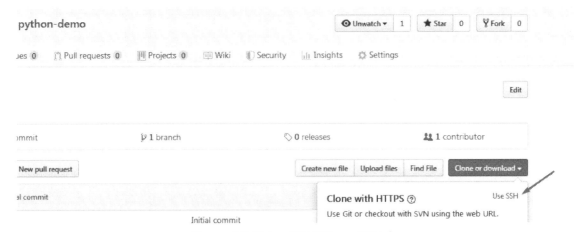

Figure 9.2: Using SSH URL on GitHub

5. Now copy the **SSH URL** on GitHub. Then, using your local Command Prompt, such as **CMD** in Windows, clone the repository:

```
git clone git@github.com:andrewbird2/python-demo.git
```

> **Note**
>
> Your command will look slightly different from the preceding command because of the different username. You need to add your SSH URL after **git clone**. Note that you may also need to add an SSH key to your GitHub account for authentication. If so, follow the instructions here to add the SSH key: https://packt.live/2qjhtKH.

6. In your new **python-demo** directory, create a Python file. It doesn't matter what it contains; for instance, create a simple one-line **test.py** file, as shown in the following code snippet:

```
echo "x = 5" >> test.py
```

7. Let's **commit** our changes:

```
git add .
git commit -m "Initial"
git push origin master
```

You should get the following output:

```
Enumerating objects: 3, done.
Counting objects: 100% (3/3), done.
Writing objects: 100% (3/3), 223 bytes | 111.00 KiB/s, done.
Total 3 (delta 0), reused 0 (delta 0)
To github.com:andrewbird2/python-demo.git
 * [new branch]      master -> master
```

Figure 9.3: Pushing our initial commit

At this point, if you are working with someone else, clone their repository, and perform the following steps on their code base to experience what collaboration feels like. If working alone, just proceed with your own repository.

8. Create a new branch called **dev**:

```
git checkout -b dev
```

You should get the following output:

```
(base) C:\Users\andrew.bird\python-demo>git checkout -b dev
Switched to a new branch 'dev'
```

Figure 9.4: Creating a dev branch

9. Create a new file called **hello_world.py**. This can be done in a text editor, or with the following simple command:

```
echo "print("Hello World!")" >> hello_world.py
```

10. **commit** the new file to the **dev** branch and **push** it to the created **python-demo** repository:

```
git add .
git commit -m "Adding hello_world"
git push --set-upstream origin dev
```

11. Go to the project repository in your web browser and click on **Compare & pull request**:

Figure 9.5: The home page of the repository on GitHub

12. Here, you can see a list of changes made on the **dev** branch that you created. You can also provide an explanation that someone else might read when reviewing your code before deciding whether or not it should be committed to the master branch:

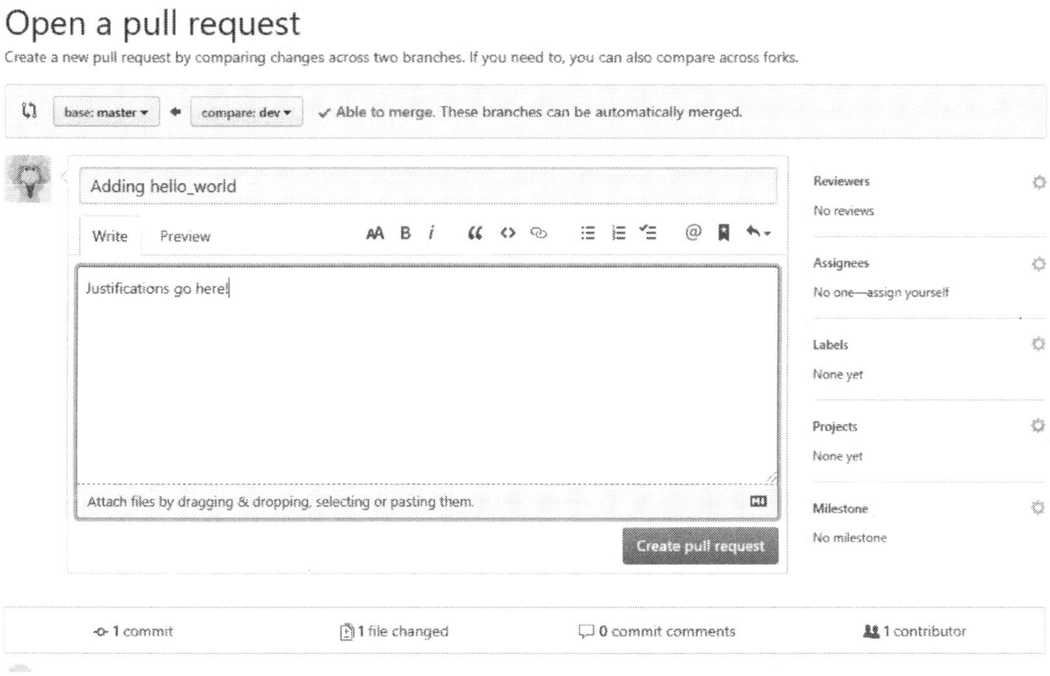

Figure 9.6: Adding justifications to the code on GitHub

13. Click on **Create pull request** to add the justifications on GitHub.

14. Now, if working with a partner, you should switch back to the original repository that you own and view their **pull** request. You could comment on it if you have any concerns regarding the **commit** request; otherwise, you can simply click on **Merge pull request**:

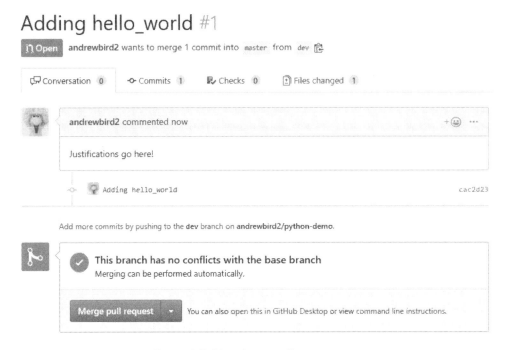

Figure 9.7: Merging a pull request

You now understand how people can work together on the same repository on GitHub, reviewing and discussing each other's code before merging into the master branch. This comes in very handy as a developer when you want to have a single repository to store your code or help a fellow developer located somewhere else in the world. In the next section, you will look at dependency management.

Dependency Management

In the IT world, most complex programs depend on libraries beyond the Python standard library. You may use **numpy** or **pandas** to deal with multidimensional data or **matplotlib** to visualize data in graphs (this will be covered in *Chapter* 10, *Data Analytics with pandas and NumPy*), or any number of other libraries available to Python developers.

Just like your own software, the libraries developed by other teams frequently change as bugs are fixed, features are added, and old code is removed or refactored, which is the process of restructuring existing code. That means it's important that your team uses the same version of a library so that it works in the same way for all of them.

Additionally, you want your customers or the servers where you deploy your software to use the same versions of the same libraries as well, so that everything works the same way on their computers, too.

There are multiple tools for solving this problem. These include **pip**, **easy_install**, **brew**, and **conda**, to name a few. You are already familiar with **pip**, and in some contexts, it suffices to use this package manager to keep track of dependencies.

For instance, try running **pip freeze** in Command Prompt. You should get the following output:

```
(base) C:\Users\andrew.bird\Python-In-Demand>pip freeze
alabaster==0.7.12
anaconda-client==1.7.2
anaconda-navigator==1.9.6
anaconda-project==0.8.2
asn1crypto==0.24.0
astroid==2.1.0
astropy==3.1
atomicwrites==1.2.1
attrs==18.2.0
Babel==2.6.0
backcall==0.1.0
backports.os==0.1.1
```

Figure 9.8: Output of pip freeze (truncated)

This package list could be saved to a **text** file with the following command: **pip freeze > requirements.txt**. This will create a file called **requirements.txt**, which will be similar to *Figure 9.9*:

```
requirements.txt - Notepad
File  Edit  Format  View  Help
alabaster==0.7.12
anaconda-client==1.7.2
anaconda-navigator==1.9.6
anaconda-project==0.8.2
asn1crypto==0.24.0
astroid==2.1.0
astropy==3.1
atomicwrites==1.2.1
attrs==18.2.0
Babel==2.6.0
backcall==0.1.0
backports.os==0.1.1
```

Figure 9.9: Viewing requirements.txt in Notepad (truncated)

Now that you have the information about the packages, you can choose to install these packages on another machine or environment with the following command: `pip install -r requirements.txt`.

In this chapter, you will focus on **conda**, which provides a complete solution for dependency management. **conda** is particularly popular among data scientists and machine learning programmers. For instance, some dependencies in machine learning environments can't be managed by **pip**, as they might not be a simple Python package. **conda** takes care of these for us.

Virtual Environments

In this chapter, you will use **conda** to create "virtual environments." When you code in Python, you have certain versions of certain packages installed. You're also using a specific version of Python itself, which is 3.7. However, what if you are working on two projects, with each requiring different versions of the packages? You would need to reinstall all of the packages when switching between these projects, which would be a hassle. Virtual environments address this problem. A virtual environment contains a set of particular packages at specific versions. By switching between virtual environments, you can switch between different packages and versions instantly. Typically, you will have a different virtual environment for each major project you are working on.

Exercise 118: Creating and Setting Up a conda Virtual Environment to Install numpy and pandas

In this exercise, you'll create a virtual environment with **conda** and execute some simple code to import basic libraries. This exercise will be performed in the **conda** environment.

> **Note**
>
> If you have not already installed Anaconda, refer to the *Preface* section for installation instructions.

Now, with **conda** installed on your system, you can create a new **conda** environment and include packages in it; for example, **numpy**.

1. Now you should run the following command using the **Anaconda Prompt** program, which is now installed on your computer:

```
conda create -n example_env numpy
```

You should get the following output:

```
(base) C:\Users\andrew.bird>conda create -n example_env numpy
Solving environment: done


==> WARNING: A newer version of conda exists. <==
  current version: 4.5.12
  latest version: 4.7.10

Please update conda by running

    $ conda update -n base -c defaults conda



## Package Plan ##

  environment location: C:\Users\andrew.bird\AppData\Local\conda\conda\envs\example_env

  added / updated specs:
    - numpy


The following packages will be downloaded:
```

Figure 9.10: Creating a new conda environment (truncated)

> **Note**
>
> If you are asked to enter **y/n** by the prompt, you need to enter **y** to proceed
> further.

2. Activate the **conda** environment:

```
conda activate example_env
```

You can add other packages to the environment with **conda install**.

3. Now, add **pandas** to the **example_env** environment:

```
conda install pandas
```

You should get the following output:

```
(example_env) C:\Users\andrew.bird>conda install pandas
Solving environment: done


==> WARNING: A newer version of conda exists. <==
  current version: 4.5.12
  latest version: 4.7.10

Please update conda by running

    $ conda update -n base -c defaults conda



## Package Plan ##

  environment location: C:\Users\andrew.bird\AppData\Local\conda\conda\envs\example_env

  added / updated specs:
    - pandas

The following packages will be downloaded:
```

Figure 9.11: The pandas output

> **Note**
>
> The preceding output is truncated.

4. Next, open a Python terminal within the virtual environment by typing in **python** and then verify that you can import **pandas** as **numpy** as expected:

```
python
import pandas as pd
import numpy as np
```

5. Now, exit the Python terminal in the virtual environment using the **exit()** method:

```
exit()
```

6. Finally, deactivate the virtual environment:

```
conda deactivate
```

> **Note**
>
> You may have noticed the **$** sign in the prompts. While working on the prompt, you need to ignore the **$** sign. The **$** sign is just to mention that the command will be executed on the terminal.

In this exercise, you created your first virtual environment using **conda**, installed packages such as **numpy** and **pandas**, and ran simple Python code to import libraries.

Saving and Sharing Virtual Environments

Now, suppose you have built an application that relies on various Python packages. You now decide that you want to run the application on a server, so you want a way of setting up the same virtual environment on the server as you have running on your local machine. As you previously encountered with `pip freeze`, the metadata defining a **conda** environment can be easily exported to a file that can be used to recreate an identical environment on another computer.

Exercise 119: Sharing Environments between a conda Server and Your Local System

In this exercise, you will export the metadata of our **example_env** conda environment, which you created in *Exercise 118, Creating and Setting Up a conda Virtual Environment to Install numpy and pandas*, to a **text** file and learn how to recreate the same environment using this file.

This exercise will be performed on the **conda** environment command line:

1. Activate your example environment, for **example_env**:

```
conda activate example_env
```

2. Now, **export** the environment to a text file:

```
conda env export > example_env.yml
```

The **env export** command produces the text metadata (which is mainly just a list of Python package versions), and the **> example_env.yml** part of the command stores this text in a file. Note that the **.yml** extension is a special easy-to-read file format that is usually used to store configuration information.

3. Now **deactivate** that environment and remove it from **conda**:

```
conda deactivate
conda env remove --name example_env
```

4. You no longer have an **example_env** environment, but you can recreate it by importing the **example_env.yml** file you created earlier in the exercise:

```
conda env create -f example_env.yml
```

You have now learned how to save your environment and create an environment using the saved file. This approach could be used when transferring your environment between your personal computers when collaborating with another developer, or even when deploying code to a server.

Deploying Code into Production

You have all of the pieces now to get your code onto another computer and get it running. You can use **PIP** (covered in *Chapter 8, Software Development*) to create a package, and **conda** to create a portable definition of the environment needed for your code to run. These tools still give users a few steps to follow to get up and running, and each step adds effort and complexity that may put them off.

A common tool for one-command setup and installation of software is **Docker**. Docker is based on Linux container technologies. However, because the Linux kernel is open source, developers have been able to make it so that Docker containers can run on both Windows and macOS. Programmers create Docker images, which are Linux filesystems containing all of the code, tools, and configuration files necessary to run their applications. Users download these images and use Docker to execute them or deploy the images into networks using **docker-compose**, **Docker Swarm**, **Kubernetes**, or similar tools.

You prepare your program for Docker by creating a **Dockerfile** file that tells Docker what goes into your image. In the case of a Python application, that's Python and your Python code.

Firstly, you need to install Docker.

> **Note**
>
> The installation steps for Docker are mentioned in the Preface.

Note that after installing, you may need to restart your computer.

To test Docker, run the **hello-world** application to confirm that Docker is correctly configured. **hello-world** is a simple Docker application that comes as part of the standard library of Docker apps:

```
docker run hello-world
```

You should get the following output:

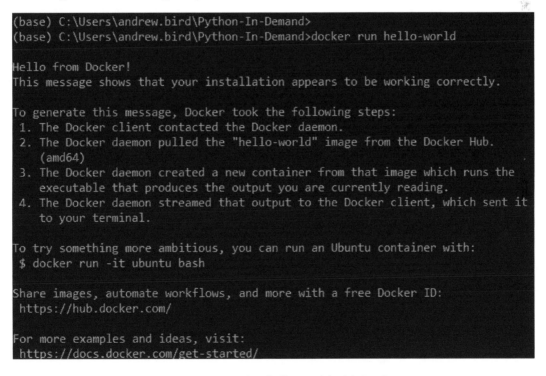

Figure 9.12: Running hello-world with Docker

You have successfully installed and run Docker on your local machine.

Exercise 120: Dockerizing Your Fizzbuzz Tool

In this exercise, you'll use Docker to create an executable version of a simple Python script that creates a sequence of numbers. However, instead of printing **3** or multiples of **3**, it will print **Fizz**, and multiples of **5** will print **Buzz**.

This exercise will be performed in the **docker** environment:

1. Create a new directory called **my_docker_app** and **cd** into this directory, as shown in the following code snippet:

    ```
    mkdir my_docker_app
    cd my_docker_app
    ```

2. Within this directory, create an empty file called **Dockerfile**. You can create this with Jupyter Notebook, or your favorite text editor. Ensure this file does not have any extensions, such as **.txt**.

3. Now, add the first line to your **Dockerfile**:

    ```
    FROM python:3
    ```

    This line tells it to use a system that has Python 3 installed. Specifically, this is going to use a Python image built on top of a minimal Linux distribution called Alpine. More details about this image can be found at https://packt.live/32oNn6E.

4. Next, create a **fizzbuzz.py** file in the **my_docker_app** directory with the following code:

    ```python
    for num in range(1,101):
        string = ""
        if num % 3 == 0:
            string = string + "Fizz"
        if num % 5 == 0:
            string = string + "Buzz"
        if num % 5 != 0 and num % 3 != 0:
            string = string + str(num)
        print(string)
    ```

5. Now **ADD** a second line to your **Dockerfile** file. This line tells Docker to include the **fizzbuzz.py** file in the application:

    ```
    ADD fizzbuzz.py /
    ```

6. Finally, add the command that Docker must run:

    ```
    CMD [ "python", "./fizzbuzz.py" ]
    ```

7. Your **Dockerfile** file should look like this:

```
FROM python:3

ADD fizzbuzz.py /

CMD [ "python", "./fizzbuzz.py" ]
```

> **Note**
>
> This Docker output file will be saved locally on your system. You shouldn't try to access such files directly.

8. Now build your **Docker** image. You will give it the name **fizzbuzz_app**:

```
$ docker build -t fizzbuzz_app .
```

This command created an **image** file on your system that contains all of the information required to execute your code in a simple Linux environment.

9. Now you can run your program inside Docker:

```
docker run fizzbuzz_app
```

You should get the following output:

```
(base) C:\Users\andrew.bird\Python-In-Demand\Lesson09\fizzbuzz_docker>docker run testapp
1
2
Fizz
4
Buzz
Fizz
7
8
Fizz
Buzz
```

Figure 9.13: Running your program inside Docker (truncated)

You can see the full list of Docker images available on your system by running **docker images**. This list should include your new **fizzbuzz_app** application.

Finally, suppose your **fizzbuzz** file imported a third-party library as part of the code. For example, perhaps it used the **pandas** library (it shouldn't need to). In this case, our code would break, because the installation of Python within the Docker image does not contain the pandas package.

10. To fix this, you can simply add a **pip install pandas** line to our **Dockerfile** file. Our updated **Dockerfile** file will look like this:

```
FROM python:3

ADD fizzbuzz.py /

RUN pip install pandas

CMD [ "python", "./fizzbuzz.py" ]
```

In this exercise, you installed and deployed your first application with Docker. In the next section, you will look at multiprocessing.

Multiprocessing

It's common to need to execute more than one thing in parallel in a modern software system. Machine learning programs and scientific simulations benefit from using the multiple cores available in a modern processor, dividing their work up between concurrent threads operating on the parallel hardware. Graphical user interfaces and network servers do their work "in the background," leaving a thread available to respond to user events or new requests.

As a simple example, suppose your program had to execute three steps: A, B, and C. These steps are not dependent on each other, meaning they can be completed in any order. Usually, you would simply execute them in order, as follows:

Figure 9.14: Processing with a single thread

However, what if you could do all of these steps at the same time, rather than waiting for one to complete before moving onto the next? Our workflow would look like this:

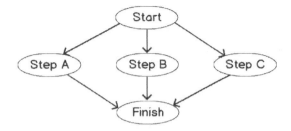

Figure 9.15: Multithreaded processing

This has the potential to be a lot faster if you have the infrastructure to execute these steps at the same time. That is, each step will need to be executed by a different thread.

Python itself uses multiple threads to do some work internally, which puts some limits on the ways in which a Python program can do multiprocessing. The three safest ways to work are as follows:

- Find a library that solves your problem and handles multiprocessing for you (which has been carefully tested).

- Launch a new Python interpreter by running another copy of your script as a completely separate process.

- Create a new thread within the existing interpreter to do some work concurrently.

The first of these is the easiest and the most likely to be a success. The second is fairly simple and imposes the most overhead on your computer as the operating system is now running two independent Python scripts. The third is very complicated, easy to get wrong, and still creates a lot of overhead as Python maintains a Global Interpreter Lock (GIL), which means that only one thread at a time can interpret a Python instruction. A quick rule of thumb to choose between the three approaches is to always pick the first one. If a library doesn't exist to address your needs, then pick the second. If you absolutely need to share memory between the concurrent processes, or if your concurrent work is related to handling I/O, then you can choose the third carefully.

Multiprocessing with execnet

It's possible to launch a new Python interpreter with the standard library's **subprocess** module. However, doing so leaves a lot of work up to you about what code to run and how to share data between the "parent" and "child" Python scripts.

An easier interface is the **execnet** library. **execnet** makes it very easy to launch a new Python interpreter running some given code, including versions such as **Jython** and **IronPython**, which integrate with the Java virtual machine and .NET common language runtime, respectively. It exposes an asynchronous communication channel between the parent and child Python scripts, so the parent can send data that the child works on and get on with its own thing until it's ready to receive the result. If the parent is ready before the child is finished, then the parent waits.

Exercise 121: Working with execnet to Execute a Simple Python Squaring Program

In this exercise, you'll create a **squaring** process that receives **x** over an **execnet** channel and responds with **x**2**. This is much too small a task to warrant multiprocessing, but it does demonstrate how to use the library.

This exercise will be performed on a Jupyter notebook:

1. First, install **execnet** using the **pip** package manager:

```
$ pip install execnet
```

2. Now write the **square** function, which receives numbers on a channel and returns their square:

```
import execnet
def square(channel):
    while not channel.isclosed():
        number = channel.receive()
        number_squared = number**2
        channel.send(number_squared)
```

> **Note**
>
> Due to the way **execnet** works, you must type the following examples into a Jupyter notebook. You cannot type them into the interactive >>> prompt.

The **while not channel.isclosed()** statement ensures that we only proceed with the calculation if there is an open channel between the parent and child Python processes. **number = channel.receive()** takes the input from the parent process that you want to **square**. It is then squared in the **number_squared = number**2** code line. Lastly, you send the squared number back to the parent process with **channel. send(number_squared)**.

3. Now set up a **gateway** channel to a remote Python interpreter running that function:

```
gateway = execnet.makegateway()
channel = gateway.remote_exec(square)
```

A **gateway** channel manages the communication between the parent and child Python processes. The channel is used to actually send and receive data between the processes.

4. Now send some integers from our parent process to the child process, as shown in the following code snippet:

```
for i in range(10):
    channel.send(i)
    i_squared = channel.receive()
    print(f"{i} squared is {i_squared}")
```

You should get the following output:

```
0 squared is 0
1 squared is 1
2 squared is 4
3 squared is 9
4 squared is 16
5 squared is 25
6 squared is 36
7 squared is 49
8 squared is 64
9 squared is 81
```

Figure 9.16: The results passed back from the child Python processes

Here, you loop through 10 integers, send them through the **square** channel, and then receive the result using the **channel.receive()** function.

5. When you are done with the remote Python interpreter, close the **gateway** channel to cause it to quit:

```
gateway.exit()
```

In this exercise, you learned how to use **execnet** to pass instructions between Python processes. In the next section, you will be looking at multiprocessing with the **multiprocessing** package.

Multiprocessing with the Multiprocessing Package

The **multiprocessing** module is built into Python's standard library. Similar to **execnet**, it allows you to launch new Python processes. However, it provides an API that is lower-level than **execnet**. This means that it's harder to use than **execnet**, but affords more flexibility. An **execnet** channel can be simulated by using a pair of multiprocessing queues.

Exercise 122: Using the Multiprocessing Package to Execute a Simple Python Program

In this exercise, you will use the **multiprocessing** module to complete the same task as in *Exercise 121, Working with execnet to Execute a Simple Python Squaring Program*:

1. Create a new text file called **multi_processing.py**.

2. Now, **import** the **multiprocessing** package:

```
import multiprocessing
```

3. Create a **square_mp** function that will continuously monitor the queue for numbers, and when it sees a number, it will take it, square it, and place it in the outbound queue:

```
def square_mp(in_queue, out_queue):
    while(True):
        n = in_queue.get()
        n_squared = n**2
        out_queue.put(n_squared)
```

4. Finally, add the following block of code to **multi_processing.py**:

```
if __name__ == '__main__':
    in_queue = multiprocessing.Queue()
    out_queue = multiprocessing.Queue()
    process = multiprocessing.Process(target=square_mp, args=(in_queue, out_queue))
    process.start()
    for i in range(10):
```

```
            in_queue.put(i)
            i_squared = out_queue.get()
            print(f"{i} squared is {i_squared}")
    process.terminate()
```

Recall that the **if name == '__main__'** line simply avoids executing this section of code if the module is being imported elsewhere in your project. In comparison, **in_queue** and **out_queue** are both queue objects through which data can be sent between the parent and child processes. Within the following loop, you can see that you add integers to **in_queue** and get the results from **out_queue**. If you look at the preceding **square_mp** function, you can see how the child process will get its values from the **in_queue** object, and pass the result back into the **out_queue** object.

5. Execute your program from the command line as follows:

```
python multi_processing.py
```

You should get the following output:

```
(base) C:\Users\andrew.bird\Python-In-Demand\Lesson09>python multi_processing.py
0 squared is 0
1 squared is 1
2 squared is 4
3 squared is 9
4 squared is 16
5 squared is 25
6 squared is 36
7 squared is 49
8 squared is 64
9 squared is 81

(base) C:\Users\andrew.bird\Python-In-Demand\Lesson09>
```

Figure 9.17: Running our multiprocessing script

In this exercise, you learned how to pass tasks between our parent and child Python processes using the **multiprocessing** package, and you found the square of a set of numbers.

Multiprocessing with the Threading Package

Whereas **multiprocessing** and **execnet** create a new Python process to run your asynchronous code, threading simply creates a new thread within the current process. It, therefore, uses fewer operating resources than alternatives. Your new thread shares all memory, including global variables, with the creating thread. The two threads are not truly concurrent, because the GIL means only one Python instruction can be running at once across all threads in a Python process.

Finally, you cannot terminate a thread, so unless you plan to exit your whole Python process, you must provide the **thread** function with a way to exit. In the following exercise, you'll use a special signal value sent to a queue to exit the thread.

Exercise 123: Using the Threading Package

In this exercise, you will use the **threading** module to complete the same task of squaring numbers as in *Exercise 121, Working with execnet to Execute a Simple Python Squaring Program*:

1. In a Jupyter notebook, **import** the **threading** and **queue** modules:

```
import threading
import queue
```

2. Create two new queues to handle the communication between our processes, as shown in the following code snippet:

```
in_queue = queue.Queue()
out_queue = queue.Queue()
```

3. Create the function that will watch the queue for new numbers and return squared numbers. The **if n == 'STOP'** line allows you to terminate the thread by passing **STOP** into the **in_queue** object:

```
def square_threading():
    while True:
        n = in_queue.get()
        if n == 'STOP':
            return
        n_squared = n**2
        out_queue.put(n_squared)
```

4. Now, create and start a new thread:

```
thread = threading.Thread(target=square_threading)
thread.start()
```

5. Loop through **10** numbers, pass them into the **in_queue** object, and receive them from the **out_queue** object as the expected output:

```
for i in range(10):
    in_queue.put(i)
    i_squared = out_queue.get()
    print(f"{i} squared is {i_squared}")
in_queue.put('STOP')
thread.join()
```

You should get the following output:

```
0 squared is 0
1 squared is 1
2 squared is 4
3 squared is 9
4 squared is 16
5 squared is 25
6 squared is 36
7 squared is 49
8 squared is 64
9 squared is 81
```

Figure 9.18: Output from the threading loop

In this exercise, you learned how to pass tasks between our parent and child Python processes using the threading package. In the next section, you will look at parsing command-line arguments in scripts.

Parsing Command-Line Arguments in Scripts

Scripts often need input from their user in order to make certain choices about what the script does or how it runs. For instance, consider a script to train a deep learning network used for image classification. A user of this script will want to tell it where the training images are, what the labels are, and may want to choose what model to use, the learning rate, where to save the trained model configuration, and other features.

It's conventional to use command-line arguments; that is, values that the user supplies from their shell or from their own script when running your script. Using command-line arguments makes it easy to automate using the script in different ways and will be familiar to users who have experience of using the Unix or Windows command shells.

Python's standard library module for interpreting command-line arguments, **argparse**, supplies a host of features, making it easy to add argument handling to scripts in a fashion that is consistent with other tools. You can make arguments required or optional, have the user supply values for certain arguments, or define default values. **argparse** creates usage text, which the user can read using the **--help argument**, and checks the user-supplied arguments for validity.

Using **argparse** is a four-step process. First, you create a **parser** object. Second, you add arguments your program accepts to the **parser** object. Third, tell the **parser** object to parse your script's **argv** (short for argument vector, the list of arguments that were supplied to the script on launch); it checks them for consistency and stores the values. Finally, use the object returned from the **parser** object in your script to access the values supplied in the arguments.

To run all of the exercises in this section, later on, you will need to type the Python code into the **.py** files and run them from your operating system's command line, not from a Jupyter notebook.

Exercise 124: Introducing argparse to Accept Input from the User

In this exercise, you'll create a program that uses **argparse** to take a single input from the user called **flag**. If the **flag** input is not provided by the user, its value is **False**. If it is provided, its value is **True**. This exercise will be performed in a Python terminal:

1. Create a new Python file called **argparse_demo.py**.

2. Import the **argparse** library:

```
import argparse
```

3. Create a new **parser** object, as shown in the following code snippet:

```
parser = argparse.ArgumentParser(description="Interpret a Boolean flag.")
```

4. Add an argument that will allow the user to pass through the **-flag** argument when they execute the program:

```
parser.add_argument('--flag', dest='flag', action='store_true', help='Set the flag
value to True.')
```

The **store_true** action means that the parser will set the value of the argument to **True** if the **flag** input is present. If the **flag** input is not present, it will set the value to **False**. The exact opposite can be achieved using the **store_false** action.

5. Now call the **parse_args()** method, which executes the actual processing of the arguments:

```
arguments = parser.parse_args()
```

6. Now, **print** the value of the argument to see whether it worked:

```
print(f"The flag's value is {arguments.flag}")
```

7. Execute the file with no arguments supplied; the value of **arguments.flag** should be **False**:

```
python argparse_example.py
```

You should get the following output:

```
(base) C:\Users\andrew.bird\Python-In-Demand\Lesson09>python argparse_demo.py
The flag's value is False
```

Figure 9.19: Running argparse_demo with no arguments

8. Run the script again, with the **--flag** argument, to set it to **True**:

```
python argparse_demo.py –flag
```

You should get the following output:

```
(base) C:\Users\andrew.bird\Python-In-Demand\Lesson09>python argparse_demo.py --flag
The flag's value is True

(base) C:\Users\andrew.bird\Python-In-Demand\Lesson09>
```

Figure 9.20: Running argparse_demo with the --flag argument

9. Now enter the following code and see the **help** text that **argparse** extracted from the description and **help** text you supplied:

```
python argparse_demo.py –help
```

You should get the following output:

```
(base) C:\Users\andrew.bird\Python-In-Demand\Lesson09>python argparse_demo.py --help
usage: argparse_demo.py [-h] [--flag]

Interpret a Boolean flag.

optional arguments:
  -h, --help  show this help message and exit
  --flag      Set the flag value to True.
```

Figure 9.21: Viewing the help text of argparse_demo

You have successfully created a script that allows an argument to be specified when it is executed. You can probably imagine how useful this can often be.

Positional Arguments

Some scripts have arguments that are fundamental to their operation. For example, a script that copies a file always needs to know the **source** file and **destination** file. It would be inefficient to repetitively type out the names of the arguments; for instance, `python copyfile.py --source infile --destination outfile`, every time you use the script.

You can use positional arguments to define arguments that the user does not name but always provides in a particular order. The difference between a positional and a named argument is that a named argument starts with a hyphen (-), such as `--flag` in *Exercise 124, Introducing argparse to Accept Input from the User*. A positional argument does **not** start with a hyphen.

Exercise 125: Using Positional Arguments to Accept Source and Destination Inputs from a User

In this exercise, you will create a program that uses **argparse** to take two inputs from the user: **source** and **destination**.

This exercise will be performed in a Python terminal:

1. Create a new Python file called **positional_args.py**.

2. Import the **argparse** library:

```
import argparse
```

3. Create a new **parser** object:

```
parser = argparse.ArgumentParser(description="Interpret positional arguments.")
```

4. Add two arguments for the **source** and **destination** values:

```
parser.add_argument('source', action='store', help='The source of an operation.')
parser.add_argument('dest', action='store', help='The destination of the
operation.')
```

5. Call the **parse_args()** method, which executes the actual processing of **arguments**:

```
arguments = parser.parse_args()
```

6. Now, **print** the value of **arguments** so that you can see whether it worked:

```
print(f"Picasso will cycle from {arguments.source} to {arguments.dest}")
```

7. Now, execute the file while using this script with no arguments, which causes an error because it expects two **positional** arguments:

```
python positional_args.py
```

You should get the following output:

```
(base) C:\Users\andrew.bird\Python-In-Demand\Lesson09>python positional_args.py
usage: positional_args.py [-h] source dest
positional_args.py: error: the following arguments are required: source, dest
```

Figure 9.22: Running the script with no arguments specified

8. Try running the script and specifying two locations as the source and destination positional arguments.

> **Note**
>
> The arguments are supplied on the command line with no names or leading hyphens.

```
$ python positional_args.py Chichester Battersea
```

You should get the following output:

```
(base) C:\Users\andrew.bird\Python-In-Demand\Lesson09>python positional_args.py Chichester Battersea
Picasso will cycle from Chichester to Battersea
```

Figure 9.23: Successfully specifying two positional arguments

In this exercise, you learned how to parameterize your scripts by accepting positional arguments using the **argparse** Python package.

Performance and Profiling

Python is not often thought of as a high-performance language, though it really should be. The simplicity of the language and the power of its standard library mean that the time from idea to result can be much shorter than in other languages with better runtime performance.

But we have to be honest. Python is not among the fastest-running programming languages in the world, and sometimes that's important. For instance, if you're writing a web server application, you need to be able to handle as many network requests as are being made, and with timeliness that satisfies the users making the requests.

Alternatively, if you're writing a scientific simulation or a deep learning inference engine, then the simulation or training time can completely dwarf the programmer time (which is your time) spent writing the code. In any situation, reducing the time spent running your application can decrease the cost, whether measured in dollars on your cloud hosting bill or in milliamp-hours on your laptop battery.

Changing Your Python

You'll learn how to use some of Python's timing and profiling tools later on in this section. Before that, you can consider whether you even need to do that. Taligent, an object-oriented software company in the 1990s, had a performance saying: "*There is no code faster than no code.*" You can generalize that idea as follows:

There is no work that can be done faster than doing no work.

The fastest way to speed up your Python program can often be to simply use a different Python interpreter. You saw earlier in this chapter that multithreaded Python is slowed down by **GIL**, which means that only one Python thread can be executing a Python instruction at any time in a given process. The **Jython** and **IronPython** environments, targeting the Java Virtual Machine and .NET common language runtime, do not have **GIL**, so they may be faster for multithreaded programs. But there are also two Python implementations that are specifically designed to perform better, so you'll look to those for assistance in later sections.

PyPy

You will now look in more detail at another Python environment. It's called **pypy**, and Guido van Rossum (Python's creator) has said: "*If you want your code to run faster, you should probably just use PyPy.*"

PyPy's secret is Just-in-time (JIT) compilation, which compiles the Python program to a machine language such as **Cython** but does it while the program is running rather than once on the developer's machine (called ahead-of-time, or AOT, compilation). For a long-running process, a JIT compiler can try different strategies to compile the same code and find the ones that work best in the program's environment. The program will quickly get faster until the best version the compiler can find is running. Take a look at PyPy in the following exercise.

Exercise 126: Using PyPy to Find the Time to Get a List of Prime Numbers

In this exercise, you will be executing a Python program to get a list of prime numbers using milliamp-hours. But remember that you are more interested in checking the amount of time needed to execute the program using **pypy**.

This exercise will be performed in a Python terminal.

> **Note**
>
> You need to install **pypy** for your operating system. Go to https://pypy.org/download.html and make sure to get the version that is compatible with Python 3.7.

1. First, run the **pypy3** command, as shown in the following code snippet:

```
pypy3
Python 3.6.1 (dab365a465140aa79a5f3ba4db784c4af4d5c195, Feb 18 2019, 10:53:27)
[PyPy 7.0.0-alpha0 with GCC 4.2.1 Compatible Apple LLVM 10.0.0 (clang-1000.11.45.5)]
on darwin
Type "help", "copyright", "credits" or "license" for more information.
And now for something completely different: ''release 1.2 upcoming''
>>>>
```

Note that you may find it easier to navigate to the folder with the **pypy3.exe** file and run the preceding command, instead of following the installation instructions to create a symlink.

2. Press **Ctrl + D** to exit **pypy**.

You're going to use the program from *Chapter 7*, *Becoming Pythonic*, again, which finds prime numbers using the *Sieve of Eratosthenes method*. There are two changes that you will introduce here: firstly, find prime numbers up to 1,000 to give the program more work to do; secondly, instrument it with Python's **timeit** module so that you can see how long it takes to run. **timeit** runs a Python statement multiple times and records how long it takes. Tell **timeit** to run your Sieve of Eratosthenes 10,000 times (the default is 100,000 times, which takes a very long time).

3. Create a **eratosthenes.py** file and enter the following code:

```python
import timeit
class PrimesBelow:
    def __init__(self, bound):
        self.candidate_numbers = list(range(2,bound))
    def __iter__(self):
        return self
    def __next__(self):
        if len(self.candidate_numbers) == 0:
            raise StopIteration
        next_prime = self.candidate_numbers[0]
        self.candidate_numbers = [x for x in self.candidate_numbers if x %
            next_prime != 0]
        return next_prime
print(timeit.timeit('list(PrimesBelow(1000))', setup='from __main__ import
    PrimesBelow', number=10000))
```

4. Run the file with the regular Python interpreter:

```
python eratosthenes.py
```

You should get the following output:

```
(base) C:\Users\andrew.bird\Python-In-Demand\Lesson09>python eratosthenes.py
17.597791835
```

Figure 9.24: Executing with the regular Python interpreter

The number will be different on your computer, but that's **17.6** seconds to execute the **list(PrimesBelow(1000))** statement 10,000 times, or 1,760 µs per iteration. Now, run the same program, using **pypy** instead of CPython:

```
$ pypy3 eratosthenes.py
```

You should get the following output:

```
4.81645076300083
```

Here, it is 482 µs per iteration.

In this exercise, you will have noticed that it only takes 30% of the time to run our code in **pypy** as it took in Python. You really can get a lot of performance boost with very little effort, just by switching to **pypy**.

Cython

A Python module can be compiled to C, with a wrapper that means it is still accessible from other Python code. Compiling code simply means it is taken from one language and put into another. In this case, the compiler takes Python code and expresses it in the C programming language. The tool that does this is called **Cython**, and it often generates modules with lower memory use and execution time than if they're left as Python.

> **Note**
>
> The standard Python interpreter, the one you've almost certainly been using to complete the exercises and activities in this course, is sometimes called "CPython." This is confusingly similar to "Cython," but the two really are different projects.

Exercise 127: Adopting Cython to Find the Time Taken to get a List of Prime Numbers

In this exercise, you will install **Cython**, and, as mentioned in *Exercise 126*, you will find a list of prime numbers, but you are more interested in knowing the amount of time it takes to execute the code using Cython.

This exercise will be performed on the command line:

1. Firstly, install **cython**, as shown in the following code snippet:

```
$ pip install cython
```

2. Now, go back to the code you wrote for *Exercise 8*, and extract the class for iterating over primes using the Sieve of Eratosthenes into a file, **sieve_module.py**:

```
class PrimesBelow:
    def __init__(self, bound):
        self.candidate_numbers = list(range(2,bound))
    def __iter__(self):
        return self
    def __next__(self):
        if len(self.candidate_numbers) == 0:
            raise StopIteration
        next_prime = self.candidate_numbers[0]
        self.candidate_numbers = [x for x in self.candidate_numbers if x %
            next_prime != 0]
        return next_prime
```

3. Compile that into a C module using **Cython**. Create a file called **setup.py** with the following contents:

```
drom distutils.core import setup
from Cython.Build import cythonize
setup(
    ext_modules = cythonize("sieve_module.py")
)
```

4. Now, on the command line, run **setup.py** to build the module, as shown in the following code snippet:

```
$ python setup.py build_ext --inplace
running build_ext
building 'sieve_module' extension
creating build
creating build/temp.macosx-10.7-x86_64-3.7
gcc -Wno-unused-result -Wsign-compare -Wunreachable-code -DNDEBUG -g -fwrapv -O3
-Wall -Wstrict-prototypes -I/Users/leeg/anaconda3/include -arch x86_64 -I/Users/
leeg/anaconda3/include -arch x86_64 -I/Users/leeg/anaconda3/include/python3.7m -c
sieve_module.c -o build/temp.macosx-10.7-x86_64-3.7/sieve_module.o
gcc -bundle -undefined dynamic_lookup -L/Users/leeg/anaconda3/lib -arch x86_64
-L/Users/leeg/anaconda3/lib -arch x86_64 -arch x86_64 build/temp.macosx-
10.7-x86_64-3.7/sieve_module.o -o /Users/leeg/Nextcloud/Documents/Python Book/
Lesson_9/sieve_module.cpython-37m-darwin.so
```

The output will look different if you're on Linux or Windows, but you should see no errors.

5. Now import the **timeit** module and use it in a script called **cython_sieve.py**:

```
import timeit
print(timeit.timeit('list(PrimesBelow(1000))', setup='from sieve_module
    import PrimesBelow', number=10000))
```

6. Run this program to see the timing:

```
$ python cython_sieve.py
```

You should get the following output:

```
3.830873068
```

Here, it is 3.83 seconds, so 383 μs per iteration. That's a little over 40% of the time taken by the CPython version, but the **pypy** Python was still able to run the code faster. The advantage of using Cython is that you are able to make a module that is compatible with CPython, so you can make your module code faster without needing to make everybody else switch to a different Python interpreter to reap the benefits.

Profiling

Having exhausted the minimum-effort options for improving your code's performance, it's time to actually put some work in if you need to go faster. There's no recipe to follow to write fast code: if there were, you could have taught you that in *Chapters 1-8* and there wouldn't need to be a section on performance now. And, of course, speed isn't the only performance goal: you might want to reduce memory use or increase the number of simultaneous operations that can be in-flight. But programmers often use "performance" as a synonym for "reducing time to completion," and that's what you'll investigate here.

Improving performance is a scientific process: you observe how your code behaves, hypothesize about a potential improvement, make the change, and then observe it again and check that you really did improve things. Good tool support exists for the observation steps in this process, and you'll look at one such tool now: cProfile.

cProfile is a module that builds an execution profile of your code. Every time your Python program enters or exits a function or other callable, cProfile records what it is and how long it takes. It's then up to you to work out how it could spend less time doing that. Remember to compare a profile recorded before your change with one recorded after, to make sure you improved things! As you'll see in the next exercise, not all "optimizations" actually make your code faster, and careful measurement and thought are needed to decide whether the optimization is worth pursuing and retaining. In practice, cProfile is often used when trying to understand why code is taking longer than expected to execute. For example, you might write an iterative calculation that suddenly takes 10 minutes to compute after scaling to 1,000 iterations. With cProfile, you might discover that this is due to some inefficient function in the pandas library, which you could potentially avoid to speed up your code.

Profiling with cProfile

The goal of this example is to learn how to diagnose code performance using cProfile. In particular, to understand which parts of your code are taking the most time to execute.

This is a pretty long example, and the point is not to make sure that you type in and understand the code but to understand the process of profiling, to consider changes, and to observe the effects those changes have on the profile. This example will be performed on the command line:

1. Start with the code you wrote in *Chapter 7, Becoming Pythonic*, to generate an infinite series of prime numbers:

```python
class Primes:
    def __init__(self):
        self.current = 2
    def __iter__(self):
        return self
    def __next__(self):
        while True:
            current = self.current
            square_root = int(current ** 0.5)
            is_prime = True
            if square_root >= 2:
                for i in range(2, square_root + 1):
                    if current % i == 0:
                        is_prime = False
                        break
            self.current += 1
            if is_prime:
                return current
```

2. You'll remember that you had to use **itertools.takewhile()** to turn this into a finite sequence. Do so to generate a large list of primes and use **cProfile** to investigate its performance:

```python
import cProfile
import itertools
cProfile.run('[p for p in itertools.takewhile(lambda x: x<10000, Primes())]')
```

You should get the following output:

```
      2466 function calls in 0.021 seconds

Ordered by: standard name

ncalls  tottime  percall  cumtime  percall filename:lineno(function)
     1    0.000    0.000    0.000    0.000 <ipython-input-1-5aedc56b5f71>:2(__init__)
     1    0.000    0.000    0.000    0.000 <ipython-input-1-5aedc56b5f71>:4(__iter__)
  1230    0.020    0.000    0.020    0.000 <ipython-input-1-5aedc56b5f71>:6(__next__)
  1230    0.000    0.000    0.000    0.000 <string>:1(<lambda>)
     1    0.001    0.001    0.021    0.021 <string>:1(<listcomp>)
     1    0.000    0.000    0.021    0.021 <string>:1(<module>)
     1    0.000    0.000    0.021    0.021 {built-in method builtins.exec}
     1    0.000    0.000    0.000    0.000 {method 'disable' of '_lsprof.Profiler' objects}
```

Figure 9.25: Investigating performance with cProfile

The __next__() function is called most often, which is not surprising as it is the iterative part of the iteration. It also takes up most of the execution time in the profile. So, is there a way to make it faster?

One hypothesis is that the method does a lot of redundant divisions. Imagine that the number 101 is being tested as a prime number. This implementation tests whether it is divisible by 2 (no), then 3 (no), and then 4, but 4 is a multiple of 2, and you know it isn't divisible by 2.

3. As a hypothesis, change the __next__() method so that it only searches the list of known prime numbers. You know that if the number being tested is divisible by any smaller numbers, at least one of those numbers is itself prime:

```
class Primes2:
    def __init__(self):
        self.known_primes=[]
        self.current=2
    def __iter__(self):
        return self
    def __next__(self):
        while True:
            current = self.current
            prime_factors = [p for p in self.known_primes if current % p
                == 0]
```

```
                    self.current += 1
                    if len(prime_factors) == 0:
                        self.known_primes.append(current)
                    return current
        cProfile.run('[p for p in itertools.takewhile(lambda x: x<10000, Primes2())]')
```

You should get the following output:

```
    23708 function calls in 0.468 seconds

  Ordered by: standard name

  ncalls  tottime  percall  cumtime  percall filename:lineno(function)
   10006    0.455    0.000    0.455    0.000 <ipython-input-2-c6ffd796f813>:10(<listcomp>)
       1    0.000    0.000    0.000    0.000 <ipython-input-2-c6ffd796f813>:2(__init__)
       1    0.000    0.000    0.000    0.000 <ipython-input-2-c6ffd796f813>:5(__iter__)
    1230    0.011    0.000    0.466    0.000 <ipython-input-2-c6ffd796f813>:7(__next__)
    1230    0.000    0.000    0.000    0.000 <string>:1(<lambda>)
       1    0.001    0.001    0.468    0.468 <string>:1(<listcomp>)
       1    0.000    0.000    0.468    0.468 <string>:1(<module>)
       1    0.000    0.000    0.468    0.468 {built-in method builtins.exec}
   10006    0.001    0.000    0.001    0.000 {built-in method builtins.len}
    1230    0.000    0.000    0.000    0.000 {method 'append' of 'list' objects}
       1    0.000    0.000    0.000    0.000 {method 'disable' of '_lsprof.Profiler' objects}
```

Figure 9.26: It took longer this time!

Now, **__next()__** isn't the most frequently called function in the profile, but that's not a good thing. Instead, you've introduced a list comprehension that gets called even more times, and the whole process takes 30 times longer than it used to.

4. One thing that changed in the switch from testing a range of factors to the list of known primes is that the upper bound of tested numbers is no longer the square root of the candidate prime. Going back to thinking about testing whether 101 is prime, the first implementation tested all numbers between 2 and 10. The new one tests all primes from 2 to 97 and is therefore doing more work. Reintroduce the square root upper limit, using **takewhile** to filter the list of primes:

```
class Primes3:
    def __init__(self):
        self.known_primes=[]
        self.current=2
    def __iter__(self):
        return self
    def __next__(self):
        while True:
            current = self.current
            sqrt_current = int(current**0.5)
```

```
                    potential_factors = itertools.takewhile(lambda x: x < sqrt_current,
        self.known_primes)
                    prime_factors = [p for p in potential_factors if current % p
                        == 0]
                    self.current += 1
                    if len(prime_factors) == 0:
                        self.known_primes.append(current)
                    return current
        cProfile.run('[p for p in itertools.takewhile(lambda x: x<10000, Primes3())]')
```

You should get the following output:

```
        291158 function calls in 0.102 seconds

Ordered by: standard name

ncalls  tottime  percall  cumtime  percall filename:lineno(function)
267345    0.023    0.000    0.023    0.000 <ipython-input-3-10d4133c7618>:11(<lambda>)
 10006    0.058    0.000    0.081    0.000 <ipython-input-3-10d4133c7618>:12(<listcomp>)
     1    0.000    0.000    0.000    0.000 <ipython-input-3-10d4133c7618>:2(__init__)
     1    0.000    0.000    0.000    0.000 <ipython-input-3-10d4133c7618>:5(__iter__)
  1265    0.018    0.000    0.100    0.000 <ipython-input-3-10d4133c7618>:7(__next__)
  1265    0.000    0.000    0.000    0.000 <string>:1(<lambda>)
     1    0.001    0.001    0.102    0.102 <string>:1(<listcomp>)
     1    0.000    0.000    0.102    0.102 <string>:1(<module>)
     1    0.000    0.000    0.102    0.102 {built-in method builtins.exec}
 10006    0.001    0.000    0.001    0.000 {built-in method builtins.len}
  1265    0.000    0.000    0.000    0.000 {method 'append' of 'list' objects}
     1    0.000    0.000    0.000    0.000 {method 'disable' of '_lsprof.Profiler' objects}
```

Figure 9.27: Getting faster this time

5. Much better. Well, much better than **Primes2** anyway. This still takes seven times longer than the original algorithm. There's still one trick to try. The biggest contribution to the execution time is the list comprehension on line 12. By turning that into a **for** loop, it's possible to break the loop early by exiting as soon as a prime factor for the candidate prime is found:

```
class Primes4:
    def __init__(self):
        self.known_primes=[]
        self.current=2
    def __iter__(self):
        return self
    def __next__(self):
        while True:
            current = self.current
            sqrt_current = int(current**0.5)
            potential_factors = itertools.takewhile(lambda x: x < sqrt_
                current, self.known_primes)
```

```
                    is_prime = True
                    for p in potential_factors:
                        if current % p == 0:
                            is_prime = False
                            break
                    self.current += 1
                    if is_prime == True:
                        self.known_primes.append(current)
                        return current
        cProfile.run('[p for p in itertools.takewhile(lambda x: x<10000, Primes4())]')
```

You should get the following output:

```
     64802 function calls in 0.033 seconds

   Ordered by: standard name

   ncalls  tottime  percall  cumtime  percall filename:lineno(function)
    61001    0.007    0.000    0.007    0.000 <ipython-input-4-4f9e19e7ebde>:11(<lambda>)
        1    0.000    0.000    0.000    0.000 <ipython-input-4-4f9e19e7ebde>:2(__init__)
        1    0.000    0.000    0.000    0.000 <ipython-input-4-4f9e19e7ebde>:5(__iter__)
     1265    0.024    0.000    0.032    0.000 <ipython-input-4-4f9e19e7ebde>:7(__next__)
     1265    0.000    0.000    0.000    0.000 <string>:1(<lambda>)
        1    0.001    0.001    0.033    0.033 <string>:1(<listcomp>)
        1    0.000    0.000    0.033    0.033 <string>:1(<module>)
        1    0.000    0.000    0.033    0.033 {built-in method builtins.exec}
     1265    0.000    0.000    0.000    0.000 {method 'append' of 'list' objects}
        1    0.000    0.000    0.000    0.000 {method 'disable' of '_lsprof.Profiler' objects}
```

Figure 9.28: An even faster output

Once again, the result is better than the previous attempt, but it is still not as good as the "naive" algorithm. This time, the biggest contribution to the runtime is the lambda expression on line 11. That tests whether one of the previously found primes is smaller than the square root of the candidate number. There's no way to remove that test from this version of the algorithm. In other words, surprisingly, in this case, doing too much work to find a prime number is faster than finding the minimum work necessary and doing just that.

6. In fact, the good news is that our effort has not been wasted. It's don't recommend running this yourself unless the instructor says it's time for a coffee break, but if you increase the number of primes your iterator searches for, there will come the point where the "optimized" algorithm will outpace the "naive" implementation:

```
cProfile.run('[p for p in itertools.takewhile(lambda x: x<10000000, Primes())]')
```

You should get the following output:

```
        1329166 function calls in 147.528 seconds

   Ordered by: standard name

   ncalls  tottime  percall  cumtime  percall filename:lineno(function)
        1    0.000    0.000    0.000    0.000 <ipython-input-1-5aedc56b5f71>:2(__init__)
        1    0.000    0.000    0.000    0.000 <ipython-input-1-5aedc56b5f71>:4(__iter__)
   664580  146.901    0.000  146.901    0.000 <ipython-input-1-5aedc56b5f71>:6(__next__)
   664580    0.101    0.000    0.101    0.000 <string>:1(<lambda>)
        1    0.514    0.514  147.516  147.516 <string>:1(<listcomp>)
        1    0.011    0.011  147.528  147.528 <string>:1(<module>)
        1    0.000    0.000  147.528  147.528 {built-in method builtins.exec}
        1    0.000    0.000    0.000    0.000 {method 'disable' of '_lsprof.Profiler' objects}
```

Figure 9.29: The result of the naive implementation

```
cProfile.run('[p for p in itertools.takewhile(lambda x: x<10000000, Primes4())]')
```

You should get the following output:

```
        317503134 function calls in 106.236 seconds

   Ordered by: standard name

   ncalls  tottime  percall  cumtime  percall filename:lineno(function)
315507795   24.815    0.000   24.815    0.000 <ipython-input-4-4f9e19e7ebde>:11(<lambda>)
        1    0.000    0.000    0.000    0.000 <ipython-input-4-4f9e19e7ebde>:2(__init__)
        1    0.000    0.000    0.000    0.000 <ipython-input-4-4f9e19e7ebde>:5(__iter__)
   665111   80.611    0.000  105.523    0.000 <ipython-input-4-4f9e19e7ebde>:7(__next__)
   665111    0.114    0.000    0.114    0.000 <string>:1(<lambda>)
        1    0.583    0.583  106.221  106.221 <string>:1(<listcomp>)
        1    0.015    0.015  106.236  106.236 <string>:1(<module>)
        1    0.000    0.000  106.236  106.236 {built-in method builtins.exec}
   665111    0.097    0.000    0.097    0.000 {method 'append' of 'list' objects}
        1    0.000    0.000    0.000    0.000 {method 'disable' of '_lsprof.Profiler' objects}
```

Figure 9.30: The result of the optimized implementation

By the end of this example, you were able to find the best-optimized method to run the code. This decision was made possible by observing the amount of time needed to run the code, allowing us to tweak the code to address inefficiencies. In the following activity, you will put all of these concepts together.

Activity 23: Generating a List of Random Numbers in a Python Virtual Environment

You work for a sports betting website and want to simulate random events in a particular betting market. In order to do so, your goal will be to create a program that is able to generate long lists of random numbers using multiprocessing.

In this activity, the aim is to create a new Python environment, install the relevant packages, and write a function using the **threading** library to generate a list of random numbers.

Here are the steps:

1. Create a new **conda** environment called **my_env**.

2. Activate the **conda** environment.

3. Install **numpy** in your new environment.

4. Next, install and run a Jupyter notebook from within your virtual environment.

5. Next, create a new Jupyter notebook and **import** libraries such as **numpy**, **cProfile**, **itertools**, and **threading**.

6. Create a function that uses the **numpy** and **threading** libraries to generate an array of random numbers. Recall that when threading, we need to be able to send a signal for the **while** statement to terminate. The function should monitor the queue for an integer that represents the number of random numbers it should return. For example, if the number **10** was passed into the queue, it should return an array of **10** random numbers.

7. Next, add a function that will start a thread and put integers into the **in_queue** object. You can optionally print the output by setting the **show_output** argument to **True**. Make this function loop through the integers **0** to **n**, where **n** can be specified when the function is called. For each integer between **0** and **n**, it will pass the integer into the queue, and receive the array of random numbers.

8. Run the numbers on a small number of iterations to test and see the output.

You should get the following output:

```
[]
[0.78155881]
[0.61671875 0.96379795]
[0.52748128 0.69182391 0.11764897]
[0.89243527 0.75566451 0.88089298 0.15782374]
[0.1140009  0.25980504 0.88632411 0.08730527 0.17493792]
[0.41370041 0.01167654 0.60758276 0.73804504 0.73648781 0.29094613]
[0.8317736  0.57914287 0.01291246 0.61011878 0.91729392 0.50898183
 0.24640681]
[0.4475645  0.94036652 0.69823962 0.37459892 0.15512432 0.15115215
 0.65882522 0.77908825]
[0.42420881 0.7135031  0.22843178 0.20624473 0.32533328 0.86108686
 0.46407033 0.81794371 0.98958707]
```

Figure 9.31: The expected sample output

9. Rerun the numbers with a large number of iterations and use **cProfile** to view a breakdown of what is taking time to execute.

> **Note**
>
> The solution for this activity is available on page 550.

Summary

In this chapter, you have seen some of the tools and skills needed to transition from being a Python programmer to a Python software engineer. You have learned how to collaborate with other programmers using `Git` and GitHub, how to manage dependencies and virtual environments with **conda**, and how to deploy Python applications using Docker. You have explored multiprocessing and investigated tools and techniques used for improving the performance of your Python code. These new skills leave you better equipped to handle the messy real world of collaborative teams working on large problems in production environments. These skills are not just academic but are essential tools for any aspiring Python developer to familiarize themselves with.

The next chapter begins the part of the book on using Python for data science. You will learn about popular libraries for working with numerical data, and techniques to import, explore, clean up, and analyze real-world data.

10

Data Analytics with pandas and NumPy

Overview

By the end of this chapter, you will be able, use pandas to view, create, analyze, and modify DataFrames; use NumPy to perform statistics and speed up matrix computations; organize and modify data using read, transpose, loc, iloc, and concatenate; clean data by deleting or manipulating NaN values and coercing column types; visualize data by constructing, modifying, and interpreting histograms and scatter plots; generate and interpret statistical models using pandas and statsmodels and solve real-world problems using data analytics techniques.

Introduction

In *Chapter 9, Practical Python – Advanced Topics*, you looked at how to use GitHub to collaborate with team members. You also used **conda** to document and set up the dependencies for Python programs and **docker** to create reproducible Python environments to run our code.

We now shift gears to data science. Data science is booming like never before. Data scientists have become among the most sought-after practitioners in the world today. Most leading corporations have data scientists to analyze and explain their data.

Data analytics focuses on the analysis of big data. As each day goes by, there is more data than ever before – far too much for any human to analyze by sight. Leading Python developers such as Wes McKinney and Travis Oliphant addressed the gap by creating specialized Python libraries, in particular, pandas and NumPy to handle big data.

Taken together, pandas and NumPy are masterful at handling big data. They are built for speed, efficiency, readability, and ease of use.

Pandas provide you with a unique framework to view and modify data. Pandas handles all data-related tasks such as creating DataFrames, importing data, scraping data from the web, merging data, pivoting, concatenating, and more.

NumPy, short for Numerical Python, is more focused on computation. NumPy interprets the rows and columns of pandas DataFrames as matrices in the form of NumPy arrays. When computing descriptive statistics such as the mean, median, mode, and quartiles, NumPy is blazingly fast.

Another key player in data analysis is Matplotlib, a graphing library that handles scatter plots, histograms, regression lines, and much more. The importance of data graphs cannot be overstated since most non-technical professionals use them to interpret results.

NumPy and Basic Stats

NumPy is designed to handle big data swiftly. It includes the following essential components according to the NumPy documentation:

- A powerful n-dimensional array object
- Sophisticated (broadcasting) functions
- Tools for integrating C/C++ and Fortran code
- Useful linear algebra, Fourier transform, and random number capabilities

You will be using NumPy for the rest of the course. Instead of using lists, you will use NumPy arrays. NumPy arrays are the basic elements of the NumPy package. NumPy arrays are designed to handle arrays of any dimension.

Numpy arrays can be indexed easily and can have many types of data, such as **float**, **int**, **string**, and **object**, but the types must be consistent to improve speed.

Exercise 128: Converting Lists to NumPy Arrays

In this exercise, you will convert a list to a **numpy** array. The following steps will enable you to complete the exercise:

1. Open a new Jupyter Notebook.

2. Firstly, you need to import **numpy**:

```
import numpy as np
```

3. Now, you'll create a list for **test_scores** and confirm the type of data:

```
test_scores = [70,65,95,88]
type(test_scores)
```

The output will be as follows:

```
list
```

> **Note**
>
> Now that **numpy** has been imported, you can access all **numpy** methods, such as **numpy** arrays. Type **np. + Tab** on your keyboard to see the breadth of options. You are looking for an array.

4. Now, you will convert the list of marks to a **numpy** array and check the **type** of the array. Enter the code in the following code snippet:

```
scores = np.array(test_scores)
type(scores)
```

The output will be as follows:

```
numpy.ndarray
```

In this exercise, you were able to convert a list of test score marks to a NumPy array. You will find the mean using these values within the NumPy array in *Exercise 129, Calculating the Mean of the Test Score.*

One of the most common statistical measures is the mean. Traditionally thought of as the average, the mean of a list is the sum of each entry divided by the number of entries. In NumPy, the mean may be computed using the .**mean** method.

Exercise 129: Calculating the Mean of the Test Score

In this exercise, you will use the **numpy** array you created to store our test scores from *Exercise 128, Converting Lists to NumPy Arrays,* and you will calculate the mean of **testscores**. The following steps will enable you to complete the exercise:

1. Continue in the same Jupyter Notebook from *Exercise 128, Converting Lists to NumPy Arrays.*

2. Now, to find the "average" of **testscore**, you can use the **mean** method, as shown here:

```
scores.mean()
```

The output will be as follows:

```
79.5
```

> **Note**
>
> The word "average" is in quotation marks. This is not an accident. The mean is only one kind of average. Another kind of average is the median.

Given our test scores of 70, 65, 95, and 88, the "average" is 79.5, which is the expected output. In this exercise, you were able to use the **mean** function of NumPy and find the average of **test_scores**. In the following exercise, you will find the median using NumPy.

The median is the number in the middle. Although not necessarily the best measure of test averages, it's an excellent measure of income average.

Exercise 130: Finding the Median from a Collection of Income Data

In this exercise, you will be finding the median from a collection of income data for a neighborhood and help a millionaire decide whether he should build his dream house in the neighborhood based on the income data. The **median** function here is a method of **numpy**.

The following steps will enable you to complete the exercise:

1. Open a new Jupyter Notebook.

2. Firstly, you need to import the **numpy** package as **np**, then create a **numpy** array and assign various pieces of **income** data, as shown in the following code snippet:

```
import numpy as np
income = np.array([75000, 55000, 88000, 125000, 64000, 97000])
```

3. Next, find the mean of the income data:

```
income.mean()
```

The output will be as follows:

```
84000
```

So far, so good. **84000** is the average **income** on your block. Now, say the millionaire decides to build his dream house on the vacant corner lot. He adds a salary of 12 million dollars.

4. Append the value of 12 million dollars to the current array and find the new mean:

```
income = np.append(income, 12000000)
income.mean()
```

The output will be as follows:

```
1786285.7142857143
```

The new average income is 1.7 million dollars. Okay. Nobody makes close to 1.7 million dollars on the block. It's not a representative average. This is where the median comes into play.

> **Note**
>
> Median here is not a method of **np.array**, but it is a method of **numpy**. (The mean may be computed in the same way, as a method of numpy.)

5. Now to find the **median** function from the **income** values you have:

```
np.median(income)
```

The output will be as follows:

```
88000
```

This result says that half of the neighborhood residents make more than 88,000, and half of the blocks make less. This would give the millionaire a fair idea of the neighborhood. In this particular case, the median is a much better estimation of average income than the mean.

In the next section, you will be covering skewed data and outliers.

Skewed Data and Outliers

Something about the 12 million salary does not sit right. It's nowhere near anyone else's income. In statistics, there is official terminology for this. You say that the data is skewed by an outlier of 12,000,000. In particular, the data is right-skewed since 12,000,000 is far to the right of every other data point.

Right-skewed data pulls the mean away from the median. In fact, if the mean greatly exceeds the median, this is clear evidence of right-skewed data. Similarly, if the mean is much less than the median, this is clear evidence of left-skewed data.

Unfortunately, there is no universal way to compute individual outliers. There are some general methods, but you won't get into them here. Just keep in mind that outliers are far removed from other data points, and they skew the data.

Standard Deviation

The standard deviation is a precise statistical measure of how spread out data points are. In the following exercise, you will use the standard deviation.

Exercise 131: Finding the Standard Deviation from Income Data

In this exercise, you will be using the income data from *Exercise 130, Finding the Median from a Collection of Income Data,* and you will find the amount of deviation you have between the income of the millionaire to the regular residents living in the neighborhood.

The following steps will enable you to complete the exercise:

1. Continue with the previous Jupyter Notebook.

2. Now check the standard deviation using the **std()** function, as mentioned in the following code snippet:

```
income.std()
```

The output will be as follows:

```
4169786.007331644
```

As you can see, the standard deviation here is a huge number, which is 4 million, and this could be practically meaningless while you plot the data. On average, the incomes are not 4 million away from each other.

Now, try to find the standard deviation from the **test_scores** data from *Exercise 128, Converting Lists to NumPy Arrays.*

3. Assign the **test_scores** list value once again as this is a new Jupyter notebook:

```
test_scores = [70,65,95,88]
```

4. Now, convert this list to a **numpy** array:

```
scores = np.array(test_scores)
```

5. Now, find the standard deviation of **test_scores** using the **std()** function:

```
scores.std()
```

The output will be as follows:

```
12.379418403139947
```

In this exercise, you observed that the income data is so skewed that the standard deviation of 4 million is practically meaningless. But the 12.4 standard deviation of the test scores is very meaningful; the mean test score of 79.5 with a standard deviation of 12.4 means that you can expect the scores to be about 12 points away from the mean on average.

What if you need to find the maximum, minimum, or sum of the **numpy** arrays? For instance, you can use the values from **test_scores** to find the maximum, minimum, and sum of **test_scores**.

You can find the maximum from the **numpy** array using the **max()** method, the minimum using the **min()** method, and the sum using the **sum()** method.

You can easily find the **max**, the **min**, and the **sum** values of **numpy** arrays.

To find the maximum, enter the following code:

```
test_scores = [70,65,95,88]
scores = np.array(test_scores)
scores.max()
```

The output will be as follows:

```
95
```

To find the minimum, enter the following code:

```
scores.min()
```

The output will be as follows:

```
65
```

To find the sum, enter the following code:

```
scores.sum()
```

The output will be as follows:

```
318
```

Matrices

A DataFrame is generally composed of rows, and each row has the same number of columns. From one point of view, it's a two-dimensional grid containing lots of numbers. It can also be interpreted as a list of lists, or an array of arrays.

In mathematics, a matrix is a rectangular array of numbers defined by the number of rows and columns. It is standard always to list rows first, and columns second. For instance, a 2 x 3 matrix consists of 2 rows and 3 columns, whereas a 3 x 2 matrix consists of 3 rows and 2 columns.

Here is a 4 x 4 matrix:

$$\begin{bmatrix} 9 & 13 & 5 & 2 \\ 1 & 11 & 7 & 6 \\ 3 & 7 & 4 & 1 \\ 6 & 0 & 7 & 10 \end{bmatrix}$$

Figure 10.1: Matrix representation of a 4 x 4 matrix

Exercise 132: Matrices

NumPy has methods for creating matrices or n-dimensional arrays. One option is to place random numbers between 0 and 1 into each entry, as follows.

In this exercise, you will implement the various **numpy** matrix methods and observe the outputs (recall that **random.seed** will allow us to reproduce the same numbers, and it's okay if you want to generate your own).

The following steps will enable you to complete the exercise:

1. Begin with a new Jupyter Notebook.

2. Now, generate a random 5 x 5 matrix, as shown in the following code snippet:

```
import numpy as np
np.random.seed(seed=60)
random_square = np.random.rand(5,5)
random_square
```

You should get the following output:

```
Out[2]:  array([[0.30087333, 0.18694582, 0.32318268, 0.66574957, 0.5669708 ],
                [0.39825396, 0.37941492, 0.01058154, 0.1703656 , 0.12339337],
                [0.69240128, 0.87444156, 0.3373969 , 0.99245923, 0.13154007],
                [0.50032984, 0.28662051, 0.22058485, 0.50208555, 0.63606254],
                [0.63567694, 0.08043309, 0.58143375, 0.83919086, 0.29301825]])
```

Figure 10.2 A random matrix being generated

In the preceding code, you have used **random.seed**. You just invoke **random. seed(seed=60)**, and whenever you run the script, you will get the same sequence of values.

This is very similar to the DataFrames that you will be dealing with for the rest of this book. You can go through some code to obtain particular rows, columns, and entries.

3. Now, find the rows and columns of the matrix that is generated.

    In general, if you omit the columns from the matrix **[row, column]**, **numpy** will select them all.

    ```
    # First row
    random_square[0]
    ```

    You should get the following output, consisting of all columns, and the first row:

    ```
    Out[4]:  array([0.30087333, 0.18694582, 0.32318268, 0.66574957, 0.5669708 ])
    ```

    Figure 10.3: The values of the matrix row

    ```
    # First column
    ```

    Now, to find the values of all the rows, and the first column of the matrix.

    ```
    random_square[:,0]
    ```

    You should get the following output, consisting of all rows, and the first column:

    ```
    Out[5]:  array([0.30087333, 0.39825396, 0.69240128, 0.50032984, 0.63567694])
    ```

    Figure 10.4: The values of the matrix column

4. Now find individual entries by specifying the value of the matrix **[row, column]**, as shown in the following code snippet:

    ```
    # First entry
    random_square[0,0]
    ```

    The output, the entry in the first row and first column, will be as follows:

    ```
    0.30087333004661876
    ```

    Here is the **first entry** using another way:

    ```
    random_square[0][0]
    ```

    The output will be as follows:

    ```
    0.30087333004661876
    ```

    Entry in 2nd row, 3rd column:

    ```
    random_square[2,3]
    ```

    The output will be as follows:

    ```
    0.9924592256795676
    ```

Now, to find the mean values of the matrix, you will find the mean of the entire matrix, individual rows, and columns using the **square.mean()** method, as shown in the following code snippet.

Here is the **mean** entry of the matrix:

```
random_square.mean()
```

The output will be as follows:

```
0.42917627159618377
```

Here is the **mean** entry of the first row:

```
random_square[0].mean()
```

The output will be as follows:

```
0.4087444389228477
```

Here is the **mean** entry of the last column:

```
random_square[:,-1].mean()
```

The output will be as follows:

```
0.35019700684996913
```

In this exercise, you created a random 5 x 5 matrix and implemented a few basic operations on the matrix.

Computation Time for Large Matrices

Now that you have gotten a hang of creating random matrices, you can see how long it takes to generate a large matrix and compute the mean:

```
%%time
np.random.seed(seed=60)
big_matrix = np.random.rand(100000, 100)
```

The output will be as follows:

```
Wall time: 101 ms
```

Figure 10.5: Computation time for a large matrix

Now, to find the computation time for the mean of the matrix.

```
%%time
big_matrix = np.random.rand(100000, 100)
big_matrix.mean()
```

You should get the following output:

`Wall time: 130 ms`

Figure 10.6: Computation time for the mean of the matrix

Your time will be different than ours, but it should be in the order of milliseconds. Not bad. It takes much less than a second to generate a matrix of 10 million entries and compute its mean.

In the next exercise, you will create arrays using NumPy and compute various values through them. One such computation you will be using is **ndarray**. **numpy.ndarray** is a (usually fixed-size) multidimensional array container of items of the same type and size.

Exercise 133: Creating an Array to Implement NumPy Computations

In this exercise, you will generate a new matrix and perform mathematical operations on it, which will be covered later in this exercise. Unlike with traditional lists, NumPy arrays allow each member of the list to be manipulated with ease. The following steps will enable you to complete the exercise:

1. Open a new Jupyter Notebook.

2. Now import **numpy** and create **ndarray** between **1** and **100**:

```
import numpy as np
np.arange(1, 101)
```

You should get the following output:

```
Out[2]: array([  1,   2,   3,   4,   5,   6,   7,   8,   9,  10,  11,  12,  13,
                14,  15,  16,  17,  18,  19,  20,  21,  22,  23,  24,  25,  26,
                27,  28,  29,  30,  31,  32,  33,  34,  35,  36,  37,  38,  39,
                40,  41,  42,  43,  44,  45,  46,  47,  48,  49,  50,  51,  52,
                53,  54,  55,  56,  57,  58,  59,  60,  61,  62,  63,  64,  65,
                66,  67,  68,  69,  70,  71,  72,  73,  74,  75,  76,  77,  78,
                79,  80,  81,  82,  83,  84,  85,  86,  87,  88,  89,  90,  91,
                92,  93,  94,  95,  96,  97,  98,  99, 100])
```

Figure 10.7: Showing ndarray with values 1 to 100

3. Reshape the array to **20** rows and **5** columns:

```
np.arange(1, 101).reshape(20,5)
```

You should get the following output:

```
Out[3]: array([[  1,   2,   3,   4,   5],
               [  6,   7,   8,   9,  10],
               [ 11,  12,  13,  14,  15],
               [ 16,  17,  18,  19,  20],
               [ 21,  22,  23,  24,  25],
               [ 26,  27,  28,  29,  30],
               [ 31,  32,  33,  34,  35],
               [ 36,  37,  38,  39,  40],
               [ 41,  42,  43,  44,  45],
               [ 46,  47,  48,  49,  50],
               [ 51,  52,  53,  54,  55],
               [ 56,  57,  58,  59,  60],
               [ 61,  62,  63,  64,  65],
               [ 66,  67,  68,  69,  70],
               [ 71,  72,  73,  74,  75],
               [ 76,  77,  78,  79,  80],
               [ 81,  82,  83,  84,  85],
               [ 86,  87,  88,  89,  90],
               [ 91,  92,  93,  94,  95],
               [ 96,  97,  98,  99, 100]])
```

Figure 10.8: Output with the reshaped array of 20 rows and 5 columns

4. Now, define **mat1** as a **20 x 5** array between **1** and **100** and then subtract **50** from **mat1**, as shown in the following code snippet:

```
mat1 = np.arange(1, 101).reshape(20,5)
mat1 - 50
```

You should get the following output:

```
Out[4]: array([[-49, -48, -47, -46, -45],
               [-44, -43, -42, -41, -40],
               [-39, -38, -37, -36, -35],
               [-34, -33, -32, -31, -30],
               [-29, -28, -27, -26, -25],
               [-24, -23, -22, -21, -20],
               [-19, -18, -17, -16, -15],
               [-14, -13, -12, -11, -10],
               [ -9,  -8,  -7,  -6,  -5],
               [ -4,  -3,  -2,  -1,   0],
               [  1,   2,   3,   4,   5],
               [  6,   7,   8,   9,  10],
               [ 11,  12,  13,  14,  15],
               [ 16,  17,  18,  19,  20],
               [ 21,  22,  23,  24,  25],
               [ 26,  27,  28,  29,  30],
               [ 31,  32,  33,  34,  35],
               [ 36,  37,  38,  39,  40],
               [ 41,  42,  43,  44,  45],
               [ 46,  47,  48,  49,  50]])
```

Figure 10.9: Output subtracting values from the array

5. Now, multiply **mat1** by **10** and observe the change in the output:

```
mat1 * 10
```

You should get the following output:

```
Out[5]: array([[  10,   20,   30,   40,   50],
               [  60,   70,   80,   90,  100],
               [ 110,  120,  130,  140,  150],
               [ 160,  170,  180,  190,  200],
               [ 210,  220,  230,  240,  250],
               [ 260,  270,  280,  290,  300],
               [ 310,  320,  330,  340,  350],
               [ 360,  370,  380,  390,  400],
               [ 410,  420,  430,  440,  450],
               [ 460,  470,  480,  490,  500],
               [ 510,  520,  530,  540,  550],
               [ 560,  570,  580,  590,  600],
               [ 610,  620,  630,  640,  650],
               [ 660,  670,  680,  690,  700],
               [ 710,  720,  730,  740,  750],
               [ 760,  770,  780,  790,  800],
               [ 810,  820,  830,  840,  850],
               [ 860,  870,  880,  890,  900],
               [ 910,  920,  930,  940,  950],
               [ 960,  970,  980,  990, 1000]])
```

Figure 10.10: Output when you multiply mat1 by 10

6. Now you need to add **mat1** to itself, as mentioned in the following code snippet:

```
mat1 + mat1
```

You should get the following output:

```
Out[6]: array([[   2,    4,    6,    8,   10],
               [  12,   14,   16,   18,   20],
               [  22,   24,   26,   28,   30],
               [  32,   34,   36,   38,   40],
               [  42,   44,   46,   48,   50],
               [  52,   54,   56,   58,   60],
               [  62,   64,   66,   68,   70],
               [  72,   74,   76,   78,   80],
               [  82,   84,   86,   88,   90],
               [  92,   94,   96,   98,  100],
               [ 102,  104,  106,  108,  110],
               [ 112,  114,  116,  118,  120],
               [ 122,  124,  126,  128,  130],
               [ 132,  134,  136,  138,  140],
               [ 142,  144,  146,  148,  150],
               [ 152,  154,  156,  158,  160],
               [ 162,  164,  166,  168,  170],
               [ 172,  174,  176,  178,  180],
               [ 182,  184,  186,  188,  190],
               [ 192,  194,  196,  198,  200]])
```

Figure 10.11: Output of adding mat1 to itself

7. Now you will multiply each entry in **mat1** by itself:

```
mat1*mat1
```

You should get the following output:

```
Out[7]: array([[    1,     4,     9,    16,    25],
               [   36,    49,    64,    81,   100],
               [  121,   144,   169,   196,   225],
               [  256,   289,   324,   361,   400],
               [  441,   484,   529,   576,   625],
               [  676,   729,   784,   841,   900],
               [  961,  1024,  1089,  1156,  1225],
               [ 1296,  1369,  1444,  1521,  1600],
               [ 1681,  1764,  1849,  1936,  2025],
               [ 2116,  2209,  2304,  2401,  2500],
               [ 2601,  2704,  2809,  2916,  3025],
               [ 3136,  3249,  3364,  3481,  3600],
               [ 3721,  3844,  3969,  4096,  4225],
               [ 4356,  4489,  4624,  4761,  4900],
               [ 5041,  5184,  5329,  5476,  5625],
               [ 5776,  5929,  6084,  6241,  6400],
               [ 6561,  6724,  6889,  7056,  7225],
               [ 7396,  7569,  7744,  7921,  8100],
               [ 8281,  8464,  8649,  8836,  9025],
               [ 9216,  9409,  9604,  9801, 10000]])
```

Figure 10.12: Output of multiplying mat1 by itself

8. Now, take the **dot** product of **mat1** and **mat1.T**:

```
np.dot(mat1, mat1.T)
```

You should get the following output:

```
Out[8]:  array([[    55,    130,    205,    280,    355,    430,    505,    580,    655,
                    730,    805,    880,    955,   1030,   1105,   1180,   1255,   1330,
                   1405,   1480],
                [    130,    330,    530,    730,    930,   1130,   1330,   1530,   1730,
                   1930,   2130,   2330,   2530,   2730,   2930,   3130,   3330,   3530,
                   3730,   3930],
                [    205,    530,    855,   1180,   1505,   1830,   2155,   2480,   2805,
                   3130,   3455,   3780,   4105,   4430,   4755,   5080,   5405,   5730,
                   6055,   6380],
                [    280,    730,   1180,   1630,   2080,   2530,   2980,   3430,   3880,
                   4330,   4780,   5230,   5680,   6130,   6580,   7030,   7480,   7930,
                   8380,   8830],
                [    355,    930,   1505,   2080,   2655,   3230,   3805,   4380,   4955,
                   5530,   6105,   6680,   7255,   7830,   8405,   8980,   9555,  10130,
                  10705,  11280],
                [    430,   1130,   1830,   2530,   3230,   3930,   4630,   5330,   6030,
                   6730,   7430,   8130,   8830,   9530,  10230,  10930,  11630,  12330,
                  13030,  13730],
                [    505,   1330,   2155,   2980,   3805,   4630,   5455,   6280,   7105,
                   7930,   8755,   9580,  10405,  11230,  12055,  12880,  13705,  14530,
                  15355,  16180],
                [    580,   1530,   2480,   3430,   4380,   5330,   6280,   7230,   8180,
                   9130,  10080,  11030,  11980,  12930,  13880,  14830,  15780,  16730,
                  17680,  18630],
                [    655,   1730,   2805,   3880,   4955,   6030,   7105,   8180,   9255,
                  10330,  11405,  12480,  13555,  14630,  15705,  16780,  17855,  18930,
                  20005,  21080],
```

Figure 10.13: Output of the dot product of mat1 and mat1.T

> **Note**
>
> The output shown in Figure 10.13 has been truncated.

In this exercise, you computed and added in values to an array, after which you implemented different NumPy computations.

When it comes to data analysis, NumPy will make your life tremendously easier. The ease with which NumPy arrays may be combined, manipulated, and used to compute standard statistical measures like the mean, median, and standard deviation make them far superior to Python lists. They also handle big data so exceptionally well, it's hard to imagine the world of data science without them.

In the next section, you will be covering pandas, which is another library available in Python to make the life of a Python developer much easier.

The pandas Library

Pandas is the Python library that handles data on all fronts. Pandas can import data, read data, and display data in an object called a **DataFrame**. A DataFrame consists of rows and columns. One way to get a feel for DataFrames is to create one.

In the IT industry, pandas is widely used for data manipulation. It is also used for stock prediction, statistics, analytics, big data, and, of course, data science.

In the following exercises, you will be working with DataFrames and learning different computations that are available with them.

Exercise 134: Using DataFrames to Manipulate Stored Student testscore Data

In this exercise, you will create a **dictionary**, which is one of many ways to create a **pandas** DataFrame. You will then manipulate this data as required. In order to use pandas, you must import **pandas**, which is universally imported as **pd**. Pandas and NumPy are so omnipresent it's a good idea to import them first before performing any kind of data analysis. The following steps will enable you to complete the exercise:

1. You'll begin by importing **pandas** as **pd**:

```
import pandas as pd
```

   Now that you have imported **pandas**, you will create a **DataFrame**.

2. First, you will create a dictionary of test scores as **test_dict**:

```
# Create dictionary of test scores
test_dict = {'Corey':[63,75,88], 'Kevin':[48,98,92], 'Akshay': [87, 86, 85]}
```

3. Next, you place the **text_dict** into the DataFrame using the **DataFrame** method:

```
# Create DataFrame
df = pd.DataFrame(test_dict)
```

4. Now, you can display the Dataframe:

```
# Display DataFrame
df
```

You should get the following output:

Out[4]:

	Corey	Kevin	Akshay
0	63	48	87
1	75	98	86
2	88	92	85

Figure 10.14: Output with the values added in the DataFrame

You can inspect the **DataFrame**. First, each dictionary key is listed as a column. Second, the rows are labeled with indices starting with **0** by default. Third, the visual layout is clear and legible.

Each column and row of **DataFrame** is officially represented as a **Series**. A series is a one-dimensional **ndarray**.

Now, you will rotate the DataFrame, which is also known as a **transpose**, a standard **pandas** method. A transpose turns rows into columns and columns into rows.

5. Copy the code shown in the following code snippet to perform a transpose on the DataFrame:

```
# Transpose DataFrame
df = df.T
df
```

You should get the following output:

Out[5]:

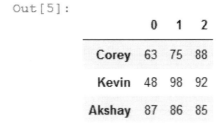

	0	1	2
Corey	63	75	88
Kevin	48	98	92
Akshay	87	86	85

Figure 10.15: The output of the transpose on the DataFrame

In this exercise, you created a DataFrame that holds the values of **testscores**, and to finish, you transposed this DataFrame to get the output. In the next exercise, you will look at renaming column names and selecting data from the DataFrame, which is an important part of working with pandas.

Exercise 135: DataFrame Computations with the Student testscore Data

In this exercise, you will rename the columns of the DataFrame, and you will then select the data to display as output from the DataFrame:

1. Open a new Jupyter Notebook.

2. Import **pandas** as **pd** and enter the student value, as shown in *Exercise 134*, *Using DataFrames to Manipulate Stored Student testscore Data*. After this, convert it to a DataFrame and have it transposed:

```
import pandas as pd
# Create dictionary of test scores
test_dict = {'Corey':[63,75,88], 'Kevin':[48,98,92], 'Akshay': [87, 86, 85]}
# Create DataFrame
df = pd.DataFrame(test_dict)
df = df.T
```

3. Now rename the columns to something more precise. You can use `.columns` on the DataFrame to rename the column names:

```
# Rename Columns
df.columns = ['Quiz_1', 'Quiz_2', 'Quiz_3']
df
```

You should get the following output:

	Quiz_1	Quiz_2	Quiz_3
Corey	63	75	88
Kevin	48	98	92
Akshay	87	86	85

Figure 10.16: Output with changed column names

Now, select a range of values from specific rows and columns. You will be using `.iloc` with the index number, which is a function present in a pandas DataFrame for selection. This is shown in the following step:

4. Select a range of rows:

```
# Access first row by index number
df.iloc[0]
```

You should get the following output:

```
Quiz_1    63
Quiz_2    75
Quiz_3    88
Name: Corey, dtype: int64
```

Figure 10.17: Output with the selected values

5. Now, select a column using its name, as shown in the following code snippet.

   You can access columns by putting the column name in quotes inside of brackets:

```
# Access first column by name
df['Quiz_1']
```

You should get the following output:

```
Corey     63
Kevin     48
Akshay    87
Name: Quiz_1, dtype: int64
```

Figure 10.18: Output while accessing it with a change in the column name

6. Now, select a column using the dot (.) notation:

```
# Access first column using dot notation
df.Quiz_1
```

You should get the following output:

```
Corey     63
Kevin     48
Akshay    87
Name: Quiz_1, dtype: int64
```

Figure 10.19: Output of selecting a column using the dot notation

> **Note**
>
> There are limitations to using dot notation, so bracket quotations are often preferable.

In this exercise, you implemented and changed the column names of the DataFrame. Next, you used `.iloc` to select data as per our requirement from the DataFrame.

In the next exercise, you will implement different computations on the DataFrame.

Exercise 136: Computing DataFrames within DataFrames

In this exercise, you will use the same **testscore** data and perform more computations on the DataFrame. The following steps will enable you to complete the exercise:

1. Open a new Jupyter Notebook.

2. Import **pandas** as **pd** and enter the student value as shown in *Exercise 135, DataFrame Computations with the Student testscore Data*. After this, convert it to a DataFrame:

```
import pandas as pd
# Create dictionary of test scores
test_dict = {'Corey':[63,75,88], 'Kevin':[48,98,92], 'Akshay': [87, 86, 85]}
# Create DataFrame
df = pd.DataFrame(test_dict)
```

3. Now, begin by arranging the rows of the DataFrame, as shown in the following code snippet.

   You can use the same bracket notation, **[]**, for rows as for lists and strings:

```
# Limit DataFrame to first 2 rows
df[0:2]
```

You should get the following output:

```
Out[3]:
```

	Corey	Kevin	Akshay
0	63	48	87
1	75	98	86

Figure 10.20: Output of arranging rows

4. Transpose the DataFrame:

```
df = df.T
df
```

5. Now, rename the columns to **Quiz_1**, **Quiz_2**, and **Quiz_3**, which was covered in *Exercise 135, DataFrame Computations with the Student testscore Data*:

```
# Rename Columns
df.columns = ['Quiz_1', 'Quiz_2', 'Quiz_3']
df
```

You should get the following output:

```
Out[6]:
```

	Quiz_1	Quiz_2	Quiz_3
Corey	63	75	88
Kevin	48	98	92
Akshay	87	86	85

Figure 10.21: Output with the renamed column names

6. Now, define a new **DataFrame** from the first two rows and the last two columns.

You can choose the rows and columns by name first, as shown in the following code snippet:

```
# Defining a new DataFrame from first 2 rows and last 2 columns
rows = ['Corey', 'Kevin']
cols = ['Quiz_2', 'Quiz_3']
df_spring = df.loc[rows, cols]
df_spring
```

You should get the following output:

```
Out[8]:
```

	Quiz_1	Quiz_2
Corey	63	75
Kevin	48	98

Figure 10.22: Output of the newly defined DataFrame

7. Now, select the first two rows and the last two columns using index numbers.

You can use **.iloc** to select rows and columns by index, as shown in the following code snippet:

```
# Select first 2 rows and last 2 columns using index numbers
df.iloc[[0,1], [1,2]]
```

You should get the following output:

```
Out[9]:
```

	Quiz_2	Quiz_3
Corey	75	88
Kevin	98	92

Figure 10.23: Output of selecting the first two rows and last two columns using index numbers

Now, add a new column to find the quiz average of our students.

You can generate new columns in a variety of ways. One way is to use available methods such as the mean. In pandas, it's important to specify the axis. An axis of 0 represents the index, and an axis of 1 represents the rows.

8. Now, create a new column as the mean, as shown in the following code snippet:

```
# Define new column as mean of other columns
df['Quiz_Avg'] = df.mean(axis=1)
df
```

You should get the following output:

```
Out[10]:
```

	Quiz_1	Quiz_2	Quiz_3	Quiz_Avg
Corey	63	75	88	75.333333
Kevin	48	98	92	79.333333
Akshay	87	86	85	86.000000

Figure 10.24: Adding a new quiz_avg column to the output

A new column can also be added as a list by choosing the rows and columns by name first.

9. Create a new column as a list, as shown in the following code snippet:

```
df['Quiz_4'] = [92, 95, 88]
df
```

You should get the following output:

```
Out[11]:
```

	Quiz_1	Quiz_2	Quiz_3	Quiz_Avg	Quiz_4
Corey	63	75	88	75.333333	92
Kevin	48	98	92	79.333333	95
Akshay	87	86	85	86.000000	88

Figure 10.25: Output with a newly added column using lists

What if you need to delete the column you created? You can do so by using the **del** function. It's easy to delete columns in pandas using **del**.

10. Now, delete the **Quiz_Avg** column as it is not needed anymore:

```
del df['Quiz_Avg']
df
```

You should get the following output:

```
Out[12]:
```

	Quiz_1	Quiz_2	Quiz_3	Quiz_4
Corey	63	75	88	92
Kevin	48	98	92	95
Akshay	87	86	85	88

Figure 10.26: Output with a deleted column

In this exercise, you implemented different ways to add and remove columns as per our requirements. In the next section, you will be looking at new rows and **NaN**, which is an official **numpy** term.

New Rows and NaN

It's not easy to add new rows to a pandas DataFrame. A common strategy is to generate a new DataFrame and then to concatenate the values.

Say you have a new student who joins the class for the fourth quiz. What values should you put for the other three quizzes? The answer is NaN. It stands for **Not a Number**

NaN is an official NumPy term. It can be accessed using **np.NaN**. It is case-sensitive. In later exercises, you will look at how NaN can be used. In the next exercise, you will look at concatenating and working with null values.

Exercise 137: Concatenating and Finding the Mean with Null Values for Our testscore Data

In this exercise, you will be concatenating and finding the mean with null values for the student **testscore** data you created in *Exercise 136, Computing DataFrames within DataFrames* with four quiz scores. The following steps will enable you to complete the exercise:

1. Open a new Jupyter Notebook.

2. Import **pandas** and **numpy** and create a dictionary with the **testscore** data to be transformed into a DataFrame, as mentioned in *Exercise 134, Using DataFrames to Manipulate Stored Student testscore Data*:

```
import pandas as pd
# Create dictionary of test scores
test_dict = {'Corey':[63,75,88], 'Kevin':[48,98,92], 'Akshay': [87, 86, 85]}
# Create DataFrame
df = pd.DataFrame(test_dict)
```

3. Transpose the DataFrame and rename the columns:

```
df = df.T
df
# Rename Columns
df.columns = ['Quiz_1', 'Quiz_2', 'Quiz_3']
df
```

You should get the following output:

```
Out[5]:
```

	Quiz_1	Quiz_2	Quiz_3
Corey	63	75	88
Kevin	48	98	92
Akshay	87	86	85

Figure 10.27: The transposed and renamed DataFrame

4. Now, add a new column, as shown in *Exercise 136, Computing DataFrames within DataFrames*:

```
df['Quiz_4'] = [92, 95, 88]
df
```

You should get the following output:

```
Out[7]:
```

	Quiz_1	Quiz_2	Quiz_3	Quiz_4
Corey	63	75	88	92
Kevin	48	98	92	95
Akshay	87	86	85	88

Figure 10.28: Output of the added Quiz_4 column

5. Now, add a new row with the value set as **Adrian**, as shown in the following code snippet:

```
import numpy as np
# Create new DataFrame of one row
df_new = pd.DataFrame({'Quiz_1':[np.NaN], 'Quiz_2':[np.NaN], 'Quiz_3': [np.NaN],
'Quiz_4':[71]}, index=['Adrian'])
```

6. Now, concatenate **Dataframe** with the added new row, **Adrian**, and display the new **Dataframe** value using **df**:

```
# Concatenate DataFrames
df = pd.concat([df, df_new])
# Display new DataFrame
df
```

You should get the following output:

```
Out[7]:
```

	Quiz_1	Quiz_2	Quiz_3	Quiz_4
Corey	63.0	75.0	88.0	92
Kevin	48.0	98.0	92.0	95
Akshay	87.0	86.0	85.0	88
Adrian	NaN	NaN	NaN	71

Figure 10.29: Output with the row added to the DataFrame

You can now compute the new mean, but you must skip the **NaN** values; otherwise, there will be no mean score for **Adrian**. This will be fixed in step 7.

7. Find the **mean** value ignoring NaN and use these values to create a new column named **Quiz-Avg**, as shown in the following code snippet:

```
df['Quiz_Avg'] = df.mean(axis=1, skipna=True)
df
```

You should get the following output:

```
Out[8]:
```

	Quiz_1	Quiz_2	Quiz_3	Quiz_4	Quiz_Avg
Corey	63.0	75.0	88.0	92	79.50
Kevin	48.0	98.0	92.0	95	83.25
Akshay	87.0	86.0	85.0	88	86.50
Adrian	NaN	NaN	NaN	71	71.00

Figure 10.30: Output with quiz_4 values added to Adrian

Notice that all values are floats except for **Quiz_4**. There will be occasions when you need to cast all values in a particular column as another type.

Cast Column Types

For the sake of consistency, you will do that here. Cast all the ints in **Quiz_4** that you used in *Exercise 137, Concatenating and Finding the Mean with Null Values for Our testscore Data* as floats using the following code snippet:

```
df.Quiz_4.astype(float)
```

You should get the following output:

```
In [9]:  df.Quiz_4.astype(float)

Out[9]:  Corey      92.0
         Kevin      95.0
         Akshay     88.0
         Adrian     71.0
         Name: Quiz_4, dtype: float64
```

Figure 10.31: Output with the cast column types

You can observe the change in values by examining the DataFrame yourself. Now, move on to the next topic: which is data.

Data

Now that you have been introduced to NumPy and pandas, you will use them to analyze some real data.

Data scientists analyze data that exists in the cloud or online. One strategy is to download data directly to your computer.

> **Note**
>
> It is recommended to create a new folder to store all of your data. You can open your Jupyter Notebook in this same folder.

Downloading Data

Data comes in many formats, and pandas is equipped to handle most of them. In general, when looking for data to analyze, it's worth searching the keyword "dataset." A dataset is a collection of data. Online, "data" is everywhere, whereas datasets contain data in its raw format.

You will start by examining the famous Boston Housing dataset from 1980, which is available on our GitHub repository.

This dataset can be found here https://packt.live/31Cd96j.

You can begin by first downloading the dataset onto our system.

Downloading the Boston Housing Data from GitHub

1. Head to the GitHub repository and download the dataset onto your system.

2. Move the downloaded dataset file into your data folder.

3. Open a Jupyter Notebook in the same folder.

Reading Data

Now that the data is downloaded, and the Jupyter Notebook is open, you are ready to read the file. The most important part of reading a file is the extension. Our file is a `.csv` file. You need a method for reading `.csv` files.

CSV stands for Comma-Separated Values. CSV files are a popular way of storing and retrieving data, and pandas handles them very well.

Here is a list of standard data files that pandas will read, along with the code for reading data:

type of file	code
csv files:	pd.read_csv('file_name')
excel files:	pd.read_excel('file_name')
feather files:	pd.read_feather('file_name')
html files:	pd.read_html('file_name')
json files:	pd.read_json('file_name')
sql database:	pd.read_sql('file_name')

Figure 10.32: Standard data files that pandas read

If the files are clean, pandas will read them properly. Sometimes, files are not clean, and changing function parameters may be required. It's advisable to copy any errors and search for solutions online.

A further point of consideration is that the data should be read into a **DataFrame**. Pandas will convert the data into a DataFrame upon reading it, but you need to save **DataFrame** as a variable.

> **Note**
>
> **df** is often used to store DataFrames, but it's not universal since you may be dealing with many DataFrames.

In *Exercise 138*, *Reading and Viewing the Boston Housing Dataset*, you will be using the Boston Housing dataset and performing basic actions on the data.

Exercise 138: Reading and Viewing the Boston Housing Dataset

In this exercise, your goal is to read and view the Boston Housing dataset in our Jupyter Notebook. The following steps will enable you to complete the exercise:

1. Open a new Jupyter Notebook.

2. Import **pandas** as **pd**:

```
import pandas as pd
```

3. Now, choose a variable to store **DataFrame** and place the **HousingData.csv** file in the folder for *Exercise 138*. Then, run the following command:

```
housing_df = pd.read_csv('HousingData.csv')
```

If no errors arise, the file has been properly read. Now you can examine and view the file.

4. Now, you need to view the file by entering the following command:

```
housing_df.head()
```

The **pandas** **.head** method does just that. By default, it selects the first five rows. You may enter more if you choose by adding a number in parentheses.

You should get the following output:

	CRIM	ZN	INDUS	CHAS	NOX	RM	AGE	DIS	RAD	TAX	PTRATIO	B	LSTAT	MEDV
0	0.00632	18.0	2.31	0.0	0.538	6.575	65.2	4.0900	1	296	15.3	396.90	4.98	24.0
1	0.02731	0.0	7.07	0.0	0.469	6.421	78.9	4.9671	2	242	17.8	396.90	9.14	21.6
2	0.02729	0.0	7.07	0.0	0.469	7.185	61.1	4.9671	2	242	17.8	392.83	4.03	34.7
3	0.03237	0.0	2.18	0.0	0.458	6.998	45.8	6.0622	3	222	18.7	394.63	2.94	33.4
4	0.06905	0.0	2.18	0.0	0.458	7.147	54.2	6.0622	3	222	18.7	396.90	NaN	36.2

Figure 10.33: Output letting us view the first five rows of the dataset

Before you explore operations performed on this dataset, you may wonder what values such as **CRIM** and **ZN** mean in the dataset.

It's always nice to view data to get a general feel for things. In this particular case, you might want to know what the columns actually mean:

```
CRIM      per capita crime rate by town
ZN        proportion of residential land zoned for lots over 25,000 sq. Ft.
INDUS     proportion of non-retail business acres per town
CHAS      Charles River dummy variable (= 1 if tract bounds river; 0 otherwise)
NOX       nitric oxides concentration (parts per 10 million)
RM        average number of rooms per dwelling
AGE       proportion of owner-occupied units built prior to 1940
DIS       weighted distances to five Boston employment centers
RAD       index of accessibility to radial highways
TAX       full-value property-tax rate per $10,000
PTRATIO   pupil-teacher ratio by town
LSTAT     % lower status of the population
MEDV      Median value of owner-occupied homes in $1000's
```

Figure 10.34: Representation of the column values of the dataset

Now that you know what the values in the dataset mean you will start performing some advanced operations on the dataset. You will cover this in the following exercise.

Exercise 139: Gaining Data Insights on the Boston Housing Dataset

In this exercise, you will be performing some more advanced operations and using pandas methods to understand the dataset and get desired insights. The following steps will enable you to complete the exercise:

1. Open a new Jupyter Notebook and copy the dataset file into a separate folder where you will perform this exercise.

2. Import pandas and choose a variable to store **DataFrame** and place the **HousingData. csv** file:

```
import pandas as pd
housing_df = pd.read_csv('HousingData.csv')
```

3. Now, use the **describe()** method to display key statistical measures of each column, including the mean, median, and quartiles, as shown in the following code snippet:

```
housing_df.describe()
```

You should get the following output:

	CRIM	ZN	INDUS	CHAS	NOX	RM	AGE	DIS	RAD	TAX	PTRATIO	B	L
count	486.000000	486.000000	486.000000	486.000000	506.000000	506.000000	486.000000	506.000000	506.000000	506.000000	506.000000	506.000000	486.00
mean	3.611874	11.211934	11.083992	0.069959	0.554695	6.284634	68.518519	3.795043	9.549407	408.237154	18.455534	356.674032	12.71
std	8.720192	23.388876	6.835896	0.255340	0.115878	0.702617	27.999513	2.105710	8.707259	168.537116	2.164946	91.294864	7.15
min	0.006320	0.000000	0.460000	0.000000	0.385000	3.561000	2.900000	1.129600	1.000000	187.000000	12.600000	0.320000	1.73
25%	0.081900	0.000000	5.190000	0.000000	0.449000	5.885500	45.175000	2.100175	4.000000	279.000000	17.400000	375.377500	7.12
50%	0.253715	0.000000	9.690000	0.000000	0.538000	6.208500	76.800000	3.207450	5.000000	330.000000	19.050000	391.440000	11.43
75%	3.560262	12.500000	18.100000	0.000000	0.624000	6.623500	93.975000	5.188425	24.000000	666.000000	20.200000	396.225000	16.95
max	88.976200	100.000000	27.740000	1.000000	0.871000	8.780000	100.000000	12.126500	24.000000	711.000000	22.000000	396.900000	37.97

Figure 10.35: Output with the desired () method

In this output, you will review the meaning of each row.

Count: The number of rows with actual values.

Mean: The sum of each entry divided by the number of entries. It is often a good estimate of the average.

Std: The number of unit entries that are expected to deviate from the mean. It is a good measure of spread.

Min: The smallest entry in each column.

25%: The first quartile. 25% of the data has a value less than this number.

50%: The median. The halfway marker of the data. It is another good estimate of the average.

75%: The third quartile. 75% of the data has a value less than this number.

Max: The largest entry in each column.

4. Now use the **info()** method to deliver a full list of columns.

info() is especially valuable when you have hundreds of columns, and it takes a long time to horizontally scroll through each one:

```
housing_df.info()
```

You should get the following output:

```
<class 'pandas.core.frame.DataFrame'>
RangeIndex: 506 entries, 0 to 505
Data columns (total 14 columns):
CRIM        486 non-null  float64
ZN          486 non-null  float64
INDUS       486 non-null  float64
CHAS        486 non-null  float64
NOX         506 non-null  float64
RM          506 non-null  float64
AGE         486 non-null  float64
DIS         506 non-null  float64
RAD         506 non-null  int64
TAX         506 non-null  int64
PTRATIO     506 non-null  float64
B           506 non-null  float64
LSTAT       486 non-null  float64
MEDV        506 non-null  float64
dtypes: float64(12), int64(2)
memory usage: 55.4 KB
```

Figure 10.36: Output with the info () method

As you can see, `.info()` reveals the count of non-null values in each column along with the column type. Since some columns have less than 506 non-null values, it's safe to assume that the other values are null values.

In this dataset, there are a of total of 506 rows and 14 columns. You can use the `.shape` attribute to obtain this information.

Now confirm the number of rows and columns in the dataset:

```
housing_df.shape
```

You should get the following output:

```
(506, 14)
```

This confirms that you have 506 rows and 14 columns. Notice that **shape** does not have any parentheses after it. This is because it's technically an attribute and pre-computed.

In this exercise, you performed basic operations on the dataset, such as describing the dataset and finding the number of rows and columns in the dataset.

In the next section, you will cover null values.

Null Values

You need to do something about the null values. There are several popular choices when dealing with null values:

1. Eliminate the rows: A great approach if null values are a very small percentage, such as 1% of the total dataset.

2. Replace with a significant value, such as the median or the mean: A great approach if the rows are valuable, and the column is reasonably balanced.

3. Replace with the most likely value, perhaps a 0 or 1: It's preferable to option 2 when the median might be useless. The median can often work here.

> **Note**
>
> **mode** is the official term for the value that occurs the greatest number of times.

As you can see, which option you choose depends on the data.

Exercise 140: Null Value Operations on the Dataset

In this exercise, you will perform a null value operation. You can only select the columns that have null values in our dataset:

1. Open a new Jupyter Notebook and copy the dataset file within a separate folder where you will perform this exercise.

2. Import **pandas** and choose a variable to store the **DataFrame** and place the **HousingData.csv** file:

```
import pandas as pd
housing_df = pd.read_csv('HousingData.csv')
```

3. Now, find values and columns in the dataset with **null** values, as shown in the following code snippet:

```
housing_df.isnull().any()
```

You should get the following output:

```
CRIM        True
ZN          True
INDUS       True
CHAS        True
NOX         False
RM          False
AGE         True
DIS         False
RAD         False
TAX         False
PTRATIO     False
B           False
LSTAT       True
MEDV        False
dtype: bool
```

Figure 10.37: Output of the columns with null values

The .**isnull()** method will display an entire **DataFrame** of **True/False** values depending on the **Null** value. Give it a try.

The .**any()** method returns the individual columns.

Take it a step further and choose the **DataFrame** with those columns.

4. Now, using the **DataFrame**, find the null columns.

You can use .**loc** to find the location of particular rows. You will select the first five rows and all of the columns that have null values, as shown in the following code snippet:

```
housing_df.loc[:5, housing_df.isnull().any()]
```

You should get the following output:

	CRIM	ZN	INDUS	CHAS	AGE	LSTAT
0	0.00632	18.0	2.31	0.0	65.2	4.98
1	0.02731	0.0	7.07	0.0	78.9	9.14
2	0.02729	0.0	7.07	0.0	61.1	4.03
3	0.03237	0.0	2.18	0.0	45.8	2.94
4	0.06905	0.0	2.18	0.0	54.2	NaN
5	0.02985	0.0	2.18	0.0	58.7	5.21

Figure 10.38: Output of the dataset with the null columns

Now for the final step. Use the `.describe` method on these particular columns but select all of the rows.

5. Use the `.describe()` method on the null columns of the dataset.

The code mentioned ahead is a long piece of the code snippet. `housing_df` is the DataFrame. `.loc` allows you to specify rows and columns. `:` selects all rows. `housing_df.isnull().any()` selects only columns with null values. `.describe()` pulls up the statistics:

```
housing_df.loc[:, housing_df.isnull().any()].describe()
```

You should get the following output:

	CRIM	ZN	INDUS	CHAS	AGE	LSTAT
count	486.000000	486.000000	486.000000	486.000000	486.000000	486.000000
mean	3.611874	11.211934	11.083992	0.069959	68.518519	12.715432
std	8.720192	23.388876	6.835896	0.255340	27.999513	7.155871
min	0.006320	0.000000	0.460000	0.000000	2.900000	1.730000
25%	0.081900	0.000000	5.190000	0.000000	45.175000	7.125000
50%	0.253715	0.000000	9.690000	0.000000	76.800000	11.430000
75%	3.560262	12.500000	18.100000	0.000000	93.975000	16.955000
max	88.976200	100.000000	27.740000	1.000000	100.000000	37.970000

Figure 10.39: Output with the .describe() method on particular columns but instead selects all of the rows

Consider the first column, CRIM. The mean is way more than the median (50%). This indicates that the data is very right-skewed with some outliers. Indeed, you can see that the maximum of 88.97 is much larger than the 3.56 value of the 75th percentile. This makes the mean a poor replacement candidate for this column.

It turns out, after examining every column, that the median is a good candidate. Although the median is clearly not better than the mean in some cases, there are a few cases where the mean is clearly worse (CRIM, ZN, and CHAS).

The choice depends on what you ultimately want to do with the data. If the goal is a straightforward data analysis, eliminating the rows with null values is worth consideration. However, if the goal is to use machine learning to predict data, then perhaps more is to be gained by changing the null values to a suitable replacement. It's impossible to know in advance.

A more thorough examination could be warranted depending on the data. For instance, if analyzing new medical drugs, it would be worth putting more time and energy into appropriately dealing with null values. You may want to perform more analysis to determine whether a value is 0 or 1, depending upon other factors.

In this particular case, replacing all the null values with the median is warranted. You can have a look at this in the following example.

Replacing Null Values

Pandas include a nice method, fillna, which can be used to replace null values. It works for individual columns and entire DataFrames. You will use three approaches, replacing the null values of a column with the mean, replacing the null values of a column with another value, and replacing all the null values in the entire dataset with the median. You will use the same Boston Housing dataset.

Replace null column values with mean:

```
housing_df['AGE'] = housing_df['AGE'].fillna(housing_df.mean())
```

Then, replace null column values with a value:

```
housing_df['CHAS'] = housing_df['CHAS'].fillna(0)
```

Replace null DataFrame values with median:

```
housing_df = housing_df.fillna(housing_df.median())
```

Finally, check that all null values have been replaced:

```
housing_df.info()
```

You should get the following output:

```
<class 'pandas.core.frame.DataFrame'>
RangeIndex: 506 entries, 0 to 505
Data columns (total 14 columns):
CRIM        506 non-null float64
ZN          506 non-null float64
INDUS       506 non-null float64
CHAS        506 non-null float64
NOX         506 non-null float64
RM          506 non-null float64
AGE         506 non-null float64
DIS         506 non-null float64
RAD         506 non-null int64
TAX         506 non-null int64
PTRATIO     506 non-null float64
B           506 non-null float64
LSTAT       506 non-null float64
MEDV        506 non-null float64
dtypes: float64(12), int64(2)
memory usage: 55.4 KB
```

Figure 10.40: Output with the null values eliminated

After eliminating all null values, the dataset is much cleaner. There may also be unrealistic outliers or extreme outliers that will lead to poor prediction. These can often be detected through visual analysis, which you will be covering in the next section.

Visual Analysis

Most people interpret the data visually. They prefer to view colorful, meaningful graphs that make sense of the data. As a data science practitioner, it's your job to create these graphs.

In this section, you will primarily focus on two kinds of graphs: histograms and scatter plots. You will use Python to create these graphs. Although software packages such as Tableau are rather popular, they are essentially drag and drop. Since Python is an all-purpose programming language, the limitations are only what you know and are capable of doing.

The matplotlib Library

A popular Python library for creating graphs is **matplotlib**. It's traditionally imported as **plt**, as shown in the following code snippet:

```
import matplotlib.pyplot as plt
%matplotlib inline
```

Note the strange second line of code. It basically shows all graphs within Jupyter Notebooks instead of exporting them to external files. It's used when you want to see the graphs right there in front of you.

Histograms

Creating a histogram is rather simple. You choose a column and place it inside of **plt. hist()**. The general idea behind a histogram is that it groups the **x** value (in our case, the median home value) into various bins. The height of the bin is determined by the number of values that fall into that particular range. By default, Matplotlib selects 10 bins.

In order to make the graph more meaningful, you should add some labels. You can also use the Seaborn library by importing **seaborn** as **sns** , which provides some nice added visuals.

Exercise 141: Creating a Histogram Using the Boston Housing Dataset

In this exercise, you will use **MEDV**, the median value of the Boston Homes dataset, a future target column for machine learning. The following steps will enable you to complete the exercise:

1. Open a new Jupyter Notebook and copy the dataset file into a separate folder where you will perform this exercise.

2. Import **pandas** as pd and choose a variable, **housing_df**, to store the **DataFrame** after reading the **HousingData** csv file.:

```
import pandas as pd
housing_df = pd.read_csv('HousingData.csv')
```

3. Next, you need to import **matplotlib** as **plt**, as shown here:

```
import matplotlib.pyplot as plt
%matplotlib inline
```

> **Note**
>
> The **%matplotlib** inline ensures that your graphs appear in the Jupyter Notebook instead of external files.

4. Now, import **seaborn** which will make the graph more visually appealing.

```
import seaborn as sns
# Set up seaborn dark grid
sns.set()
```

5. Now plot the histogram for the dataset.

```
plt.hist(housing_df['MEDV'])
plt.show()
```

You should get the following output:

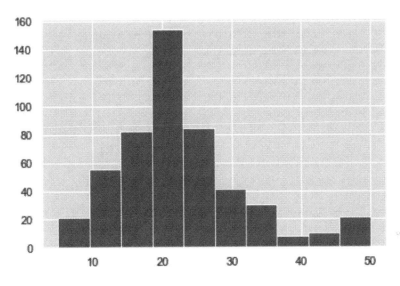

Figure 10.41: Output of the histogram

6. Now, plot the changes onto the histogram, as shown in the following code snippet:

```
plt.hist(housing_df['MEDV'])
plt.title('Median Boston Housing Prices')
plt.xlabel('1980 Median Value in Thousands')
plt.ylabel('Count')
plt.show()
```

You should get the following output:

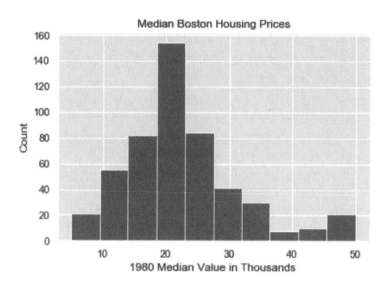

Figure 10.42: Histogram with meaningful values using seaborn

Now, this is a bit clearer. But in the Jupyter Notebook, the entry is a little small. You can make the graph and the title larger. You can also save the figure using the title of the graph.

7. Make the histogram clearer by increasing the **dpi(dots per inch)** and the **fontsize**. This indicates that the output is really flexible, as per our needs. Copy the following code snippet and observe the change in the output:

```
title = 'Median Boston Housing Prices'
plt.figure(figsize=(10,6))
plt.hist(housing_df['MEDV'])
plt.title(title, fontsize=15)
plt.xlabel('1980 Median Value in Thousands')
plt.ylabel('Count')
plt.savefig(title, dpi=300)
plt.show()
```

You should get the following output:

Figure 10.43: Output of an ideal histogram

By the end of this exercise, you were able to achieve a solid histogram, which can help to communicate your results to a wider audience.

Now, say you want to create another histogram. Should you keep copying the same code? Copying code repeatedly is never a good idea. It's better to write functions.

Histogram Functions

Define a histogram function, as mentioned in the following code snippet:

```
def my_hist(column, title, xlab, ylab):
    plt.figure(figsize=(10,6))
    plt.hist(column)
    plt.title(title, fontsize=15)
    plt.xlabel(xlab)
    plt.ylabel(ylab)
    plt.savefig(title, dpi=300)
    plt.show()
```

It's not easy to create functions with Matplotlib, so you should go over the parameters carefully. The **figsize** allows you to establish the size of the figure. The **column** is the essential parameter. It's what you are going to be graphing. Next, you have the title, followed by the label for the x and y axes. Finally, you save the figure and show the plot. Inside of the function is basically the same code that you ran before. You can try it on a new column – the number of rooms.

Do this by calling the histogram function, as mentioned in the following code snippet:

```
my_hist(housing_df['RM'], 'Average Number of Rooms in Boston Households', 'Average Number
of Rooms', 'Count')
```

You should get the following output:

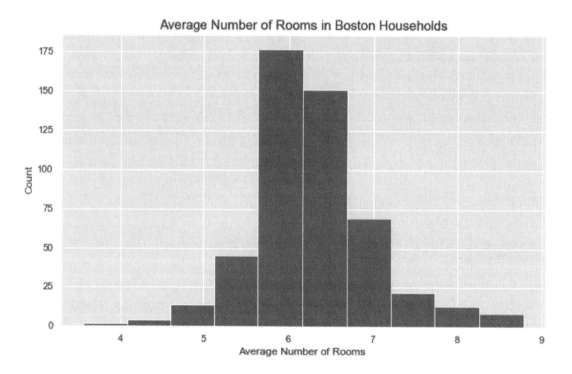

Figure 10.44: Output with the histogram function

Okay. It's not bad, but there's one glaring issue. It's the distribution of bins. It seems most rooms have an average of six, but how many of those are closer to seven? Our graph could be improved if each histogram was clearly between two numbers on the plot. A survey of the preceding data (check **max** and **min** from .**describe()**), reveals that the average number of rooms is between three and nine.

In addition to changing the bins, you can also add options to change the color, and the alpha, or transparency.

You can improve the built histogram function, as mentioned in the following code snippet:

```
def my_hist(column, title, xlab, ylab, bins=10, alpha=0.7, color='c'):
    title = title
    plt.figure(figsize=(10,6))
    plt.hist(column, bins=bins, range=(3,9), alpha=alpha, color=color)
    plt.title(title, fontsize=15)
    plt.xlabel(xlab)
    plt.ylabel(ylab)
    plt.savefig(title, dpi=300)
    plt.show()
```

The number of bins is 10 by default, so you can change it whenever you desire. **alpha** is a convenient tool that can be used to make the bars transparent. 1.0 has no transparency, and 0.0 has full transparency. Play around with this to select the number that you like.

Call the improved histogram function:

```
my_hist(housing_df['RM'], 'Average Number of Rooms in Boston',
'Average Number of Rooms', 'Count', bins=6)
```

You should get the following output:

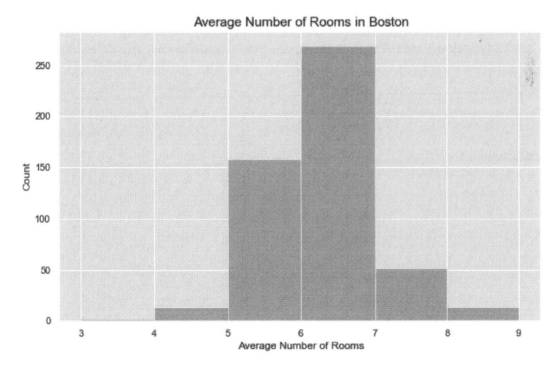

Figure 10.45: Output of the improved histogram function being called

Now it's clear that the highest average is between six and seven. Also, note that this dataset is surveying groups of houses, not individual houses. This is why the average number of rooms is between 6 and 7.

Now that you have understood histograms you can have a look at another type of visual data analysis, called scatter plots.

Scatter Plots

Scatter plots are hugely important in data analysis. They require an x value, and a y value, typically taken from two numeric columns of a DataFrame. You can use the average number of rooms as our x value and the average median income as our y value.

Exercise 142: Creating a Scatter Plot for the Boston Housing Dataset

In this exercise, you will create a scatter plot for our Boston housing dataset.

The following steps will enable you to complete the exercise:

1. Open a new Jupyter file and copy the dataset file into a separate folder.

2. Import **pandas** and choose a variable to store the **DataFrame** and place the **HousingData.csv** file:

```
import pandas as pd
housing_df = pd.read_csv('HousingData.csv')
```

3. Next, you need to import **matplotlib** as **plt**, as shown here:

```
import matplotlib.pyplot as plt
%matplotlib inline
```

4. Now you need to plot the scatter plot data, as shown in the following code snippet:

```
x = housing_df['RM']
y = housing_df['MEDV']
plt.scatter(x, y)
plt.show()
```

You should get the following output:

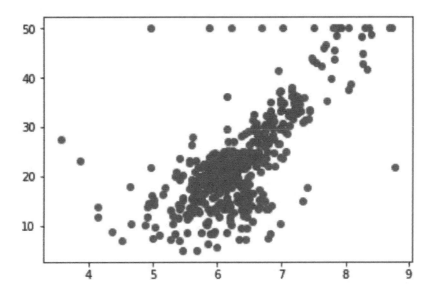

Figure 10.46: Scatter plot output of the dataset

There is a definite positive association. This means that as the x value goes up, the y value goes up.

In statistics, there is a particular concept to determine association; it's called **correlation**.

Correlation

Correlation is a statistical measure between –1 and +1 that indicates how closely two variables are related. A correlation of –1 or +1 means that variables are dependent, and they fall in a perfectly straight line. A correlation of 0 indicates that an increase in one variable gives no information whatsoever about the other variable. Visually, this would be points all over the place. Correlations usually fall somewhere in the middle. For instance, a correlation of 0.75 represents a fairly strong relationship, whereas a correlation of 0.25 is a reasonably weak relationship. Positive correlations go up (meaning as x goes up, y goes up), and negative correlations go down.

In the following exercise, you will find the correlation values from the Boston Housing dataset.

Exercise 143: Correlation Values from the Dataset

In this exercise, you will find the correlation values from the Boston Housing dataset. The following steps will enable you to complete the exercise:

1. Open a new Jupyter Notebook and copy the **dataset** file into a separate folder where you will perform this exercise.

2. Import **pandas** and choose a variable to store **DataFrame** and place the **HousingData. csv** file:

```
import pandas as pd
housing_df = pd.read_csv('HousingData.csv')
```

3. Next, you need to import **matplotlib** as **plt**, as shown here:

```
import matplotlib.pyplot as plt
%matplotlib inline
```

4. Now, find the correlation value of the dataset, as shown in the following code snippet:

```
housing_df.corr()
```

You should get the following output:

	CRIM	ZN	INDUS	CHAS	NOX	RM	AGE	DIS	RAD	TAX	PTRATIO	B	LSTAT	MEDV
CRIM	1.000000	-0.191178	0.401863	-0.054355	0.417130	-0.219150	0.354342	-0.374166	0.624765	0.580595	0.281110	-0.381411	0.444943	-0.391363
ZN	-0.191178	1.000000	-0.531871	-0.037229	-0.513704	0.320800	-0.563801	0.656739	-0.310919	-0.312371	-0.414046	0.171303	-0.414193	0.373136
INDUS	0.401863	-0.531871	1.000000	0.059859	0.764866	-0.390234	0.638431	-0.711709	0.604533	0.731055	0.390954	-0.360532	0.590690	-0.481772
CHAS	-0.054355	-0.037229	0.059859	1.000000	0.075097	0.104885	0.078831	-0.093971	0.001468	-0.032304	-0.111304	0.051264	-0.047424	0.181391
NOX	0.417130	-0.513704	0.764866	0.075097	1.000000	-0.302188	0.731548	-0.769230	0.611441	0.668023	0.188933	-0.380051	0.582641	-0.427321
RM	-0.219150	0.320800	-0.390234	0.104885	-0.302188	1.000000	-0.247337	0.205246	-0.209847	-0.292048	-0.355501	0.128069	-0.614339	0.695360
AGE	0.354342	-0.563801	0.638431	0.078831	0.731548	-0.247337	1.000000	-0.744844	0.458349	0.509114	0.269226	-0.275303	0.602891	-0.394656
DIS	-0.374166	0.656739	-0.711709	-0.093971	-0.769230	0.205246	-0.744844	1.000000	-0.494588	-0.534432	-0.232471	0.291512	-0.493328	0.249929
RAD	0.624765	-0.310919	0.604533	0.001468	0.611441	-0.209847	0.458349	-0.494588	1.000000	0.910228	0.464741	-0.444413	0.479541	-0.381626
TAX	0.580595	-0.312371	0.731055	-0.032304	0.668023	-0.292048	0.509114	-0.534432	0.910228	1.000000	0.460853	-0.441808	0.536110	-0.468536
PTRATIO	0.281110	-0.414046	0.390954	-0.111304	0.188933	-0.355501	0.269226	-0.232471	0.464741	0.460853	1.000000	-0.177383	0.375966	-0.507787
B	-0.381411	0.171303	-0.360532	0.051264	-0.380051	0.128069	-0.275303	0.291512	-0.444413	-0.441808	-0.177383	1.000000	-0.369889	0.333461
LSTAT	0.444943	-0.414193	0.590690	-0.047424	0.582641	-0.614339	0.602891	-0.493328	0.479541	0.536110	0.375966	-0.369889	1.000000	-0.735822
MEDV	-0.391363	0.373136	-0.481772	0.181391	-0.427321	0.695360	-0.394656	0.249929	-0.381626	-0.468536	-0.507787	0.333461	-0.735822	1.000000

Figure 10.47: Correlation value output

This tells us the exact correlation values. For instance, to see what variables are the most correlated with the **Median Value Home**, you can examine the values under the **MEDV** column. There, you will find that **RM** is the largest at **0.695360**. But you also see a value of **-0.735822** for **LSTAT**, which is the percentage of the lower status of the population. Seaborn provides a nice way to view correlations, called a heatmap. You can have a look at a heatmap in the following step.

Now, you need to get the heatmap for the correlation values.

5. Begin by importing the **seaborn** module as **sns**:

```
import seaborn as sns
# Set up seaborn dark grid
sns.set()
```

6. Now find the **heatmap**, as shown in the following code snippet:

```
corr = housing_df.corr()
plt.figure(figsize=(8,6))
sns.heatmap(corr, xticklabels=corr.columns.values,
yticklabels=corr.columns.values, cmap="Blues", linewidths=1.25, alpha=0.8)
plt.show()
```

You should get the following output:

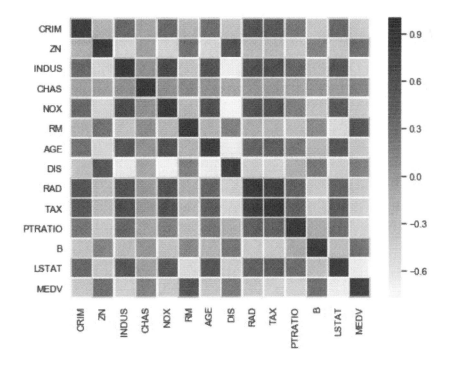

Figure 10.48: Heatmap for the correlation values

The darker the squares, the higher the correlation, and the lighter the squares, the lower the correlation. Now when examining the MEDV column, it's much easier to find the darkest square RM, and the lightest square LSTAT. You may have noticed that technically the MEDV square is the darkest. This has to be true because MEDV is perfectly correlated with itself. The same holds for each column along the diagonal.

In this exercise, you were able to work with correlation values from the dataset and get a visual aid for the data output.

In the next section, you will have a look at regression.

Regression

Perhaps the most important addition to a scatter plot is the regression line. The idea of regression came from Sir Francis Galton, who measured the heights of the offspring of very tall and very short parents. The offspring were not taller or shorter than these parents on average, but rather closer to the mean height of all people. Sir Francis Galton used the term "regression to the mean," meaning that the heights of the offspring were closer to the mean of their very tall or very short parents. The name stuck.

In statistics, a regression line is a line that tries to fit the values of a scatter plot as closely as possible. Generally speaking, half of the points are above the line, and half of the points are below. The most popular regression line method is ordinary least squares, which sums the square of the distance from each point to the line.

There are a variety of methods to compute and display regression lines using Python.

Plotting a Regression Line

To create a regression line of our Boston dataset, the following code steps need to be followed:

```
plt.figure(figsize=(10, 7))
sns.regplot(x,y)
plt.show()
```

You should get the following output:

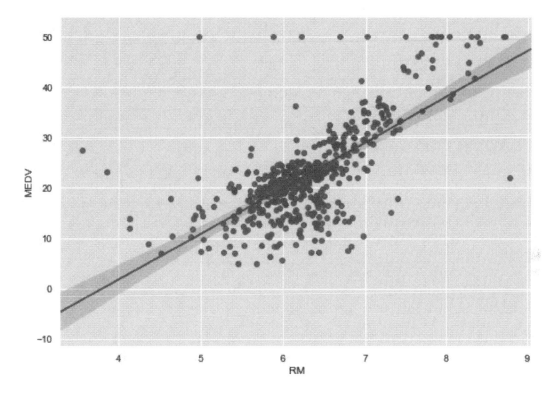

Figure 10.49: Example output of a regression line

You may wonder about the shaded part of the line. It represents a 95% confidence interval, meaning that Python is 95% confident that the actual regression line falls within that range. Since the shaded area is fairly small in relation to the plot, this means that the regression line is reasonably accurate.

The general idea behind regression lines is that they can be used to predict new y values from new x values. For instance, if there is an eight-room house, you can use regression to get an estimate of its value. You will use this general philosophy in a more sophisticated manner in *Chapter 11, Machine Learning*, using the machine learning version of linear regression.

Although this is not a course on statistics, you want to provide enough of an introduction so that you can analyze data on your own. In this respect, there is one more key piece to the regression that is worth sharing. It's the data about the line itself.

StatsModel Regression Output

You will import **StatsModel** and use its methods to print out a summary of the regression line:

```
import statsmodels.api as sm
X = sm.add_constant(x)
model = sm.OLS(y, X)
est = model.fit()
print(est.summary())
```

The strangest part of the code is adding the constant. This is basically the y-intercept. When the constant is not added, the y-intercept is 0. In our case, it makes sense that the y-intercept would be 0; if there are 0 rooms, the house should have no value. In general, however, it's a good idea to keep a y-intercept, and it's the default choice of the preceding Seaborn graph. It's a good idea to try both methods and compare the results of the data. A comparative analysis will definitely improve your background in statistics:

```
                            OLS Regression Results
==============================================================================
Dep. Variable:                   MEDV   R-squared:                       0.484
Model:                            OLS   Adj. R-squared:                  0.483
Method:                 Least Squares   F-statistic:                     471.8
Date:                Wed, 16 Oct 2019   Prob (F-statistic):           2.49e-74
Time:                        14:42:27   Log-Likelihood:                -1673.1
No. Observations:                 506   AIC:                             3350.
Df Residuals:                     504   BIC:                             3359.
Df Model:                           1
Covariance Type:            nonrobust
==============================================================================
                 coef    std err          t      P>|t|      [0.025      0.975]
------------------------------------------------------------------------------
const        -34.6706      2.650    -13.084      0.000     -39.877     -29.465
RM             9.1021      0.419     21.722      0.000       8.279       9.925
==============================================================================
Omnibus:                      102.585   Durbin-Watson:                   0.684
Prob(Omnibus):                  0.000   Jarque-Bera (JB):              612.449
Skew:                           0.726   Prob(JB):                     1.02e-133
Kurtosis:                       8.190   Cond. No.                         58.4
==============================================================================

Warnings:
[1] Standard Errors assume that the covariance matrix of the errors is correctly specified.
```

Figure 10.50: Summary of the regression line

There's a lot of important information in this table. The first is the value of **R^2** at 0.484. This suggests that 48% of the data can be explained by the regression line. The second is the coefficient constant of **-34.6706**. This is the y-intercept. The third is the RM coefficient of **9.1021**. This suggests that for every one-bedroom increase, the value of the house increased by 9,102. (Keep in mind that this dataset is from 1980.)

The standard error suggests how far off the actual values are from the line on average, and the numbers underneath the [0.025 0.975] column give the 95% **Confidence Interval** of the value, meaning `statsmodel` is 95% confident that the true increase in the value of the average house for every one-bedroom increase is between 8,279 and 9,925.

Additional Models

There's a great deal of data analysis in Python — far more than you can adequately cover in an introductory text. Thus far, you have covered histograms and scatter plots in considerable detail. Two additional types of plots will be highlighted before moving on to machine learning.

Exercise 144: Box Plots

A box plot provides a nice visual of the mean, median, quartiles, and outliers of a given column of data.

In this exercise, you will create box plots using the Boston Housing dataset. The following steps will enable you to complete the exercise:

1. Open a new Jupyter Notebook and copy the dataset file within a separate folder where you will perform this exercise.

2. Import **pandas** and choose a variable to store the DataFrame and place the **HousingData.csv** file:

```
import pandas as pd
housing_df = pd.read_csv('HousingData.csv')
import matplotlib.pyplot as plt
%matplotlib inline
import seaborn as sns
# Set up seaborn dark grid
sns.set()
```

3. Now, enter the following code in the code snippet to create a box plot:

```
x = housing_df['RM']
y = housing_df['MEDV']
plt.boxplot(x)
plt.show()
```

You should get the following output:

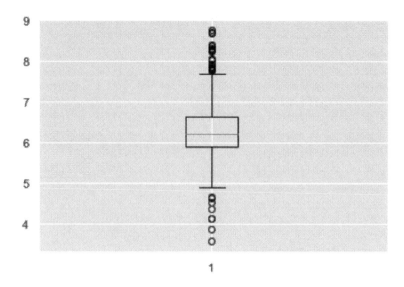

Figure 10.51: Box plot output

Note that the open circles are considered outliers. The orange bar in the middle is the median, and the bars at the end of the black box are the 25th and 75th percentiles, or the 1st and 3rd quartiles, respectively. The end bars represent the quartiles plus or minus 1.5 times the interquartile range. The value of 1.5 times the interquartile range is a standard limit in statistics used to define outliers. In this exercise, you created a box plot graph to represent the graph.

Violin Plots

A violin plot is a different type of plot that conveys similar information:

```
plt.violinplot(x)
plt.show()
```

You should get the following output:

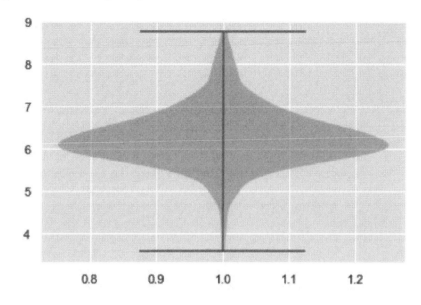

Figure 10.52: Violin plot output

In the violin plot, the upper and lower bars define the minimum and maximum values, and the width of the plot indicates how many rows contain that particular value. The difference between the violin plot and the box plot is that the violin plot shows the overall distribution of the data.

Now, you will have a look at an activity to see whether you are able to implement the concepts covered in this chapter.

Activity 24: Data Analysis to Find the Outliers in Pay versus the Salary Report in the UK Statistics Dataset

You are working as a data scientist, and you come across a government dataset that seems really interesting with regard to pay. But as the dataset values are cluttered, you need to use visual data analysis to study the data and come to a conclusion to understand whether there are any outliers in the dataset.

In this activity, you will be performing visual data analysis using histograms and scatter plots and creating a regression line to come to a certain conclusion.

Follow these steps to complete this activity:

1. First, you need to copy the **UKStatistics.csv** dataset file into a specific folder.

2. Now, import the necessary data visualization packages.

3. View the dataset file and find the number of rows and columns in the dataset file.

4. Plot the histogram for **Actual Pay Floor (£)**.

5. Plot the scatter plot using the values for **x** as **Salary Cost of Reports (£)** and **y** as **Actual Pay Floor (£)**.

6. Now get the box plot for the **x** and **y** values, as shown in *Step 5*.

> **Note**
>
> **UKStatistics.csv** is available for download on GitHub here: https://packt.live/2Pf7al4.
>
> More information on the **UKStatistics** dataset can be found at https://packt.live/2BzBwqF.

Here is the expected output with the outliers in the box plot:

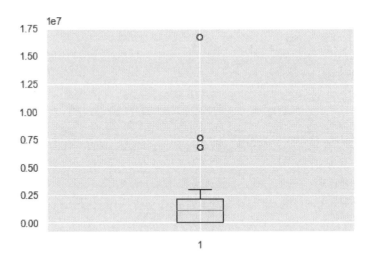

Figure 10.53: The expected output with the outliers in the x and y data

> **Note**
>
> The solution for this activity is available on page 554.

Summary

You began our introduction to data analysis with `NumPy`, Python's incredibly fast library for handling massive matrix computations. Next, you learned about the fundamentals of pandas, Python's library for handling DataFrames. Taken together, you used NumPy and pandas to analyze the Boston Housing dataset, which included descriptive statistical methods and Matplotlib and Seaborn's graphical libraries. Along the way, you learned about fundamental statistical concepts, including the mean, standard deviation, median, quartiles, correlation, skewed data, and outliers. You also learned about advanced methods for creating clean, clearly labeled, publishable graphs.

In *Chapter 11, Machine Learning*, you will come across interesting machine learning concepts such as regression, different types of classifications, decision trees. You will use Python to build efficient machine learning models and predict new results.

11

Machine Learning

Overview

By the end of this chapter, you will be able to, apply machine learning algorithms to solve different problems; compare, contrast, and apply different types of machine learning algorithms, including linear regression, logistic regression, decision trees, random forests, Naive Bayes, and AdaBoost; analyze overfitting and implement regularization; work with `GridSearchCV` and `RandomizedSearchCV` to adjust hyperparameters; evaluate algorithms using a confusion matrix and cross-validation and solve real-world problems using the machine learning algorithms outlined here.

Introduction

Computer algorithms enable machines to learn from data. The more data an algorithm receives, the more capable the algorithm is of detecting underlying patterns within the data. In *Chapter 10, Data Analytics with pandas and NumPy,* you learned how to view and analyze big data with pandas and NumPy. In this chapter, we will now extend these concepts to building algorithms that learn from data.

Consider how a child learns to identify a cat. Generally speaking, a child learns by having someone point out "That's a cat," "No, that's a dog," and so on. After enough cats and non-cats have been pointed out, the child knows how to identify a cat.

Machine learning implements the same general approach. A convolutional neural network is a machine learning algorithm that distinguishes between images. Upon receiving images labeled cats and non-cats, the algorithm looks for underlying patterns within the pixels by adjusting the parameters of an equation until it finds an equation that minimizes the error.

After the algorithm has selected the best possible equation, given the data it has received, this equation is used to predict future data. When a new image arrives, the new image is placed within the algorithm to determine whether the image is a cat or not.

In this chapter, on machine learning, you will learn how to construct linear regression, logistic regression, decision tree, random forest, Naive Bayes, and AdaBoost algorithms. These algorithms can be used to solve a wide range of problems, from predicting rainfall to detecting credit card fraud and identifying diseases.

Then, you will learn about Ridge and Lasso, two regularized machine learning algorithms that are variations of Linear Regression. You will learn about using regularization and cross-validation to obtain accurate results with data that the algorithm has never seen before.

After learning how to build a machine learning model in scikit-learn through an extended example with linear regression, you will take a similar approach to build models based on k-nearest neighbors, decision trees, and random forests. You will learn how to extend these models with hyperparameter turning, a way of fine-tuning models to meet the specifications of the data at hand.

Next, you will move onto classification problems, where the machine learning model is used to determine whether an email is a spam and whether a celestial object is a planet. All classification problems can be tackled with Logistic Regression, a machine learning algorithm that you will learn about here. In addition, you will solve classification problems with Naïve Bayes, Random Forests, and other types of algorithms. Classification results can be interpreted with a confusion matrix and a classification report, both of which we will explore in-depth.

Finally, you will learn how to implement boosting methods that transform weak learners into strong learners. In particular, you will learn how to implement AdaBoost, one of the most successful machine learning algorithms in history.

To sum it up, after completing this chapter, you will be able to apply multiple machine learning algorithms to solve classification and regression problems. You will be capable of using advanced tools such as a confusion matrix and a classification report to interpret results. You will also be able to refine your models using regularization and hyperparameter tuning. In short, you will have the tools to use machine learning to solve real-world problems, including predicting cost and classifying objects.

Introduction to Linear Regression

Machine learning is the ability of computers to learn from data. The power of machine learning comes from making future predictions based on the data received. Today, machine learning is used all over the world to predict the weather, stock prices, movie recommendations, profits, errors, clicks, purchases, words to complete a sentence, and many more things.

The unparalleled success of machine learning has led to a paradigm shift in the way businesses make decisions. In the past, businesses made decisions based on who had the most influence. But now, the new idea is to make decisions based on data. Decisions are constantly being made about the future, and machine learning is the best tool at our disposal to convert raw data into actionable decisions.

The first step in building a machine learning algorithm is deciding what you want to predict. When looking at a DataFrame, the idea is to choose one column as the **target** column or **predictor** column. The target column, by definition, is what the algorithm will be trained to predict.

Recall the Boston Housing dataset introduced in *Chapter 10, Data Analytics with pandas and NumPy*. The median value of a home is a desirable target column since real estate agents, buyers, and sellers often want to know how much a house is worth. People usually determine this information based on the size of the house, the location, the number of bedrooms, and many other factors.

Here is the Boston Housing DataFrame from *Chapter 10, Data Analytics with pandas and NumPy*. Each column includes features about houses in the neighborhood, such as crime, the average age of the house, and notably, in the last column, the median value:

	CRIM	ZN	INDUS	CHAS	NOX	RM	AGE	DIS	RAD	TAX	PTRATIO	B	LSTAT	MEDV
0	0.00632	18.0	2.31	0.0	0.538	6.575	65.2	4.0900	1	296	15.3	396.90	4.98	24.0
1	0.02731	0.0	7.07	0.0	0.469	6.421	78.9	4.9671	2	242	17.8	396.90	9.14	21.6
2	0.02729	0.0	7.07	0.0	0.469	7.185	61.1	4.9671	2	242	17.8	392.83	4.03	34.7
3	0.03237	0.0	2.18	0.0	0.458	6.998	45.8	6.0622	3	222	18.7	394.63	2.94	33.4
4	0.06905	0.0	2.18	0.0	0.458	7.147	54.2	6.0622	3	222	18.7	396.90	NaN	36.2

Figure 11.1: Sample from the Boston Housing dataset

You may be wondering what the values **CRIM**, **NOX**, and so on mean in the dataset. Don't worry – have a look at the following figure:

```
CRIM      per capita crime rate by town
ZN        proportion of residential land zoned for lots over 25,000 sq. Ft.|
INDUS     proportion of non-retail business acres per town
CHAS      Charles River dummy variable (= 1 if tract bounds river; 0 otherwise)
NOX       nitric oxides concentration (parts per 10 million)
RM        average number of rooms per dwelling
AGE       proportion of owner-occupied units built prior to 1940
DIS       weighted distances to five Boston employment centers
RAD       index of accessibility to radial highways
TAX       full-value property-tax rate per $10,000
PTRATIO   pupil-teacher ratio by town
LSTAT     % lower status of the population
MEDV      Median value of owner-occupied homes in $1000's
```

Figure 11.2: Dataset value representation

We want to come up with an equation that uses every other column to predict the last column, which will be our target column. What kind of equation should we use? Before we answer this question, let's have a look at a simplified version.

Simplify the Problem

It's often helpful to simplify a problem. What if we take just one column, such as the number of bedrooms, and use it to predict the median house value?

It's clear that the more bedrooms a house has, the more valuable it will be. As the number of bedrooms goes up, so does the house value. A standard way to represent this positive association is with a straight line.

In *Chapter 10, Data Analytics with pandas and NumPy*, we modeled the relationship between the number of bedrooms and the median house value with the linear regression line, as shown in *Figure 11.3*:

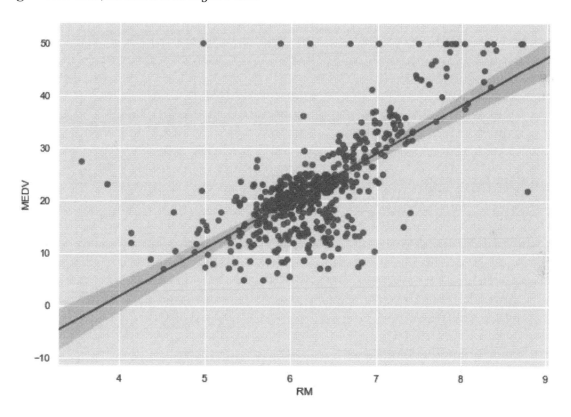

Figure 11.3: Linear regression line for the median value and the number of bedrooms

It turns out that linear regression is a very popular machine learning algorithm. Linear regression is worth trying whenever the target column is a continuous value, as in this dataset. The value of a home is generally considered to be continuous. There is technically no limit to how high the cost of a home may be. It could take any value between two numbers, despite often rounding up.

By contrast, if we predict whether a house will sell after one month on the market, the possible answers are yes and no. In this case, the target column is not continuous but binary.

> **Note**
>
> Whenever the target column is binary, linear regression will not produce strong results.

From One to N-Dimensions

Dimensionality is an important concept in machine learning. In math, it's common to work with two dimensions, x, and y, in the coordinate plane. In physics, it's common to work with three dimensions, the x, y, and z axes. When it comes to spatial dimensions, three is the limit because we live in a three-dimensional universe. In mathematics, however, there is no restriction on the number of dimensions we can use theoretically. In superstring theory, 12 or 13 dimensions are often used. In machine learning, however, the number of dimensions is often the number of **predictor** columns.

There is no need to limit ourselves to one-dimension with linear regression. Additional dimensions – in this case, additional columns – will give us more information about the median house value and make our model more valuable.

In one-dimensional linear regression, the slope-intercept equation is $y = mx + b$, where y is the target column, x is the input, m is the slope, and b is the y-intercept. This equation is now extended to an arbitrary number of dimensions using $Y = MX + B$, where Y, M, and X are vectors of arbitrary length. Instead of the slope, M is referred to as the weight.

> **Note**
>
> It's not essential to comprehend the linear algebra behind vector mathematics to run machine learning algorithms; however, it is essential to comprehend the underlying ideas. The underlying idea here is that linear regression can be extended to an arbitrary number of dimensions.

In the Boston Housing dataset, the linear regression model will select weights for each of the columns. In order to predict the median house value for each row (our target column), the weights will be multiplied by the column entries and then summed to get as close as possible to the value.

We will have a look at how this works in practice.

The Linear Regression Algorithm

Before implementing the algorithm, let's take a brief look at the libraries that we will **import** and use in our programs:

- **pandas** – You learned how to use **pandas** in *Chapter 10, Data Analytics with pandas and NumPy*. When it comes to machine learning, all data will be handled through **pandas**. Loading data, reading data, viewing data, cleaning data, and manipulating data all require **pandas**, so **pandas** will always be our first **import**.

- **NumPy** – **NumPy** was introduced in *Chapter 10, Data Analytics with pandas and NumPy*, as well. This will be used for mathematical computations on the dataset. It's always a good idea to import **NumPy** when performing machine learning.

- **LinearRegression** – The **LinearRegression** library should be implemented every time linear regression is used. The **LinearRegression** library will allow you to build linear regression models and test them in very few steps. Machine learning libraries do the heavy lifting for you. In this case, **LinearRegression** will place weights on each of the columns and adjust them until it finds an optimal solution to predict the **target** column, which in our case would be the median house value.

- **Mean_squared_error** – In order to find optimal values, the algorithm needs a measure to test how well it's doing. Measuring how far the model's predicted value is from the target value is a standard place to start. In order to avoid negatives canceling out positives, we can use **mean_squared_error**. To compute the **mean_squared_error**, the prediction of each row is subtracted from the target column or actual value, and the result is squared. Each result is summed, and the mean is computed. Finally, taking the square root keeps the units the same.

- **Train_test_split** – Python provides **train_test_split** to split data into a **training** set and a **test** set. Splitting the data into a training set and test set is essential because it allows users to test the model right away. Testing the model on data the machine has never seen before is the most important part of building the model because it shows how well the model will perform in the real world.

Most of the data is included in the training set because more data leads to a more robust model. A smaller portion – around **20%** – is held back for the test set. The **80-20** split is the default, though you may adjust it as you see fit. The model is optimized on the training set, and after completion, it is scored against the test set.

These libraries are a part of **scikit-learn**. **scikit-learn** has a wealth of excellent online resources for beginners. See https://scikit-learn.org/stable/ for more information.

Exercise 145: Using Linear Regression to Predict the Accuracy of the Median Values of Our Dataset

The goal of this exercise is to build a machine learning model using linear regression. Your model will predict the median value of Boston houses and, based on this, we will come to a conclusion about whether the value is optimal or not.

This exercise will be performed on a Jupyter Notebook.

> **Note**
>
> To proceed with the exercises in the chapter, you will need the **scikit-learn** library that is mentioned in the Preface.

1. Open a new notebook file.

2. Now, **import** all the necessary libraries, as shown in the following code snippet:

```
import pandas as pd
import numpy as np
from sklearn.linear_model import LinearRegression
from sklearn.metrics import mean_squared_error
from sklearn.model_selection import train_test_split
```

Now that we have imported the libraries, we will load the data.

3. Load the dataset and view the DataFrames to look at the first five rows:

```
# load data
housing_df = pd.read_csv('HousingData.csv')
housing_df.head()
```

Recall that, as mentioned in *Chapter 10, Data Analytics with pandas and NumPy*, **housing_df = pd.read_cs('HousingData.csv')** will read the **CSV** file in parentheses and store it in a DataFrame called **housing_df**. Then, **housing_df.head()** will display the first five rows of the **housing_df** DataFrame by default.

You should get the following output:

	CRIM	ZN	INDUS	CHAS	NOX	RM	AGE	DIS	RAD	TAX	PTRATIO	B	LSTAT	MEDV
0	0.00632	18.0	2.31	0.0	0.538	6.575	65.2	4.0900	1	296	15.3	396.90	4.98	24.0
1	0.02731	0.0	7.07	0.0	0.469	6.421	78.9	4.9671	2	242	17.8	396.90	9.14	21.6
2	0.02729	0.0	7.07	0.0	0.469	7.185	61.1	4.9671	2	242	17.8	392.83	4.03	34.7
3	0.03237	0.0	2.18	0.0	0.458	6.998	45.8	6.0622	3	222	18.7	394.63	2.94	33.4
4	0.06905	0.0	2.18	0.0	0.458	7.147	54.2	6.0622	3	222	18.7	396.90	NaN	36.2

Figure 11.4: Output with the dataset displayed

4. Next, enter the following code to clean the dataset of null values using .dropna():

```
# drop null values
housing_df = housing_df.dropna()
```

In *Chapter 10, Data Analytics with pandas and NumPy*, we cleared the **null** values by counting them and comparing them to measures of central tendency. In this chapter, however, we will use a swifter approach in order to expedite testing for machine learning. The **housing_df.dropna()** code will drop all null values from the **housing_df** DataFrame.

Now that the data is clean, it's time to prepare our **X** and **y** values.

5. Now, declare the **X** and **y** variables, where you use **X** for the **predictor** columns and **y** for the **target** column:

```
# declare X and y
X = housing_df.iloc[:,:-1]
y = housing_df.iloc[:, -1]
```

The target column is **MEDV**, which is the median value of the Boston house prices. The predictor columns include every other column. The standard notation is to use **X** for the predictor columns and **y** for the target column.

Since the last column is the target column, which is **y**, it should be eliminated from the predictor column, that is, **X**. We can achieve this split by indexing.

6. Now we build the actual linear regression model.

Although many machine learning models are incredibly sophisticated, they can be built using very few lines of code. In this case, it takes three steps. We are going to build a model that will predict the median house value given all of the input columns.

The first line uses **train_test_split()** to split **X** and **y**, the predictor and target columns, into **training** and **test** sets. The model will be built using the training set.

Split **X** and **y** into training and test sets as follows:

```
#Create training and test sets
X_train, X_test, y_train, y_test = train_test_split(X, y, test_size = 0.2)
```

test_size = 0.2 reflects the percentage of rows held back for the **test** set. This is the default setting and does not need to be added explicitly. It is presented so that you know how to change it.

> **Note**
>
> The output values may differ from the values mentioned in the book. We have chosen not use a random seed so that you can get accustomed to diverse outputs.

Next, create an empty **LinearRegression()** model, as shown in the following code snippet:

```
#Create the regressor: reg
reg = LinearRegression()
```

Finally, we **fit** the model to the data using the **.fit()** method:

```
#Fit the regressor to the training data
reg.fit(X_train, y_train)
```

The parameters are **X_train** and **y_train**, which is the training set that we have defined. **reg.fit(X_train, y_train)** is where machine learning actually happens. In this line, the **LinearRegression()** model adjusts itself to the training data. The model keeps changing weights, according to the machine learning algorithm, until the weights minimize the error.

You should get the following output:

```
LinearRegression(copy_X=True, fit_intercept=True, n_jobs=None, normalize=False)
```

Figure 11.5: Output when the model adjusts itself to the training data

At this point, **reg** is a machine learning model with specified weights. There is one weight for each **X** column. These weights are multiplied by the entry in each row to get as close as possible to the target column, **y**, which is the median house value.

7. Now, find how accurate the model is. Here, we can test it on unseen data:

```
# Predict on the test data: y_pred
y_pred = reg.predict(X_test)
```

To make a prediction, we implement a method, **.predict()**. This method takes specified rows of data as the input and produces the corresponding predicted values as the output. The input is **X_test**, the **X-values** that were held back for our test set. The output is the predicted **y**-values.

8. We can now test the prediction by comparing the predicted **y-values**, which is **y_pred**, to the actual **y-values**, which is **y_test**, as shown in the following code snippet:

```
# Compute and print RMSE
rmse = np.sqrt(mean_squared_error(y_test, y_pred))
print("Root Mean Squared Error: {}".format(rmse))
```

The error, the difference between the two **np.array**, may be computed as **mean_squared_error**. We take the square root of the mean squared error to keep the same units as the target column.

You should get the following output:

Root Mean Squared Error: 5.561132474524558

Figure 11.6: Output on the accuracy of the dataset model

Note that there are other errors to choose from. The square root of **mean_squared_error** is a standard choice with linear regression. **rmse**, short for "root mean squared error," will give us the error of the model on the test set.

A root mean squared error of **5.56** means that, on average, the machine learning model predicts values approximately **5.56** units away from the target value, which is not bad in terms of accuracy. Since the median value (from 1980) is in the thousands, the predictions are about **5.56** thousand off. Lower errors are always better, so we will see if can improve the error going forward.

In this very first exercise, we were able to load our dataset, clean it, and use linear regression, and we were able to train the model to make predictions and find out exactly how accurate it is.

Linear Regression Function

In the first exercise, you were able to see how accurate your Boston Housing median value predictions were. What if you enter the entire code in a function and then run it multiple times? Will you get different results?

You do this as shown in the following example using the same Boston Housing dataset.

Let's put all the machine learning code in a function and run it again.

```
def regression_model(model):
    # Create training and test sets
    X_train, X_test, y_train, y_test = train_test_split(X, y, test_size = 0.2)
    # Create the regressor: reg_all
    reg_all = model
    # Fit the regressor to the training data
    reg_all.fit(X_train, y_train)
    # Predict on the test data: y_pred
    y_pred = reg_all.predict(X_test)
    # Compute and print RMSE
    rmse = np.sqrt(mean_squared_error(y_test, y_pred))
    print("Root Mean Squared Error: {}".format(rmse))
```

Now run the function multiple times to see the results:

```
regression_model(LinearRegression())
```

You should get the following output:

```
Root Mean Squared Error: 4.085279539934423
```

Now, run the function once again:

```
regression_model(LinearRegression())
```

You should get the following output:

```
Root Mean Squared Error: 4.317496624587608
```

And finally, run it one more time:

```
regression_model(LinearRegression())
```

You should get the following output:

```
Root Mean Squared Error: 4.7884343211684435
```

This is troublesome, right? The score is always different. Your scores are also likely to differ from ours.

The scores are different because we are splitting the data into a different training set and test set each time, and the model is based on different training sets. Furthermore, it's being scored against a different test set.

In order for machine learning scores to be meaningful, we want to minimize fluctuation and maximize accuracy. We will see how to do this in the next section.

Cross-Validation

In cross-validation, also known as CV, the training data is split into five folds (any number will do, but **five is standard**). The machine learning algorithm is fit on one fold at a time and tested on the remaining data. The result is five different training and test sets that are all representative of the same data. The mean of the scores is usually taken as the accuracy of the model.

> **Note**
>
> Five is only one suggestion. Any natural number may be used.

Cross-validation is a core tool for machine learning. Mean test scores on different folds will always be more reliable than one mean test score on the entire set, which we performed in the first exercise. When examining one test score, there is no way of knowing whether it is low or high. Five test scores give a better picture of the accuracy of the model.

Cross-validation can be implemented in a variety of ways. A standard approach is to use **cross_val_score**, which returns an array of scores for each fold; **cross_val_score** breaks **X** and **y** into the training set and test set for you.

Let's modify our regression machine learning function to include **cross_val_score** in the following exercise.

Exercise 146: Using the cross_val_score Function to Get Accurate Results on the Dataset

The goal of this exercise is to use cross-validation to obtain more accurate machine learning results from the dataset compared to the previous exercise.

1. Continue using the same Jupyter Notebook from *Exercise 145, Using Linear Regression to Predict the Accuracy of the Median Values of Our Dataset*.

2. Now, **import cross_val_score**:

```
from sklearn.model_selection import cross_val_score
```

3. Define the **regression_model_cv** function, which takes a fitted model as one parameter. The **k = 5** hyperparameter gives the number of folds. Enter the code shown in the following code snippet:

```
def regression_model_cv(model, k=5):
    scores = cross_val_score(model, X, y, scoring='neg_mean_squared_
        error', cv=k)
    rmse = np.sqrt(-scores)
    print('Reg rmse:', rmse)
    print('Reg mean:', rmse.mean ())
```

In **sklearn**, the scoring options are sometimes limited. Since **mean_squared_error** is not an option for **cross_val_score**, we choose the **neg_mean_squared_error**. **cross_val_score** takes the highest value by default, and the highest negative mean squared error is 0.

4. Use the **regression_model_cv** function on the **LinearRegression()** model defined in the previous exercise:

```
regression_model_cv(LinearRegression())
```

You may get something similar to the following output:

```
Reg rmse: [3.26123843 4.42712448 5.66151114 8.09493087 5.24453989]
Reg mean: 5.337868962878373
```

5. Use the **regression_model_cv** function on the **LinearRegression()** model with 3 folds and then **6** folds, as shown in the following code snippet, for **3** folds:

```
regression_model_cv(LinearRegression(), k=3)
```

You may get something similar to the following output:

```
Reg rmse: [ 3.72504914 6.01655701 23.20863933]
Reg mean: 10.983415161090695
```

6. Now, test the values for **6** folds:

```
regression_model_cv(LinearRegression(), k=6)
```

You may get something similar to the following output:

```
Reg rmse: [3.23879491 3.97041949 5.58329663 3.92861033 9.88399671
           3.91442679]
Reg mean: 5.08659081080109
```

You have found out that there is a large discrepancy between the number of folds. One reason is that we have a reasonably small dataset to begin with. In the real world, with a huge amount of data, this generally does not make a huge difference to the results when we compare results with different folds.

Regularization: Ridge and Lasso

Regularization is an important concept in machine learning; it's used to counteract overfitting. In the world of big data, it's easy to overfit data to the training set. When this happens, the model will often perform badly on the test set as indicated by `mean_squared_error`, or some other error.

You may wonder why a test set is kept aside at all. Wouldn't the most accurate machine learning model come from fitting the algorithm on all the data?

The answer, generally accepted by the machine learning community after years of research and experimentation, is probably not.

There are two main problems with fitting a machine learning model on all the data:

- There is no way to test the model on unseen data. Machine learning models are powerful when they make good predictions on new data. Models are trained on known results, but they perform in the real world on data that has never been seen before. It's not vital to see how well a model fits known results (the training set), but it's absolutely crucial to see how well it performs on unseen data (the test set).

- The model may overfit the data. Models exist that may fit any set of data points perfectly. Consider the 14 green points in the following diagram. A 14th-degree polynomial exists that fits these points almost perfectly. But it's a poor predictor of the new data. The green line is a much better predictor of the new data. Have a look at the following figure to get a better understanding:

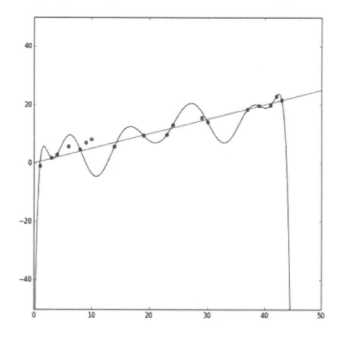

Figure 11.7: Model fitting the data points

There are many models and approaches to counteract overfitting. Let's go over a couple of models now.

Ridge is a simple alternative to linear regression, designed to counteract overfitting. Ridge includes an L2 penalty term (L2 is based on Euclidean Distance) that shrinks the linear coefficients based on their size. The coefficients are the weights, numbers that determine how influential each column is on the output. Larger weights carry greater penalties in Ridge.

Lasso is another regularized alternative to linear regression. Lasso adds a penalty equal to the absolute value of the magnitude of coefficients. This L1 regularization (L1 is taxicab distance.) can eliminate some columns and result in a model that is sparse by comparison.

Let's look at an example to check how Ridge and Lasso perform on our Boston Housing dataset.

In this example, we perform regularization on the dataset using Ridge and Lasso to counteract overfitting. You can continue on the notebook from *Exercise 146, Using the cross_val_score Function to Get Accurate Results on the Dataset*, to work on this example.

We begin by setting `Ridge()` as a parameter for `regression_model_cv`, as shown in the following code snippet:

```
from sklearn.linear_model import Ridge
regression_model_cv(Ridge())
```

You should get the following output:

```
Reg rmse: [3.52479283 4.72296032 5.54622438 8.00759231 5.26861171]
Reg mean: 5.414036309884279
```

It's not surprising that Ridge has a slightly better score than linear regression. This is because both algorithms use Euclidean distance and the linear regression model is overfitting the data by a slight amount. Your results may be different from ours, however, and the scores are very close.

Another basis of comparison is the worst score of the five. In Ridge, we obtained **8.00759** as the worst score. In linear regression, we obtained **23.20863933** as the worst score. This suggests that **23.20863933** is badly overfitting the training data. In Ridge, this overfitting is compensated.

Now, set **Lasso()** as the parameter for `regression_model_cv`:

```
from sklearn.linear_model import Lasso
regression_model_cv(Lasso())
```

You should get the following output:

```
Reg rmse: [4.712548    5.83933857 8.02996117 7.89925202 4.38674414]
Reg mean: 6.173568778640692
```

Whenever you're trying `LinearRegression()`, it's always worth trying Lasso and Ridge as well, since overfitting the data is common, and they only actually take a few lines of code to test. Lasso does not perform as well here because the L1 distance metric, taxicab distance, was not used in our model.

Regularization is an essential tool when implementing machine learning algorithms. Whenever you choose a particular model, be sure to research regularization methods to improve your results, as you observed in the preceding example.

Now, let's get to know a developer's doubt. Although we have focused on overfitting the data, underfitting the data is also possible, right? It's less common in the world of big data, though. Underfitting can occur if the model is a straight line, but a higher degree polynomial will fit the data better. By trying multiple models, you are more likely to find optimal results.

So far, you have learned how to implement linear regression as a machine learning model. You have learned how to perform cross-validation to get more accurate results, and you have learned about using two additional models, Ridge and Lasso, to counteract overfitting.

Now that you understand how to build machine learning models using `scikit-learn`, let's take a look at some different kinds of models that will also work on regression.

K-Nearest Neighbors, Decision Trees, and Random Forests

Are there other machine learning algorithms, besides `LinearRegression()`, that is suitable for the Boston Housing dataset? Absolutely. There are many regressors in the `scikit-learn` library that may be used. Regressors are generally considered a class of machine learning algorithms that are suitable for continuous target values. In addition to Linear Regression, Ridge, and Lasso, we can try K-Nearest Neighbors, Decision Trees, and Random Forests. These models perform well on a wide range of datasets. Let's try them out and analyze them individually.

K-Nearest Neighbors

The idea behind K-Nearest Neighbors (KNN) is straightforward. When choosing the output of a row with an unknown label, the prediction is the same as the output of its k-nearest neighbors, where k may be any whole number.

For instance, let's say that k=3. Given an unknown label, we take n columns for this row and place them in n-dimensional space. Then we look for the three closest points.

These points already have labels. We assume the majority label for our new point.

KNN is commonly used for classification since classification is based on grouping values, but it can be applied to regression as well. When determining the value of a home, for instance, in our Boston Housing dataset, it makes sense to compare the values of homes in a similar location, with a similar number of bedrooms, a similar amount of square footage, and so on.

You can always choose the number of neighbors for the algorithm and adjust it accordingly. The number of neighbors denoted here is **k**, which is also called a **hyperparameter**. In machine learning, the model parameters are derived during training, whereas the hyperparameters are chosen in advance.

Fine-tuning hyperparameters is an essential task to master when building machine learning models. Learning the ins and outs of hyperparameter tuning takes time, practice, and experimentation.

Exercise 147: Using K-Nearest Neighbors to Find the Median Value of the Dataset

The goal of this exercise is to use K-Nearest Neighbors to predict the optimal median value of homes in Boston. We will use the same function, **regression_model_cv**, with an input of **KNeighborsRegressor()**:

1. Continue with the same Jupyter Notebook from the previous *Exercise 146*.

2. Set and **import KNeighborsRegressor()** as the parameter on the **regression_model_cv** function:

```
from sklearn.neighbors import KNeighborsRegressor
regression_model_cv(KNeighborsRegressor())
```

You should get the following output:

```
Reg rmse: [ 8.24568226  8.81322798 10.58043836  8.85643441  5.98100069]
Reg mean: 8.495356738515685
```

K-Nearest Neighbors did not perform as well as **LinearRegression()**, but it performed respectably. Recall that **rmse** stands for root mean squared error. So, the mean error is about **8.50** (or 85,000 since the units are ten of thousands of dollars).

We can change the number of neighbors to see if we can get better results. The default number of neighbors is **5**. Let's change the number of neighbors to **4**, **7**, and **10**.

3. Now, change the **n_neighbors** hyperparameter to **4**, **7**, and **10**. For **4** neighbors, enter the following code:

```
regression_model_cv(KNeighborsRegressor(n_neighbors=4))
```

You should get an output similar to the following:

```
Reg rmse: [ 8.44659788  8.99814547 10.97170231  8.86647969  5.72114135]
Reg mean: 8.600813339223432
```

Change **n_neighbors** to 7:

```
regression_model_cv(KNeighborsRegressor(n_neighbors=7))
```

You should get the following output:

```
Reg rmse: [ 7.99710601  8.68309183 10.66332898  8.90261573  5.51032355]
Reg mean: 8.351293217401393
```

Change **n_neighbors** to 10:

```
regression_model_cv(KNeighborsRegressor(n_neighbors=10))
```

You should get the following output:

```
Reg rmse: [ 7.47549287  8.62914556 10.69543822  8.91330686  6.52982222]
Reg mean: 8.448641147609868
```

The best results so far come from 7 neighbors. But how do we know if 7 neighbors give us the best results? How many different scenarios do we have to check?

Scikit-learn provides a nice option to check a wide range of hyperparameters, which is **GridSearchCV**. The idea behind **GridSearchCV** is to use cross-validation to check all possible values in a grid. The value in the grid that gives the best result is then accepted as a hyperparameter.

Exercise 148: K-Nearest Neighbors with GridSearchCV to Find the Optimal Number of Neighbors

The goal of this exercise is to use **GridSearchCV** to find the optimal number of neighbors for K-Nearest Neighbors to predict the median housing value in Boston. In the previous exercise, if you recall, we used only three neighbor values. Here, we will increase the number using **GridSearchCV**:

1. Continue with the Jupyter Notebook from the previous exercise.

2. Import **GridSearchCV**, as shown in the following code snippet:

```
from sklearn.model_selection import GridSearchCV
```

3. Now, choose the grid. The grid is the range of numbers – in this case, neighbors – that will be checked. Set up a hyperparameter grid for between **1** and **20** neighbors:

```
neighbors = np.linspace(1, 20, 20)
```

We achieve this with **np.linspace(1, 20, 20)**, where the **1** is the first number, the first **20** is the last number, and the second **20** in the brackets is the number of intervals to count.

4. Convert floats to **int** (required by **knn**):

```
k = neighbors.astype(int)
```

5. Now, place the grid in a dictionary, as shown in the following code snippet:

```
param_grid = {'n_neighbors': k}
```

6. Build the model for each neighbor:

```
knn = KNeighborsRegressor()
```

7. Instantiate the **GridSearchCV** object – **knn_tuned**:

```
knn_tuned = GridSearchCV(knn, param_grid, cv=5, scoring='neg_mean_squared_error')
```

8. Fit **knn_tuned** to the data using **.fit**:

```
knn_tuned.fit(X, y)
```

9. Finally, you **print** the best parameter results, as shown in the following code snippet:

```
k = knn_tuned.best_params_
print("Best n_neighbors: {}".format(k))
score = knn_tuned.best_score_
rsm = np.sqrt(-score)
print("Best score: {}".format(rsm))
```

You should get the following output:

```
Best n_neighbors: {'n_neighbors': 7}
Best score: 8.523048500643897
```

Figure 11.8: Output showing the best score using n_neighbors

In our case, 7 gave the best results. Your results may differ. Now, moving on, let's look at the different types of decision trees and random forests.

Decision Trees and Random Forests

The best way to understand a concept is to relate it to something. You may be familiar with the game Twenty Questions. It's a game in which someone is asked to think of something or someone, perhaps a person. The questioner asks them binary yes or no questions, gradually narrowing down the search in order to determine exactly who they are thinking of.

Twenty Questions is a decision tree. Every time a question is asked, there are two possible branches that the tree may take depending upon the answer. For every new question, new branching occurs, until the branches end at a prediction, called a leaf.

Here is a mini-Decision Tree that predicts whether a Titanic passenger survived:

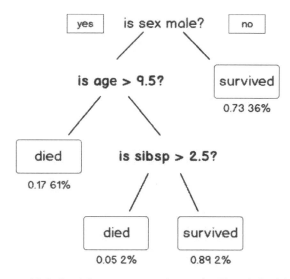

Figure 11.9: Decision tree sample on the Titanic incident

This decision tree starts by determining whether the passenger was male. If the passenger was male, the branch is followed that asks the question was their age greater than 9.5. If the passenger was not male, we reach the end of a branch, and we find out that the probability of survival is 0.73. The other number, 36%, indicates that 36% of the passengers end up at this leaf.

Decision Trees are very good machine learning algorithms, but they are prone to overfitting. A random forest is an ensemble of decision trees. Random forests consistently outperform decision trees because their predictions generalize to data much better. A random forest may consist of hundreds of decision trees.

A random forest is a great machine-learning algorithm to try on almost any dataset. Random forests work well with both regression and classification, and they often perform well out of the box.

Let's try Decision Trees and Random Forests on our data.

Exercise 149: Decision Trees and Random Forests

The goal of this exercise is to use decision trees and random forests to predict median house values in Boston:

1. Continue with the same Jupyter Notebook from the previous exercise.

2. Use **DecisionTreeRegressor()** as the input for **regression_model_cv**.

```
from sklearn import tree
regression_model_cv(tree.DecisionTreeRegressor())
```

You should get the following output:

```
Reg rmse: [3.84098484 5.67885262 7.7328741  6.53263473 5.78903694]
Reg mean: 5.914876645128473
```

> **Note**
>
> The output values may differ from the values mentioned in the book.

3. Use **RandomForestRegressor()** as the input for **regression_model_cv**:

```
from sklearn.ensemble import RandomForestRegressor
regression_model_cv(RandomForestRegressor())
```

You should get the following output:

```
Reg rmse: [3.49719743 3.86463108 4.60294622 6.7640934  3.73856719]
Reg mean: 4.493487064599419
```

As you can see, the random forest regressor gives the best results yet. Let's see if we can improve these results by examining random forest hyperparameters.

Random Forest Hyperparameters

Random forests have a lot of hyperparameters. Instead of going over them all, we will highlight the most important ones:

- **n_jobs(default=None)**: The number of jobs has to do with internal processing. **None** means 1. It's ideal to set **n_jobs = -1** to permit the use of all processors. Although this does not improve the accuracy of the model, it does improve the speed.

- **n_estimators(default=10)**: The number of trees in the forest. The more trees, the better. The more trees, the more RAM is required. It's worth increasing this number until the algorithm moves too slowly. Although 1,000,000 trees may give better results than 1,000, the gain might be small enough to be negligible. A good starting point is 100, and 500 if time permits.

- **max_depth(default=None)**: The max depth of the trees in the forest. The deeper the trees, the more information is captured about the data, but the more prone the trees are to overfitting. When set to the default **max_depth** of **None**, there are no limitations, and each tree goes as deep as necessary. The max depth may be reduced to a smaller number of branches.

- **min_samples_split(default=2)**: This is the minimum number of samples required for a new branch or split to occur. This number can be increased to constrain the trees as they require more samples to make a decision.

- **min_samples_leaf(default=1)**: This is the same as **min_samples_split**, except it's the minimum number of samples at the leaves or the base of the tree. By increasing this number, the branch will stop splitting when it reaches this parameter.

- **max_features(default="auto")**: The number of features to consider when looking for the best split. The default for regression is to consider the total number of columns. For classification random forests, **sqrt** is recommended.

Exercise 150: Random Forest Tuned to Improve the Prediction on Our Dataset

The goal of this exercise is to tune a random forest to improve the median house value predictions for Boston:

1. Continue with the same Jupyter Notebook from *Exercise 149, Decision Trees and Random Forests*:

2. Set **n_jobs = -1** and **n_estimators=100** for **RandomForestRegressor** as the input of **regression_model_cv**. We can always use **n_jobs** to speed up the algorithm, and we can increase **n_estimators** to achieve better results:

```
regression_model_cv(RandomForestRegressor(n_jobs=-1, n_estimators=100))
```

You should get the following output:

```
Reg rmse: [3.29260656 3.61943542 4.83755526 6.49556195 3.76565343]
Reg mean: 4.402162523852732
```

We could try **GridSearchCV** on the other hyperparameters to see if we can find a better combination than the defaults, but checking every possible combination of hyperparameters could reach the order of thousands and take way too long.

> **Note**
>
> The output values may differ from the values mentioned in the book.

Sklearn provides **RandomizedSearchCV** to check a wide range of hyperparameters. Instead of exhaustively going through a list, **RandomizedSearchCV** will check a set amount of random combinations and return the best results.

3. Use **RandomizedSearchCV** to look for better Random Forest hyperparameters:

```
from sklearn.model_selection import RandomizedSearchCV
```

4. Set up the hyperparameter grid using **max_depth**, as shown in the following code snippet:

```
param_grid = {'max_depth': [None, 10, 30, 50, 70, 100, 200, 400],
              'min_samples_split': [2, 3, 4, 5],
              'min_samples_leaf': [1, 2, 3],
              'max_features': ['auto', 'sqrt']}
```

5. Instantiate the **knn** regressor:

```
reg = RandomForestRegressor(n_jobs = -1)
```

6. Instantiate the **RandomizedSearchCV** object – **reg_tuned**:

```
reg_tuned = RandomizedSearchCV(reg, param_grid, cv=5,
    scoring='neg_mean_squared_error')
```

7. Fit **reg_tuned** to the data:

```
reg_tuned.fit(X, y)
```

8. Now, **print** the **tuned** parameters and **score**:

```
p = reg_tuned.best_params_
print("Best n_neighbors: {}".format(p))
score = reg_tuned.best_score_
rsm = np.sqrt(-score)
print("Best score: {}".format(rsm))
```

You should get the following output:

```
Best n_neighbors: {'min_samples_split': 4, 'min_samples_leaf': 1, 'max_features': 'auto', 'max_depth': 70}
Best score: 4.571319583949792
```

Figure 11.10: Output of the tuned parameters and score

Keep in mind that with **RandomizedSearchCV**, there is no guarantee that the hyperparameters will produce the best results. Although the randomized search did well, it did not perform as well as the defaults with **n_jobs** = -1 and **n_estimators** = **100**.

9. Now, run a random forest regressor with **n_jobs** = -1 and **n_estimators** = **500**:

```
# Setup the hyperparameter grid
regression_model_cv(RandomForestRegressor(n_jobs=-1, n_estimators=500))
```

You should get the following output:

```
Reg rmse: [3.17315086 3.77060192 4.77587747 6.45161665 3.9681246 ]
Reg mean: 4.427874301108916
```

> **Note**
>
> Increasing **n_estimators** every time will produce more accurate results, but the model takes longer to build.

Hyperparameters are a primary key to building excellent machine learning models. Anyone with basic machine learning training can build machine learning models using default hyperparameters. Using **GridSearchCV** and **RandomizedSearchCV** to fine-tune hyperparameters to create more efficient models distinguishes advanced users from beginners.

Classification Models

The Boston Housing dataset was great for regression because the target column took on continuous values without limit. There are many cases when the target column takes on one or two values, such as **TRUE** or **FALSE**, or possibly a grouping of three or more values, such as **RED, BLUE,** or **GREEN**. When the target column may be split into distinct categories, the group of machine learning models that you should try are referred to as **classification**.

To make things interesting, let's load a new dataset used to detect pulsar stars in outer space. Go to https://packt.live/33SD0IM and click on **Data Folder**. Then, click on **HTRU2.zip**.

Index of /ml/machine-learning-databases/00372

- Parent Directory
- HTRU2.zip

Apache/2.4.6 (CentOS) OpenSSL/1.0.2k-fips SVN/1.7.14 Phusion_Passenger/4.0.53 mod_perl/2.0.10 Perl/v5.16.3 Server at archive.ics.uci.edu Port 443

Figure 11.11: Dataset directory on the UCI website

The dataset consists of 17,898 potential pulsar stars in space. But what are these pulsars? Pulsar stars rotate very quickly, so they have periodic light patterns. Radio frequency interference and noise, however, are attributes that make pulsars very hard to detect. This dataset contains 16,259 non-pulsars and 1,639 real pulsars.

> **Note**
>
> The dataset is from Dr. Robert Lyon, University of Manchester, School of Physics and Astronomy, Alan Turing Building, Manchester M13 9PL, United Kingdom, Robert.lyon'@'manchester.ac.uk, 2017.

The columns include information about an integrated pulse profile and a DM–SNR curve. All pulsars produce a unique pattern of emissions, commonly known as their "pulse profile." A pulse profile is similar to a fingerprint, but it is not consistent like a pulsar rotational period. An integrated pulse profile consists of a matrix of an array of continuous values describing the pulse intensity and phase of the pulsar. DM stands for Dispersion Measure, a constant that relates the frequency of light to the extra time required to reach the observer, and SNR stands for Signal to Noise Ratio, which relates how well an object has been measured compared to its background noise.

Here is the official list of columns in the dataset:

- Mean of the integrated profile
- Standard deviation of the integrated profile
- Excess kurtosis of the integrated profile
- Skewness of the integrated profile
- Mean of the DM–SNR curve
- Standard deviation of the DM–SNR curve
- Excess kurtosis of the DM–SNR curve
- Skewness of the DM–SNR curve
- Class

In this dataset, potential pulsars have already been classified as pulsars and non-pulsars by the astronomy community. The goal here is to see if machine learning can detect patterns within the data to correctly classify new potential pulsars that emerge.

The methods that you learn for this topic will be directly applicable to a wide range of classification problems, including spam classifiers, user churn in markets, quality control, product identification, and others.

Exercise 151: Preparing the Pulsar Dataset and Checking for Null Values

The goal of this exercise is to prepare the pulsar dataset for machine learning. The exercises from here on will be on the same notebook file:

1. Open a new Jupyter Notebook.

2. Import the libraries, load the data, and display the first five rows, as shown in the following code snippet:

```
import pandas as pd
import numpy as np
df = pd.read_csv('HTRU_2.csv')
df.head()
```

You should get the following output:

	140.5625	55.68378214	-0.234571412	-0.699648398	3.199832776	19.11042633	7.975531794	74.24222492	0
0	102.507812	58.882430	0.465318	-0.515088	1.677258	14.860146	10.576487	127.393580	0
1	103.015625	39.341649	0.323328	1.051164	3.121237	21.744669	7.735822	63.171909	0
2	136.750000	57.178449	-0.068415	-0.636238	3.642977	20.959280	6.896499	53.593661	0
3	88.726562	40.672225	0.600866	1.123492	1.178930	11.468720	14.269573	252.567306	0
4	93.570312	46.698114	0.531905	0.416721	1.636288	14.545074	10.621748	131.394004	0

Figure 11.12: The first five rows of the pulsar dataset

Looks interesting, and problematic. Notice that the column headers appear to be another row. It's impossible to analyze data without knowing what the columns are supposed to be, right?

Note that the last column is all 0's in the DataFrame. This suggests that this is the Class column, which is our target column. When detecting the presence of something – in this case, pulsar stars – it's common to use a 1 for positive identification, and a 0 for a negative identification.

Since Class is last in the list, let's assume that the columns are given in the correct order presented in the Attribute Information list. We can also assume that losing the current column headers, a negative identification among 17,898 rows is virtually meaningless. The easiest way forward is simply to change the column headers to match the attribute list.

3. Now, change column headers to match the official list and print the first five rows, as shown in the following code snippet:

```
df.columns = [['Mean of integrated profile', 'Standard deviation of integrated
profile',
                'Excess kurtosis of integrated profile', 'Skewness of integrated
profile',
                'Mean of DM-SNR curve', 'Standard deviation of DM-SNR curve',
                'Excess kurtosis of DM-SNR curve', 'Skewness of DM-SNR curve',
'Class' ]]
df.head()
```

You should get the following output:

	Mean of integrated profile	Standard deviation of integrated profile	Excess kurtosis of integrated profile	Skewness of integrated profile	Mean of DM-SNR curve	Standard deviation of DM-SNR curve	Excess kurtosis of DM-SNR curve	Skewness of DM-SNR curve	Class
0	102.507812	58.882430	0.465318	-0.515088	1.677258	14.860146	10.576487	127.393580	0
1	103.015625	39.341649	0.323328	1.051164	3.121237	21.744669	7.735822	63.171909	0
2	136.750000	57.178449	-0.068415	-0.636238	3.642977	20.959280	6.896499	53.593661	0
3	88.726562	40.672225	0.600866	1.123492	1.178930	11.468720	14.269573	252.567306	0
4	93.570312	46.698114	0.531905	0.416721	1.636288	14.545074	10.621748	131.394004	0

Figure 11.13: Check for null values using df.info() and len(df)

4. Now, let's find the info of the dataset using `.info()`:

```
df.info()
```

You should get the following output:

```
<class 'pandas.core.frame.DataFrame'>
RangeIndex: 17897 entries, 0 to 17896
Data columns (total 9 columns):
(Mean of integrated profile,)                    17897 non-null float64
(Standard deviation of integrated profile,)      17897 non-null float64
(Excess kurtosis of integrated profile,)         17897 non-null float64
(Skewness of integrated profile,)                17897 non-null float64
(Mean of DM-SNR curve,)                          17897 non-null float64
(Standard deviation of DM-SNR curve,)            17897 non-null float64
(Excess kurtosis of DM-SNR curve,)               17897 non-null float64
(Skewness of DM-SNR curve,)                       17897 non-null float64
(Class,)                                         17897 non-null int64
dtypes: float64(8), int64(1)
memory usage: 1.2 MB
```

Figure 11.14: Information based on the pulsar dataset

5. Finally, use **len(df)** and match all columns of **df.info()** with only the non-null entries:

```
len(df)
```

You should get the following output:

```
17897
```

We know that there are no null values. If there were null values, we would need to eliminate the rows or fill them in by taking the mean, the median, the mode, or another value from the columns.

When it comes to preparing data for machine learning, it's essential to have clean, numerical data with no null values. Further data analysis is often warranted, depending upon the goal at hand. If the goal is simply to try out some models and check them for accuracy, it's fine to go ahead. If the goal is to uncover deep insights about the data, further statistical analysis, as introduced in the previous chapter, is always warranted. Now that we have all this basic information, we can proceed ahead on the same notebook file.

Logistic Regression

When it comes to datasets that classify points, logistic regression is one of the most popular and successful machine learning algorithms. Logistic regression utilizes the sigmoid function to determine whether points should approach one value or the other. As the following diagram indicates, it's a good idea to classify the target values as 0 and 1 when utilizing logistic regression. In the pulsar dataset, the values are already classified as 0s and 1s. If the dataset was labeled as **Red** and **Blue**, converting them in advance to 0 and 1 would be essential (you will practice converting categorical to numerical values in the activity at the end of his chapter):

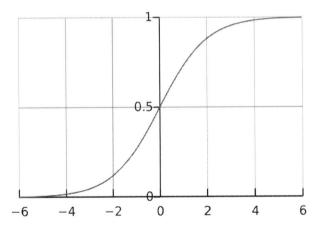

Figure 11.15: Sigmoid curve on a plot

The sigmoid curve in figure 11.14 approaches 1 from the left and 0 from the right, without ever reaching 0 or 1. In this respect, 0 and 1 function as horizontal asymptotes. Basically, every positive **x** value is given an output of 1, and every negative **x** value is given an output of 0. Furthermore, the higher up the graph, the higher the probability of a 1, and the lower down the graph, the higher the probability of 0.

Let's see how logistic regression works in action by using a similar function as before.

By default, classifiers use percentage accuracy as the score output.

Exercise 152: Using Logistic Regression to Predict Data Accuracy

The goal of this exercise is to use logistic regression to predict the classification of pulsar stars:

1. Import **LogisticRegression**:

```
from sklearn.model_selection import cross_val_score
from sklearn.linear_model import LogisticRegression
```

2. Set up matrices **X** and **y** to store the predictors and response variables, respectively:

```
X = df.iloc[:, 0:8]
y = df.iloc[:, 8]
```

3. Write a classifier function that takes a model as its input:

```
def clf_model(model):
```

4. Create the **clf** classifier, as shown in the following code snippet:

```
clf = model
scores = cross_val_score(clf, X, y)
print('Scores:', scores)
print('Mean score:', scores.mean())
```

5. Run the **clf_model** function with **LogisticRegression()** as the input:

```
clf_model(LogisticRegression())
```

You should get the following output:

```
Scores: [0.97385621 0.98239732 0.97686505]
Mean score: 0.9777061909796982
```

Figure 11.16: Mean score using logistic regression

These numbers represent accuracy. A mean score of `0.977706` means that the logistic regression model is classifying `97.8%` of pulsars correctly.

Logistic regression is very different than linear regression. Logistic regression uses the sigmoid function to classify all instances into one group or the other. Generally speaking, all cases that are above 0.5 are classified as a 1, and all cases that fall below 0.5 are classified as a 0, with decimals that are close to 1 more likely to be a 1, and decimals that are close to 0 more likely to be a 0. Linear regression, by contrast, finds a straight line that minimizes the error between the straight line and the individual points. Logistic regression classifies all points into two groups; all new points will fall into one of these groups. By contrast, linear regression finds a line of best fit; all new points may fall anywhere on the line and take on any value.

Other Classifiers

There are other classifiers that we can try, including K-Nearest Neighbors (KNN), Decision Trees, Random Forests, and Naive Bayes.

We used KNN, Decision Trees, and Random Forests as regressors before. This time, we need to implement them as classifiers. For instance, there is `RandomForestRegressor`, and there is `RandomForestClassifier`. Both are random forests, but they are implemented differently to meet the output of the data. Recall that classifiers have an output of two or more end values, whereas regression has an output of continuous values. The general setup is the same, but the output is different. In the next section, we will have a look at Naive Bayes.

Naive Bayes

Naive Bayes is a model based on Bayes' theorem, a famous probability theorem based on a conditional probability that assumes independent events. Similarly, Naive Bayes assumes independent attributes or columns. The mathematical details of Naive Bayes are beyond the scope of this book, but we can still apply it to our dataset.

There is a small family of machine learning algorithms based on Naive Bayes. The one that we will use here is `GaussianNB`. Gaussian Naïve Bayes assumes that the likelihood of features is `Gaussian`. Other options that you may consider trying include `MultinomialNB`, used for multinomial distributed data (such as text), and `ComplementNB`, an adaptation of `MultinomialNB` that is used for imbalanced datasets.

Let's try Naive Bayes, in addition to the KNN, Decision Tree, and Random Forest classifiers mentioned previously.

Exercise 153: Using GaussianNB, KneighborsClassifier, DecisionTreeClassifier, and RandomForestClassifier to Predict Accuracy in Our Dataset

The goal of this exercise is to predict pulsars using a variety of classifiers, including GaussianNB, KneighborsClassifier, DecisionTreeClassifier, and RandomForestClassifier.

1. Begin this exercise on the same notebook file from the previous exercise.

2. Run the **clf_model** function with **GaussianNB()** as the input:

```
from sklearn.naive_bayes import GaussianNB
clf_model(GaussianNB())
```

You should get the following output:

```
Scores: [0.95692978 0.92472758 0.94836547]
Mean score: 0.9433409410695212
```

Figure 11.17: Mean score using GaussianNB

3. Now, run the **clf_model** function with **KNeighborsClassifier()** as the input:

```
from sklearn.neighbors import KNeighborsClassifier
clf_model(KNeighborsClassifier())
```

You should get the following output:

```
Scores: [0.96899615 0.97200335 0.97082984]
Mean score: 0.9706097796987464
```

Figure 11.18: Mean score using KNeighborsClassifier

4. Run the **clf_model** function with **DecisionTreeClassifier()** as the input:

```
from sklearn.tree import DecisionTreeClassifier
clf_model(DecisionTreeClassifier())
```

You should get the following output:

```
Scores: [0.96849338 0.96043588 0.96697402]
Mean score: 0.9653010904297002
```

Figure 11.19: Mean score using DecisionTreeClassifier

> **Note**
>
> The output values may differ from the values mentioned in the book.

5. Run the `clf_model` function with `RandomForestClassifier()` as the input:

```
from sklearn.ensemble import RandomForestClassifier
clf_model(RandomForestClassifier())
```

You should get the following output:

```
Scores: [0.97670521 0.97837385 0.97619447]
Mean score: 0.9770911757237218
```

Figure 11.20: Mean score using RandomForestClassifier

All classifiers have achieved between 94% and 98% accuracy. It's unusual for this many classifiers to all perform this well. There must be clear patterns within the data, or something is going on behind the scenes.

You may also wonder how to know when to use these classifiers. The bottom line is that whenever you have a classification problem, meaning that the data has a target column with a finite number of options, such as three kinds of wine, most classifiers are worth trying. Naive Bayes is known to work well with text data, and random forests are known to work well generally. New machine learning algorithms are often being developed to handle special cases. Practice and research will help to uncover more nuanced cases.

Confusion Matrix

When discussing classification, it's important to know whether the dataset is imbalanced, as we had some doubts about the results from *Exercise 153, Using GaussianNB, KneighborsClassifier, DecisionTreeClassifier and RandomForestClassifier to Predict Accuracy in Our Dataset*. An imbalance occurs if the majority of data points have one label rather than another.

Exercise 154: Finding the Pulsar Percentage from the Dataset

The goal of this exercise is to count the percentage of pulsars in our dataset. We will use the `Class` column. Although we have primarily been using `df['Class']` as a way to reference a particular column, `df.Class` will work as well (except in limited cases, such as setting values):

1. Begin this exercise on the same notebook you used in the previous exercise.

2. Use the `count.()` method on `df.Class` to obtain the number of potential pulsars:

```
df.Class.count()
```

You should get the following output:

```
Out[24]:  Class     17897
          dtype: int64
```

Figure 11.21: Output of the potential pulsars in the dataset

3. Use the .count() method on df[df.Class == 1] to obtain the number of actual pulsars:

```
df[df.Class == 1].Class.count()
```

You should get the following output:

```
Out[25]:  Class     1639
          dtype: int64
```

Figure 11.22: Output of the total actual pulsars in the dataset

4. Divide step 2 by step 1 to obtain the percentage of pulsars:

```
df[df.Class == 1].Class.count()/df.Class.count()
```

You should get the following output:

```
Out[26]:  Class     0.09158
          dtype: float64
```

Figure 11.23: Output showing the percentage of pulsars

The results show that 0.09158 or 9% of the data are pulsars. The other 91% are not pulsars. This means that it's very easy to make a machine learning algorithm in this case with 91% accuracy to predict that every row is not a pulsar.

Imagine that the situation is even more extreme. Imagine that we are trying to detect exoplanets, and our dataset has only classified 1% of the data as exoplanets. This means that 99% are not exoplanets. This also means that it's super easy to develop an algorithm with 99% accuracy! Just claim that everything is not an exoplanet!

The confusion matrix was designed to reveal the truth behind imbalanced datasets:

	Total population	True Condition	
		Condition positive	Condition negative
Predicted condition	Predicted condition positive	True positive	False positive, Type I error
	Predicted condition negative	False negative, Type II error	True negative

Figure 11.24: Overview of the confusion matrix

As you can see from figure 11.24, the confusion matrix is designed to show you what happened to each of the outputs. Every output will fall into one of four boxes, labeled "True positive," "False positive," "False negative," and "True negative":

True positive	Prediction positive and label positive
True negative	Prediction negative and label negative
False positive	Prediction positive but label negative
False negative	Prediction negative but label positive

Figure 11.25: Prediction of the confusion matrix based on conditions

Consider the following example. This is the confusion matrix for the decision tree classifier we used earlier. You will see the code to obtain this shortly. First, we want to focus on the interpretation:

```
[[3985    91]
 [  65   334]]
```

Figure 11.26: Confusion matrix

In sklearn, the default order is 0, 1. This means that the zeros or negative values are actually listed first. So, in effect, the confusion matrix is interpreted as follows:

```
        0      1
0  [[3985    91]
1   [  65   334]]
```

Figure 11.27: Confusion matrix with the default orders

In this particular case, 3,985 non-pulsars have been identified correctly, and 334 pulsars have been identified correctly. The 91 in the upper-right corner indicates that the model classified 91 pulsars incorrectly, and the 65 in the bottom-left corner indicates that 65 non-pulsars were misclassified as pulsars.

It can be challenging to interpret the confusion matrix, especially when positives and negatives do not always line up in the same columns. Fortunately, a classification report may be displayed along with it.

The classification report includes the total number of labels, along with various percentages to help make sense of the numbers and analyze the data.

Here is the classification report with the confusion matrix for the decision tree classifier:

```
Confusion Matrix:  [[3985    91]
                    [  65   334]]


Classification Report:
                   precision  recall   f1-score    support

          0          0.98      0.98      0.98         4076
          1          0.79      0.84      0.81          399

   avg / total       0.97      0.97      0.97         4475
```

Figure 11.28: Classification report on the confusion matrix

In the classification report, the columns on the two ends are the easiest to interpret. On the far right, **support** is the number of labels in the dataset. It matches the indexed column on the far left, labeled 0 and 1. Support reveals that there are 4,076 non-pulsars (0s) and 399 pulsars (1s). This number is less than the total because we are only looking at the test set.

Precision is the true positives divided by all the positive predictions. In the case of the zeros, this is 3985 / (3985 + 65), and in the case of the ones, this is 334 / (334 + 91).

Recall is the true positives divided by all the positive labels. For the zeros, this is 3985 / (3985 + 91) and for the ones this is 334 / (334 + 65).

The **f1-score** is the harmonic mean of the precision and recall scores. Note that the f1 scores are very different for the zeros than the ones.

The most important number in the classification report depends on what you are trying to accomplish. Consider the case of the pulsars. Is the goal to identify as many potential pulsars as possible? If so, a lower precision is okay, provided that the recall is higher. Or perhaps an investigation would be expensive. In this case, a higher precision than recall would be desirable.

Exercise 155: Confusion Matrix and Classification Report for the Pulsar Dataset

The goal of this exercise is to build a function that displays the confusion matrix along with the classification report:

1. Continue on the same notebook file from the previous exercise.

2. Now, **import** the **confusion_matrix** and the **classification_report** libraries:

```
from sklearn.metrics import classification_report
from sklearn.metrics import confusion_matrix
from sklearn.cross_validation import train_test_split
```

To use the confusion matrix and classification report, we need a designated test set. We can accomplish this using **train_test_split**.

3. Split the data into a training set and a test set:

```
X_train, X_test, y_train, y_test = train_test_split(X, y, test_size = 0.25)
```

Now, build a function called **confusion** that takes a model as the input and prints the confusion matrix and classification report. The **clf** classifier should be the output:

```
def confusion(model):
```

4. Create a **model** classifier:

```
clf = model
```

5. Fit the classifier to the data:

```
clf.fit(X_train, y_train)
```

6. Predict the labels of the y_pred test set:

```
y_pred = clf.predict(X_test)
```

7. Compute and **print** the confusion matrix:

```
print('Confusion Matrix:', confusion_matrix(y_test, y_pred))
```

8. Compute and print the classification report:

```
print('Classification Report:', classification_report(y_test, y_pred))
return clf
```

Now let's try the function on our various classifiers.

9. Run the **confusion()** function with **LogisticRegression** as the input:

```
confusion(LogisticRegression())
```

You should get the following output:

```
Confusion Matrix: [[4029    23]
 [  81   342]]
Classification Report:               precision    recall   f1-score    support

           0          0.98       0.99      0.99        4052
           1          0.94       0.81      0.87         423

   micro avg          0.98       0.98      0.98        4475
   macro avg          0.96       0.90      0.93        4475
weighted avg          0.98       0.98      0.98        4475
```

Figure 11.29: Output of the confusion matrix on LogisticRegression

As you can see, the precision of classifying actual pulsars, the 1 in the classification report, is 94%, whereas the total is 98%. Perhaps more significantly, the f1-score, which is the average of the precision and recall scores, is 98% overall, but only 87% for the pulsars, or ones.

10. Now, run the **confusion()** function with **KNeighborsClassifier()** as the input:

```
confusion(KNeighborsClassifier())
```

You should get the following output:

```
Confusion Matrix: [[4019    33]
 [  94   329]]
Classification Report:               precision    recall   f1-score    support

           0          0.98       0.99      0.98        4052
           1          0.91       0.78      0.84         423

   micro avg          0.97       0.97      0.97        4475
   macro avg          0.94       0.88      0.91        4475
weighted avg          0.97       0.97      0.97        4475
```

Figure 11.30: Output of the confusion matrix on KNeighborsClassifier

They're all high scores overall, but the 78% recall and 84% f1-score for the pulsars are a little lacking.

11. Run the **confusion()** function with **GaussianNB()** as the input:

```
confusion(GaussianNB())
```

You should get the following output:

```
Confusion Matrix: [[3884  168]
 [  62  361]]
Classification Report:              precision    recall   f1-score    support

           0      0.98       0.96       0.97      4052
           1      0.68       0.85       0.76       423

   micro avg      0.95       0.95       0.95      4475
   macro avg      0.83       0.91       0.86      4475
weighted avg      0.96       0.95       0.95      4475
```

Figure 11.31: Output of the confusion matrix on GaussianNB

In this particular case, the 68% precision of correctly identifying pulsars is not up to par.

12. Run the **confusion()** function with **RandomForestClassifer()** as the input:

```
confusion(RandomForestClassifier())
```

You should get the following output:

```
Confusion Matrix: [[4024   28]
 [  75  348]]
Classification Report:              precision    recall   f1-score    support

           0      0.98       0.99       0.99      4052
           1      0.93       0.82       0.87       423

   micro avg      0.98       0.98       0.98      4475
   macro avg      0.95       0.91       0.93      4475
weighted avg      0.98       0.98       0.98      4475
```

Figure 11.32: Output of the confusion matrix on RandomForestClassifier

We've now finished this exercise, and you can see that, in this case, the f1-score of 87% is the highest that we have seen.

Which classifier would give the best results if we want to detect pulsars? **RandomForestClassifier()** is great because it has the highest precision and recall for pulsar identification. If the goal is to detect pulsars, **RandomForestClassifier** is the best bet.

Boosting Methods

Random Forests are a type of bagging method. A **bagging** method is a machine learning method that aggregates a large sum of machine learning models. In the case of Random Forests, the aggregates are decision trees.

Another machine learning method is boosting. The idea behind boosting is to transform a weak learner into a strong learner by modifying the weights for the rows that the learner got wrong. A weak learner may have an error of 49%, hardly better than a coin flip. A strong learner, by contrast, may have an error rate of 1 or 2 %. With enough iterations, very weak learners can be transformed into very strong learners.

The success of boosting methods caught the attention of the machine learning community. In 2003, Yoav Fruend and Robert Shapire won the 2003 Godel Prize for developing AdaBoost, short for adaptive boosting.

Like many boosting methods, AdaBoost has both a classifier and a regressor. AdaBoost adjusts weak learners toward instances that were previously misclassified. If one learner is 45% correct, the sign can be flipped to become 55% correct. By switching the signs of negatives to positives, the only problematic instances are those that are exactly 50% correct because changing the sign will not change anything. The larger the percentage that is correct, the larger the weight given is given out to sensitive outliers.

Let's see how the AdaBoost classifier performs on our datasets.

Exercise 156: Using AdaBoost to Predict the Best Optimal Values

The goal of this exercise is to predict pulsars and median housing prices in Boston using AdaBoost:

1. Begin this exercise on the same notebook you used in the previous exercise.

2. Now, **import AdaBoostClassifier** and use it as the input for **clf_model()**:

```
from sklearn.ensemble import AdaBoostClassifier
clf_model(AdaBoostClassifier())
```

You should get the following output:

```
Scores: [0.97519692 0.98122381 0.97652976]
Mean score: 0.9776501596069993
```

Figure 11.33: Mean score output using AdaBoostClassifier

As you can see, the AdaBoost classifier gave one of the best results yet. Let's see how it performs on the confusion matrix.

3. Use **AdaBoostClassifer()** as the input for the **confusion()** function:

```
confusion(AdaBoostClassifier())
```

You should get the following output:

```
Confusion Matrix: [[4020    32]
 [   77   346]]
Classification Report:                 precision    recall   f1-score    support

                 0          0.98        0.99      0.99       4052
                 1          0.92        0.82      0.86        423

         micro avg          0.98        0.98      0.98       4475
         macro avg          0.95        0.91      0.93       4475
      weighted avg          0.97        0.98      0.98       4475
```

Figure 11.34: Output of the confusion matrix on AdaBoostClassifier

Totals of 98% for precision, recall, and the f1-score are outstanding. The f1-score of the positive pulsar classification, the 1's, is 86%, nearly performing as well as **RandomForestClassifier**.

> **Note**
>
> Now, head to the notebook file for *exercises 146-150* and execute the following steps.

4. Set **X** and **y** equal to **housing_df.iloc[:, :-1]** and **housing_df.iloc[:, -1]**:

```
X = housing_df.iloc[:,:-1]
y = housing_df.iloc[:, -1]
```

5. Now, **import AdaBoostRegressor** and use **AdaBoostRegressor()** as the input for the **regression_model_cv** function:

```
from sklearn.ensemble import AdaBoostRegressor
regression_model_cv(AdaBoostRegressor())
```

You should get the following output:

```
Reg rmse: [3.75023024 3.48211969 5.46911888 6.30026928 4.13913715]
Reg mean: 4.628175048702711
```

Figure 11.35: Mean score output using AdaBoostRegressor

It's no surprise that AdaBoost also gives one of the best results on the housing dataset. It has a great reputation for a reason.

AdaBoost is one example of many reputable boosters. XGBoost, and its successor, LightGBM, followed in the footsteps of AdaBoost. They are not part of the sklearn library, however, so we will not implement them in this book.

Activity 25: Using Machine Learning to Predict Customer Return Rate Accuracy

In this activity, you will use machine learning to solve a real-world problem. A bank wants to predict whether customers will return, also known as churn. They want to know which customers are most likely to leave. They give you their data, and they ask you to create a machine-learning algorithm to help them target the customers most likely to leave.

The overview for this activity will be for you to first prepare the data in the dataset, then run a variety of machine learning algorithms that were covered in this chapter to check their accuracy. You will then use the confusion matrix and classification report to help find the best algorithm to identify cases of user churn. You will select one final machine learning algorithm along with its confusion matrix and classification report for your output.

Here are the steps to achieve this goal:

1. Download the dataset from https://packt.live/35NRn2C.

2. Open **CHURN.csv** in a Jupyter Notebook and observe the first five rows.

3. Check for **NaN** values and remove any that you find in the dataset.

4. In order to use machine learning on all the columns, the predictive column should be in terms of numbers, not **'No'** and **'Yes'**. You may replace **'No'** and **'Yes'** with **0** and **1** as follows:

```
df['Churn'] = df['Churn'].replace(to_replace=['No', 'Yes'], value=[0, 1])
```

5. Set **X**, the predictor columns, equal to all columns except the first and the last. Set **y**, the target column, equal to the last column.

6. You want to transform all of the predictive columns into numeric columns. This can be achieved as follows:

```
X = pd.get_dummies(X)
```

7. Write a function called **clf_model** that uses **cross_val_score** to implement a classifier. Recall that **cross_val_score** must be imported.

8. Run your function on five different machine learning algorithms. Choose the top three models.

9. Build a similar function using the confusion matrix and the classification report that uses **train_test_split**. Compare your top three models using this function.

10. Choose your best model, look at the hyperparameters, and optimize at least one hyperparameter.

    You should get an output similar to the following:

    ```
    Confusion Matrix: [[1147  158]
     [ 192  264]]
    Classification Report:              precision    recall  f1-score   support

                0         0.86      0.88      0.87      1305
                1         0.63      0.58      0.60       456

        avg / total       0.80      0.80      0.80      1761
    ```

    ```
    Out[22]: AdaBoostClassifier(algorithm='SAMME.R', base_estimator=None,
                  learning_rate=1.0, n_estimators=25, random_state=None)
    ```

    Figure 11.36: Expected confusion matrix output

> **Note**
>
> The solution for this activity is available on page 559.

Summary

In this chapter, you have learned how to build a variety of machine learning models to solve regression and classification problems. You have implemented Linear Regression, Ridge, Lasso, Logistic Regression, Decision Trees, Random Forests, Naive Bayes, and AdaBoost. You have learned about the importance of using cross-validation to split up your training set and test set. You have learned about the dangers of overfitting and how to correct it with regularization. You have learned how to fine-tune hyperparameters using **GridSearchCV** and **RandomizedSearchCV**. You have learned how to interpret imbalanced datasets with a confusion matrix and a classification report. You have also learned how to distinguish between bagging and boosting, and precision and recall.

The truth is that you have only scratched the surface of machine learning. In addition to classification and regression, there are many other popular classes of machine learning algorithms, such as recommenders, which are used to recommend what movies or books a user may like based on their preferences and what they have liked before, and unsupervised algorithms, which group data in unpredictable ways.

With this chapter, we come to the end of our journey in this book. We've learned the basics of Python and how to get started from opening a Jupyter Notebook and loading the necessary libraries, to working with lists, dictionaries, and sets; after which, we moved on to visually outputting data using Python, which is an essential part of presenting data. We saw not only how to code in Python, but also how to be Pythonic, which is the smarter way to code in Python. We then covered using unit testing and debugging techniques to handle errors. Lastly, we saw how to learn from big data in this last chapter on machine learning.

Appendix

About

This section is included to assist you in performing the activities present in the book. It includes detailed steps that are to be performed by the students to complete and achieve the objectives of the book.

Chapter 1: Vital Python – Math, Strings, Conditionals, and Loops

Activity 1: Assigning Values to Variables

Solution:

1. We begin with the first step, where **x** has been assigned the value of **14**:

```
x = 14
```

2. Now we use the **+=** operator to set **x** equal to **x + 1** in the same step:

```
x += 1
```

3. In this step, **x** is divided by **5**, and the result is squared:

```
(x/5) ** 2
```

You should get the following output:

```
9.0
```

With this activity, you have learned how to perform multiple mathematical operations on a variable. This is very common in Python. For example, in machine learning, covered in *Chapter 11, Machine Learning*, the input may be a matrix, **X**, and multiple mathematical operations will be performed on the **X** matrix until predictive results are obtained. Although the mathematics behind machine learning is more sophisticated, the core ideas are the same.

Activity 2: Finding a Solution Using Pythagorean Theorem in Python

Solution:

1. Open your Jupyter Notebook.

2. In this step, you need to write a docstring that describes the code as follows:

```
"""
This document determines the Pythagorean Distance
between three given points
"""
```

3. Now, in the following code snippet, you have set **x**, **y**, and **z** equal to **2**, **3**, and **4**:

```
# Initialize variables
x, y, z = 2, 3, 4
```

4. In the following steps, 4 and 5, you determine the Pythagorean distance between the three points by squaring each value using the **w_squared** variable and taking the square root of the sum. And in the final step, you add comments to clarify each line of code:

```
# Pythagorean Theorem in 3 dimensions
w_squared = x**2 + y**2 + z**2
```

5. Now, we take the square root of the sum, which will give us the distance in the final step:

```
# The square root gives the distance
w = w_squared ** 0.5
```

6. To print the distance, we simply enter the **w** variable to output the final distance:

```
#Show the distance
w
```

You should get the following output:

```
5.385164807134504
```

In this activity, you have written a mini program that determines the Pythagorean distance between three points. Significantly, you have added a docstring and comments to clarify the code. There is never a correct answer for comments. It's up to the writer to determine how much information to give. A general goal is to be terse but informative. Comprehension is the most important thing. Adding comments and docstrings will always make your code look more professional and easier to read.

Congratulations on making it through the first topic in your Python journey! You are well on your way to becoming a developer or data scientist.

Activity 3: Using the input() Function to Rate Your Day

Solution:

1. We begin this activity by opening up a new Jupyter Notebook.

2. In this step, a question is displayed, prompting a user to rate their day on a number scale:

```
# Choose a question to ask
print('How would you rate your day on a scale of 1 to 10?')
```

3. In this step, the user input is saved as a variable:

```
# Set a variable equal to input()
day_rating = input()
```

You should get the following output:

```
In [*]:  day_rating = input()
         9
```

Figure 1.20: Output asking the user for an input value

4. In this step, a statement is displayed that includes the provided number:

```
# Select an appropriate output.
print('You feel like a ' + day_rating + ' today. Thanks for letting me know')
```

You should get the following output:

```
In [5]:  print('You feel like a ' + day_rating + ' today. Thanks for letting me know')
         You feel like a 9 today. Thanks for letting me know
```

Figure 1.21: Output displaying the user's day rating on a scale of 1 to 10

In this activity, you prompted the user for a number and used that number to display a statement back to the user that includes the number. Communicating directly with users depending upon their input is a core developer skill.

Activity 4: Finding the Least Common Multiple (LCM)

Solution:

1. We begin by opening a new Jupyter Notebook.

2. Here, you begin by setting the variables equal to **24** and **36**:

```
# Find the Least Common Multiple of Two Divisors
first_divisor = 24
second_divisor = 36
```

3. In this step, you have initialized a **while** loop based on the counting Boolean, which is **True**, with an iterator, **i**:

```
counting = True
i = 1
while counting:
```

4. This step sets up a conditional to check whether the iterator divides both numbers:

```
if i % first_divisor == 0 and i % second_divisor == 0:
```

5. This step breaks the **while** loop:

```
break
```

6. This step increments the iterator at the end of the loop:

```
i += 1
print('The Least Common Multiple of', first_divisor, 'and', second_divisor, 'is', i,
'.')
```

The aforementioned code snippet prints the results.

You should get the following output:

```
The Least Common Multiple of 24 and 36 is 72.
```

In this activity, you used a **while** loop to run a program that computes the LCM of two numbers. Using **while** loops to complete tasks is an essential ability for all developers.

Activity 5: Building Conversational Bots Using Python

Solution:

For the first bot, the solution is as follows:

1. This step shows the first question asked of the user:

```
print('What is your name?')
```

2. This step shows the response with the answer:

```
name = input()
print('Fascinating.', name, 'is my name too.')
```

You should get the following output:

```
In [*]: name = input()
        print('Fascinating.', name, 'is my name too.')

        Corey
```

Figure 1.22: Using the input() function to ask the user to enter a value

Once you enter the value, in this case, your name, the output will be as follows:

```
In [2]: name = input()
        print('Fascinating.', name, 'is my name too.')

        Corey
        Fascinating. Corey is my name too.
```

Figure 1.23: Output once the user has entered the values

3. This step shows the second question asked of the user:

```
print('Have you thought about black holes today?')
```

You should get the following output:

```
Have you thought about black holes today?
```

4. This step shows the response with the answer:

```
yes_no = input()
print('I am so glad you said', yes_no, '. I was thinking the same thing.')
```

You should get the following output:

```
In [4]: yes_no = input()
        print('I am so glad you said', yes_no, '. I was thinking the same thing.')

        Yes
        I am so glad you said Yes . I was thinking the same thing.
```

Figure 1.24: Using the input() function asks the user to enter the value

Once you enter the value, in this case, your name, the output will be as follows:

```
In [4]: yes_no = input()
        print('I am so glad you said', yes_no, '. I was thinking the same thing.')

        Yes
        I am so glad you said Yes . I was thinking the same thing.
```

Figure 1.25: Printing the input() function statements

5. This step shows the response with the answer:

```
print('We\'re kindred spirits,', name, '. Talk later.')
```

You should get the following output:

```
We're kindred spirits, Corey.Talk later.
```

Now, moving on to the second bot:

6. Create an **input()** function for a **smart** variable and change the type to **int**:

```
print('How intelligent are you? 0 is very dumb. And 10 is a genius')
smarts = input()
smarts = int(smarts)
```

7. Create an **if** loop so that if the user enters a value equal to or less than **3**, we print **I don't believe you**. If not, then print the next statement:

```
if smarts <= 3:
    print('I don\'t believe you.')
    print('How bad of a day are you having? 0 is the worst, and 10 is the best.')
```

8. Create an **input()** function for the **day** variable and change the type to **int**:

```
day = input()
day = int(day)
```

9. Now, create an **if else** loop where if the user entered a value less than or equal to 5, we **print** the output statement. If not, then we **print** the output **else** statement:

```
if day <= 5:
    print('If I was human, I would give you a hug.')
else:
    print('Maybe I should try your approach.')
```

10. Continue the loop using **elif**, also called **else-if**, where if the user enters a value less than or equal to **6**, we print the corresponding statement:

```
elif smarts <= 6:
    print('I think you\'re actually smarter.')
    print('How much time do you spend online? 0 is none and 10 is 24 hours a day.')
```

11. Now, build another **input()** function for the **hours** variable and change the type to **int**. Use the **if-else** loop so that if the user enters a value less than or equal to **4**, we print the corresponding statement. If not, print the other statement:

```
hours = input()
hours = int(hours)
if hours <= 4:
    print('That\'s the problem.')
else:
    print('And I thought it was only me.')
```

12. Using the **elif** loop, we check the **smart** variable and output the corresponding **print** statement. We also use **if-else** to find out whether the user has entered a value less than or equal to **5**:

```
elif smarts <= 8:
    print('Are you human by chance? Wait. Don\'t answer that.')
    print('How human are you? 0 is not at all and 10 is human all the way.')
    human = input()
    human = int(human)
    if human <= 5:
        print('I knew it.')
    else:
        print('I think this courtship is over.')
```

13. We continue with the **else** loop from the **if-else** from step 7 and set the appropriate conditions and **print** statements:

```
else:
    print('I see... How many operating systems do you run?')
```

14. Set the **input()** functions once again to the **os** variable and change the type to **int**, after which we output the corresponding **print** statement depending on the user's input values:

```
os = input()
os = int(os)
if os <= 2:
    print('Good thing you\'re taking this course.')
else:
    print('What is this? A competition?')
```

You should get the following output:

```
How intelligent are you? 0 is very dumb. And 10 is a genius
8
Are you human by chance? Wait. Don't answer that.
How human are you? 0 is not at all and 10 is human all the way.
8
I think this courtship is over.
```

Figure 1.26: Expected outcome from one of the possible values entered by the user

Congratulations! By completing this activity, you have created two conversational bots using nested conditionals and **if-else** loops where we also used changing types, using the **input()** function to get values from the user and then respectively displaying the output.

Chapter 2: Python Structures

Activity 6: Using a Nested List to Store Employee Data

Solution:

1. Begin by creating a list, adding data, and assigning it to **employees**:

```
employees = [['John Mckee', 38, 'Sales'], ['Lisa Crawford', 29, 'Marketing'],
['Sujan Patel', 33, 'HR']]
print(employees)
```

You should get the following output:

```
[['John Mckee', 38, 'Sales'], ['Lisa Crawford', 29, 'Marketing'], ['Sujan Patel', 33, 'HR']]
```

Figure 2.31: Output when we print the content of employees

2. Next, we can utilize the **for..in** loop to print each of the record's data within **employee**:

```
for employee in employees:
    print(employee)
```

```
['John Mckee', 38, 'Sales']
['Lisa Crawford', 29, 'Marketing']
['Sujan Patel', 33, 'HR']
```

Figure 2.32: Output when printing each of the records inside employees

3. To have the data presented in a structured version of the **employee** record, add the following lines of code:

```
for employee in employees:
    print("Name:", employee[0])
    print("Age:", employee[1])
    print("Department:", employee[2])
    print('-' * 20)
```

```
Name: John Mckee
Age: 38
Department: Sales
--------------------
Name: Lisa Crawford
Age: 29
Department: Marketing
--------------------
Name: Sujan Patel
Age: 33
Department: HR
--------------------
```

Figure 2.33: Output when printing each of the records inside employees with a structure

4. Lastly, if we were to print the details of **Lisa Crawford**, we would need to use the indexing method. Lisa's record is in position 1, so we would write:

```python
employee = employees[1]
print(employee)
print("Name:", employee[0])
print("Age:", employee[1])
print("Department:", employee[2])
print('-' * 20)
```

```
['Lisa Crawford', 29, 'Marketing']
Name: Lisa Crawford
Age: 29
Department: Marketing
--------------------
```

Figure 2.34: Output when printing the details of Lisa Crawford

Having successfully completed this activity, you will be able to work with lists and nested lists. As mentioned in the activity, this is just one instance where this concept could come in handy, that is, to store data in lists and then access them as required.

Activity 7: Storing Company Employee Table Data Using a List and a Dictionary

Solution:

1. Open a Jupyter Notebook and enter the following code in it:

```
employees = [
    {"name": "John Mckee", "age":38, "department":"Sales"},
    {"name": "Lisa Crawford", "age":29, "department":"Marketing"},
    {"name": "Sujan Patel", "age":33, "department":"HR"}
]
print(employees)
```

You should get the following output:

```
[{'name': 'John Mckee', 'age': 38, 'department': 'Sales'}, {'name': 'Lisa Crawford', 'age': 29, 'department': 'Market
ing'}, {'name': 'Sujan Patel', 'age': 33, 'department': 'HR'}]
```

Figure 2.35: Output when we print the employees list

In step 1, we created a list, **employee**, and added values to it, such as **name**, **age**, and **department**.

2. Now, we will be adding a **for** loop to our **employee** list using the * operator. To do this, we will use a dictionary to **print** the **employee** details in a presentable structure:

```
for employee in employees:
    print("Name:", employee['name'])
    print("Age:", employee['age'])
    print("Department:", employee['department'])
    print('-' * 20)
```

You should get the following output:

```
Name: John Mckee
Age: 38
Department: Sales
--------------------
Name: Lisa Crawford
Age: 29
Department: Marketing
--------------------
Name: Sujan Patel
Age: 33
Department: HR
--------------------
```

Figure 2.36: Output when we print an individual employee in a structured format

> **Note**
>
> You can compare this method with the previous activity, where we printed from a nested list. Using a dictionary gives us a more concise syntax, as we access the data using a key instead of a positional index. This is particularly helpful when we are dealing with objects with many keys.

3. The final step is to print the **employee** details of **Sujan Patel**. To do this, we will access the **employees** dictionary and will only **print** the value of one **employee** from a list of **employee** names:

```python
for employee in employees:
    if employee['name'] == 'Sujan Patel':
        print("Name:", employee['name'])
        print("Age:", employee['age'])
        print("Department:", employee['department'])
        print('-' * 20)
```

You should get the following output:

```
Name: Sujan Patel
Age: 33
Department: HR
--------------------
```

Figure 2.37: Output when we only print the employee details of Sujan Patel

Having completed this activity, you are able to work with lists and dictionaries. As you have seen, lists are very useful for storing and accessing data, which very often comes in handy in the real world when handling data in Python. Using dictionaries along with lists proves to be very useful, as you have seen in this activity.

Chapter 3: Executing Python – Programs, Algorithms, Functions

Activity 8: What's the Time?

Solution:

In the following, you will find the solution code to *Activity 8, What's the Time?*

To make it easier to understand, the code has been broken down with explanations:

`current_time.py`:

```
"""
This script returns the current system time.
"""
```

1. Firstly, we import the **datetime** library, which contains a range of useful utilities for working with dates:

```
import datetime
```

2. Using the **datetime** library, we can get the current **datetime** stamp, and then call the **time()** function in order to retrieve the time:

```
time = datetime.datetime.now().time()
```

3. If the script is being executed, this **if** statement will be true, and, therefore, the time will be printed:

```
if __name__ == '__main__':
    print(time)
```

You should get the following output:

Anaconda Prompt

```
(base) C:\Users\andrew.bird\Python-In-Demand\Lesson03\Activities>python current_time.py
16:48:22.416000

(base) C:\Users\andrew.bird\Python-In-Demand\Lesson03\Activities>
```

Figure 3.35: The output in the datetime format

At the end of this activity, you are able to import the **datetime** module and execute the Python script to tell the time. Additionally, you are able to import the time to use it elsewhere in your code if necessary.

Activity 9: Formatting Customer Names

Solution:

The `customer.py` file should look like the steps mentioned below. Note that there are many different valid ways to write this function:

1. The `format_customer` function takes two required positional arguments, `first_name` and `last_name`, and one optional keyword argument, `location`:

```
def format_customer(first, last, location=None):
```

2. It then uses the `%` string formatting notation to create a `full_name` variable:

```
full_name = '%s %s' % (first, last)
```

3. The third line checks whether a location has been specified and, if so, appends the location details to the full name. If no location was specified, just the full name is returned:

```
if location:
    return '%s (%s)' % (full_name, location)
else:
    return full_name
```

By the end of this activity, you are able to create a function that takes in various arguments for names and returns a string as you require.

Activity 10: The Fibonacci Function with an Iteration

Solution:

1. This `fibonacci_iterative` function starts with the first two values of the Fibonacci sequence, `0` and `1`:

```
def fibonacci_iterative(n):
    previous = 0
    current = 1
```

2. For each loop in the iteration, it updates these values to represent the previous two numbers in the sequence. After reaching the final iteration, the loop terminates, and returns the value of the `current` variable:

```
    for i in range(n - 1):
        current_old = current
        current = previous + current
        previous = current_old
    return current
```

3. Now you can try running a few examples in Jupyter Notebook by importing the **fibonacci_iterative** function:

```
from fibonacci import fibonacci_iterative
fibonacci_iterative(3)
```

You should get the following output:

```
2
```

Let's try another example:

```
fibonacci_iterative(10)
```

You should get the following output:

```
55
```

In this activity, you were able to work with iterations and return the nth value in the Fibonacci sequence.

Activity 11: The Fibonacci Function with Recursion

Solution:

1. Open the **fibonacci.py** file.

2. Define a **fibonacci_recursive** function that takes a single input named **n**:

```
def fibonacci_recursive(n):
```

3. Now check whether the value of **n** is equal to 0 or 1. If the condition is satisfied, the value of **n** is returned. Write the following code to implement this step:

```
if n == 0 or n == 1:
    return n
```

4. Otherwise, in case the condition is not satisfied it will return the same function, but the argument will be decremented by 2 and 1 and the respective differences will be added:

```
else:
    return fibonacci_recursive(n - 2) + fibonacci_recursive(n - 1)
```

5. Once the function is created, try running the examples in the compiler using the following command:

```
from fibonacci import fibonacci_recursive
fibonacci_recursive(3)
```

You should get the following output:

```
2
```

You can now work with recursive functions. We implemented this on our **fibonnacci.py** file to get the expected output. Recursive functions are helpful in many cases in order to reduce the lines of code that you will be using if it is repetitive.

Activity 12: The Fibonacci Function with Dynamic Programming

Solution:

1. We begin by keeping a dictionary of Fibonacci numbers in the **stored** variable. The keys of the dictionary represent the index of the value in the sequence (such as the first, second, and fifth number), and the value itself:

```
stored = {0: 0, 1: 1}  # We set the first 2 terms of the Fibonacci sequence here.
```

2. When calling the **fibonacci_dynamic** function, we check to see whether we have already computed the result; if so, we simply return the value from the dictionary:

```
def fibonacci_dynamic(n):
    if n in stored:
        return stored[n]
```

3. Otherwise, we revert to the recursive logic by calling the function to compute the previous two terms:

```
    else:
        stored[n] = fibonacci_dynamic(n - 2) + fibonacci_dynamic(n - 1)
        return stored[n]
```

4. Now, run the following:

```
from fibonacci import fibonacci_recursive
fibonacci_dynamic(100)
```

You should get the following output:

```
354224848179261915075
```

In this activity, we used a function with dynamic programming that takes a single positional argument representing the number term in the sequence that we want to return.

Chapter 4: Extending Python, Files, Errors, and Graphs

Activity 13: Visualizing the Titanic Dataset Using a Pie Chart and Bar Plots

Solution

1. Import all the lines from the **csv** file in the **titanic_train.csv** dataset file and store it in a list:

```
import csv
lines = []
with open('titanic_train.csv') as csv_file:
    csv_reader = csv.reader(csv_file, delimiter=',')
    for line in csv_reader:
        lines.append(line)
```

2. Generate a collection of **passengers** objects. This step is designed to facilitate the subsequent steps where we need to extract values of different properties into a list for generating charts:

```
data = lines[1:]
passengers = []
headers = lines[0]
```

3. Create a simple **for** loop for the **d** variable in **data**, which will store the values in a list:

```
for d in data:
    p = {}
    for i in range(0,len(headers)):
        key = headers[i]
        value = d[i]
        p[key] = value
    passengers.append(p)
```

4. Extract the **survived**, **pclass**, **age**, and **gender** values of survived passengers into respective lists. We need to utilize list comprehension in order to extract the values; for the passengers who survived, we will need to convert **survived** into an integer and filter **survived == 1**, that is, passengers who survived:

```
survived = [p['Survived'] for p in passengers]
pclass = [p['Pclass'] for p in passengers]
age = [float(p['Age']) for p in passengers if p['Age'] != '']
gender_survived = [p['Sex'] for p in passengers if int(p['Survived']) == 1]
```

5. Now, **import** all the necessary libraries, such as **matplotlib**, **seaborn**, and **numpy**, and draw a pie chart using **plt.pie** to visualize the passengers who survived:

```
import matplotlib.pyplot as plt
import seaborn as sns
import numpy as np
from collections import Counter
plt.title("Survived")
plt.pie(Counter(survived).values(), labels=Counter(survived).keys(),
autopct='%1.1f%%',
        colors=['lightblue', 'lightgreen', 'yellow'])
plt.show()
```

Execute the cell twice, and you should get the following output:

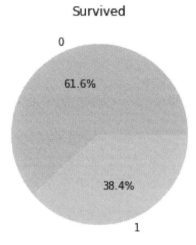

Figure 4.28: Pie chart showing the survival rate of the passengers

6. Draw a column bar plot using **plt.bar** to visualize the passengers who survived based on their gender:

```
plt.title("surviving passengers count by gender")
plt.bar(Counter(gender_survived).keys(), Counter(gender_survived).values())
plt.show()
```

You should get the following output:

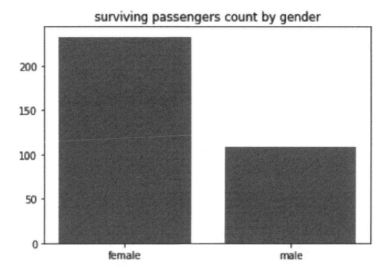

Figure 4.29: A bar plot showing the variation in gender of those who survived the incident

In this activity, we have used the interesting Titanic dataset to visualize data. We imported the dataset and stored the data in a list. Then, we used the **matplotlib**, **seaborn**, and **numpy** libraries to plot the various data and get the outputs as needed using the two plotting techniques: pie charts and bar plots.

Chapter 5: Constructing Python – Classes and Methods

Activity 14: Creating Classes and Inheriting from a Parent Class

Solution:

1. Firstly, define the parent class, **Polygon**. We add an **init** method that allows the user to specify the lengths of the sides when creating the polygon:

```
class Polygon():
    """A class to capture common utilities for dealing with shapes"""
    def __init__(self, side_lengths):
        self.side_lengths = side_lengths


    def __str__(self):
        return 'Polygon with %s sides' % self.num_sides
```

2. Add two properties to the **Polygon** class – one that computes the number of sides of the polygon, and another that returns the perimeter:

```
class Polygon():
    """A class to capture common utilities for dealing with shapes"""
    def __init__(self, side_lengths):
        self.side_lengths = side_lengths


    def __str__(self):
        return 'Polygon with %s sides' % self.num_sides

    @property
    def num_sides(self):
        return len(self.side_lengths)


    @property
    def perimeter(self):
            return sum(self.side_lengths)
```

3. Create a child class of **Polygon** called **Rectangle**. Add an **init** method that allows the user to specify the height and the width of the rectangle. Add a property that computes the area of the rectangle:

```python
class Rectangle(Polygon):
    def __init__(self, height, width):
        super().__init__([height, width, height, width])

    @property
    def area(self):
        return self.side_lengths[0] * self.side_lengths[1]
```

4. Test your **Rectangle** class by creating a new rectangle and checking the value of its properties – the **area** and the **perimeter**:

```python
r = Rectangle(1, 5)
r.area, r.perimeter
```

You should get the following output:

```python
(5, 12)
```

5. Create a child class of **Rectangle** called **Square** that takes a single **height** parameter in its initialization:

```python
class Square(Rectangle):
    def __init__(self, height):
        super().__init__(height, height)
```

6. Test your **Square** class by creating a new square and checking the value of its properties – the **area** and the **perimeter**:

```python
s = Square(5)
s.area, s.perimeter
```

You should get the following output:

```python
(25, 20)
```

Chapter 6: The Standard Library

Activity 15: Calculating the Time Elapsed to Run a Loop

Solution:

1. We begin by opening a new Jupyter file and importing the **random** and **time** modules:

```
import random
import time
```

2. Then, we use the **time.time** function to get the **start** time:

```
start = time.time()
```

3. Now, by using the aforementioned code, we will find the time in nanoseconds. Here, the range is set from 1 to 999:

```
l = [random.randint(1, 999) for _ in range(10 * 3)]
```

4. Now, we record the finish time and subtract this time to get the delta:

```
end = time.time()
print(end - start)
```

You should get the following output:

```
0.0019025802612304688
```

5. But this will give us a float. For measurements higher than 1 second, the precision might be good enough, but we can also use **time.time_ns** to get the time as the number of nanoseconds elapsed. This will give us a more precise result, without the limitations of floating-point numbers:

```
start = time.time_ns()
l = [random.randint(1, 999) for _ in range(10 * 3)]
end = time.time_ns()
print(end - start)
```

You should get the following output:

```
187500
```

> **Note**
>
> This is a good solution when using the **time** module and for common applications.

Activity 16: Testing Python Code

Solution:

The line, `compile("1" + "+1" * 10 ** 6, "string", "exec")`, will crash the interpreter; we will need to run it with the following code:

1. First, import the **sys** and **subprocess** modules as we are going to use them in the following steps:

```
import sys
import subprocess
```

2. We save the code that we were given in the **code** variable:

```
code = 'compile("1" + "+1" * 10 ** 6, "string", "exec")'
```

3. Run the code by calling **subprocess.run** and **sys.executable** to get the Python interpreter we are using:

```
result = subprocess.run([
    sys.executable,
    "-c", code
])
```

The preceding code takes a code line, which compiles Python code that will crash and runs it in a subprocess by executing the same interpreter (retrieved via **sys. executable**) with the **-c** option to run Python code inline.

4. Now, we print the final result using **result.resultcode**. This will return the value **-11**, which means the process has crashed:

```
print(result.returncode)
```

The output will be as follows:

```
-11
```

This line of code just prints the return code of the **subprocess** call.

In this activity, we have executed a small program that can run the requested code line and checked whether it would crash without breaking the current process. It did end up crashing, hence outputting the value **-11**, which corresponded to an abort in the program.

Activity 17: Using partial on class Methods

Solution:

You need to explore the **functools** module and realize a specific **helper** for methods, which can be used as explained in the following steps:

1. When you execute the mentioned code, you will get the following error message:

```
TypeError                               Traceback (most recent call last)
<ipython-input-2-3b1898c093f2> in <module>
      4      hero.rename("Batman")
      5      assert hero.name == "Batman"
----> 6      hero.reset_name()
      7      assert hero.name == "Batman"

TypeError: rename() missing 1 required positional argument: 'new_name'
```

Figure 6.52: Error output with a missing required positional argument

Now, to fix this, let's check for an alternative by observing the following steps.

2. Import the **functools** module:

```
import functools
```

3. Create the **Hero** class, which uses **partialmethod** to set **reset_name**:

```
class Hero:
    DEFAULT_NAME = "Superman"
    def __init__(self):
        self.name = Hero.DEFAULT_NAME

    def rename(self, new_name):
        self.name = new_name

    reset_name = functools.partial(rename, DEFAULT_NAME)

    def __repr__(self):
        return f"Hero({self.name!r})"
```

The code makes use of a different version of **partial**, **partialmethod**, which allows the creation of **partial** for a method class. By using this utility on the **rename** method and setting the name to the default name, we can create **partial**, which will be used as a method. The name of the method is the one that is set in the scope of the **Hero** class definition, which is **reset_name**.

Wrong Assumptions with Date and Time

Wrong assumption	Reasoning
Years have 365 days.	There are years that have 366 days as a result of leap days, or calendars that have a different number of days. Never assume that 365 days is equivalent to a year.
Days have 24 hours.	Due to DST changes or any other changes in time zones, it is not safe to assume that 24 hours are equivalent to a day, especially if not dealing with UTC.
Weeks start on Monday and weekdays are Monday to Friday.	This totally depends on the culture. Multiple calendars start the week on Sunday, and the weekend also varies between countries.
Given a date and time in the future and a location, I can safely change the time zone of an object.	When working with wall times, there are many developers who try to convert everything to UTC. This is a common mistake as, if a country decides to change their time zone, which happens every other month, your conversions will not be valid anymore, and if you did not save the original time you will basically have corrupted data. When working with future wall times, never convert them. Just save the date and time with the time zone separate if needed, as many databases will force you to save in UTC.
All seconds have equal durations	Due to how NTP works, your clock will synchronize and perform changes that can change the duration of a second. A common scenario is to slow down seconds around a leap second. If your application is really sensitive to time, consider using a more precise clock.
Time always moves forward.	It can happen that you call time. This can happen due to NTP synchronizations. If you were planning on using time as some kind of ever-increasing counter, just don't. Python comes with another function, time.monotic, for that exact use case.

Figure 6.53: Wrong assumptions of date and time along with its reasoning

Chapter 7: Becoming Pythonic

Activity 18: Building a Chess Tournament

Solution:

1. Open the Jupyter Notebook.

2. Define the list of player names in Python:

```
names = ["Magnus Carlsen", "Fabiano Caruana", "Yifan Hou", "Wenjun Ju"]
```

3. The list comprehension uses the list of names twice because each person can either be player 1 or player 2 in a match (that is, they can play with the white or the black pieces). Because we don't want the same person to play both sides in a match, add an **if** clause that filters out the situation where the same name appears in both elements of the comprehension:

```
fixtures = [f"{p1} vs. {p2}" for p1 in names for p2 in names if p1 != p2]
```

4. Finally, print the resulting list so that the match officials can see who will be playing whom:

```
print(fixtures)
```

You should get the following output:

```
In [1]: names = ["Magnus Carlsen", "Fabiano Caruana", "Yifan Hou", "Wenjun Ju"]
        fixtures = [f"{p1} vs. {p2}" for p1 in names for p2 in names if p1 != p2]
        print(fixtures)

['Magnus Carlsen vs. Fabiano Caruana', 'Magnus Carlsen vs. Yifan Hou', 'Magnus Carlsen vs. Wenjun Ju', 'Fabiano Caruana vs.
Magnus Carlsen', 'Fabiano Caruana vs. Yifan Hou', 'Fabiano Caruana vs. Wenjun Ju', 'Yifan Hou vs. Magnus Carlsen', 'Yifan H
ou vs. Fabiano Caruana', 'Yifan Hou vs. Wenjun Ju', 'Wenjun Ju vs. Magnus Carlsen', 'Wenjun Ju vs. Fabiano Caruana', 'Wenju
n Ju vs. Yifan Hou']
```

Figure 7.30: The sorted fixtures' output using a list comprehension

In this activity, we used list comprehension to sort out players and create a fixture that was in the form of a string.

Activity 19: Building a Scorecard Using Dictionary Comprehensions and Multiple Lists

Solution:

1. The solution is to iterate through both collections at the same time, using an index. First, define the collections of names and their scores:

```
students = ["Vivian", "Rachel", "Tom", "Adrian"]
points = [70, 82, 80, 79]
```

Now build the dictionary. The comprehension is actually using the third collection; that is, the range of integers from 0 to 100.

2. Each of these numbers can be used to index into the list of names and scores so that the correct name is associated with the correct **points** value:

```
scores = { students[i]:points[i] for i in range(4) }
```

3. Finally, print out the dictionary you just created:

```
print(scores)
```

You should get the following output:

```
In [3]: print(scores)
        {'Vivian': 70, 'Rachel': 82, 'Tom': 80, 'Adrian': 79}
```

Figure 7.31: A dictionary indicating names and scores as a key-value pair

In this activity, we worked on dictionary comprehension and multiple lists. We executed the code to print out a scorecard with two separate lists of names and scores and outputted their values.

Activity 20: Using Random Numbers to Find the Value of Pi

Solution:

1. You will need the **math** and **random** libraries to complete this activity:

```
import math
import random
```

2. Define the **approximate_pi** function:

```
def approximate_pi():
```

3. Set the counters to zero:

```
total_points = 0
within_circle = 0
```

4. Calculate the approximation multiple times:

```
for i in range (10001):
```

Here, **x** and **y** are random numbers between **0** and **1**, which, together, represent a point in the unit square (you can refer to *Figure 7.25*):

```
x = random.random()
y = random.random()
total_points += 1
```

5. Use Pythagoras' Theorem to work out the distance between the point and the origin, (0,0):

```
distance = math.sqrt(x**2+y**2)
if distance < 1:
```

If the distance is less than 1, then this point is both inside the square and inside a circle of radius 1, centered on the origin. You can refer to *Figure 7.25*:

```
within_circle += 1
```

6. Yield a result every 1,000 points. There's no reason why this couldn't yield a result after each point, but the early estimates will be very imprecise, so let's assume that users want to draw a large sample of random values:

```
if total_points % 1000 == 0:
```

7. The ratio of points within the circle to total points generated should be approximately π/4 because the points are uniformly distributed across the square. Only some of the points are both in the square and the circle, and the ratio of areas between the circle segment and the square is π/4:

```
pi_estimate = 4 * within_circle / total_points
if total_points == 10000:
```

8. After **10000** points are generated, return the estimate to complete the iteration. Using what you have learned about **itertools** in this chapter, you could turn this generator into an infinite sequence if you want to:

```
        return pi_estimate
else:
```

Yield successive approximations to π:

```
    yield pi_estimate
```

9. Use the generator to find estimates for the value of π. Additionally, use a list comprehension to find the errors: the difference between the estimated version and the "actual" value in Python's **math** module ("actual" is in scare quotes because it too is only an approximate value). Approximate values are used because Python cannot be exactly expressed in the computer's number system without using infinite memory:

```
estimates = [estimate for estimate in approximate_pi()]
errors = [estimate - math.pi for estimate in estimates]
```

10. Finally, print out our values and the errors to see how the generator performs:

```
print(estimates)
print(errors)
```

You should get the following output:

```
print(estimates)
print(errors)
```

```
[3.236, 3.232, 3.2106666666666666, 3.206, 3.1824, 3.1633333333333336, 3.1582857142857144, 3.1645, 3.1577777777777776]
[0.0944073464102071, 0.09040734641020709, 0.06907401307687344, 0.06440734641020684, 0.04080734641020678, 0.0217406797435404
36, 0.016693060695921247, 0.022907346410206753, 0.01618512418798457]
```

Figure 7.32: The output showing the generator yielding successive estimates of π

By completing this activity, you are now able to explain the working of generators. You successfully generated a plot of points, using which you were able to calculate the value of π. In the following section, we will learn about regular expressions.

Activity 21: Regular Expressions

Solution:

1. First, create the list of names:

    ```
    names = ["Xander Harris", "Jennifer Smith", "Timothy Jones", "Amy Alexandrescu",
    "Peter Price", "Weifung Xu"]
    ```

2. Using the list comprehension syntax from this chapter makes finding the winners as easy as a single line of Python:

    ```
    winners = [name for name in names if re.search("[Xx]", name)]
    ```

3. Finally, print the list of winners:

    ```
    print(winners)
    ```

    You should get the following output:

    ```
    print(winners)
    ```

    ```
    ['Xander Harris', 'Amy Alexandrescu', 'Weifung Xu']
    ```

Figure 7.33: The output showing the winners list indicating the presence of "Xx" in the customer name

In this activity, we used regular expressions and Python's **re** module to find customers from a list whose name contains the value of **Xx**.

Chapter 8: Software Development

Activity 22: Debugging Sample Python Code for an Application

Solution:

1. First, you need to copy the source code, as demonstrated in the following code snippet:

```python
DEFAULT_INITIAL_BASKET = ["orange", "apple"]
def create_picnic_basket(healthy, hungry,    initial_basket=DEFAULT_INITIAL_BASKET):
    basket = initial_basket
    if healthy:
        basket.append("strawberry")
    else:
        basket.append("jam")
    if hungry:
        basket.append("sandwich")
    return basket
```

For the first step, the code creates a list of food that is based on an initial list that can be passed as an argument. There are then some flags that control what gets added. When **healthy** is true, a strawberry will get added. On the other hand, if it is false, the jam will be added instead. Finally, if the **hungry** flag is set to true, a sandwich will be added as well.

2. Run the code in your Jupyter Notebook, along with the reproducers, as demonstrated in the following code snippet:

```python
# Reproducer
print("First basket:", create_picnic_basket(True, False))
print("Second basket:", create_picnic_basket(False, True, ["tea"]))
print("Third basket:", create_picnic_basket(True, True))
```

3. Observe the output; the issue will show up in the third basket, where there is one extra strawberry.

    You should get the following output:

```
In [2]: print("First basket:", create_picnic_basket(True, False))

        First basket: ['orange', 'apple', 'strawberry']

In [3]: print("Second basket:", create_picnic_basket(False, True, ["tea"]))

        Second basket: ['tea', 'jam', 'sandwich']

In [4]: print("Third basket:", create_picnic_basket(True, True))

        Third basket: ['orange', 'apple', 'strawberry', 'strawberry', 'sandwich']
```

Figure 8.19: The output with the additional item in the third basket

4. You will need to fix this by setting the basket value to **None** and using the **if-else** logic, as demonstrated in the following code snippet:

```python
def create_picnic_basket(healthy, hungry, basket=None):
    if basket is None:
        basket = ["orange", "apple"]
    if healthy:
        basket.append("strawberry")
    else:
        basket.append("jam")
    if hungry:
        basket.append("sandwich")
    return basket
```

Note that default values in functions should not be mutable, as the modifications will persist across calls. The default basket should be set to None in the function declaration, and the constant should be used within the function. This is a great exercise to debug.

5. Now, run the reproducers once again, and it will be fixed.

The debugged output is as follows:

```
In [6]: print("First basket:", create_picnic_basket(True, False))

        First basket: ['orange', 'apple', 'strawberry']

In [7]: print("Second basket:", create_picnic_basket(False, True, ["tea"]))

        Second basket: ['tea', 'jam', 'sandwich']

In [8]: print("Third basket:", create_picnic_basket(True, True))

        Third basket: ['orange', 'apple', 'strawberry', 'sandwich']

In [ ]:
```

Figure 8.20: Debugging the activity with the correct output

In this activity, you have implemented debugging to understand the source code, after which you were able to print the test cases (reproducers) and find the issue. You were then able to debug the code and fix it to achieve the desired output.

Chapter 9: Practical Python – Advanced Topics

Activity 23: Generating a List of Random Numbers in a Python Virtual Environment

Solution

1. Create a new **conda** environment called **my_env**:

```
conda create -n my_env
```

You should get the following output:

```
(base) C:\Users\andrew.bird\python-demo>conda create my_env

CondaValueError: either -n NAME or -p PREFIX option required,
try "conda create -h" for more details


(base) C:\Users\andrew.bird\python-demo>conda create -n my_env
Solving environment: done


==> WARNING: A newer version of conda exists. <==
  current version: 4.5.12
  latest version: 4.7.10
```

Figure 9.32: Creating a new conda environment (truncated)

2. Activate the **conda** environment:

```
conda activate my_env
```

3. Install **numpy** in your new environment:

```
conda install numpy
```

You should get the following output:

```
(my_env) C:\Users\andrew.bird\Python-In-Demand\Lesson09>conda install numpy
Solving environment: done


==> WARNING: A newer version of conda exists. <==
  current version: 4.5.12
  latest version: 4.7.10

Please update conda by running

    $ conda update -n base -c defaults conda



## Package Plan ##

  environment location: C:\Users\andrew.bird\AppData\Local\conda\conda\envs\my_env

  added / updated specs:
    - numpy
```

Figure 9.33: Installing numpy (truncated)

4. Next, install and run a **jupyter** Notebook from within your virtual environment:

```
conda install jupyter
jupyter notebook
```

5. Create a new **jupyter** Notebook and start with the following imports:

```
import threading
import queue
import cProfile
import itertools
import numpy as np
```

6. Create a function that uses the **numpy** library to generate an array of random numbers. Recall that when threading, we need to be able to send a signal for the **while** statement to terminate:

```
in_queue = queue.Queue()
out_queue = queue.Queue()
def random_number_threading():
    while True:
        n = in_queue.get()
        if n == 'STOP':
            return
```

```
        random_numbers = np.random.rand(n)
        out_queue.put(random_numbers)
```

7. Next, let's add a function that will start a thread and put integers into the **in_queue** object. We can optionally print the output by setting the **show_output** argument to **True**:

```
def generate_random_numbers(show_output, up_to):
    thread = threading.Thread(target=random_number_threading)
    thread.start()
    for i in range(up_to):
        in_queue.put(i)
        random_nums = out_queue.get()
        if show_output:
            print(random_nums)
    in_queue.put('STOP')
    thread.join()
```

8. Run the numbers on a small number of iterations to test and see the output:

```
generate_random_numbers(True, 10)
```

You should get the following output:

```
[]
[0.78155881]
[0.61671875 0.96379795]
[0.52748128 0.69182391 0.11764897]
[0.89243527 0.75566451 0.88089298 0.15782374]
[0.1140009  0.25980504 0.88632411 0.08730527 0.17493792]
[0.41370041 0.01167654 0.60758276 0.73804504 0.73648781 0.29094613
[0.8317736  0.57914287 0.01291246 0.61011878 0.91729392 0.50898183
 0.24640681]
[0.4475645  0.94036652 0.69823962 0.37459892 0.15512432 0.15115215
 0.65882522 0.77908825]
[0.42420881 0.7135031  0.22843178 0.20624473 0.32533328 0.86108686
 0.46407033 0.81794371 0.98958707]
```

Figure 9.34: Generating lists of random numbers with numpy

9. Rerun the numbers with a large number of iterations and use **cProfile** to view a breakdown of what is taking time to execute:

```
cProfile.run('generate_random_numbers(False, 20000)')
```

You should get the following output:

```
        740056 function calls in 3.461 seconds

   Ordered by: standard name

   ncalls  tottime  percall  cumtime  percall filename:lineno(function)
        1    0.051    0.051    3.461    3.461 <ipython-input-4-04f1b90debed>:1(generate_random_numbers)
        1    0.000    0.000    3.461    3.461 <string>:1(<module>)
        1    0.000    0.000    0.000    0.000 _weakrefset.py:38(_remove)
        1    0.000    0.000    0.000    0.000 _weakrefset.py:81(add)
    20001    0.063    0.000    0.200    0.000 queue.py:121(put)
    20000    0.137    0.000    3.209    0.000 queue.py:153(get)
    40000    0.019    0.000    0.026    0.000 queue.py:208(_qsize)
    20001    0.009    0.000    0.012    0.000 queue.py:212(_put)
    20000    0.008    0.000    0.012    0.000 queue.py:216(_get)
        1    0.000    0.000    0.000    0.000 threading.py:1000(join)
        1    0.000    0.000    0.000    0.000 threading.py:1038(_wait_for_tstate_lock)
        1    0.000    0.000    0.000    0.000 threading.py:1096(daemon)
        2    0.000    0.000    0.000    0.000 threading.py:1206(current_thread)
        1    0.000    0.000    0.000    0.000 threading.py:216(__init__)
    40002    0.016    0.000    0.024    0.000 threading.py:240(__enter__)
    40002    0.021    0.000    0.028    0.000 threading.py:243(__exit__)
    20001    0.008    0.000    0.010    0.000 threading.py:249(_release_save)
    20001    0.014    0.000    0.023    0.000 threading.py:252(_acquire_restore)
    60002    0.023    0.000    0.043    0.000 threading.py:255(_is_owned)
    20001    0.074    0.000    2.941    0.000 threading.py:264(wait)
    40001    0.088    0.000    0.165    0.000 threading.py:335(notify)
```

Figure 9.35: cProfile output (truncated)

Having completed this activity, you now know how to execute programs in a **conda** virtual environment and get the final output as a set amount of time to execute the code. You also used **CProfiling** to analyze the time taken by various parts of your code, giving you the opportunity to diagnose which parts of your code were the least efficient.

Chapter 10: Data Analytics with pandas and NumPy

Activity 24: Data Analysis to Find the Outliers in Pay versus the Salary Report in the UK Statistics Dataset

Solution

1. You begin with a new Jupyter Notebook.

2. Copy the UK Statistics dataset file into a specific folder where you will be performing this activity.

3. Import the necessary data visualization packages, which include **pandas** as **pds**, **matplotlib** as **plt**, and **seaborn** as **sns**:

```
import pandas as pd
import matplotlib.pyplot as plt
%matplotlib inline
import seaborn as sns
# Set up seaborn dark grid
sns.set()
```

4. Choose a variable to store **DataFrame** and place the **UKStatistics.csv** file within the folder of your Jupyter Notebook. In this case, it would be as follows:

```
statistics_df = pd.read_csv('UKStatistics.csv')
```

5. Now, to display the dataset, we will be calling the **statistics_df** variable, and **.head()** will show us the output of the entire dataset:

```
statistics_df.head()
```

The output will be as follows:

```
Out[3]:
```

	Post Unique Reference	Name	Grade (or equivalent)	Job Title	Job/Team Function	Parent Department	Organisation	Unit	Contact Phone	Contact E-mail	Reports to Senior Post
0	1	John Pullinger	SCS4	Permanent Secretary	National Statistician, Head of GSS	UK Statistics Authority	UK Statistics Authority	UK Statistics Authority	01633 455036	national.statistician@statistics.gsi.gov.uk	Board
1	2	Glen Watson	SCS3	Director General	Head Of ONS	UK Statistics Authority	UK Statistics Authority	Office For National Statistics	0845 601 3034	info@statistics.gov.uk	1
2	4	Nick Vaughan	SCS2	Director	Production of statistical outputs from Nationa...	UK Statistics Authority	UK Statistics Authority	National Accounts & Ecomonic Statistics	0845 601 3034	info@statistics.gov.uk	2
3	5	Ian Cope	SCS2	Director	Population and Demography	UK Statistics Authority	UK Statistics Authority	Population and Demography	0845 601 3034	info@statistics.gov.uk	2
4	6	Guy Goodwin	SCS2	Director	Analysis and Dissemination	UK Statistics Authority	UK Statistics Authority	Analysis and Dissemination	0845 601 3034	info@statistics.gov.uk	2

Figure 10.54: Dataset output to view

6. To find the shape that is the number of rows and columns in the dataset, we use the **.shape** method:

```
statistics_df.shape
```

The output will be as follows:

```
(51, 19)
```

7. Now, to plot a histogram of the data for **Actual Pay Floor (£)**, we use the **.hist** method, as mentioned in the following code snippet. Here, you will see the difference in **Pay Floor** in the histogram:

```
plt.hist(statistics_df['Actual Pay Floor (£)'])
plt.show()
```

The output will be as follows:

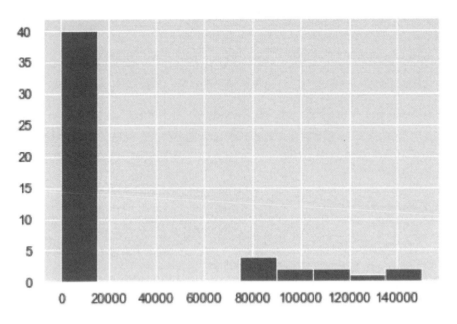

Figure 10.55: Output as a histogram

8. To plot the scatter plot, we use the `.scatter` method, and we will be comparing the x values as **Salary Cost of Reports (£)**, and **y** as **Actual Pay Floor (£)**:

```
x = statistics_df['Salary Cost of Reports (£)']
y = statistics_df['Actual Pay Floor (£)']
plt.scatter(x, y)
plt.show()
```

The output will be as follows:

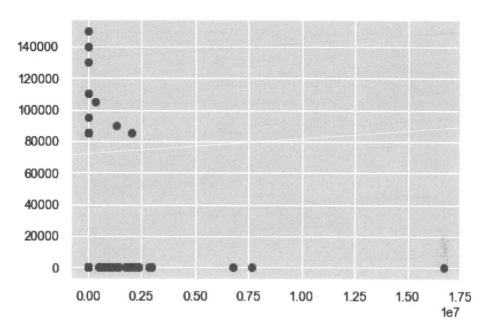

Figure 10.56: Output of the scatter plot

9. Next, you need to find the difference in data, which is the data that is vastly apart from each other for **x** as **Salary Cost of Reports (£)** and **y** as **Actual Pay Floor (£)** using the box plot graph. We first assign the values of **x** and **y**, as mentioned in the following code snippet:

```
x = statistics_df['Salary Cost of Reports (£)']
y = statistics_df['Actual Pay Floor (£)']
```

10. Now, to create the end outcome and check the amount of data that is closely stuck together within the box and the outliers that are presented away from the box in the graph, we use the .**boxplot** method to plot the graph:

```
plt.boxplot(x)
plt.show()
```

The output will be as follows:

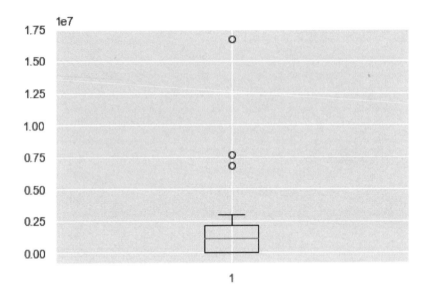

Figure 10.57: Output of the box plot

In this activity, we compared two specific pieces of data from the dataset, that is, **Salary Cost of Reports (£)** and **Actual Pay Floor (£)**. We then used various graphs and observed the vast difference between **Salary cost reports** and **Actual Pay Floor**. The box plot graph clearly shows us that there are three outliers in the data of **x** and **y** that make it prone to inconsistencies with regard to pay from the government.

Chapter 11: Machine Learning

Activity 25: Using Machine Learning to Predict Customer Return Rate Accuracy

Solution:

1. The first step asks you to download the dataset and display the first five rows.

   Import the necessary **pandas** and **numpy** libraries to begin with:

```
import pandas as pd
import numpy as np
```

2. Next, load the **CHURN.csv** file:

```
df = pd.read_csv('CHURN.csv')
```

3. Now, display the headers using **.head()**:

```
df.head()
```

You should get the following output:

Out[3]:

	customerID	gender	SeniorCitizen	Partner	Dependents	tenure	Phone Service	MultipleLines	InternetService	Online Security	...	DeviceProtection	TechSu
0	7590-VHVEG	Female	0	Yes	No	1	No	No phone service	DSL	No	...	No	No
1	5575-GNVDE	Male	0	No	No	34	Yes	No	DSL	Yes	...	Yes	Yes
2	3668-QPYBK	Male	0	No	No	2	Yes	No	DSL	Yes	...	Yes	No
3	7795-CFOCW	Male	0	No	No	45	No	No phone service	DSL	Yes	...	Yes	Yes
4	9237-HQITU	Female	0	No	No	2	Yes	No	Fiber optic	No	...	No	No

5 rows × 21 columns

Figure 11.37: Dataset displaying the data as output

4. The next step asks you to check for **NaN** values. The following code reveals that there are none:

```
df.info()
```

You should get the following output:

```
<class 'pandas.core.frame.DataFrame'>
RangeIndex: 7043 entries, 0 to 7042
Data columns (total 21 columns):
customerID          7043 non-null object
gender              7043 non-null object
SeniorCitizen       7043 non-null int64
Partner             7043 non-null object
Dependents          7043 non-null object
tenure              7043 non-null int64
PhoneService        7043 non-null object
MultipleLines       7043 non-null object
InternetService     7043 non-null object
OnlineSecurity      7043 non-null object
OnlineBackup        7043 non-null object
DeviceProtection    7043 non-null object
TechSupport         7043 non-null object
StreamingTV         7043 non-null object
StreamingMovies     7043 non-null object
Contract            7043 non-null object
PaperlessBilling    7043 non-null object
PaymentMethod       7043 non-null object
MonthlyCharges      7043 non-null float64
TotalCharges        7043 non-null object
Churn               7043 non-null object
dtypes: float64(1), int64(2), object(18)
memory usage: 1.1+ MB
```

Figure 11.38: Information on the dataset

5. The next step is done for you. The following code converts **'No'** and **'Yes'** into **0** and **1**:

```
df['Churn'] = df['Churn'].replace(to_replace=['No', 'Yes'], value=[0, 1])
```

6. The next step asks you to correctly define **X** and **y**. The correct solution is as follows. Note that the first column is eliminated because a customer ID would not be useful in making predictions:

```
X = df.iloc[:,1:-1]
y = df.iloc[:, -1]
```

7. In order to transform all of the predictive columns into numeric columns, the following code will work:

```
X = pd.get_dummies(X)
```

8. This step asks you to write a classifier function with **cross_val_score**. This is done as follows:

```
from sklearn.model_selection import cross_val_score
def clf_model (model, cv=3):
    clf = model

    scores = cross_val_score(clf, X, y, cv=cv)

    print('Scores:', scores)
    print('Mean score', scores.mean())
```

9. The following code and output show the implementation of five classifiers, as required in this step:

By using logistic regression:

```
from sklearn.linear_model import LogisticRegression
clf_model(LogisticRegression())
```

You should get the following output:

```
Scores:  [0.8032368   0.80195911 0.80400511]
Mean score  0.8030670081080226
```

Figure 11.39: Mean score output using LogisticRegression

By using **KNeighborsClassifier**:

```
from sklearn.neighbors import KNeighborsClassifier
clf_model(KNeighborsClassifier())
```

You should get the following output:

```
Scores:  [0.77938671 0.76320273 0.77290158]
Mean score  0.7718303381000114
```

Figure 11.40: Mean score output using KNeighborsClassifier

By using **GaussianNB**:

```
from sklearn.naive_bayes import GaussianNB
clf_model(GaussianNB())
```

You should get the following output:

```
Scores: [0.27725724 0.28109029 0.27652322]
Mean score 0.2782902503153228
```

Figure 11.41: Mean score output using GaussianNB

By using **RandomForestClassifier**:

```
from sklearn.ensemble import RandomForestClassifier
clf_model(RandomForestClassifier())
```

You should get the following output:

```
Scores: [0.78236797 0.77214651 0.786536  ]
Mean score 0.7803501612724885
```

Figure 11.42: Mean score output using RandomForestClassifier

By using **AdaBoostClassifier**:

```
from sklearn.ensemble import AdaBoostClassifier
clf_model(AdaBoostClassifier())
```

You should get the following output:

```
Scores: [0.80366269 0.80451448 0.80059651]
Mean score 0.8029245594131428
```

Figure 11.43: Mean score output using AdaBoostClassifier

You may or may not have the same warning as us in your notebook files. Generally speaking, warnings that do not interfere with code are okay. They are often used to warn the developer of future changes. The top three performing models, in this case, are **AdaBoostClassifer**, **RandomForestClassifier**, and **Logistic Regression**.

10. In this step, you are asked to build a function using the confusion matrix and the classification report and run it on your top three models. The following code does just that:

```
from sklearn.metrics import classification_report
from sklearn.metrics import confusion_matrix
from sklearn.model_selection import train_test_split
```

```
X_train, X_test ,y_train, y_test = train_test_split(X, y, test_size = 0.25)
def confusion(model):
    clf = model
    clf.fit(X_train, y_train)
    y_pred = clf.predict(X_test)
    print('Confusion Matrix:', confusion_matrix(y_test, y_pred))
    print('Classfication Report:', classification_report(y_test, y_pred))

    return clf
```

11. Now, build a function for the confusion matrix using **AdaBoostClassifier**:

```
confusion(AdaBoostClassifier())
```

You should get the following output:

```
Confusion Matrix: [[1157  130]
 [ 219  255]]
Classfication Report:              precision    recall  f1-score   support

           0        0.84      0.90      0.87      1287
           1        0.66      0.54      0.59       474

   micro avg        0.80      0.80      0.80      1761
   macro avg        0.75      0.72      0.73      1761
weighted avg        0.79      0.80      0.79      1761


AdaBoostClassifier(algorithm='SAMME.R', base_estimator=None,
          learning_rate=1.0, n_estimators=50, random_state=None)
```

Figure 11.44: Output of the confusion matrix on AdaBoostClassifier

Confusion matrix using **RandomForestClassifier**:

```
confusion(RandomForestClassifier())
```

You should get the following output:

```
Confusion Matrix: [[1168  119]
 [ 287  187]]
Classfication Report:                 precision    recall  f1-score   support

           0       0.80      0.91      0.85      1287
           1       0.61      0.39      0.48       474

   micro avg       0.77      0.77      0.77      1761
   macro avg       0.71      0.65      0.67      1761
weighted avg       0.75      0.77      0.75      1761


RandomForestClassifier(bootstrap=True, class_weight=None, criterion='gini',
            max_depth=None, max_features='auto', max_leaf_nodes=None,
            min_impurity_decrease=0.0, min_impurity_split=None,
            min_samples_leaf=1, min_samples_split=2,
            min_weight_fraction_leaf=0.0, n_estimators=10, n_jobs=None,
            oob_score=False, random_state=None, verbose=0,
            warm_start=False)
```

Figure 11.45: Output of the confusion matrix on RandomForestClassifier

Confusion matrix using **LogisticRegression**:

```
confusion(LogisticRegression())
```

You should get the following output:

```
Confusion Matrix: [[1162  125]
 [ 210  264]]
Classfication Report:                 precision    recall  f1-score   support

           0       0.85      0.90      0.87      1287
           1       0.68      0.56      0.61       474

   micro avg       0.81      0.81      0.81      1761
   macro avg       0.76      0.73      0.74      1761
weighted avg       0.80      0.81      0.80      1761


LogisticRegression(C=1.0, class_weight=None, dual=False, fit_intercept=True,
            intercept_scaling=1, max_iter=100, multi_class='warn',
            n_jobs=None, penalty='12', random_state=None, solver='warn',
            tol=0.0001, verbose=0, warm_start=False)
```

Figure 11.46: Output of the confusion matrix on LogisticRegression

12. In this step, you are asked to optimize one hyperparameter for your best model. We looked up **AdaBoostClassifier()** and discovered the **n_estimators** hyperparameter, similar to the **n_estimators** of Random Forests. We tried several out and came up with the following result for **n_estimators=250**:

```
confusion(AdaBoostClassifier(n_estimators=250))
```

You should get the following output:

```
Confusion Matrix: [[1162  125]
 [ 219  255]]
Classfication Report:                 precision    recall  f1-score   support

              0           0.84         0.90       0.87       1287
              1           0.67         0.54       0.60        474

    micro avg           0.80         0.80       0.80       1761
    macro avg           0.76         0.72       0.73       1761
 weighted avg           0.80         0.80       0.80       1761


AdaBoostClassifier(algorithm='SAMME.R', base_estimator=None,
          learning_rate=1.0, n_estimators=250, random_state=None)
```

Figure 11.47: Output of the confusion matrix using n_estimators=250

13. For **n_estimators=25** using the **AdaBoostClassifier**:

```
confusion(AdaBoostClassifier(n_estimators=25))
```

You should get the following output:

```
Confusion Matrix: [[1155  132]
 [ 217  257]]
Classfication Report:                 precision    recall  f1-score   support

              0           0.84         0.90       0.87       1287
              1           0.66         0.54       0.60        474

    micro avg           0.80         0.80       0.80       1761
    macro avg           0.75         0.72       0.73       1761
 weighted avg           0.79         0.80       0.80       1761


AdaBoostClassifier(algorithm='SAMME.R', base_estimator=None,
          learning_rate=1.0, n_estimators=25, random_state=None)
```

Figure 11.48: Output of the confusion matrix using n_estimators=25

14. For **n_estimators=15** using the **AdaBoostClassifier**:

```
confusion(AdaBoostClassifier(n_estimators=15))
```

You should get the following output:

```
Confusion Matrix: [[1162   125]
 [ 240   234]]
Classfication Report:                  precision    recall   f1-score   support

              0        0.83       0.90       0.86      1287
              1        0.65       0.49       0.56       474

      micro avg        0.79       0.79       0.79      1761
      macro avg        0.74       0.70       0.71      1761
   weighted avg        0.78       0.79       0.78      1761


AdaBoostClassifier(algorithm='SAMME.R', base_estimator=None,
          learning_rate=1.0, n_estimators=15, random_state=None)
```

Figure 11.49: Output of the confusion matrix using n_estimators=15

As you will see by the end of this activity, when it comes to predicting user churn, **AdaBoostClassifier(n_estimators = 25)** gives the best predictions.

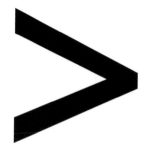

Index

About

All major keywords used in this book are captured alphabetically in this section. Each one is accompanied by the page number of where they appear.

Printed in Great Britain
by Amazon